BEST OF
Betty Crocker®
2012

BEST OF
Betty Crocker®
2012

For more great recipes and ideas, go to bettycrocker.com

PUBLISHED BY
Taste of Home Books
Reiman Media Group, LLC
5400 S. 60th St., Greendale WI 53129
www.tasteofhome.com

Printed in the U.S.A.

Taste of Home® is a registered trademark of Reiman Media Group, LLC

The trademarks referred to herein are trademarks of General Mills, Inc., or its affiliates, except as noted.

All recipes were originally published in different form by Betty Crocker® Magazine, a trademark of General Mills, Inc.

International Standard Book Number (10):
0-89821-907-8

International Standard Book Number (13):
978-0-89821-907-4

International Standard Serial Number:
1947-234X

CREDITS

General Mills, Inc.
EDITORIAL DIRECTOR: Jeff Nowak
PUBLISHING MANAGER: Christine Gray
COOKBOOK EDITOR: Grace Wells
EDITORIAL ASSISTANT: Kelly Gross
DIGITAL ASSETS MANAGER: Carrie Jacobson
RECIPE DEVELOPMENT AND TESTING:
Betty Crocker Kitchens
PHOTOGRAPHY: General Mills Photography Studio

Reiman Media Group, LLC
EDITOR: Heidi Reuter Lloyd
ASSOCIATE EDITOR: Victoria Soukup Jensen
SENIOR EDITOR/BOOKS: Mark Hagen
ASSOCIATE CREATIVE DIRECTOR: Edwin Robles Jr.
ART DIRECTOR: Gretchen Trautman
CONTENT PRODUCTION MANAGER: Julie Wagner
LAYOUT DESIGNER: Nancy Novak

COVER PHOTOGRAPHY:
Taste of Home Photo Studio
PHOTOGRAPHER: Rob Hagen
FOOD STYLIST: Diane Armstrong
SET STYLIST: Stephanie Marchese

EDITOR-IN-CHIEF: Catherine Cassidy
VICE PRESIDENT, EXECUTIVE EDITOR, BOOKS:
Heidi Reuter Lloyd
NORTH AMERICAN CHIEF MARKETING OFFICER:
Lisa Karpinski
VICE PRESIDENT/BOOK MARKETING: Dan Fink
CREATIVE DIRECTOR/CREATIVE MARKETING:
James Palmen

The Reader's Digest Association, Inc.
PRESIDENT & CHIEF EXECUTIVE OFFICER:
Tom Williams
EXECUTIVE VICE PRESIDENT, RDA, AND
PRESIDENT, NORTH AMERICA:
Dan Lagani

Front Cover Photographs, clockwise from top:
Chocolate-Chip Toffee Cheesecake, p. 211; Pecan-Bourbon Italian Cream Cups, p. 188; Black Bean and Corn Salad, p 139; Sticky Ginger Garlic Chicken Wings, p. 32; Chicken and Grilled Vegetable Stacked Sandwiches, p. 96.

Back Cover Photographs, clockwise from upper left:
Seaside BLT Pasta, p. 147; Easy Hamburger Pot Pie, p. 49; Farmer's Crostini, p. 22; Dark Chocolate-Glazed Orange Macaroons, p. 265.

table
OF CONTENTS

9

22

49

71

97

112

135

166

187

220

265

287

387

311 Reasons to Love This Cookbook—
BETTY CROCKER OFFERS UP HER BEST YET!

The third time is the charm for Betty Crocker! Yes, this third edition of our popular annual cookbook series is the best and biggest yet, with 311 recipes in all.

The name "Betty Crocker" has been trusted by home cooks for decades. Her recipes and products bring to mind high-quality ingredients, delicious food and the simple joy of sharing a meal with family and friends.

When Betty is in the mix, a holiday dinner becomes an event to remember, and even a weeknight supper brings smiles and sighs of satisfaction.

We've compiled 311 mouthwatering recipes from Betty's popular magazines for this big, beautiful book. Each recipe has been tested for both taste and accuracy in the Betty Crocker Kitchens.

Every recipe has a color photo, and most have tips from Betty's cooking experts. These tips offer ingredient substitution suggestions, how-to advice and success hints. They're all designed to get your family's meal on the table faster and easier than ever before!

p. 183

p. 167

p. 77

LOOK FOR THE ICONS

At-a-glance icons tell you which recipes will best fit your family's needs. If you're facing a time crunch, we've got you double-covered:

The **EASY** icon means that dish preps in just 15 or less minutes.

The **QUICK** icon means the recipe goes together from start to finish in a mere 30 minutes.

In fact, if your family is living in the too-fast lane, our Quick Meals chapter beginning on page 67 is one you'll want to turn to right away. There are more than 2 dozen family favorites that go together in a snap.

If someone in your family is watching fat or calorie intake, the **LOW FAT** icon will help. It identifies main dishes with 10 grams of fat or less and side dishes and desserts with 3 grams of fat or less. Because nutritional information is

offered with every recipe in this cookbook, it's easy to plan a menu that meets any health concerns.

If you're looking for recipes for a gathering of family and friends, start with our Appetizers For All Occasions chapter (p. 19), then turn to Oven Entrees (p. 47) or From the Grill (p. 95); and then finish off with any of our six luscious dessert chapters, starting on page 155.

Where else can you find an entire collection of dreamy cheesecakes and a bonanza of cupcake creations plus dozens of cakes, pies, crisps, cookies, brownies and bars? No sweet tooth can pass up these goodies!

Welcome to our third edition of *Best of Betty Crocker*. We think you'll agree that it's Betty's proudest moment yet!

BREAKFAST & BRUNCH

p.9

13

6

7

banana-chocolate chip coffee cake

Prep Time: 15 Minutes
Start to Finish: 1 Hour 15 Minutes
Servings: 9

EASY

Coffee Cake

2-1/4	cups Original Bisquick® mix
1	cup mashed ripe bananas (about 2 medium)
1/2	cup miniature semisweet chocolate chips
1/4	cup granulated sugar
1/3	cup milk
2	tablespoons butter or margarine, softened

1/2	teaspoon ground cinnamon
1	egg

Glaze

1	cup powdered sugar
1	tablespoon milk
1/2	teaspoon vanilla

1 Heat oven to 375°F. Spray 8-inch square pan with cooking spray. In medium bowl, stir all coffee cake ingredients with wire whisk or fork until blended. Spread in pan.

2 Bake 26 to 30 minutes or until golden brown and toothpick inserted in center comes out clean. Cool 30 minutes.

3 In small bowl, mix all glaze ingredients until smooth. If necessary, add additional milk, 1 teaspoon at a time, for desired consistency. Drizzle glaze over warm coffee cake. Serve warm.

High Altitude (3500-6500 ft): No change.

Nutritional Info: 1 Serving: Calories 310 (Calories from Fat 90); Total Fat 10g (Saturated Fat 5g, Trans Fat 1g); Cholesterol 30mg; Sodium 400mg; Total Carbohydrate 51g (Dietary Fiber 2g, Sugars 28g); Protein 4g. % Daily Value: Vitamin A 2%; Vitamin C 0%; Calcium 6%; Iron 8%. Exchanges: 1 Starch, 2-1/2 Other Carbohydrate, 2 Fat. Carbohydrate Choices: 3-1/2.

Betty's Kitchen Tip

• For more chocolate delight, omit the glaze and drizzle with 2 tablespoons melted white or semi-sweet chocolate instead.

cinnamon streusel coffee cake

Prep Time: 10 Minutes
Start to Finish: 35 Minutes
Servings: 6

EASY

Streusel Topping
- 1/3 cup Original Bisquick® mix
- 1/3 cup packed brown sugar
- 1/2 teaspoon ground cinnamon
- 2 tablespoons firm butter or margarine

Coffee Cake
- 2 cups Original Bisquick® mix
- 2/3 cup milk or water
- 2 tablespoons granulated sugar
- 1 egg

1 Heat oven to 375°F. Grease bottom and side of 9-inch round pan with shortening or cooking spray. In small bowl, mix 1/3 cup Bisquick mix, the brown sugar and cinnamon. Cut in butter, using fork or pastry blender, until mixture is crumbly; set aside.

2 In medium bowl, stir all coffee cake ingredients until blended. Spread in pan. Sprinkle with topping.

3 Bake 18 to 22 minutes or until golden brown. Serve warm or cool.

High Altitude (3500-6500 ft): No change.

Nutritional Info: 1 Serving: Calories 310 (Calories from Fat 110); Total Fat 12g (Saturated Fat 4.5g, Trans Fat 1.5g); Cholesterol 50mg; Sodium 720mg; Total Carbohydrate 46g (Dietary Fiber 0g, Sugars 21g); Protein 5g. % Daily Value: Vitamin A 4%; Vitamin C 0%; Calcium 15%; Iron 10%. Exchanges: 1-1/2 Starch, 1-1/2 Other Carbohydrate, 2 Fat. Carbohydrate Choices: 3.

Betty's Kitchen Tip
• Top with a dollop of whipped cream and fresh raspberries or peaches.

chocolate chip scones

Prep Time: 10 Minutes
Start to Finish: 25 Minutes
Servings: 8 scones

EASY QUICK

2 cups Original Bisquick® mix	1 egg
1/2 cup semisweet chocolate chips	1 teaspoon vanilla
1/3 cup whipping (heavy) cream	Additional whipping (heavy) cream
3 tablespoons sugar	Additional sugar

1 Heat oven to 425°F. Spray cookie sheet with cooking spray or grease with shortening. Stir the Bisquick mix, chocolate chips, 1/3 cup whipping cream, 3 tablespoons sugar, the egg and vanilla in medium bowl until soft dough forms.

2 Pat into 8-inch circle on cookie sheet (if dough is sticky, dip fingers in Bisquick mix). Brush circle with additional whipping cream; sprinkle with additional sugar. Cut into 8 wedges, but do not separate.

3 Bake about 12 minutes or until golden brown; carefully separate. Serve warm.

High Altitude (3500-6500 ft): No change.

Nutritional Info: 1 Scone: Calories 260 (Calories from Fat 110); Total Fat 12g (Saturated Fat 6g, Trans Fat 1.5g); Cholesterol 45mg; Sodium 380mg; Total Carbohydrate 33g (Dietary Fiber 1g, Sugars 13g); Protein 3g. % Daily Value: Vitamin A 4%; Vitamin C 0%; Calcium 4%; Iron 6%. Exchanges: 1 Starch, 1 Other Carbohydrate, 2-1/2 Fat. Carbohydrate Choices: 2.

Betty's Kitchen Tip

• Make it even easier by making drop scones. Heat oven to 400°F. Drop dough into 8 mounds onto cookie sheet; pat to slightly flatten. Bake 10 to 12 minutes or until golden brown.

apricot-oatmeal muffins

Prep Time: 15 Minutes
Start to Finish: 40 Minutes
Servings: 6 muffins

EASY

3/4	cup Gold Medal® all-purpose flour
1/2	cup quick-cooking or old-fashioned oats
1	teaspoon baking powder
1/4	teaspoon salt
1/2	cup packed brown sugar
1/3	cup milk
3	tablespoons vegetable oil
1/2	teaspoon vanilla
1	egg
1/3	cup finely chopped dried apricots
1	tablespoon quick-cooking or old-fashioned oats, if desired

1 Heat oven to 400°F. Grease bottoms only of 6 regular-size muffin cups with shortening or cooking spray, or line with paper baking cups.

2 In medium bowl, mix flour, 1/2 cup oats, the baking powder and salt. In small bowl, mix brown sugar, milk, oil, vanilla and egg with fork or wire whisk until blended. Stir milk mixture into flour mixture just until flour is moistened. Fold in apricots. Divide evenly among muffin cups. Sprinkle each with 1/2 teaspoon oats.

3 Bake 23 to 25 minutes or until toothpick inserted in center comes out clean. Remove from pan to cooling rack. Serve warm or cool.

High Altitude (3500-6500 ft): No change.

Nutritional Info: 1 Muffin: Calories 260; Total Fat 9g (Saturated Fat 1.5g); Sodium 230mg; Total Carbohydrate 40g (Dietary Fiber 1g); Protein 4g. Exchanges: 1-1/2 Starch, 1 Other Carbohydrate, 1-1/2 Fat. Carbohydrate Choices: 2-1/2.

Betty's Kitchen Tips

Success Hint: To avoid soggy muffins, take them out of the pan immediately after removing them from the oven.

How-To: Use an ice cream scoop, if you have one, to fill the muffin cups with batter.

honey-bran muffins

Prep Time: 15 Minutes
Start to Finish: 35 Minutes
Servings: 6 muffins

EASY

1/4 cup wheat bran
3 tablespoons boiling water
1/4 cup milk
1/4 cup honey
3 tablespoons vegetable oil
1 egg

1-1/2 cups Gold Medal® all-purpose flour
1-1/2 teaspoons baking powder
1/2 teaspoon ground cinnamon
1/4 teaspoon salt
Granulated sugar, if desired

1 Heat oven to 400°F. Place paper baking cup in each of 6 regular-size muffin cups; spray baking cups with cooking spray.

2 In small bowl, mix wheat bran and boiling water. In medium bowl, beat milk, honey, oil and egg with spoon until well mixed. Stir in bran mixture, flour, baking powder, cinnamon and salt just until the flour is moistened. Divide the batter evenly among the muffin cups. Sprinkle with granulated sugar.

3 Bake 15 to 20 minutes or until golden brown and tops spring back when touched lightly in center. Immediately remove from pan to cooling rack.

High Altitude (3500-6500 ft): No change.

Nutritional Info: 1 Muffin: Calories 250; Total Fat 8g (Saturated Fat 1.5g); Sodium 240mg; Total Carbohydrate 38g (Dietary Fiber 2g); Protein 5g. Exchanges: 1-1/2 Starch, 1 Other Carbohydrate, 1-1/2 Fat. Carbohydrate Choices: 2-1/2.

Betty's Kitchen Tips

Substitution: Oat bran or wheat germ can be used instead of the wheat bran.

Serve-With: Try serving these yummy muffins with honey butter. To make, simply combine 3 tablespoons softened butter with 1 tablespoon of honey.

crowd-pleasing impossibly easy breakfast bake

Prep Time: 20 Minutes
Start to Finish: 1 Hour 10 Minutes
Servings: 12

2	packages (12 oz each) bulk pork sausage
1	medium bell pepper, chopped (1 cup)
1	medium onion, chopped (1/2 cup)
3	cups frozen hash brown potatoes
2	cups shredded Cheddar cheese (8 oz)
1	cup Original Bisquick® mix
2	cups milk
1/4	teaspoon pepper
4	eggs

1 Heat oven to 400°F. Grease 13x9x2-inch (3-quart) glass baking dish. Cook sausage, bell pepper and onion in 10-inch skillet over medium heat, stirring occasionally, until sausage is no longer pink; drain. Stir together sausage mixture, potatoes and 1-1/2 cups of the cheese in baking dish.

2 Stir Bisquick mix, milk, pepper and eggs until blended. Pour into baking dish.

3 Bake uncovered 40 to 45 minutes or until knife inserted in center comes out clean. Sprinkle with remaining cheese. Bake 1 to 2 minutes longer or just until cheese is melted. Cool 5 minutes.

High Altitude (3500-6500 ft): No change.

Nutritional Info: 1 Serving: Calories 300 (Calories from Fat 160); Total Fat 18g (Saturated Fat 8g, Trans Fat 0g); Cholesterol 115mg; Sodium 490mg; Total Carbohydrate 20g (Dietary Fiber 1g, Sugars 4g); Protein 15g. % Daily Value: Vitamin A 8%; Vitamin C 10%; Calcium 20%; Iron 6%. Exchanges: 1-1/2 Starch, 1-1/2 High-Fat Meat, 1 Fat. Carbohydrate Choices: 1.

Betty's Kitchen Tip

• Make it Supreme! Add 1 jar (4.5 oz) Green Giant® sliced mushrooms, drained, with the potatoes and sprinkle with 2 tablespoons chopped green onions or minced chives just before serving.

caramel-spice french breakfast muffins

Prep Time: 20 Minutes
Start to Finish: 50 Minutes
Servings: 18 muffins

Merry Graham
Newhall, CA
Celebrate the Season-Fall Baking Contest

Muffins

1/2	cup butter or margarine, softened
1/2	cup sugar
1/2	cup caramel topping or caramel apple dip (4 oz)
2	eggs
3/4	cup milk
2	cups Gold Medal® unbleached flour
1-1/2	teaspoons baking powder

1/2	teaspoon salt
1/2	teaspoon ground cinnamon
1/2	teaspoon ground nutmeg

Topping

3/4	cup butter or margarine
3/4	cup sugar
1-1/2	teaspoons pumpkin pie spice

Caramel topping or caramel apple dip

1 Heat oven to 375°F. Spray 18 regular-size muffin cups with cooking spray.

2 In large bowl, beat 1/2 cup butter, 1/2 cup sugar, 1/2 cup caramel topping, the eggs and milk with electric mixer on low speed (mixture will appear curdled). Stir in remaining muffin ingredients just until moistened. Fill muffin cups 2/3 full.

3 Bake 20 to 25 minutes or until toothpick inserted in center comes out clean. Cool 5 minutes. Meanwhile, in medium microwavable bowl, microwave 3/4 cup butter on High until melted. In small bowl, mix 3/4 cup sugar and the pumpkin pie spice. Remove muffins from pan. Roll in melted butter, then in sugar mixture. Drizzle with caramel topping. Serve warm.

High Altitude (3500-6500 ft): No change.

Nutritional Info: 1 Muffin: Calories 260; Total Fat 14g (Saturated Fat 8g); Sodium 240mg; Total Carbohydrate 31g (Dietary Fiber 0g); Protein 2g. Exchanges: 1/2 Starch, 1-1/2 Other Carbohydrate, 2-1/2 Fat. Carbohydrate Choices: 2.

Betty's Kitchen Tips

Substitution: All-purpose flour can be used in place of unbleached flour.

Purchasing: You can make your own pumpkin pie spice blend by mixing 4 tablespoons ground cinnamon, 4 teaspoons ground nutmeg, 4 teaspoons ground ginger and 3 teaspoons ground allspice. Store tightly covered and keep on hand to use in this recipe and others that call for it.

peanut butter waffle toast

Prep Time: 20 Minutes
Start to Finish: 20 Minutes
Servings: 6 to 8

QUICK

- 1-1/4 cups milk
- 1 cup Original Bisquick® mix
- 1/2 cup peanut butter
- 2 tablespoons granulated sugar
- 1 teaspoon vanilla
- 1 egg
- 6 to 8 slices bread
- 6 to 8 tablespoons miniature semisweet chocolate chips

Powdered sugar, if desired

1 Heat waffle iron; grease with shortening if necessary (or spray with cooking spray before heating).

2 In medium bowl, stir milk, Bisquick mix, peanut butter, granulated sugar, vanilla and egg until well blended. Carefully dip bread into batter on both sides. Place in waffle iron; close lid.

3 Bake about 2 minutes or until steaming stops and "toast" is golden. Carefully remove waffle toast. Sprinkle each waffle with 1 tablespoon chocolate chips and powdered sugar.

High Altitude (3500-6500 ft): No change.

Nutritional Info: 1 Serving: Calories 400 (Calories from Fat 180); Total Fat 20g (Saturated Fat 6g, Trans Fat 0.5g); Cholesterol 40mg; Sodium 550mg; Total Carbohydrate 43g (Dietary Fiber 3g, Sugars 17g); Protein 12g. % Daily Value: Vitamin A 2%; Vitamin C 0%; Calcium 15%; Iron 15%. Exchanges: 1-1/2 Starch, 1-1/2 Other Carbohydrate, 1 High-Fat Meat, 2 Fat. Carbohydrate Choices: 3.

Betty's Kitchen Tip

• The peanutty batter covering the bread is thick so it clings to the bread. If it seems a little too thick, add a small amount of milk. When you coat the bread, use your fingers to turn the slices (messy) or try using a spatula (less messy). Either way, the toast turns out delicious!

cheesy sausage and egg bake

Prep Time: 25 Minutes
Start to Finish: 1 Hour
Servings: 12

- -

1	lb bulk pork sausage, cooked and drained
1-1/2	cups sliced fresh mushrooms (4 oz)
8	medium green onions, sliced (1/2 cup)
2	medium tomatoes, chopped (1-1/2 cups)
2	cups shredded mozzarella cheese (8 oz)
1-1/4	cups Original Bisquick® mix

1	cup milk
1-1/2	teaspoons salt
1-1/2	teaspoons chopped fresh oregano leaves or 1/2 teaspoon dried oregano leaves
1/2	teaspoon pepper
12	eggs

- -

1 Heat oven to 350°F. Grease 13x9x2-inch (3-quart) glass baking dish. Layer sausage, mushrooms, onions, tomatoes and cheese in baking dish.

2 Stir remaining ingredients until blended. Pour over cheese.

3 Bake uncovered 30 to 35 minutes or until golden brown and set.

High Altitude (3500-6500 ft): No change.

Nutritional Info: 1 Serving: Calories 260 (Calories from Fat 150); Total Fat 16g (Saturated Fat 6g, Trans Fat 0.5g); Cholesterol 240mg; Sodium 750mg; Total Carbohydrate 12g (Dietary Fiber 0g, Sugars 3g); Protein 17g. % Daily Value: Vitamin A 15%; Vitamin C 4%; Calcium 20%; Iron 8%. Exchanges: 1 Starch, 2 High-Fat Meat. Carbohydrate Choices: 1.

Betty's Kitchen Tip

• Wake up to a healthy breakfast! Use turkey sausage instead of the pork and reduced-fat mozzarella cheese. Serve with a fresh spinach salad and fresh fruit.

pancakes with yogurt topping

Prep Time: 25 Minutes
Start to Finish: 25 Minutes
Servings: 6 (2 pancakes each)

QUICK

Pancakes

- 2 cups Original Bisquick® mix
- 1 teaspoon ground cinnamon
- 1 cup milk
- 1 teaspoon vanilla
- 2 eggs

Yogurt Topping

- 2 containers (6 oz each) Yoplait® Original 99% Fat Free French vanilla yogurt
- 1/2 cup strawberry or other flavor fruit preserves

1. Brush griddle or skillet with vegetable oil or spray with cooking spray; heat griddle to 375°F or heat skillet over medium heat. In large bowl, stir Bisquick mix, cinnamon, milk, vanilla and eggs with wire whisk or fork until blended.

2. For each pancake, pour 1/4 cup batter onto hot griddle. Cook until edges are dry. Turn; cook other sides until golden brown.

3. In medium bowl, mix topping ingredients. Serve hot pancakes with topping; if desired, sprinkle with additional cinnamon. Cover and refrigerate any remaining topping.

High Altitude (3500-6500 ft): No change.

Nutritional Info: 1 Serving (2 pancakes): Calories 340 (Calories from Fat 70); Total Fat 8g (Saturated Fat 3g, Trans Fat 1.5g); Cholesterol 75mg; Sodium 560mg; Total Carbohydrate 58g (Dietary Fiber 1g, Sugars 25g); Protein 8g. % Daily Value: Vitamin A 8%; Vitamin C 2%; Calcium 15%; Iron 8%. Exchanges: 1-1/2 Starch, 2 Other Carbohydrate, 1/2 Skim Milk, 1 Fat. Carbohydrate Choices: 4.

Betty's Kitchen Tip

- A few sliced strawberries, banana slices or chopped walnuts are pretty, tasty toppers for these pancakes.

oatmeal-brown sugar pancakes with banana-walnut syrup

Prep Time: 30 Minutes
Start to Finish: 30 Minutes
Servings: 6

Banana-Walnut Syrup

2	tablespoons butter or margarine
1/4	cup chopped walnuts
2	bananas, sliced
1	cup maple-flavored syrup

Pancakes

2	cups Original Bisquick® mix
1/2	cup old-fashioned or quick-cooking oats
2	tablespoons packed brown sugar
1-1/4	cups milk
2	eggs

1 In 1-1/2-quart saucepan, melt butter over medium heat. Add walnuts; cook, stirring occasionally, just until walnuts and butter begin to brown. Add bananas; stir to coat with butter. Stir in syrup. Reduce heat to low; cook until warm. Keep warm while making pancakes.

2 Heat griddle or skillet over medium heat or to 375°F. Grease griddle with vegetable oil if necessary (or spray with cooking spray before heating). In medium bowl, stir all of the pancake ingredients with spoon until blended.

3 For each pancake, pour 1/4 cup batter onto hot griddle. Cook until edges are dry. Turn; cook other sides until golden. Serve with warm syrup.

High Altitude (3500-6500 ft): No change.

Nutritional Info: 1 Serving: Calories 520 (Calories from Fat 140); Total Fat 16g (Saturated Fat 5g, Trans Fat 1g); Cholesterol 85mg; Sodium 700mg; Total Carbohydrate 86g (Dietary Fiber 2g, Sugars 35g); Protein 9g. % Daily Value: Vitamin A 8%; Vitamin C 4%; Calcium 15%; Iron 10%. Exchanges: 2-1/2 Starch, 1 Fruit, 2 Other Carbohydrate, 3 Fat. Carbohydrate Choices: 6.

Betty's Kitchen Tip

• Watch the butter carefully when it's browning so it turns an even golden brown color that just begins to smell toasty.

carrot-walnut coffee cake

Prep Time: 15 Minutes
Start to Finish: 1 Hour 20 Minutes
Servings: 9

EASY

Streusel

1/2	cup Original Bisquick® mix
1/3	cup packed brown sugar
2	tablespoons cold butter or margarine

Coffee Cake

2	cups Original Bisquick® mix
2	tablespoons granulated sugar
1-1/2	teaspoons pumpkin pie spice
1/2	cup chopped walnuts
1/2	cup shredded carrots
1/2	cup raisins
2/3	cup milk
2	tablespoons vegetable oil
1	egg

1. Heat oven to 375°F. In small bowl, mix 1/2 cup Bisquick mix and the brown sugar until well blended. Cut in butter, using pastry blender or fork, until mixture is crumbly; set aside.

2. In large bowl, stir 2 cups Bisquick mix, the granulated sugar, pumpkin pie spice, walnuts, carrots and raisins. Stir in milk, oil and egg with wire whisk or fork until blended. Pour into ungreased 8-inch square pan. Sprinkle with streusel.

3. Bake 30 to 35 minutes or until toothpick inserted in center comes out clean. Cool 30 minutes before serving. Serve warm, with honey, if desired.

High Altitude (3500-6500 ft): No change.

Nutritional Info: 1 Serving: Calories 320 (Calories from Fat 140); Total Fat 15g (Saturated Fat 4g, Trans Fat 1.5g); Cholesterol 30mg; Sodium 450mg; Total Carbohydrate 41g (Dietary Fiber 2g, Sugars 18g); Protein 5g. % Daily Value: Vitamin A 25%; Vitamin C 0%; Calcium 8%; Iron 8%. Exchanges: 1-1/2 Starch, 1 Other Carbohydrate, 3 Fat. Carbohydrate Choices: 3.

Betty's Kitchen Tip

• Try dried cranberries or cut-up dried apples in place of the raisins.

double-ginger pumpkin muffins with sweet candied pecans

Prep Time: 30 Minutes
Start to Finish: 1 Hour 55 Minutes
Servings: 33 muffins

Laura Lufkin, Essex, MA
Celebrate the Season-Fall Baking Contest
2nd Place Winner

Candied Pecans

1-1/2	cups chopped pecans
1	tablespoon egg white
3	tablespoons granulated sugar
2	teaspoons ground ginger
1/2	to 1 teaspoon kosher (coarse) salt

Muffins

1	can (15 oz) pumpkin (not pumpkin pie mix)
4	eggs
1	cup canola oil

1/3	cup water
2-1/2	cups granulated sugar
3	teaspoons vanilla
3-1/2	cups Gold Medal® all-purpose flour
2	tablespoons ground cinnamon
2	teaspoons baking soda
1	teaspoon salt
1	teaspoon ground ginger
1/2	teaspoon ground nutmeg
1/2	cup crystallized ginger, finely chopped

1 Heat oven to 350°F. Line 15x10x1-inch pan with cooking parchment paper. Spray regular-size muffin cups with cooking spray.

2 In medium bowl, toss pecans with egg white until well coated. Add 3 tablespoons granulated sugar, 2 teaspoons ground ginger and the kosher salt; toss until coated. Spread in single layer on parchment-lined pan. Bake 10 to 12 minutes, stirring once, until golden brown. Cool completely, about 30 minutes. Coarsely chop; set aside.

3 In large bowl, beat pumpkin, eggs, oil, water, 2-1/2 cups granulated sugar and the vanilla with electric mixer on low speed. Stir in flour, cinnamon, baking soda, salt, 1 teaspoon ground ginger and the nutmeg. Stir in crystallized ginger. Fill muffin cups 3/4 full. Top each muffin cup with 2 teaspoons candied pecans.

4 Bake 23 to 25 minutes or until toothpick inserted in center comes out clean. Cool 5 minutes; remove from pan to cooling rack.

High Altitude (3500-6500 ft): No change.

Nutritional Info: 1 Muffin: Calories 230; Total Fat 11g (Saturated Fat 1g); Sodium 190mg; Total Carbohydrate 29g (Dietary Fiber 1g); Protein 3g. Exchanges: 1/2 Starch, 1-1/2 Other Carbohydrate, 2 Fat. Carbohydrate Choices: 2.

Betty's Kitchen Tip

• Using freshly grated nutmeg in these muffins adds great flavor!

appetizers
FOR ALL OCCASIONS

p. 22

25

27

26

broccoli-cheddar appetizers

Prep Time: 15 Minutes
Start to Finish: 1 Hour 10 Minutes
Servings: 30 appetizers

EASY

1 box (9 oz) Green Giant® Simply Steam™ broccoli cuts, thawed, drained
1 can (7 oz) Green Giant® Niblets® whole kernel sweet corn, drained
1 small onion, chopped (about 1/4 cup)
1/2 cup coarsely chopped walnuts

1/2 cup Original Bisquick® mix
1/4 teaspoon garlic salt
1/2 cup milk
1/4 cup butter or margarine, melted
2 eggs
1 cup shredded Cheddar cheese (4 oz)

1 Heat oven to 375°F. Spray 9-inch square pan with cooking spray. In pan, mix broccoli, corn, onion and walnuts.

2 In medium bowl, stir all remaining ingredients except cheese with wire whisk or fork until blended. Pour into pan.

3 Bake 23 to 25 minutes or until knife inserted in center comes out clean. Sprinkle with cheese. Bake 2 to 3 minutes longer or until cheese is melted. Cool 30 minutes. To serve, cut into 5 rows by 3 rows; cut each rectangle diagonally in half.

High Altitude (3500-6500 ft): No change.

Nutritional Info: 1 Appetizer: Calories 70 (Calories from Fat 45); Total Fat 5g (Saturated Fat 2g, Trans Fat 0g); Cholesterol 20mg; Sodium 90mg; Total Carbohydrate 4g (Dietary Fiber 0g, Sugars 0g); Protein 2g. % Daily Value: Vitamin A 4%; Vitamin C 4%; Calcium 4%; Iron 0%. Exchanges: 1/2 Other Carbohydrate, 1 Fat. Carbohydrate Choices: 0.

Betty's Kitchen Tip

• Add about 1/4 cup crisply cooked and crumbled bacon with the broccoli for even more great taste.

apricot-glazed coconut-chicken bites

Prep Time: 15 Minutes
Start to Finish: 50 Minutes
Servings: About 3 dozen appetizers

EASY

1/4	cup butter or margarine, melted
1/2	cup sweetened condensed milk
2	tablespoons Dijon mustard
1-1/2	cups Original Bisquick® mix
2/3	cup flaked coconut
1/2	teaspoon salt
1/2	teaspoon paprika
1	lb boneless, skinless chicken breasts, cut into 1-inch pieces
1/2	cup apricot spreadable fruit
2	tablespoons honey
2	tablespoons Dijon mustard
1	tablespoon white vinegar

Hot mustard, if desired

1 Heat oven to 425°F. Spread 2 tablespoons of the melted butter in a 15x10x1-inch baking pan.

2 Mix sweetened condensed milk and 2 tablespoons Dijon mustard. Mix Bisquick, coconut, salt and paprika. Dip chicken into milk mixture, then coat with Bisquick mixture. Place coated chicken in pan. Drizzle remaining butter over chicken. Bake uncovered 20 minutes.

3 Meanwhile, in small bowl, stir together spreadable fruit, honey, 2 tablespoons Dijon mustard and the vinegar. Turn chicken; brush with apricot mixture. Bake 10 to 15 minutes longer or until chicken is no longer pink in center and glaze is bubbly. Serve with hot mustard.

High Altitude (3500-6500 ft): No change.

Nutritional Info: 1 Appetizer: Calories 90 (Calories from Fat 35); Total Fat 4g (Saturated Fat 2g, Trans Fat 0g); Cholesterol 15mg; Sodium 160mg; Total Carbohydrate 10g (Dietary Fiber 0g, Sugars 6g); Protein 3g. % Daily Value: Vitamin A 0%; Vitamin C 0%; Calcium 2%; Iron 2%. Exchanges: 1 Starch, 1/2 Fat. Carbohydrate Choices: 1/2.

Betty's Kitchen Tip

• Simplify clean-up by lining pan with foil before spreading butter in pan.

farmer's crostini

Prep Time: 40 Minutes
Start to Finish: 40 Minutes
Servings: 20 (2 crostini each)

1 baguette (14 oz), cut into 40 (1/4-inch) slices
Nonstick cooking spray
2 packages (3 oz each) cream cheese, softened
1/4 cup crumbled blue cheese (from a 5-oz container)
1/4 cup mayonnaise or salad dressing

1/4 teaspoon garlic powder
1/4 teaspoon salt
1/8 teaspoon pepper
1/2 medium cucumber, finely chopped
1 small ripe tomato, finely chopped
1/2 medium red or yellow bell pepper, cut into matchsticks
Fresh flat-leaf (Italian) parsley leaves, if desired

1 Heat oven to 325°F. Place bread slices on ungreased cookie sheet; spray lightly with nonstick cooking spray. Bake 6 to 9 minutes or until crispy. Remove to cooling rack; cool completely.

2 In medium bowl, beat cream cheese, blue cheese, mayonnaise, garlic powder, salt and pepper with electric mixer on medium speed until well blended.

3 In small bowl, stir together cucumber, tomato and bell pepper.

4 Spread about 1 teaspoon cheese mixture on top of each slice of baguette. Top with cucumber and tomato mixture. Garnish with parsley.

High Altitude (3500-6500 ft): No change.

Nutritional Info: 1 Serving (2 crostini): Calories 120; Total Fat 6g (Saturated Fat 2.5g); Sodium 230mg; Total Carbohydrate 12g (Dietary Fiber 0g); Protein 3g. Exchanges: 1 Starch, 1 Fat. Carbohydrate Choices: 1.

Betty's Kitchen Tips

Substitution: Other fresh vegetable options might include tiny broccoli florets, sliced fresh mushrooms, shredded carrot, sliced green onions or small cauliflower florets.

Special Touch: Garnish with fresh dill sprigs or fresh thyme sprigs.

Success Hint: Grilled vegetables including summer squash, red onion strips and peppers are great on these crostini. Allow grilled vegetables to cool slightly before placing on the cheese mixture.

sausage-stuffed mushrooms

Prep Time: 20 Minutes
Start to Finish: 35 Minutes
Servings: 36 appetizers

LOW FAT

36	large fresh mushrooms (about 2 lb)
1	lb bulk pork sausage
1/4	cup freeze-dried chopped chives
2	tablespoons chopped onion
1	clove garlic, finely chopped
3/4	cup Original Bisquick® mix
1/4	cup Italian-style dry bread crumbs
1/4	cup grated Parmesan cheese

1 Heat oven to 350°F. Remove stems from mushrooms; finely chop stems.

2 In 10-inch skillet, cook sausage, chopped mushroom stems, chives, onion and garlic until sausage is no longer pink; drain, reserving drippings. Stir Bisquick mix and bread crumbs into sausage mixture until mixture holds together. (If mixture is dry, add 1 to 2 tablespoons reserved drippings.)

3 Spoon about 1 rounded tablespoon sausage mixture into each mushroom cap. In ungreased 15x10x1-inch pan, place filled mushrooms; sprinkle with cheese.

4 Bake about 15 minutes or until hot. Serve immediately.

High Altitude (3500-6500 ft): No change.

Nutritional Info: 1 Appetizer: Calories 45 (Calories from Fat 20); Total Fat 2.5g (Saturated Fat 1g, Trans Fat 0g); Cholesterol 5mg; Sodium 100mg; Total Carbohydrate 3g (Dietary Fiber 0g, Sugars 0g); Protein 2g. % Daily Value: Vitamin A 0%; Vitamin C 0%; Calcium 0%; Iron 0%. Exchanges: 1/2 High-Fat Meat. Carbohydrate Choices: 0.

Betty's Kitchen Tip

• Buy frozen chopped onions, which can be found near the frozen breaded onion rings, to save time. This also eliminates leftover freshly-chopped onion, which can happen when a recipe calls for only a small amount, such as this recipe.

crab cakes

Prep Time: 30 Minutes
Start to Finish: 40 Minutes
Servings: About 2 dozen appetizers

LOW FAT

Robert Cowling
Blog Chef
www.blogchef.net

1	tablespoon butter or margarine
1/3	cup chopped onion
1/3	cup chopped celery
1/3	cup chopped red and green bell pepper
1	cup soft bread crumbs
1/2	cup Original Bisquick® mix

2	teaspoons Worcestershire sauce
1/4	teaspoon pepper
1/4	teaspoon salt
2	eggs, slightly beaten
1	package (14 oz) imitation crabmeat flakes, chopped
1/2	cup cocktail sauce

1 Heat oven to 400°F. Generously grease 2 cookie sheets. Melt butter in 10-inch skillet over medium heat. Cook onion, celery and bell peppers in butter 3 minutes, stirring occasionally; remove from skillet.

2 Mix vegetable mixture and remaining ingredients except cocktail sauce. Shape mixture into 2 dozen 1-1/2-inch patties.

3 Place on cookie sheets. Bake about 12 minutes, turning once, until golden. Serve with cocktail sauce.

High Altitude (3500-6500 ft): No change.

Nutritional Info: 1 Appetizer: Calories 60 (Calories from Fat 15); Total Fat 1.5g (Saturated Fat 0.5g, Trans Fat 0g); Cholesterol 25mg; Sodium 310mg; Total Carbohydrate 8g (Dietary Fiber 0g, Sugars 3g); Protein 4g. % Daily Value: Vitamin A 4%; Vitamin C 4%; Calcium 0%; Iron 2%. Exchanges: 1/2 Starch, 1/2 Lean Meat. Carbohydrate Choices: 1/2.

Betty's Kitchen Tip

• Try other types of sauces, such as sweet and sour, tartar or horseradish sauce.

buffalo wings

Prep Time: 50 Minutes
Start to Finish: 50 Minutes
Servings: 16 appetizers

- 2 quarts oil for frying
- 1/2 cup Gold Medal® all-purpose flour
- 1/4 teaspoon paprika
- 1/4 teaspoon ground red pepper (cayenne)
- 1/4 teaspoon salt
- 2 packages (1 lb each) chicken drummettes
- 1/4 cup butter
- 1/4 cup red pepper sauce
- 1/8 teaspoon black pepper
- 1/8 teaspoon garlic powder

1 In deep fryer or 3-quart heavy saucepan, heat oil to 375°F.

2 In 1-gallon resealable food-storage plastic bag, mix flour, paprika, red pepper and salt. Add chicken, seal bag and shake until chicken is coated with flour.

3 Carefully fry chicken in batches (to avoid over-crowding) about 10 minutes each or until brown and no longer pink in center. Drain on paper towels.

4 Meanwhile, in 1-quart saucepan combine butter, pepper sauce, black pepper and garlic powder; cook over medium-high heat, 3 to 5 minutes, stirring occasionally, until the butter is melted and the mixture is blended.

5 In large bowl, toss chicken with butter mixture until completely coated.

High Altitude (3500-6500 ft): No change.

Nutritional Info: 1 Appetizer: Calories 120; Total Fat 8g (Saturated Fat 3g); Sodium 170mg; Total Carbohydrate 3g (Dietary Fiber 0g); Protein 7g. Exchanges: 1 Lean Meat, 1 Fat. Carbohydrate Choices: 0.

Betty's Kitchen Tips

Serve-With: Try serving these spicy wings with blue cheese dressing and celery sticks.

Time-Saver: Fry wings up to 8 hours ahead of time and store in refrigerator. To serve, heat oven to 450°F. Place chicken on an ungreased 15x10x1-inch baking pan. Bake 6 to 8 minutes, or until thoroughly heated. Toss with pepper sauce mixture.

cheesy bacon potato skins

Prep Time: 1 Hour
Start to Finish: 1 Hour
Servings: 8 (1 potato skin each)

Robert Cowling
Blog Chef
www.blogchef.net

8	slices bacon, cut into 1/2 inch pieces	1	tablespoon grated parmesan cheese
4	large baking potatoes (about 2 lb)	1/8	teaspoon pepper
3	tablespoons vegetable oil		Vegetable oil for deep frying
1/2	teaspoon salt	2	cups shredded Cheddar cheese (8 oz)
1/4	teaspoon garlic powder	1/2	cup sour cream
1/4	teaspoon paprika	2	large green onions, sliced (1/3 cup)

1 In 10-inch skillet, cook bacon over medium heat, stirring occasionally, until bacon is crisp; drain on paper towels.

2 Meanwhile, gently scrub potatoes, but do not peel. Pierce potatoes to allow steam to escape. Place on microwavable paper towels. Arrange in spoke pattern with narrow ends in center. Microwave 12 to 14 minutes, turning once, until tender. Cover; let stand 5 minutes.

3 When potatoes are cool enough to handle, cut lengthwise in halves; carefully scoop out pulp, leaving ¼-inch shells. Save potato pulp for another use.

4 In small bowl, mix oil, salt, garlic powder, paprika, cheese and pepper. Brush mixture over skins.

5 In deep fryer or 3-quart heavy saucepan, heat oil to 365°F. Fry in batches for 5 minutes. Drain on paper towels. (Make Ahead tip: Potatoes can be prepared up to this point and refrigerated for up to 24 hours before continuing to Step 6.)

6 One hour before serving allow potatoes to come to room temperature. Heat oven to 450°F. Lightly spray 13x9-inch (3 quart) glass baking dish. Place potato skins, skin side up, in baking dish. Bake 8 minutes. Turn potato skins over and fill with cheese and bacon.

7 Bake 7 to 8 minutes or until cheese is melted. Top with sour cream and green onions.

High Altitude (3500-6500 ft): No change.

Nutritional Info: 1 Appetizer: Calories 400; Total Fat 23g (Saturated Fat 10g); Sodium 550mg; Total Carbohydrate 33g (Dietary Fiber 3g); Protein 14g. Exchanges: 2 Starch, 1 High-Fat Meat, 3 Fat. Carbohydrate Choices: 2.

Betty's Kitchen Tip

• Bake the potato skins instead of frying them. Heat oven to 450°F. Place skins in lightly greased 13x9-inch glass baking dish; bake 8 minutes per side. Turn potato skins over and fill. Bake 7 minutes or until cheese is melted.

coconut shrimp

Prep Time: 30 Minutes
Start to Finish: 30 Minutes
Servings: 6

QUICK

1	lb uncooked deveined peeled medium shrimp (31 to 35), thawed if frozen, tail shells removed
1	cup Original Bisquick® mix
3/4	cup milk
1	egg
1	cup vegetable oil
2-1/2	cups flaked coconut
1/2	cup chili sauce
1/2	cup apricot preserves

1 Pat shrimp dry with paper towels. In medium bowl, stir Bisquick mix, milk and egg with wire whisk or fork until blended. Add shrimp; gently stir to coat well.

2 In 10-inch skillet, heat oil over medium heat to 375°F. In shallow dish, place half of the coconut (add remaining coconut after coating half of the shrimp). Cooking in batches, remove shrimp one at a time from batter and coat with coconut; place in oil in single layer.

3 Cook 3 to 4 minutes, turning once, until coating is crispy and golden brown and shrimp are pink (cut 1 shrimp open to check doneness). Drain on paper towels.

4 In small bowl, mix chili sauce and apricot preserves. Serve shrimp with the sauce for dipping.

High Altitude (3500-6500 ft): No change.

Nutritional Info: 1 Serving: Calories 440 (Calories from Fat 190); Total Fat 21g (Saturated Fat 11g, Trans Fat 0g); Cholesterol 110mg; Sodium 520mg; Total Carbohydrate 50g (Dietary Fiber 3g, Sugars 27g); Protein 15g. % Daily Value: Vitamin A 6%; Vitamin C 6%; Calcium 4%; Iron 20%. Exchanges: 1 Starch, 2 Other Carbohydrate, 1-1/2 Very Lean Meat, 4 Fat. Carbohydrate Choices: 3.

Betty's Kitchen Tip

• For a great supper salad, serve these crispy shrimp on a bed of mixed salad greens, orange slices and thinly sliced onions. Add enough water to the dipping sauce so you can drizzle it over the salad as a dressing.

caramelized onion and goat cheese crostini

Prep Time: 20 Minutes
Start to Finish: 1 Hour
Servings: 24

2 tablespoons olive or vegetable oil
2 medium sweet onions, thinly sliced (about 2 cups)
1 teaspoon salt
1 tablespoon packed brown sugar
1 tablespoon balsamic vinegar
24 slices (1/4-inch thick) French bread baguette

Nonstick cooking spray
1 package (4 oz) chèvre (goat) cheese, softened
1 package (3 oz) cream cheese, softened
1 teaspoon chopped fresh thyme or oregano leaves

1 In 12-inch nonstick skillet, heat oil over medium-high heat. Stir in onions; cook uncovered 10 minutes, stirring every 3 to 4 minutes.

2 Reduce heat to medium-low. Stir in salt, brown sugar and vinegar. Cook 30 to 35 minutes longer, stirring every 5 minutes, until onions are deep golden brown (onions will shrink during cooking). Cool slightly.

3 Heat oven to 325°F. Place bread slices on ungreased cookie sheet; spray lightly with nonstick cooking spray. Bake 6 to 9 minutes or until crispy.

4 Meanwhile, in small bowl, combine goat cheese and cream cheese; blending until smooth; set aside.

5 Place 1 teaspoon caramelized onions onto each bread slice; top with 1 rounded teaspoon cheese mixture. Sprinkle with chopped herbs.

High Altitude (3500-6500 ft): No change.

Nutritional Info: 1 Serving: Calories 70; Total Fat 4g (Saturated Fat 2g); Sodium 180mg; Total Carbohydrate 5g (Dietary Fiber 0g); Protein 2g. Exchanges: 1/2 Starch, 1 Fat. Carbohydrate Choices: 1/2.

Betty's Kitchen Tip

• Caramelized onions can be made ahead. Prepare as directed, then cover and refrigerate; allow to come to room temperature before serving. For longer storage, caramelized onions can be frozen. Spoon the caramelized onions into freezer storage containers, seal, label, date and freeze. Thaw overnight in the refrigerator, then let stand until onions are room temperature before serving.

grilled antipasti platter with lemon aioli

Prep Time: 35 Minutes
Start to Finish: 1 Hour 35 Minutes
Servings: 10

Lemon Aioli

1   cup mayonnaise or salad dressing
1   teaspoon grated lemon peel
2   tablespoons fresh lemon juice
1   to 2 cloves garlic, finely chopped

Antipasti

1   medium zucchini, cut into 4-inch sticks
1   medium yellow summer squash or crookneck squash, cut into 4-inch sticks
1   medium red bell pepper, cut into 2-inch pieces
2   cups cherry tomatoes
1   cup small whole mushrooms
1   medium red onion, cut into 1/2-inch wedges
2   tablespoons olive or vegetable oil
1   teaspoon salt
20   thin slices hard salami (about 1/4 lb)
1/2   lb mozzarella cheese, cut into 1/2-inch cubes

1 In small bowl, stir all aioli ingredients until well mixed. Cover and refrigerate at least 1 hour before serving.

2 Heat coals or gas grill for direct heat.

3 In large bowl, toss vegetables with oil and salt. Heat grill basket (grill "wok") on grill until hot. Add vegetables to grill basket. Cover and grill vegetables 6 to 10 minutes, shaking basket or stirring vegetables occasionally, until vegetables are crisp-tender and lightly charred.

4 Arrange salami around edge of large serving platter. Mound grilled vegetables onto center of serving platter. Sprinkle cheese cubes over vegetables. Serve with aioli for dipping.

High Altitude (3500-6500 ft): No change.

Nutritional Info: 1 Serving: Calories 320; Total Fat 28g (Saturated Fat 7g); Sodium 690mg; Total Carbohydrate 7g (Dietary Fiber 1g); Protein 9g. Exchanges: 1 Vegetable, 1 High-Fat Meat, 4 Fat. Carbohydrate Choices: 1/2.

Betty's Kitchen Tip

• Make this a cold antipasti platter by omitting the grilling step. Add 1 cup pitted whole ripe olives and 10 pepperoncini peppers (bottled Italian peppers), drained, with cheese cubes.

margarita fruit dip

Prep Time: 15 Minutes
Start to Finish: 1 Hour 15 Minutes
Servings: 28 (2 tablespoons each) **EASY**

- 2 packages (8 oz each) cream cheese, softened
- 2/3 cup frozen (thawed) margarita drink mix (from 10-oz can)
- 1/4 cup orange juice
- 2 teaspoons grated lime peel
- 1/2 cup whipping (heavy) cream

Whole strawberries

1 Beat cream cheese, margarita mix, orange juice and lime peel in large bowl with electric mixer on low speed until smooth.

2 Beat whipping cream in chilled small bowl with electric mixer on high speed until stiff. Fold into cream cheese mixture. Cover and refrigerate 1 hour.

3 Serve dip with strawberries.

High Altitude (3500-6500 ft): No change.

Nutritional Info: 1 Serving (2 tablespoons): Calories 70; Total Fat 7g (Saturated Fat 4g); Sodium 55mg; Total Carbohydrate 2g (Dietary Fiber 0g); Protein 1g. Exchanges: 1-1/2 Fat. Carbohydrate Choices: 0.

Betty's Kitchen Tips

Substitution: For an authentic margarita flavor, use 2 tablespoons tequila and 2 tablespoons orange juice instead of the 1/4 cup orange juice.

Special Touch: Rub rim of a serving bowl with a lemon, lime or orange half, then dip the rim of the bowl into a shallow dish of colored sugar.

Health Twist: To reduce fat to 4g and calories to 60 per serving, use reduced-fat cream cheese instead of regular cream cheese and 1 cup frozen (thawed) fat-free whipped topping instead of the whipping cream.

sticky ginger garlic chicken wings

Prep Time: 20 Minutes
Start to Finish: 1 Hour 20 Minutes
Servings: 20 (about 2 wings each)

John Mitzewich
Food Wishes Video Recipes
www.foodwishes.com

Glaze

1/2	cup packed brown sugar
1/2	cup rice vinegar
2	tablespoons grated gingerroot
1	tablespoon Sriracha hot chili sauce, or 1/2 teaspoon crushed red pepper flakes
3	cloves garlic, finely chopped
1	teaspoon soy sauce

Chicken

3	tablespoons red pepper sauce
2	tablespoons vegetable oil
1/2	teaspoon salt
1/2	teaspoon pepper
5	lb chicken wing drummettes
1	cup Gold Medal® all-purpose flour

1 In 1-quart saucepan, combine all glaze ingredients; bring to a simmer, stirring frequently over medium heat until sugar is dissolved, about 5 minutes. Remove from heat; set aside.

2 In 2-gallon resealable food-storage plastic bag, mix pepper sauce, oil, salt, pepper and chicken. Seal bag; shake to coat. Add flour, seal bag and shake until chicken is coated with flour.

3 Heat oven to 375°F. Line two cookie sheets with heavy-duty foil; spray with cooking spray.

4 Place chicken on cookie sheets. Bake uncovered 30 minutes, turn chicken over and rotate pans. Bake 20 to 30 minutes longer or until golden brown and juice of chicken is no longer pink when centers of thickest piece are cut.

5 In large bowl, toss chicken with glaze.

High Altitude (3500-6500 ft): No change.

Nutritional Info: 1 Serving (2 wings): Calories 170; Total Fat 7g (Saturated Fat 2g); Sodium 170mg; Total Carbohydrate 11g (Dietary Fiber 0g); Protein 15g. Exchanges: 1/2 Starch, 1-1/2 Medium-Fat Meat. Carbohydrate Choices: 1.

Betty's Kitchen Tip

• Fresh gingerroot will last up to 2 months when covered with dry sherry and stored in a tightly-covered jar in the refrigerator.

blt tomato cups

Prep Time: 30 Minutes
Start to Finish: 30 Minutes
Servings: 24 appetizers

QUICK LOW FAT

6	slices bacon, cut into 1/2 inch slices
12	small plum (Roma) tomatoes
3	cups coarsely chopped romaine lettuce (6 leaves)
2	tablespoons ranch dressing
2	tablespoons coarsely crushed garlic and butter flavor croutons

1 In 10-inch nonstick skillet over medium heat, cook bacon 5 to 7 minutes until crisp; drain on paper towels.

2 With serrated knife, cut each tomato in half crosswise. Using teaspoon, scoop out seeds and pulp from each tomato half, leaving enough tomato for a firm shell. If necessary, cut small slice from bottom so tomato half stands upright.

3 In medium bowl, combine lettuce and ranch dressing. Using small tongs or fingers, fill tomato shells evenly with lettuce mixture. Sprinkle with bacon and croutons. Serve immediately or refrigerate for up to 1 hour before serving.

High Altitude (3500-6500 ft): No change.

Nutritional Info: 1 Appetizer: Calories 25; Total Fat 1.5g (Saturated Fat 0g); Sodium 60mg; Total Carbohydrate 1g (Dietary Fiber 0g); Protein 1g. Exchanges: 1/2 Vegetable, 1/2 Fat. Carbohydrate Choices: 0.

Betty's Kitchen Tip
• If desired, sprinkle evenly with about 2 tablespoons of finely shredded Cheddar cheese.

chicken salad roll-ups

Prep Time: 35 Minutes
Start to Finish: 1 Hour 35 Minutes
Servings: 24

2	cups chopped cooked chicken
3	medium green onions, chopped (3 tablespoons)
1/4	cup chopped walnuts
1/2	cup creamy poppy seed dressing

1/2	cup reduced-fat cream cheese spread (from 8-oz container)
2	flour tortillas (10 inch)
6	leaves Bibb lettuce
1/2	cup finely chopped strawberries

1 In food processor bowl, mix chicken, onions and walnuts. Cover and process by using quick on-and-off motions until finely chopped. Add 1/3 cup of the poppy seed dressing; process only until mixed. In small bowl, mix remaining dressing and cream cheese spread with spoon until smooth.

2 Spread cream cheese mixture evenly over entire surface of tortillas. Remove white rib from lettuce leaves. Press lettuce into cream cheese, tearing to fit and leaving top 2 inches of tortillas uncovered. Spread chicken mixture over lettuce. Sprinkle strawberries over chicken.

3 Firmly roll up tortillas, beginning at bottom. Wrap each roll in plastic wrap. Refrigerate for at least 1 hour. Trim the ends of each roll. Cut rolls into 1/2- to 3/4-inch slices.

High Altitude (3500-6500 ft): No change.

Nutritional Info: 1 Serving: Calories 80; Total Fat 4g (Saturated Fat 1g); Sodium 170mg; Total Carbohydrate 5g (Dietary Fiber 0g); Protein 4g. Exchanges: 1/2 Other Carbohydrate, 1/2 Lean Meat, 1/2 Fat. Carbohydrate Choices: 1/2.

Betty's Kitchen Tips

Time-Saver: Use leftover cooked chicken, or purchase chopped cooked chicken from the freezer case in your supermarket.

Variation: Use escarole or leaf lettuce in place of the Bibb lettuce.

mango-pepper salsa crostini

Prep Time: 30 Minutes
Start to Finish: 1 Hour 30 Minutes
Servings: 32 crostini

- 1/2 medium mango, pitted, peeled and diced (1/2 cup)
- 1 medium green onion, thinly sliced (1 tablespoon)
- 1/4 cup diced red bell pepper
- 2 tablespoons chopped fresh cilantro
- 1/4 jalapeño chile, seeded, finely chopped
- 2 tablespoons lime juice
- 1 container (8 oz) pineapple cream cheese spread
- 32 thin slices baguette French bread

1 In medium glass or plastic bowl, mix all ingredients except cream cheese and bread. Cover; refrigerate 1 hour to blend flavors.

2 Spread cream cheese on baguette slices. Spoon about 1 teaspoon salsa over cream cheese, using slotted spoon.

High Altitude (3500-6500 ft): No change.

Nutritional Info: 1 Crostini: Calories 40; Total Fat 2g (Saturated Fat 1.5g); Sodium 80mg; Total Carbohydrate 4g (Dietary Fiber 0g); Protein 1g. Exchanges: 1/2 Starch. Carbohydrate Choices: 0.

LOW FAT

Betty's Kitchen Tips

Do-Ahead: Make the fruit salsa a day ahead of time and refrigerate it.

Serve-With: Peel and dice the remaining mango, and spoon it over ice cream for a mango sundae.

smoked salmon deviled eggs

Prep Time: 30 Minutes
Start to Finish: 1 Hour
Servings: 24

Rachel Rappaport
Coconut & Lime
www.coconutlime.blogspot.com

12	eggs	1/8	teaspoon white pepper
3	tablespoons mayonnaise or salad dressing	1.5	oz smoked salmon (lox) (from a 4-oz package), chopped (about 1/4 cup)
2	tablespoons Dijon mustard	1	teaspoon capers
2	tablespoons sour cream	Fresh dill weed	
1	teaspoon finely chopped fresh dill weed		

1 In 3-quart saucepan, place eggs in single layer; add enough cold water to cover eggs by 1 inch. Cover; heat to boiling. Remove from heat; let stand covered 15 minutes. Immediately cool eggs about 10 minutes in cold water to prevent further cooking.

2 Tap egg to crack shell; roll egg between hands to loosen shell, then peel. Cut eggs lengthwise in half. Slip out yolk into medium bowl; reserve egg white halves. Mash yolks with fork. Stir in mayonnaise, mustard, sour cream, dill weed and pepper until well blended. Stir in salmon.

3 Spoon yolk mixture in 1-quart resealable freezer plastic bag or pastry bag fitted with tip; seal bag. Cut small hole in bottom corner of plastic bag. Squeeze bag to pipe yolk mixture into egg white halves.

4 Refrigerate at least 30 minutes or up to 24 hours before serving. Just before serving top with capers and dill weed.

High Altitude (3500-6500 ft): No change.

Nutritional Info: 1 Serving: Calories 60; Total Fat 4.5g (Saturated Fat 1g); Sodium 90mg; Total Carbohydrate 0g (Dietary Fiber 0g); Protein 3g. Exchanges: 1/2 High-Fat Meat. Carbohydrate Choices: 0.

Betty's Kitchen Tip

• Cut a very thin slice off the bottom of each egg white before filling to help the eggs stay in place on the serving plate.

asparagus with basil pesto mayonnaise

Prep Time: 20 Minutes
Start to Finish: 20 Minutes
Servings: 16 (3 spears and 1 tablespoon mayonnaise)

QUICK

48	fresh asparagus spears (about 1-1/2 lb)
1	cup mayonnaise or salad dressing
2	tablespoons refrigerated basil pesto
1	tablespoon grated Parmesan cheese
1	tablespoon finely chopped fresh basil leaves
1	teaspoon fresh lemon juice
1	clove garlic, finely chopped (1/2 teaspoon)

Fresh basil leaves, if desired

1 Snap or cut off tough ends of asparagus spears. In 12-inch skillet, heat 1/2 inch water (salted if desired) to boiling. Add asparagus; reduce heat to medium-low. Cover; simmer 2 to 3 minutes or until crisp-tender. Drain. Plunge asparagus into bowl of ice water to cool; drain on paper towels. Refrigerate until ready to serve.

2 In small bowl, mix remaining ingredients, except basil leaves.

3 Spoon mayonnaise mixture into small serving bowl; garnish with basil leaves. Serve with blanched asparagus.

High Altitude (3500-6500 ft): No change.

Nutritional Info: 1 Serving: Calories 130; Total Fat 12g (Saturated Fat 2g); Sodium 100mg; Total Carbohydrate 3g (Dietary Fiber 1g); Protein 1g. Exchanges: 1/2 Vegetable, 2-1/2 Fat. Carbohydrate Choices: 0.

Betty's Kitchen Tip

• Leftover Basil Pesto Mayonnaise makes a flavorful sandwich spread.

cucumber mango salsa

Prep Time: 25 Minutes
Start to Finish: 2 Hours 25 Minutes
Servings: 18 (1/4 cup salsa and about 10 chips)

Shreya Sasaki
RecipeMatcher
www.recipematcher.com

3	ripe medium mangoes, seeds removed, peeled and coarsely chopped
1	large cucumber, peeled, seeded, coarsely chopped
2	jalapeños, seeded, finely chopped
1	small onion, finely chopped (1/4 cup)
1	clove garlic, finely chopped

1/4	cup chopped fresh cilantro
1	tablespoon lime juice
1/4	teaspoon salt
1/8	teaspoon pepper
18	oz tortilla chips (from two 12-oz bags)

1 In medium bowl, stir together all ingredients except tortilla chips.

2 Cover; refrigerate at least 2 hours or overnight to allow flavors to blend. Serve with tortilla chips.

High Altitude (3500-6500 ft): No change.

Nutritional Info: 1 Serving: Calories 170; Total Fat 7g (Saturated Fat 1g); Sodium 135mg; Total Carbohydrate 24g (Dietary Fiber 1g); Protein 2g. Exchanges: 1 Starch, 1/2 Fruit, 1-1/2 Fat. Carbohydrate Choices: 1-1/2.

Betty's Kitchen Tip

• To peel a mango, use a sharp knife to cut through one side of mango, sliding knife next to seed. Repeat on the other side of seed, making 2 large pieces. Make cuts in crosshatch fashion through flesh just to peel; bend peel back and carefully slide knife between peel and flesh to separate. Discard peel; dice flesh.

spinach-cheese balls

Prep Time: 10 Minutes
Start to Finish: 25 Minutes
Servings: 30 cheese balls

- -

1 box (9 oz) Green Giant® frozen chopped spinach, thawed, squeezed to drain
1 cup Original Bisquick® mix
2 cups shredded mozzarella cheese (8 oz)
1 egg
2 teaspoons Italian seasoning
1 teaspoon garlic salt
1 cup tomato pasta sauce, if desired

- -

1 Heat oven to 400°F. Spray cookie sheet with cooking spray. In large bowl, mix all ingredients, except pasta sauce. Shape mixture into 1-inch balls; place on cookie sheet.

2 Bake 10 to 15 minutes or until golden brown. Immediately remove from pan. Serve with pasta sauce.

High Altitude (3500-6500 ft): No change.

Nutritional Info: 1 Cheese Ball: Calories 45 (Calories from Fat 20); Total Fat 2g (Saturated Fat 1g, Trans Fat 0g); Cholesterol 10mg; Sodium 130mg; Total Carbohydrate 3g (Dietary Fiber 0g, Sugars 0g); Protein 3g. % Daily Value: Vitamin A 15%; Vitamin C 0%; Calcium 8%; Iron 0%. Exchanges: 1/2 High-Fat Meat. Carbohydrate Choices: 0.

EASY QUICK LOW FAT

Betty's Kitchen Tip

- For an easy way to serve these cheese balls, place a pretzel stick into each appetizer.

bacon, lettuce and tomato dip

Prep Time: 30 Minutes
Start to Finish: 30 Minutes
Servings: 16 (2 slices baguette and 2 tablespoons dip each)

QUICK

1 cup sour cream with chives and onions	1/2 cup chopped Roma (plum) tomatoes
1/4 cup mayonnaise or salad dressing	1 tablespoon chopped fresh chives
1/2 cup crumbled cooked bacon (about 8 slices)	32 slices (1/4-inch-thick) baguette-style French bread (from 10-oz loaf)
1-1/2 cups shredded romaine lettuce	

1 In small bowl, mix sour cream and mayonnaise until blended. Stir in bacon.

2 Arrange lettuce in shallow bowl or on small platter. Spoon sour cream mixture over lettuce. Top with tomatoes; sprinkle with chives. Serve with baguette slices.

High Altitude (3500-6500 ft): No change.

Nutritional Info: 1 Serving: Calories 120; Total Fat 7g (Saturated Fat 2.5g); Sodium 200mg; Total Carbohydrate 11g (Dietary Fiber 0g); Protein 3g. Exchanges: 1 Starch, 1 Fat. Carbohydrate Choices: 1.

Betty's Kitchen Tips

Substitution: You can use iceberg lettuce instead of the romaine if you like.

Variation: Precooked bacon can be purchased in strips or chopped. You'll find packages of it with the sandwich meats or at the deli.

Time-Saver: This dip can be prepared up to 24 hours in advance, but refrigerate the components separately. When you are at your destination and ready to serve it, assemble as directed.

mushroom and bacon mini pocket pies

Prep Time: 50 Minutes
Start to Finish: 1 Hour 25 Minutes
Servings: 16 appetizers

Louise Felice
Felice in the Kitchen
www.felicekitchen.blogspot.com

1	package (1 lb) bacon, cut into 1/4-inch pieces
1	package (8 oz) sliced mushrooms, chopped
1	large onion, finely chopped (1 cup)
2-2/3	cups Gold Medal® all-purpose flour
1	cup shredded Cheddar cheese (4 oz)
3/4	cup plus 2 tablespoons butter, cut into pieces

10	oz cream cheese, cut into pieces
3	egg yolks
2	tablespoons Gold Medal® all-purpose flour
1	egg, beaten
1	teaspoon sesame seeds

1 In 12-inch skillet, cook bacon over medium heat for 4 to 6 minutes until crisp; drain on paper towels. Cook mushrooms and onion in 2 tablespoons bacon drippings over medium heat, stirring occasionally, until tender. In small bowl, combine bacon, mushrooms and onion. Set aside.

2 Heat oven to 400°F. Spray large cookie sheet with cooking spray.

3 In food processor with metal blade, place flour and cheese. Cover; process using quick on-and-off motions, until well mixed. Add butter; process until mixture looks like coarse crumbs. Add cream cheese and egg yolks, continue to process just until blended and dough begins to form a ball.

4 On floured surface, knead the dough 10 times. Roll dough until 1/4-inch thick. Cut into 16 rounds with floured 4-inch round cutter.

5 Spoon about 1 tablespoon bacon mixture onto each round. Fold each in half; seal edges with fork tines. Place on cookie sheet. Brush each pocket with beaten egg; sprinkle with sesame seeds. Bake 15 to 20 minutes or until golden brown.

High Altitude (3500-6500 ft): No change.

Nutritional Info: 1 Appetizer: Calories 340; Total Fat 25g (Saturated Fat 13g); Sodium 370mg; Total Carbohydrate 19g (Dietary Fiber 1g); Protein 9g. Exchanges: 1-1/2 Starch, 1/2 High-Fat Meat, 4 Fat. Carbohydrate Choices: 1.

buffalo chex® mix

Prep Time: 15 Minutes
Start to Finish: 15 Minutes
Servings: 24 (1/2 cup each)

EASY QUICK

- 4 cups Rice Chex® cereal
- 4 cups Wheat Chex® cereal
- 2 cups bite-size Parmesan-flavored crackers
- 2 cups small pretzel twists
- 6 tablespoons butter or margarine
- 2-1/2 tablespoons hot sauce
- 1 envelope (1 oz) ranch dressing and seasoning mix
- 2 teaspoons celery seed

1 In large microwavable bowl, mix cereals, crackers and pretzels; set aside.

2 In small microwavable bowl, microwave butter uncovered on High about 40 seconds or until melted. Stir in hot sauce, dressing mix and celery seed. Pour over cereal mixture; stir until evenly coated.

3 Microwave uncovered on High 4 to 5 minutes, thoroughly stirring every 2 minutes. Spread on paper towels to cool. Store in airtight container.

High Altitude (3500-6500 ft): No change.

Nutritional Info: 1 Serving: Calories 110; Total Fat 4g (Saturated Fat 2g); Sodium 330mg; Total Carbohydrate 16g (Dietary Fiber 1g); Protein 2g. Exchanges: 1/2 Starch, 1/2 Other Carbohydrate, 1 Fat. Carbohydrate Choices: 1.

Betty's Kitchen Tips

Purchasing: You'll find the Parmesan-flavored crackers in the snack cracker aisle of your grocery store. Look for those little cheesy cracker squares that come in an endless variety of flavors.

Do-Ahead: To ease the load of last-minute prep, make the mix up to 2 weeks ahead and store in an airtight container.

oven caramel corn

Prep Time: 20 Minutes
Start to Finish: 1 Hour 20 Minutes
Servings: 15 (1 cup each)

12	cups popped popcorn	1/2	teaspoon baking soda
1	cup packed brown sugar	2	cups sweetened dried cranberries
1/2	cup butter or margarine	1-1/2	cups white vanilla baking chips
1/4	cup light corn syrup		
1/2	teaspoon salt		

1 Heat oven to 200°F. Divide popcorn between 2 ungreased 13x9-inch pans.

2 In 3-quart heavy saucepan, heat brown sugar, butter, corn syrup and salt over medium heat, stirring occasionally, until bubbly around edges. Cook 5 minutes longer, stirring occasionally; remove from heat. Stir in baking soda.

3 Pour caramel mixture over popcorn; stir until well coated. Add 1 cup cranberries and 3/4 cup baking chips to each pan; toss until well coated. Bake 1 hour, stirring every 15 minutes. Spread on waxed paper or foil to cool. Store in airtight container.

High Altitude (3500-6500 ft): No change.

Nutritional Info: 1 Serving: Calories 350; Total Fat 16g (Saturated Fat 9g); Sodium 250mg; Total Carbohydrate 49g (Dietary Fiber 1g); Protein 2g. Exchanges: 1/2 Fruit, 3 Other Carbohydrate, 3 Fat. Carbohydrate Choices: 3.

Betty's Kitchen Tip

• When planning your menus and grocery list, check that you have enough storage containers for the recipes you'll be making for future use. Resealable food-storage plastic bags are great for storing snack mixes like this caramel corn.

mini chinese chicken snacks

Prep Time: 25 Minutes
Start to Finish: 50 Minutes
Servings: 2 dozen appetizers

- 1-1/4 cups Original Bisquick® mix
- 1/4 cup butter or margarine, softened
- 2 tablespoons boiling water
- 1/2 cup half-and-half
- 1 egg
- 1/3 cup finely shredded carrot
- 1/3 cup drained sliced water chestnuts (from 8-oz can), chopped
- 1 tablespoon grated lemon peel
- 1/2 teaspoon salt
- 1/2 teaspoon garlic powder
- 1/2 teaspoon five-spice powder
- 1 medium green onion, thinly sliced (1 tablespoon)
- 1 can (5 oz) chunk chicken, drained

1 Heat oven to 375°F. Generously grease 24 miniature muffin cups. Stir Bisquick and butter until blended. Add boiling water; stir vigorously until soft dough forms. Press rounded teaspoonful of dough on bottom and up side of each cup.

2 Beat half-and-half and egg in medium bowl. Stir in remaining ingredients. Spoon about 1 tablespoon mixture into each cup.

3 Bake 20 to 25 minutes or until edges are golden brown and centers are set. Serve warm. Store covered in refrigerator.

High Altitude (3500-6500 ft): No change.

Nutritional Info: 1 Appetizer: Calories 60 (Calories from Fat 30); Total Fat 3.5g (Saturated Fat 2g, Trans Fat 0g); Cholesterol 20mg; Sodium 170mg; Total Carbohydrate 5g (Dietary Fiber 0g, Sugars 0g); Protein 2g. % Daily Value: Vitamin A 6%; Vitamin C 0%; Calcium 0%; Iron 0%. Exchanges: 1/2 Starch, 1/2 Fat. Carbohydrate Choices: 1/2.

Betty's Kitchen Tip

• For a pretty presentation, sprinkle tops of appetizers with chopped peanuts and chopped fresh cilantro just before serving.

pear and blue cheese tart

Prep Time: 20 Minutes
Start to Finish: 1 Hour 10 Minutes
Servings: 12

Crust
1-1/2   cups Original Bisquick® mix
1/3   cup very hot water

Filling
2   tablespoons butter or margarine
2   shallots, finely chopped (about 1/3 cup)

2   medium pears, peeled, cut into 1/4-inch slices (about 2 cups)
1/4   cup chopped walnuts
1/2   cup crumbled blue cheese (2 oz)
2   tablespoons chopped fresh parsley

1 Heat oven to 425°F. Spray 9-inch tart pan with removable bottom with cooking spray.

2 In medium bowl, stir Bisquick mix and hot water until soft dough forms. Press dough in bottom and up side of tart pan, using fingers coated with Bisquick mix. Bake 10 minutes.

3 Meanwhile, in 8-inch skillet, melt butter over medium heat. Add shallots; cook 2 to 4 minutes, stirring occasionally, until tender; remove from heat.

4 Arrange pear slices on crust. Spread butter mixture over pears. Bake 20 minutes.

5 Sprinkle walnuts over pears. Bake about 10 minutes longer or until tart is golden brown.

6 Remove from oven; sprinkle with cheese. Cool 10 minutes on cooling rack. Sprinkle with parsley. Serve the tart warm or at room temperature.

High Altitude (3500-6500 ft): No change.

Nutritional Info: 1 Serving: Calories 130 (Calories from Fat 60); Total Fat 7g (Saturated Fat 3g, Trans Fat 0.5g); Cholesterol 10mg; Sodium 260mg; Total Carbohydrate 15g (Dietary Fiber 1g, Sugars 3g); Protein 3g. % Daily Value: Vitamin A 4%; Vitamin C 0%; Calcium 4%; Iron 4%. Exchanges: 1 Starch, 1 Fat. Carbohydrate Choices: 1.

Betty's Kitchen Tip

• Pour a glass of port or other red wine to enjoy with this savory appetizer.

OVEN ENTREES

p.49

59

58

57

impossibly easy tuna, tomato and cheddar pie

Prep Time: 20 Minutes
Start to Finish: 1 Hour
Servings: 6

- -

1	tablespoon butter or margarine
1	large onion, chopped (1 cup)
1	can (6 oz) tuna, drained
1	cup shredded Cheddar cheese (4 oz)
1/2	cup Original Bisquick® mix

1	cup milk
1/8	teaspoon pepper
2	eggs
1	medium tomato, thinly sliced

- -

1 Heat oven to 400°F. Spray 9-inch glass pie plate with cooking spray. Melt butter in 10-inch skillet over low heat. Cook onion in butter, stirring occasionally, until tender. Sprinkle tuna, 1/2 cup of the cheese and the onion in pie plate.

2 Stir remaining ingredients except tomato in medium bowl with wire whisk or fork until blended. Pour into pie plate.

3 Bake 25 to 30 minutes or until knife inserted in center comes out clean. Top with tomato slices and remaining 1/2 cup cheese. Bake 3 to 5 minutes longer or until cheese is melted. Let stand 5 minutes before serving.

High Altitude (3500-6500 ft): No change.

Nutritional Info: 1 Serving: Calories 220 (Calories from Fat 110); Total Fat 12g (Saturated Fat 6g, Trans Fat 0.5g); Cholesterol 105mg; Sodium 410mg; Total Carbohydrate 12g (Dietary Fiber 0g, Sugars 5g); Protein 17g. % Daily Value: Vitamin A 15%; Vitamin C 4%; Calcium 20%; Iron 6%. Exchanges: 1 Starch, 2 Medium-Fat Meat. Carbohydrate Choices: 1.

Betty's Kitchen Tip

• For a Tuna Melt Pie, use 2 tablespoons butter or margarine instead of 1 tablespoon, and substitute 1 cup cubed process cheese spread loaf (4 oz) for the shredded Cheddar cheese.

easy hamburger pot pie

Prep Time: 15 Minutes
Start to Finish: 50 Minutes
Servings: 6 (1 cup each)

EASY

1	lb lean (at least 80%) ground beef
1-1/2	teaspoons onion powder
1/2	teaspoon salt
3/4	teaspoon pepper
1	bag (1 lb) frozen mixed vegetables, thawed, drained
1	can (10-3/4 oz) condensed tomato soup
1	cup Original Bisquick® mix
1/2	cup milk
1	egg

1 Heat oven to 375°F. In 12-inch skillet, cook beef, onion powder, salt and pepper over medium-high heat 5 to 7 minutes, stirring frequently, until the beef is thoroughly cooked; drain.

2 Stir vegetables and soup into beef; heat to boiling. Spoon mixture into an ungreased 2-quart casserole.

3 In small bowl, stir remaining ingredients with wire whisk or fork until blended. Pour over hot beef mixture.

4 Bake 28 to 33 minutes or until crust is golden brown.

High Altitude (3500-6500 ft): No change.

Nutritional Info: 1 Serving: Calories 320 (Calories from Fat 120); Total Fat 13g (Saturated Fat 4.5g, Trans Fat 1.5g); Cholesterol 85mg; Sodium 820mg; Total Carbohydrate 32g (Dietary Fiber 4g, Sugars 8g); Protein 19g. % Daily Value: Vitamin A 70%; Vitamin C 6%; Calcium 8%; Iron 15%. Exchanges: 1/2 Starch, 1-1/2 Other Carbohydrate, 1 Vegetable, 2 Medium-Fat Meat, 1/2 Fat. Carbohydrate Choices: 2.

Betty's Kitchen Tip

• This retro recipe has it all—easy, economical, kid-friendly and great tasting!

quick cheeseburger bake

Prep Time: 10 Minutes
Start to Finish: 40 Minutes
Servings: 8

EASY

1 lb lean (at least 80%) ground beef	1/4 cup milk
3/4 cup chopped onion	2 cups Original Bisquick® mix
1 can (11 oz) condensed Cheddar cheese soup	3/4 cup water
1 cup Green Giant® Valley Fresh Steamers™ frozen mixed vegetables	1 cup shredded Cheddar cheese (4 oz)

1 Heat oven to 400°F. Generously grease 13x9x2-inch (3-quart) glass baking dish. Cook ground beef and onion in 10-inch skillet over medium heat, stirring occasionally, until beef is brown; drain. Stir in soup, vegetables and milk.

2 Stir Bisquick mix and water in baking dish until moistened; spread evenly. Spread beef mixture over batter. Sprinkle with cheese.

3 Bake casserole for 30 minutes.

High Altitude (3500-6500 ft): No change.

Nutritional Info: 1 Serving: Calories 350 (Calories from Fat 170); Total Fat 19g (Saturated Fat 8g, Trans Fat 1.5g); Cholesterol 55mg; Sodium 850mg; Total Carbohydrate 28g (Dietary Fiber 2g, Sugars 5g); Protein 18g. % Daily Value: Vitamin A 40%; Vitamin C 0%; Calcium 15%; Iron 15%. Exchanges: 1 Starch, 1 Other Carbohydrate, 2 High-Fat Meat, 1/2 Fat. Carbohydrate Choices: 2.

Betty's Kitchen Tip

• Make it a California Bake by topping each serving with chopped fresh tomatoes, chopped lettuce and a thin slice of onion.

ham and cheese sandwich bake

Prep Time: 10 Minutes
Start to Finish: 1 Hour
Servings: 6

EASY

- 2   cups Original Bisquick® mix
- 1   cup milk
- 2   tablespoons mustard
- 1   egg
- 1   package (6 oz) thinly sliced fully cooked lean ham, chopped
- 1   cup shredded Cheddar cheese (4 ounces)

1 Heat oven to 350°F. Grease 8-inch square (2-quart) glass baking dish.

2 Mix baking mix, milk, mustard and egg until blended. Pour half of the batter into baking dish. Top with half of the ham and 1/2 cup of the cheese. Top with remaining ham. Pour remaining batter over ham.

3 Bake 45 to 50 minutes or until golden brown and set. Sprinkle with remaining 1/2 cup cheese. Let stand for 5 minutes before cutting.

High Altitude (3500-6500 ft): No change.

Nutritional Info: 1 Serving: Calories 310 (Calories from Fat 130); Total Fat 15g (Saturated Fat 7g, Trans Fat 1.5g); Cholesterol 75mg; Sodium 1030mg; Total Carbohydrate 29g (Dietary Fiber 1g, Sugars 3g); Protein 16g. % Daily Value: Vitamin A 6%; Vitamin C 0%; Calcium 20%; Iron 10%. Exchanges: 2 Starch, 1 Lean Meat, 2 Fat. Carbohydrate Choices: 2.

Betty's Kitchen Tip

• Vary the meat and cheese to suit your taste buds. You can use corned beef, smoked turkey or roast beef and American, Swiss or provolone cheese.

easy herb-chicken bake

Prep Time: 20 Minutes
Start to Finish: 50 Minutes
Servings: 8

Filling

1	tablespoon butter or margarine
1/2	cup chopped onion (1 medium)
1/2	cup chopped celery
1/2	cup chopped red bell pepper
1/2	teaspoon seasoned salt
2	cups cut-up cooked chicken or turkey
1	bag (12 oz) Green Giant® Valley Fresh Steamers™ Extra Sweet Niblets® frozen corn

1	can (10 3/4 oz) condensed cream of chicken soup

Crust

1	cup Original Bisquick® mix
1/4	cup milk
3/4	cup shredded Cheddar cheese (3 oz)
3/4	teaspoon dried thyme leaves

1 Heat oven to 400°F. Spray 8-inch square (2-quart) glass baking dish with cooking spray.

2 In 10-inch skillet, melt butter over medium-high heat. Add onion, celery, bell pepper and seasoned salt; cook about 5 minutes, stirring occasionally, until vegetables are tender. Stir in chicken, corn and soup; cook and stir until hot.

3 In medium bowl, mix Bisquick mix, milk, 1/2 cup of the cheese and the thyme. With floured fingers, press crust mixture evenly in bottom and 1 inch up sides of baking dish. Spoon hot filling into crust.

4 Bake 22 to 30 minutes or until crust is golden brown. Sprinkle top with remaining 1/4 cup cheese. Cut into squares; serve hot.

High Altitude (3500-6500 ft): No change.

Nutritional Info: 1 Serving: Calories 270 (Calories from Fat 110); Total Fat 12g (Saturated Fat 5g, Trans Fat 1g); Cholesterol 50mg; Sodium 660mg; Total Carbohydrate 23g (Dietary Fiber 2g, Sugars 3g); Protein 16g. % Daily Value: Vitamin A 15%; Vitamin C 10%; Calcium 10%; Iron 8%. Exchanges: 1 Starch, 1/2 Other Carbohydrate, 2 Medium-Fat Meat. Carbohydrate Choices: 1-1/2.

Betty's Kitchen Tip

• Try dried rubbed sage or poultry seasoning in place of the thyme.

chicken enchilada pie

Prep Time: 15 Minutes
Start to Finish: 50 Minutes
Servings: 6

EASY

- 2 cups cut-up cooked chicken
- 1 can (4.5 oz) Old El Paso® chopped green chiles
- 1/2 cup Old El Paso® enchilada sauce (from 10-oz can)
- 1/2 cup Original Bisquick® mix
- 1/2 cup cornmeal
- 1/2 cup milk
- 1 large egg
- 1 can (11 oz) Green Giant® Mexicorn® whole kernel corn with red and green peppers, drained
- 1 cup shredded Mexican cheese blend (4 oz)
- 1 medium tomato, chopped (3/4 cup)

1 Place sheet of foil on lowest oven rack. Heat oven to 400°F.

2 In 10-inch skillet over medium-high heat, cook chicken, chiles and enchilada sauce 3 to 4 minutes, stirring occasionally, until hot and bubbly. Pour into ungreased 9-inch glass pie plate.

3 In medium bowl, stir Bisquick mix, cornmeal, milk and egg with wire whisk or fork until blended. Stir in corn. Spoon over chicken mixture.

4 Place pie plate on rack above foil. Bake uncovered 22 to 27 minutes or until toothpick inserted in topping comes out clean. Top with cheese and tomato. Let stand 5 minutes before serving.

High Altitude (3500-6500 ft): No change.

Nutritional Info: 1 Serving: Calories 290 (Calories from Fat 100); Total Fat 11g (Saturated Fat 5g, Trans Fat 0g); Cholesterol 85mg; Sodium 870mg; Total Carbohydrate 29g (Dietary Fiber 2g, Sugars 6g); Protein 20g. % Daily Value: Vitamin A 10%; Vitamin C 10%; Calcium 20%; Iron 6%. Exchanges: 2 Starch, 2 Very Lean Meat, 1-1/2 Fat. Carbohydrate Choices: 2.

Betty's Kitchen Tip

• Garnish with a dollop of sour cream and sprinkle with chopped green onions.

california pizza

Prep Time: 20 Minutes
Start to Finish: 45 Minutes
Servings: 8

1 can (8 oz) tomato sauce	2 cups Original Bisquick® mix
1 teaspoon dried oregano leaves	1/2 cup cold water
1/2 teaspoon dried basil leaves	1-1/2 cups shredded Monterey Jack cheese (6 oz)
1/2 teaspoon salt	2 cups cut-up cooked chicken
1/4 teaspoon garlic powder or onion powder	1/2 cup sliced ripe olives
1/8 teaspoon pepper	1 medium avocado, sliced

1 Heat oven to 425°F. Grease 12-inch pizza pan. Stir together tomato sauce, oregano, basil, salt, garlic powder and pepper; set aside.

2 Stir Bisquick and cold water until soft dough forms. Press dough in pizza pan, using fingers dipped in Bisquick; pinch edge to form 1/2-inch rim. Sprinkle 1/2 cup of the cheese over dough.

3 Spread tomato sauce over top. Top with chicken and olives. Sprinkle with remaining 1 cup cheese.

4 Bake 20 to 25 minutes or until crust is golden brown and cheese is bubbly. Garnish with avocado slices.

High Altitude (3500-6500 ft): No change.

Nutritional Info: 1 Serving: Calories 310 (Calories from Fat 150); Total Fat 16g (Saturated Fat 6g, Trans Fat 1.5g); Cholesterol 50mg; Sodium 880mg; Total Carbohydrate 23g (Dietary Fiber 2g, Sugars 2g); Protein 18g. % Daily Value: Vitamin A 8%; Vitamin C 4%; Calcium 20%; Iron 10%. Exchanges: 1-1/2 Starch, 2 Lean Meat, 2 Fat. Carbohydrate Choices: 1-1/2.

Betty's Kitchen Tip

• One cup of pizza sauce can be used instead of the tomato sauce, oregano, basil, salt, garlic powder and pepper.

lemon-apricot chicken

Prep Time: 30 Minutes
Start to Finish: 1 Hour
Servings: 4

1	egg
2	tablespoons water
1	cup Original Bisquick® mix
1	tablespoon grated lemon peel
1/4	teaspoon garlic powder
4	boneless skinless chicken breasts
3	tablespoons butter or margarine, melted
2/3	cup apricot preserves
2	tablespoons lemon juice
1/2	teaspoon soy sauce
1/4	teaspoon ground ginger

1 Heat oven to 425°F. Spray 15x10-inch baking pan with cooking spray. Beat egg and water slightly. Stir together baking mix, lemon peel and garlic powder.

2 Dip chicken into egg mixture, then coat with baking mix mixture. Place in pan. Drizzle with melted butter.

3 Bake uncovered 20 minutes; turn chicken. Bake about 10 minutes longer or until juice is no longer pink when centers of thickest pieces are cut. Heat remaining ingredients in 1-quart saucepan over low heat, stirring occasionally, until warm. Spoon over chicken.

High Altitude (3500-6500 ft): No change.

Nutritional Info: 1 Serving: Calories 510 (Calories from Fat 160); Total Fat 18g (Saturated Fat 8g, Trans Fat 1.5g); Cholesterol 150mg; Sodium 570mg; Total Carbohydrate 57g (Dietary Fiber 1g, Sugars 27g); Protein 30g. % Daily Value: Vitamin A 8%; Vitamin C 8%; Calcium 6%; Iron 10%. Exchanges: 2 Starch, 2 Other Carbohydrate, 3 Lean Meat, 1-1/2 Fat. Carbohydrate Choices: 4.

Betty's Kitchen Tip

• Leftover chicken can be sliced and served on a bed of greens with Asian dressing, crunchy chow mein noodles, chopped green onions and mandarin orange slices.

italian beef bake

Prep Time: 15 Minutes
Start to Finish: 40 Minutes
Servings: 6

EASY

1 lb lean (at least 80%) ground beef	3/4 cup milk
1-1/4 cups tomato pasta sauce	1/4 cup grated Parmesan cheese
1 cup shredded mozzarella cheese (4 oz)	Additional heated tomato pasta sauce, if desired
2 cups Original Bisquick® mix	

1 Heat oven to 400°F. Spray 8-inch square (2-quart) glass baking dish with cooking spray. In 10-inch skillet, cook beef over medium-high heat 5 to 7 minutes, stirring occasionally, until thoroughly cooked; drain.

2 Stir 1-1/4 cups pasta sauce into beef. Heat to boiling. Spoon into baking dish; top with mozzarella cheese.

3 Meanwhile, in medium bowl, stir Bisquick mix, milk and Parmesan cheese until soft dough forms.

4 Drop dough by 12 tablespoonfuls onto beef mixture.

5 Bake uncovered 20 to 24 minutes or until topping is golden brown and toothpick inserted in topping comes out clean. Serve topped with additional warm pasta sauce.

High Altitude (3500-6500 ft): No change.

Nutritional Info: 1 Serving: Calories 430 (Calories from Fat 190); Total Fat 21g (Saturated Fat 8g, Trans Fat 1.5g); Cholesterol 65mg; Sodium 1050mg; Total Carbohydrate 36g (Dietary Fiber 1g, Sugars 8g); Protein 24g. % Daily Value: Vitamin A 10%; Vitamin C 6%; Calcium 30%; Iron 15%. Exchanges: 2 Starch, 1/2 Other Carbohydrate, 2-1/2 Medium-Fat Meat, 1-1/2 Fat. Carbohydrate Choices: 2-1/2.

Betty's Kitchen Tip

• Sausage lovers can substitute 1 pound hot or mild Italian sausage for the ground beef.

impossibly easy chili pie

Prep Time: 20 Minutes
Start to Finish: 1 Hour
Servings: 6

- -

1 lb lean (at least 80%) ground beef
1 can (14-1/2 oz) diced tomatoes, drained
1 medium onion, chopped (1/2 cup)
1 envelope (1-1/4 oz) chili seasoning mix
1 can (2-1/4 oz) sliced ripe olives, drained
1 cup shredded Cheddar cheese (4 oz)

1/2 cup Original Bisquick® mix
1 cup milk
2 eggs
Sour cream, if desired
Salsa, if desired

- -

1 Heat oven to 400°F. Spray 9-inch glass pie plate with cooking spray. Cook beef in 10-inch skillet over medium heat 8 to 10 minutes, stirring occasionally, until brown; drain. Stir in tomatoes, onion and chili seasoning mix. Spread in pie plate. Sprinkle with olives and 1/2 cup of the cheese.

2 Stir Bisquick mix, milk and eggs in medium bowl with wire whisk or fork until blended. Pour into pie plate.

3 Bake 30 minutes. Top with remaining cheese. Bake 2 to 3 minutes longer until cheese is melted. Let stand 5 minutes before serving. Serve with sour cream and salsa.

High Altitude (3500-6500 ft): No change.

Nutritional Info: 1 Serving: Calories 270 (Calories from Fat 100); Total Fat 11g (Saturated Fat 4g, Trans Fat 0.5g); Cholesterol 50mg; Sodium 810mg; Total Carbohydrate 18g (Dietary Fiber 2g, Sugars 8g); Protein 24g. % Daily Value: Vitamin A 20%; Vitamin C 10%; Calcium 25%; Iron 15%. Exchanges: 1 Starch, 1 Vegetable, 3 Medium-Fat Meat, 1 Fat. Carbohydrate Choices: 1.

Betty's Kitchen Tip

• Crank up the heat by substituting shredded pepper-Jack cheese.

pesto and cheese pizza

Prep Time: 20 Minutes
Start to Finish: 45 Minutes
Servings: 8

3	cups Original Bisquick® mix
2/3	cup very hot water
2	tablespoons olive or vegetable oil
4	sticks (1 oz each) mozzarella string cheese, cut in half lengthwise
1/3	cup refrigerated basil pesto (from 7-oz container)
1	bag (7 oz) shredded mozzarella cheese with sun-dried tomatoes and basil or plain mozzarella cheese (1-3/4 cups)
1-1/2	cups 1/8-inch strips yellow, red and green bell peppers

1 Move oven rack to lowest position. Heat oven to 450°F. Spray 12-inch pizza pan with cooking spray. In large bowl, stir Bisquick mix, water and oil with fork until soft dough forms; beat vigorously 20 strokes. Cover; let stand 8 minutes.

2 Pat or press dough in bottom and 1 inch over side of pizza pan. Place string cheese along edge of dough, overlapping if necessary. Fold 1-inch edge of dough over and around cheese; press to seal.

3 Bake 6 to 7 minutes or until lightly browned around edges.

4 Spread pesto over warm crust. Sprinkle with 1 cup of the mozzarella cheese; top with bell peppers and remaining 3/4 cup cheese. Bake 11 to 14 minutes or until crust is golden brown and cheese is melted.

High Altitude (3500-6500 ft): No change.

Nutritional Info: 1 Serving: Calories 380 (Calories from Fat 210); Total Fat 23g (Saturated Fat 8g, Trans Fat 1g); Cholesterol 25mg; Sodium 930mg; Total Carbohydrate 30g (Dietary Fiber 1g, Sugars 4g); Protein 14g. % Daily Value: Vitamin A 10%; Vitamin C 20%; Calcium 40%; Iron 10%. Exchanges: 1-1/2 Starch, 1/2 Other Carbohydrate, 1-1/2 Medium-Fat Meat, 3 Fat. Carbohydrate Choices: 2.

Betty's Kitchen Tip

• For a heartier version, add 1/4 cup diced smoked ham or cut-up chicken to the pizza toppings.

impossibly easy blt pie

Prep Time: 20 Minutes
Start to Finish: 55 Minutes
Servings: 6

12 slices bacon	1/8 teaspoon pepper
1 cup shredded Swiss cheese (4 oz)	2 eggs
1/2 cup Original Bisquick® mix	2 tablespoons mayonnaise or salad dressing
1/3 cup mayonnaise or salad dressing	1 cup shredded lettuce
3/4 cup milk	6 thin slices tomato

1 Heat oven to 400°F. Spray 9-inch glass pie plate with cooking spray. Line microwavable plate with microwavable paper towel. Place 6 slices of the bacon on paper towel; cover with another paper towel. Microwave 4 to 6 minutes or until crisp. Repeat with remaining 6 slices bacon. Crumble bacon. Layer bacon and cheese in pie plate.

2 In medium bowl, beat Bisquick mix, 1/3 cup mayonnaise, the milk, pepper and eggs with wire whisk until blended. Pour into pie plate.

3 Bake 25 to 30 minutes or until top is golden brown and knife inserted in center comes out clean. Let stand 5 minutes before serving. Spread 2 tablespoons mayonnaise over top of pie. Sprinkle with lettuce; top with tomato.

High Altitude (3500-6500 ft): No change.

Nutritional Info: 1 Serving: Calories 350 (Calories from Fat 250); Total Fat 28g (Saturated Fat 8g, Trans Fat 0g); Cholesterol 110mg; Sodium 620mg; Total Carbohydrate 10g (Dietary Fiber 0g, Sugars 4g); Protein 14g. % Daily Value: Vitamin A 10%; Vitamin C 0%; Calcium 20%; Iron 6%. Exchanges: 1/2 Starch, 2 High-Fat Meat, 2-1/2 Fat. Carbohydrate Choices: 1/2.

Betty's Kitchen Tip

• You can trim the fat in this pie by reducing the bacon to 8 slices, and using fat-free (skim) milk and reduced-fat mayonnaise or salad dressing.

ultimate chicken fingers

Prep Time: 20 Minutes
Start to Finish: 35 Minutes
Servings: 4

2/3	cup Original Bisquick® mix
1/2	cup grated Parmesan cheese
1/2	teaspoon salt or garlic salt
1/2	teaspoon paprika
3	boneless skinless chicken breasts, cut crosswise into 1/2-inch strips
1	egg, slightly beaten
3	tablespoons butter or margarine, melted

1 Heat oven to 450°F. Line cookie sheet with foil; spray with cooking spray.

2 Mix Bisquick mix, cheese, salt and paprika in 1-gallon resealable plastic food-storage bag. Dip half the chicken strips into egg; place in bag of Bisquick mixture. Seal bag; shake to coat. Place chicken on cookie sheet. Repeat with remaining chicken. Drizzle butter over chicken.

3 Bake 12 to 14 minutes, turning after 6 minutes with pancake turner, until no longer pink in center.

High Altitude (3500-6500 ft): No change.

Nutritional Info: 1 Serving: Calories 340 (Calories from Fat 170); Total Fat 19g (Saturated Fat 9g, Trans Fat 1g); Cholesterol 140mg; Sodium 930mg; Total Carbohydrate 13g (Dietary Fiber 0g, Sugars 2g); Protein 28g. % Daily Value: Vitamin A 15%; Vitamin C 0%; Calcium 25%; Iron 10%. Exchanges: 1 Starch, 3-1/2 Very Lean Meat, 3 Fat. Carbohydrate Choices: 1.

Betty's Kitchen Tip

• Serve with a variety of dipping sauces, such as barbecue sauce, honey-mustard or ranch dressing.

chili con queso casserole

Prep Time: 10 Minutes
Start to Finish: 50 Minutes
Servings: 6

EASY

- 2 cans (4.5 oz each) Old El Paso® chopped green chiles, drained
- 2 large tomatoes, seeded and chopped (2 cups)
- 2 cups shredded Cheddar cheese (8 oz)
- 1 cup Original Bisquick® baking mix
- 1/2 cup sour cream
- 3 eggs

1 Heat oven to 375°F. Grease 8-inch square pan.

2 Sprinkle chiles and tomato evenly in pan. Beat remaining ingredients with wire whisk or hand beater until smooth; pour over top.

3 Bake uncovered 35 to 40 minutes or until knife inserted in center comes out clean.

High Altitude (3500-6500 ft): No change.

Nutritional Info: 1 Serving: Calories 330 (Calories from Fat 190); Total Fat 22g (Saturated Fat 12g, Trans Fat 1g); Cholesterol 160mg; Sodium 620mg; Total Carbohydrate 19g (Dietary Fiber 1g, Sugars 5g); Protein 15g. % Daily Value: Vitamin A 25%; Vitamin C 15%; Calcium 25%; Iron 8%. Exchanges: 1 Starch, 1/2 Vegetable, 1-1/2 High-Fat Meat, 2 Fat. Carbohydrate Choices: 1.

Betty's Kitchen Tip

- To make ahead, cover unbaked casserole tightly and refrigerate no longer than 24 hours. About 45 minutes before serving, heat oven to 375°F. Bake uncovered 35 to 40 minutes or until knife inserted in center comes out clean.

easy chicken pot pie

Prep Time: 15 Minutes
Start to Finish: 45 Minutes
Servings: 6

EASY LOW FAT

1-2/3 cups Green Giant® Valley Fresh Steamers™ frozen mixed vegetables, thawed
1 cup cut-up cooked chicken
1 can (10 3/4 oz) condensed cream of chicken soup
1 cup Original Bisquick® mix
1/2 cup milk
1 egg

1 Heat oven to 400°F. In ungreased 9-inch pie plate, stir vegetables, chicken and soup.

2 In medium bowl, stir all of the remaining ingredients until blended. Pour into pie plate.

3 Bake uncovered about 30 minutes or until crust is golden brown.

High Altitude (3500-6500 ft): No change.

Nutritional Info: 1 Serving: Calories 230 (Calories from Fat 80); Total Fat 9g (Saturated Fat 3g, Trans Fat 1g); Cholesterol 60mg; Sodium 670mg; Total Carbohydrate 25g (Dietary Fiber 3g, Sugars 3g); Protein 12g. % Daily Value: Vitamin A 50%; Vitamin C 0%; Calcium 6%; Iron 8%. Exchanges: 1 Starch, 1/2 Other Carbohydrate, 1 Vegetable, 1 Lean Meat, 1 Fat. Carbohydrate Choices: 1-1/2.

Betty's Kitchen Tip

• Update this classic with a cheesy-herb crust. Add 1/4 cup finely shredded Parmesan cheese and 1/2 teaspoon dried rosemary with the Bisquick mix.

oven-fried ranch drumsticks

Prep Time: 10 Minutes
Start to Finish: 1 Hour
Servings: 6 to 8

EASY

3/4 cup Original Bisquick® mix	1 tablespoon water
1 package (1 oz) ranch dressing and seasoning mix	2-1/2 to 3 lb chicken drumsticks (12 to 15 pieces)
1 teaspoon paprika	1 cup ranch dressing, if desired
1 egg, slightly beaten	

1 Heat oven to 425°F. Line 13x9-inch pan with foil. Generously spray foil with cooking spray.

2 In shallow dish, mix Bisquick mix, dressing mix (dry) and paprika. In another shallow dish, mix egg and water. Dip chicken into egg mixture, then coat with Bisquick mixture. Place chicken in pan.

3 Bake 35 minutes. Turn; bake about 15 minutes longer or until juice of chicken is clear when thickest part is cut to bone (180°F). Serve with prepared ranch dressing.

High Altitude (3500-6500 ft): No change.

Nutritional Info: 1 Serving: Calories 270 (Calories from Fat 110); Total Fat 12g (Saturated Fat 4g, Trans Fat 1g); Cholesterol 110mg; Sodium 610mg; Total Carbohydrate 13g (Dietary Fiber 0g, Sugars 2g); Protein 28g. % Daily Value: Vitamin A 6%; Vitamin C 0%; Calcium 8%; Iron 15%. Exchanges: 1 Starch, 3-1/2 Lean Meat. Carbohydrate Choices: 1.

Betty's Kitchen Tip

• For an easy appetizer, use 2 lb chicken drummettes instead of the drumsticks. Drummettes are chicken wings that are trimmed to resemble small chicken legs, and they make perfect bite-size appetizers.

impossibly easy hot dog 'n cheese pie

Prep Time: 15 Minutes
Start to Finish: 50 Minutes
Servings: 6

EASY

1/2	lb hot dogs, cut into 1/4-inch pieces
1/4	cup chopped onion, if desired
1/2	cup Original Bisquick® mix
1	cup milk
2	eggs
1	cup shredded Cheddar cheese (4 oz)

Ketchup and mustard, if desired

1 Heat oven to 400°F. Spray 9-inch glass pie plate with cooking spray. Layer hot dog pieces and onion in pie plate.

2 Stir Bisquick mix, milk and eggs in medium bowl with wire whisk or fork until blended. Pour into pie plate. Sprinkle with shredded cheese.

3 Bake 25 to 30 minutes or until knife inserted in center comes out clean. Let stand 5 minutes before serving. Serve with ketchup and mustard.

High Altitude (3500-6500 ft): No change.

Nutritional Info: 1 Serving: Calories 280 (Calories from Fat 190); Total Fat 21g (Saturated Fat 9g, Trans Fat 0.5g); Cholesterol 115mg; Sodium 750mg; Total Carbohydrate 10g (Dietary Fiber 0g, Sugars 5g); Protein 13g. % Daily Value: Vitamin A 8%; Vitamin C 0%; Calcium 20%; Iron 6%. Exchanges: 1/2 Starch, 1-1/2 High-Fat Meat, 2 Fat. Carbohydrate Choices: 1/2.

Betty's Kitchen Tip

• Serve with pickle relish, sauerkraut and spicy brown mustard for hot dog aficionados.

sausage and pineapple pizza

Prep Time: 20 Minutes
Start to Finish: 35 Minutes
Servings: 8 (1/4 pizza each)

- -

1 lb bulk mild Italian sausage	2/3 cup very hot water
1 medium onion, chopped (1/2 cup)	2 tablespoons olive or vegetable oil
1 can (20 oz) pineapple tidbits	1 can (15 oz) pizza sauce
3 cups Original Bisquick® mix	3 cups shredded mozzarella cheese (12 oz)

- -

1 Move oven rack to lowest position. Heat oven to 450°F. Spray two 12-inch pizza pans with cooking spray.

2 In 10-inch skillet, cook sausage and onion over medium heat, stirring occasionally, until sausage is no longer pink; drain. Drain pineapple.

3 In large bowl, stir Bisquick mix, hot water and oil with fork until soft dough forms; beat vigorously 20 strokes. Divide dough in half. Pat or press half of dough in each pizza pan, using fingers dipped in Bisquick mix; pinch edge to form 1/2-inch rim.

4 Spread half of the pizza sauce on each pizza crust. Top each with half of the sausage and pineapple. Sprinkle each pizza with 1-1/2 cups cheese.

5 Bake 12 to 15 minutes or until crust is golden brown and cheese is melted.

High Altitude (3500-6500 ft): No change.

Nutritional Info: 1 Serving: Calories 530 (Calories from Fat 260); Total Fat 29g (Saturated Fat 11g, Trans Fat 1.5g); Cholesterol 55mg; Sodium 1480mg; Total Carbohydrate 43g (Dietary Fiber 2g, Sugars 15g); Protein 24g. % Daily Value: Vitamin A 6%; Vitamin C 8%; Calcium 40%; Iron 20%. Exchanges: 2 Starch, 1/2 Fruit, 1/2 Other Carbohydrate, 2-1/2 High-Fat Meat, 1-1/2 Fat. Carbohydrate Choices: 3.

Betty's Kitchen Tip

• To freeze and bake at a later time, drain and press pineapple with paper towels to remove excess moisture. Wrap unbaked assembled pizza(s) with heavy-duty foil. Freeze up to 2 months. To bake, remove foil and bake at 450°F for 15 to 23 minutes or until crust is golden brown, cheese is melted and center is heated through.

quick
MEALS

p. 71

70

74

81

breaded chicken with tomatoes

Prep Time: 30 Minutes
Start to Finish: 30 Minutes
Servings: 4

QUICK

4	boneless skinless chicken breasts (1 lb)
1/2	cup Progresso® panko crispy bread crumbs
1/4	cup grated Parmesan cheese
1/2	teaspoon salt
1/4	teaspoon pepper
3	tablespoons olive or vegetable oil

3	large tomatoes, chopped (3 cups)
2	medium green onions, chopped (2 tablespoons)
1	clove garlic, finely chopped
1	tablespoon balsamic vinegar
1	tablespoon chopped fresh oregano leaves

1 Between pieces of plastic wrap or waxed paper, place each chicken breast smooth side down; gently pound with flat side of meat mallet or rolling pin until about 1/4 inch thick.

2 In shallow medium bowl or pie plate, mix bread crumbs, cheese, salt and pepper. Coat chicken with crumb mixture, pressing to coat well on both sides.

3 In 12-inch nonstick skillet, heat 2 tablespoons of the oil over medium-high heat. Cook chicken in oil 6 to 10 minutes, turning once, until golden brown on outside and no longer pink in center. Remove chicken from skillet; cover to keep warm.

4 To skillet, add remaining 1 tablespoon oil, 2 cups of the tomatoes, the onions and garlic; cook and stir 2 minutes. Stir in vinegar; cook 30 seconds longer. Remove from heat; stir in remaining 1 cup tomatoes and the oregano. Serve over chicken. Garnish with additional fresh oregano sprigs, if desired.

High Altitude (3500-6500 ft): No change.

Nutritional Info: 1 Serving: Calories 350; Total Fat 17g (Saturated Fat 3.5g); Sodium 490mg; Total Carbohydrate 17g (Dietary Fiber 2g); Protein 30g. Exchanges: 1/2 Starch, 1/2 Other Carbohydrate, 4 Very Lean Meat, 3 Fat. Carbohydrate Choices: 1.

Betty's Kitchen Tips

Success Hint: Panko bread crumbs are coarser than regular bread crumbs. With a bit of pressing, the coating sticks to the chicken on its own, making this chicken very crunchy, yet light too.

How-To: If the chicken browns too quickly, simply turn down the heat a little bit.

italian stew with spinach dumplings

Prep Time: 10 Minutes
Start to Finish: 30 Minutes
Servings: 4

EASY QUICK

- 1 lb lean (at least 80%) ground beef
- 1 jar (26 oz) vegetable primavera tomato pasta sauce
- 1 jar (4.5 oz) Green Giant® sliced mushrooms, drained
- 1 cup water
- 2 cups Bisquick Heart Smart® or Original Bisquick® mix
- 1/4 cup Green Giant® frozen (thawed) chopped spinach, squeezed to drain
- 1/4 cup grated Parmesan cheese
- 1/2 cup milk

1 In 4-quart Dutch oven, cook beef over medium-high heat 5 to 7 minutes, stirring occasionally, until thoroughly cooked; drain. Stir in pasta sauce, mushrooms and water. Heat to boiling; reduce heat.

2 In medium bowl, mix Bisquick mix, spinach, cheese and milk until soft dough forms. Drop dough by 10 spoonfuls onto simmering beef mixture. Cook uncovered over low heat 10 minutes. Cover; cook 10 minutes longer.

High Altitude (3500-6500 ft): No change.

Nutritional Info: 1 Serving: Calories 540; Total Fat 20g (Saturated Fat 6g); Sodium 1320mg; Total Carbohydrate 59g (Dietary Fiber 4g); Protein 31g. Exchanges: 2-1/2 Starch, 1 Other Carbohydrate, 1 Vegetable, 3-1/2 Medium-Fat Meat. Carbohydrate Choices: 4.

Betty's Kitchen Tips

Success Hint: The secret to the best fluffy dumplings is to cook them uncovered for 10 minutes, then covered for 10 minutes.

Time-Saver: To speed the prep, thaw the spinach in the microwave.

sweet-and-sour pork

Prep Time: 20 Minutes
Start to Finish: 20 Minutes
Servings: 4

QUICK

1 lb boneless pork loin chops, cut into 1-inch cubes
1 egg, beaten
3/4 cup Original Bisquick® mix
1/2 teaspoon salt
1/8 teaspoon pepper

1/2 cup vegetable oil
1-1/2 cups frozen bell pepper and onion stir-fry (from 1-lb bag)
1 can (8 oz) pineapple chunks, drained
1 jar (11-1/2 oz) sweet-and-sour sauce

1 In medium bowl, toss pork with egg. In 1-gallon resealable food-storage plastic bag, place Bisquick mix, salt and pepper; seal bag and shake to mix. Drain excess egg from pork. Place pork cubes in plastic bag; seal bag and shake to coat.

2 In 12-inch nonstick skillet, heat oil over medium heat. Add pork in a single layer; cook 6 to 8 minutes, turning occasionally, until brown and crispy on outside and no longer pink in center. Drain on paper towels. Cover to keep warm.

3 Reserve 1 tablespoon oil in skillet; discard any remaining oil. Add bell pepper mix and pineapple; cook over medium-high heat 2 to 3 minutes, stirring frequently, until vegetables are crisp-tender. Stir in the sweet-and-sour sauce and pork; heat to boiling.

High Altitude (3500-6500 ft): No change.

Nutritional Info: 1 Serving: Calories 670 (Calories from Fat 380); Total Fat 42g (Saturated Fat 8g, Trans Fat 0.5g); Cholesterol 125mg; Sodium 960mg; Total Carbohydrate 43g (Dietary Fiber 2g, Sugars 22g); Protein 29g. % Daily Value: Vitamin A 6%; Vitamin C 25%; Calcium 8%; Iron 15%. Exchanges: 1-1/2 Starch, 1-1/2 Other Carbohydrate, 3-1/2 Lean Meat, 6 Fat. Carbohydrate Choices: 3.

Betty's Kitchen Tip

• If you can't find the frozen stir-fry mix, use 3/4 cup bell pepper strips and 3/4 cup thin onion wedges.

cheesy hamburger hash

Prep Time: 25 Minutes
Start to Finish: 25 Minutes
Servings: 4

QUICK

- 1 lb lean (at least 80%) ground beef
- 1 tablespoon butter or margarine
- 1 bag (20 oz) refrigerated cooked diced potatoes with onions
- 1 can (14.5 oz) diced tomatoes with Italian-style herbs, undrained
- 1 tablespoon pizza seasoning or Italian seasoning
- 1-1/2 cups shredded pizza cheese blend (6 oz)
- 2 tablespoons chopped fresh parsley

1 In 12-inch nonstick skillet, cook beef over medium heat 8 to 10 minutes, stirring occasionally, until thoroughly cooked; drain. Remove beef from skillet.

2 In same skillet, melt butter. Add potatoes. Cover; cook over medium heat about 5 minutes, stirring occasionally, until almost tender. Stir in beef, tomatoes and pizza seasoning. Cook uncovered about 5 minutes, stirring occasionally, until thoroughly heated.

3 Sprinkle with cheese and parsley. Cover; heat until cheese is melted.

High Altitude (3500-6500 ft): No change.

Nutritional Info: 1 Serving: Calories 620; Total Fat 36g (Saturated Fat 16g); Sodium 1000mg; Total Carbohydrate 41g (Dietary Fiber 5g); Protein 33g. Exchanges: 2-1/2 Starch, 1/2 Vegetable, 3-1/2 Medium-Fat Meat, 3-1/2 Fat. Carbohydrate Choices: 3.

Betty's Kitchen Tips

Variation: Any variety of canned seasoned diced tomatoes can be used.

Substitution: Can't find pizza cheese blend? Substitute 3/4 cup each shredded Cheddar and mozzarella.

skillet chicken nachos

Prep Time: 20 Minutes
Start to Finish: 20 Minutes
Servings: 6

1	tablespoon olive or vegetable oil	1	can (15 oz) Progresso® black beans, drained, rinsed
1-1/4	lb boneless skinless chicken breasts, cut into 1/4-inch pieces	1	can (7 oz) Green Giant® Niblets® whole kernel sweet corn, drained
1	package (1 oz) Old El Paso® taco seasoning mix	2	cups shredded Mexican cheese blend (8 oz)
1	can (8 oz) tomato sauce	6	oz tortilla chips (about 42 chips)
1	medium red bell pepper, chopped (1 cup)	1/4	cup chopped fresh cilantro

1 In 12-inch nonstick skillet, heat oil over medium-high heat. Cook chicken in oil 3 to 5 minutes, stirring occasionally, until no longer pink in center.

2 Stir in taco seasoning mix, tomato sauce, bell pepper, beans, corn and 1 cup of the cheese. Reduce heat to medium; cook 3 to 5 minutes, stirring occasionally, until heated through and cheese is melted.

3 Divide tortilla chips between 6 plates. Spoon chicken mixture evenly over chips. Sprinkle with remaining 1 cup cheese and the cilantro.

High Altitude (3500-6500 ft): No change.

Nutritional Info: 1 Serving: Calories 520; Total Fat 24g (Saturated Fat 9g); Sodium 1320mg; Total Carbohydrate 38g (Dietary Fiber 5g); Protein 36g. Exchanges: 2 Starch, 1/2 Other Carbohydrate, 1/2 Vegetable, 4 Very Lean Meat, 4 Fat. Carbohydrate Choices: 2-1/2.

Betty's Kitchen Tips

Success Hint: This recipe is versatile. Serve it as a fun appetizer, a hearty after-school snack for a group of kids or as a main dish.

Substitution: For Skillet Beef Nachos, substitute 1-1/4 lb ground beef for the chicken. In Step 1, cook beef 5 to 7 minutes or until thoroughly cooked. Drain and proceed as directed.

beer-battered fish

Prep Time: 10 Minutes
Start to Finish: 15 Minutes
Servings: 4

EASY QUICK LOW FAT

Vegetable oil
- 1   lb fish fillets, thawed if frozen
- 3   to 4 tablespoons Original Bisquick® mix
- 1   cup Original Bisquick® mix
- 1/2   cup regular or nonalcoholic beer
- 1/2   teaspoon salt
- 1   egg

Tartar sauce, if desired

1 Heat oil (1-1/2 inches) in heavy 3-quart saucepan or deep fryer to 350°F. Lightly coat fish with 3 to 4 tablespoons Bisquick mix.

2 Beat 1 cup Bisquick mix, the beer, salt and egg with hand beater until smooth. (If batter is too thick, stir in additional beer, 1 tablespoon at a time, until desired consistency.) Dip fish into batter, letting excess batter drip into bowl.

3 Fry fish in oil about 2 minutes on each side or until golden brown; drain. Serve hot with tartar sauce.

High Altitude (3500-6500 ft): No change.

Nutritional Info: 1 Serving: Calories 300 (Calories from Fat 90); Total Fat 10g (Saturated Fat 2.5g, Trans Fat 1.5g); Cholesterol 115mg; Sodium 890mg; Total Carbohydrate 26g (Dietary Fiber 1g, Sugars 1g); Protein 26g. % Daily Value: Vitamin A 2%; Vitamin C 0%; Calcium 6%; Iron 8%. Exchanges: 2 Starch, 2-1/2 Lean Meat, 1/2 Fat. Carbohydrate Choices: 2.

Betty's Kitchen Tip

• These fillets are awesome sandwiched in burger buns. Add tangy tartar sauce, crisp lettuce leaves and a tomato slice for the Ultimate Fish Sandwich.

summer chicken stir-fry

Prep Time: 30 Minutes
Start to Finish: 30 Minutes
Servings: 4

1 cup uncooked regular long-grain white rice
2 cups water
2 tablespoons olive or vegetable oil
1 lb boneless skinless chicken breasts, cut into 1-inch pieces
1 large onion, chopped (1 cup)

2 medium yellow summer squash, cut in half lengthwise, then cut crosswise into 1/2-inch pieces (about 2 cups)
4 oz fresh sugar snap peas (about 1 cup)
2 cloves garlic, finely chopped
1/2 cup stir-fry sauce
1 large tomato, chopped (1 cup)

1 Cook rice in water as directed on package. Meanwhile, in 12-inch nonstick skillet, heat 1 tablespoon of the oil over medium-high heat. Cook chicken in oil 6 to 8 minutes, stirring occasionally, until no longer pink in center. Remove chicken from skillet; cover to keep warm.

2 In same skillet, heat remaining 1 tablespoon oil. Cook onion, squash and peas in oil 5 minutes, stirring occasionally. Add garlic; cook 1 minute longer. Add stir-fry sauce and chicken; cook 2 to 3 minutes longer or until heated through.

3 Remove from heat. Stir in tomato. Serve over rice.

High Altitude (3500-6500 ft): No change.

Nutritional Info: 1 Serving: Calories 490; Total Fat 13g (Saturated Fat 2.5g); Sodium 1930mg; Total Carbohydrate 59g (Dietary Fiber 3g); Protein 32g. Exchanges: 2-1/2 Starch, 1 Other Carbohydrate, 1 Vegetable, 3 Lean Meat, 1/2 Fat. Carbohydrate Choices: 4.

Betty's Kitchen Tips

Substitution: This recipe can be altered to fit any family's taste buds. Just substitute 4 cups of your favorite chopped fresh vegetables for the onion, squash and sugar snap peas.

Variation: Instead of serving the stir-fry over rice, try mixing the chicken and vegetables with the rice and rolling it up in tortillas!

skillet ground beef stew

Prep Time: 15 Minutes
Start to Finish: 30 Minutes
Servings: 4

EASY QUICK

1	lb lean (at least 80%) ground beef
1/2	teaspoon salt
1/2	teaspoon pepper
2	tablespoons Gold Medal® all-purpose flour
1	package (8 oz) sliced fresh mushrooms (about 3 cups)
1-1/2	cups Progresso® beef-flavored broth (from 32-oz carton)
1/3	cup whipping (heavy) cream
4	teaspoons Dijon mustard
1	lb unpeeled Yukon Gold or red potatoes, cut into 1/2-inch cubes (3 medium)
2	medium carrots, thinly sliced (1 cup)
2	tablespoons chopped fresh parsley

1 In 12-inch nonstick skillet, cook beef over medium-high heat 5 to 7 minutes, stirring occasionally, until thoroughly cooked; drain. Stir in salt, pepper and flour. Add mushrooms; cook 3 minutes, stirring occasionally.

2 In small bowl, mix broth, whipping cream and mustard with wire whisk. Add to beef mixture. Stir in potatoes and carrots.

3 Reduce heat to medium-low. Cover; cook 15 minutes until vegetables are tender and sauce is slightly thickened. Sprinkle with chopped parsley.

High Altitude (3500-6500 ft): No change.

Nutritional Info: 1 Serving: Calories 410; Total Fat 21g (Saturated Fat 9g); Sodium 830mg; Total Carbohydrate 30g (Dietary Fiber 4g); Protein 25g. Exchanges: 2 Starch, 2-1/2 High-Fat Meat. Carbohydrate Choices: 2.

Betty's Kitchen Tips

How-To: If the sauce is too thin at the end of the cooking process, increase the heat to medium-high and cook uncovered another few minutes until the liquid reduces and is slightly thickened.

Time-Saver: Purchase presliced carrots in the refrigerated case of the produce department to shave a few minutes off prep time.

super-quick salsa chicken

Prep Time: 30 Minutes
Start to Finish: 30 Minutes
Servings: 4

QUICK

1	cup uncooked regular long-grain white rice
2	cups water
4	boneless skinless chicken breasts (1-1/4 lb)
2	tablespoons olive or vegetable oil
1/2	teaspoon salt
1/4	teaspoon pepper

1	medium zucchini, chopped (2 cups)
1	cup Old El Paso® Thick 'n Chunky salsa
1	can (11 oz) Green Giant® Niblets® whole kernel sweet corn, drained
1/4	cup sour cream
2	tablespoons chopped fresh cilantro

1 Cook rice in water as directed on package. Meanwhile, between pieces of plastic wrap or waxed paper, place each chicken breast smooth side down; gently pound with flat side of meat mallet or rolling pin until about 1/4 inch thick.

2 In 12-inch nonstick skillet, heat 1 tablespoon of the oil over medium-high heat. Sprinkle chicken with salt and pepper. Cook chicken in oil 6 to 10 minutes, turning once, until golden brown on outside and no longer pink in center. Remove chicken from skillet; cover to keep warm.

3 In same skillet, heat remaining 1 tablespoon oil. Cook zucchini in oil 3 minutes, stirring occasionally. Stir in salsa and corn. Reduce heat to medium; cook 2 minutes longer or until thoroughly heated.

4 Serve chicken over rice; top with vegetable mixture, sour cream and cilantro.

High Altitude (3500-6500 ft): No change.

Nutritional Info: 1 Serving: Calories 520; Total Fat 15g (Saturated Fat 4g); Sodium 1580mg; Total Carbohydrate 58g (Dietary Fiber 2g); Protein 38g. Exchanges: 2-1/2 Starch, 1/2 Other Carbohydrate, 2-1/2 Vegetable, 3-1/2 Very Lean Meat, 2 Fat. Carbohydrate Choices: 4.

Betty's Kitchen Tips

Time-Saver: If you're short on time, skip flattening and cooking the chicken breasts. Substitute 4 cups cubed cooked chicken; add with the salsa and corn in Step 3.

Do-Ahead: If you have leftovers, serve them the next day as a Mini Tortilla-Topped Snack. Just chop up leftover chicken; spoon chicken and vegetables into a large custard cup and refrigerate. To serve, microwave covered until hot and sprinkle with crushed tortilla chips.

beef, summer squash and sweet potato curry

Prep Time: 20 Minutes
Start to Finish: 30 Minutes
Servings: 6

QUICK LOW FAT

1 cup uncooked regular long-grain white rice
2 cups water
1 lb lean (at least 80%) ground beef
1 medium onion, chopped (1/2 cup)
1 tablespoon grated gingerroot
2 tablespoons curry powder
1 teaspoon ground cumin
1 teaspoon salt

1 large sweet potato, peeled, cut into 1/2-inch cubes (3 cups)
1 can (14.5 oz) diced tomatoes, undrained
1 cup Progresso® reduced-sodium chicken broth (from 32-oz carton)
2 medium zucchini, cut in half lengthwise, then cut crosswise into 1/2-inch slices (2 cups)
1/2 cup plain yogurt

1 Cook rice in water as directed on package. Meanwhile, in 12-inch skillet, cook beef and onion over medium-high heat 5 to 7 minutes, stirring occasionally, until the beef is thoroughly cooked and the onion is tender; drain.

2 Add gingerroot, curry powder, cumin and salt to skillet; cook 1 minute, stirring occasionally. Stir in sweet potato, tomatoes and broth. Heat to boiling; reduce heat. Cover; simmer 10 minutes or until potato is almost tender. Stir in zucchini. Cover; cook 5 to 10 minutes longer or until potato and zucchini are just tender.

3 Serve beef mixture over rice. Top each serving with about 1 tablespoon yogurt.

High Altitude (3500-6500 ft): No change.

Nutritional Info: 1 Serving: Calories 420; Total Fat 10g (Saturated Fat 4g); Sodium 1030mg; Total Carbohydrate 58g (Dietary Fiber 4g); Protein 22g. Exchanges: 3-1/2 Starch, 1 Vegetable, 1 High-Fat Meat. Carbohydrate Choices: 4.

Betty's Kitchen Tips

Storage: Fresh unpeeled gingerroot, tightly wrapped, can be frozen up to 6 months. To use, slice off a piece of frozen ginger and return the rest to the freezer.

Did You Know? Curry powder is a blend of several spices, such as turmeric, coriander, cumin and fenugreek. Keep ground spices for only 1 year.

barbecued beef and bow-tie dinner

Prep Time: 15 Minutes
Start to Finish: 30 Minutes
Servings: 4

EASY QUICK

1	lb lean (at least 80%) ground beef
1	medium red bell pepper, chopped (1 cup)
1-1/2	cups uncooked mini bow-tie (mini farfalle) pasta (5 oz)
2-1/2	cups Progresso® beef-flavored broth (from 32-oz carton)
1/2	cup barbecue sauce
1/2	teaspoon salt
1/4	teaspoon pepper
1	cup Green Giant® Niblets® frozen corn (from 12-oz bag), thawed
1-1/2	cups shredded Cheddar cheese (6 oz)

1 In 12-inch nonstick skillet, cook beef over medium-high heat 5 to 7 minutes, stirring occasionally, until thoroughly cooked; drain beef.

2 Add bell pepper; cook and stir 1 minute. Stir in pasta, broth, barbecue sauce, salt and pepper. Heat to boiling; reduce heat to medium-low. Cover; cook 15 minutes, stirring occasionally, until pasta is tender.

3 Stir in corn and 1 cup of the cheese. Top with remaining 1/2 cup cheese. Cover; cook 3 to 4 minutes longer, until corn is hot and cheese is melted.

High Altitude (3500-6500 ft): No change.

Nutritional Info: 1 Serving: Calories 680; Total Fat 28g (Saturated Fat 14g); Sodium 1470mg; Total Carbohydrate 66g (Dietary Fiber 4g); Protein 40g. Exchanges: 4 Starch, 1/2 Vegetable, 3 High-Fat Meat, 1 Fat. Carbohydrate Choices: 4-1/2.

Betty's Kitchen Tips

Purchasing: Buy a block of Cheddar cheese when it's on sale; shred and store, tightly sealed, in the freezer. It will be handy whenever you need it for a recipe.

Health Twist: Store-bought beef broth can be overly salty. Always look for the reduced-sodium varieties.

thai peanut noodle and beef skillet

Prep Time: 30 Minutes
Start to Finish: 30 Minutes
Servings: 6

QUICK

8 oz uncooked spaghetti
4 medium carrots, thinly sliced (2 cups)
8 oz fresh sugar snap peas
1 can (14 oz) coconut milk
(not cream of coconut)
1 tablespoon packed brown sugar
2 to 3 teaspoons Thai red curry paste

1 tablespoon soy sauce
1/2 cup crunchy peanut butter
2 tablespoons lime juice
1 lb lean (at least 80%) ground beef
1 tablespoon grated gingerroot
1/2 teaspoon salt

1 In 5- to 6-quart Dutch oven, cook spaghetti as directed on package, adding carrots and peas during last 5 minutes of cooking time. Rinse with cold water; drain and set aside.

2 In microwavable bowl, mix coconut milk, brown sugar, curry paste, soy sauce and peanut butter. Microwave on High 2 minutes or until hot. Add lime juice; stir with wire whisk until smooth. Set aside.

3 In 12-inch nonstick skillet, cook beef over medium-high heat 5 to 7 minutes, stirring occasionally, until thoroughly cooked; drain. Stir in gingerroot and salt; cook 1 minute longer.

4 Stir in reserved spaghetti, vegetables and peanut sauce; toss until coated. Cook 2 to 3 minutes or until thoroughly heated.

High Altitude (3500-6500 ft): No change.

Nutritional Info: 1 Serving: Calories 620; Total Fat 34g (Saturated Fat 18g); Sodium 760mg; Total Carbohydrate 51g (Dietary Fiber 6g); Protein 27g. Exchanges: 3 Starch, 1/2 Vegetable, 3 High-Fat Meat, 1-1/2 Fat. Carbohydrate Choices: 3-1/2.

Betty's Kitchen Tips

Purchasing: Thai red curry paste can be found in the Asian-foods section of most grocery stores. Add the lower amount first until you've tasted it—it's spicy!

Success Hint: If you will be using leftover spaghetti or making the spaghetti ahead of time, toss with 2 teaspoons sesame oil to prevent the noodles from sticking together.

quick chicken scampi

Prep Time: 25 Minutes
Start to Finish: 25 Minutes
Servings: 4

QUICK

8	oz uncooked linguine
1-1/4	lb boneless skinless chicken breasts, cut into bite-size pieces
1/2	teaspoon salt
1/4	teaspoon pepper
2	tablespoons butter
2	medium green onions, chopped (2 tablespoons)
2	cloves garlic, finely chopped
1/4	cup finely chopped drained roasted red peppers (from 7-oz jar)
1/2	lb fresh thin asparagus spears, trimmed, cut into 2-inch pieces
3/4	cup Progresso® chicken broth (from 32-oz carton)

Grated peel of 1 medium lemon
(2 to 3 teaspoons)

1 Cook linguine as directed on package. Meanwhile, sprinkle chicken with salt and pepper. In 12-inch nonstick skillet, heat 1 tablespoon of the butter over medium-high heat until melted.

2 Cook chicken in butter 5 to 7 minutes, stirring occasionally. Add onions, garlic, roasted peppers and asparagus; cook 2 to 3 minutes longer, stirring occasionally, until asparagus is crisp-tender and chicken is no longer pink in center. Stir in broth and remaining 1 tablespoon butter; cook until butter is melted.

3 Drain linguine. Serve chicken mixture over linguine. Sprinkle lemon peel over each serving.

High Altitude (3500-6500 ft): No change.

Nutritional Info: 1 Serving: Calories 500; Total Fat 12g (Saturated Fat 5g); Sodium 800mg; Total Carbohydrate 54g (Dietary Fiber 4g); Protein 43g. Exchanges: 3-1/2 Starch, 1/2 Vegetable, 4-1/2 Very Lean Meat, 1-1/2 Fat. Carbohydrate Choices: 3-1/2.

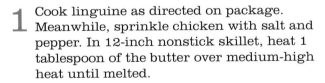

Betty's Kitchen Tips

Variation: If you're not in the mood for pasta, try serving the chicken mixture over your favorite variety of rice.

Success Hint: When grating the lemon peel, be careful to avoid the pith—the soft white layer between the peel and flesh of the fruit—as it can be bitter.

fried pork cutlets with apple slaw

Prep Time: 10 Minutes
Start to Finish: 30 Minutes
Servings: 4

Pork Cutlets

4	boneless pork loin chops, 1/2 inch thick (about 1 lb)
8	saltine crackers, finely crushed (1/3 cup)
1/2	cup Original Bisquick® mix
1/2	teaspoon paprika
1/4	teaspoon pepper
1	egg or 1/4 cup fat-free egg product
1	tablespoon water

Cooking spray

Apple Slaw

4	cups coleslaw mix (shredded cabbage and carrots)
1	small tart red apple, coarsely chopped (1 cup)
1/4	cup chopped onion (1 small)
1/3	cup fat-free coleslaw dressing
1/8	teaspoon celery seed

1 Heat oven to 425°F. Generously spray 15x10x1-inch pan with cooking spray. Between pieces of plastic wrap or waxed paper, place each pork chop; gently pound with flat side of meat mallet or rolling pin until about 1/4 inch thick.

2 In small shallow dish, mix crackers, Bisquick mix, paprika and pepper. In another shallow dish, beat egg and water.

3 Dip pork chops into egg mixture, then coat with cracker mixture. Repeat dipping coated pork in egg and in cracker mixture. Place in pan. Generously spray tops of pork with cooking spray.

4 Bake about 20 minutes or until pork chops are golden brown and no longer pink in the center.

5 Meanwhile, in large bowl, toss apple slaw ingredients. Serve slaw with pork cutlets.

High Altitude (3500-6500 ft): No change.

Nutritional Info: 1 Serving: Calories 360 (Calories from Fat 130); Total Fat 14g (Saturated Fat 4.5g, Trans Fat 1g); Cholesterol 125mg; Sodium 480mg; Total Carbohydrate 29g (Dietary Fiber 3g, Sugars 9g); Protein 29g. % Daily Value: Vitamin A 8%; Vitamin C 20%; Calcium 8%; Iron 15%. Exchanges: 1/2 Starch, 1 Other Carbohydrate, 1 Vegetable, 3-1/2 Lean Meat, 1 Fat. Carbohydrate Choices: 2.

Betty's Kitchen Tip

• Any type of cracker crumbs can be used. Try veggie-flavored or whole-grain crackers.

ham and swiss cheese bake

Prep Time: 15 Minutes
Start to Finish: 30 Minutes
Servings: 8

EASY QUICK

2	cups Bisquick Heart Smart® mix
1/3	cup honey mustard
1/3	cup milk
2	cups cubed cooked ham (12 oz)
4	medium green onions, sliced (1/4 cup)
1/4	cup chopped bell pepper (any color)
1/4	cup sour cream
1	cup shredded Swiss cheese (4 oz)

1 Heat oven to 450°F. Spray 13x9-inch pan with cooking spray. In medium bowl, stir Bisquick mix, mustard and milk until soft dough forms; press on bottom of pan. Bake 8 to 10 minutes or until crust is golden brown.

2 In medium bowl, mix ham, onions, bell pepper and sour cream; spread over crust. Sprinkle with cheese.

3 Bake uncovered 5 to 6 minutes or until mixture is hot and cheese is melted.

High Altitude (3500-6500 ft): No change.

Nutritional Info: 1 Serving: Calories 250 (Calories from Fat 100); Total Fat 11g (Saturated Fat 4.5g, Trans Fat 0g); Cholesterol 45mg; Sodium 380mg; Total Carbohydrate 23g (Dietary Fiber 0g, Sugars 4g); Protein 16g. % Daily Value: Vitamin A 8%; Vitamin C 6%; Calcium 30%; Iron 8%. Exchanges: 1-1/2 Starch, 1-1/2 Lean Meat, 1 Fat. Carbohydrate Choices: 1-1/2.

Betty's Kitchen Tip

• You can use smoked turkey or smoked chicken instead of the ham.

barbecue beef cheese melts

Prep Time: 15 Minutes
Start to Finish: 30 Minutes
Servings: 8

2 cups Original Bisquick® mix	1/2 cup chopped green bell pepper
1/2 teaspoon ground mustard	1/4 cup chopped onion
1 cup milk	1 cup barbecue sauce
1 egg, beaten	3/4 lb cooked roast beef (from deli), chopped
1 teaspoon vegetable oil	2 cups shredded Cheddar cheese (8 oz)

1 Heat oven to 350°F. Spray 13x9-inch pan with cooking spray. In large bowl, stir Bisquick mix, mustard, milk and egg until mixed. Pour and spread in pan.

2 Bake 15 to 17 minutes or until toothpick inserted in center comes out clean. (Top will not brown.) Remove from oven.

3 Meanwhile, in 10-inch nonstick skillet, heat oil over medium heat. Add bell pepper and onion. Cook 3 to 4 minutes, stirring occasionally, until crisp-tender. Stir in barbecue sauce and beef. Cook until hot. Spread over baked bread base. Top with cheese.

4 Bake 4 to 5 minutes longer or until cheese is melted. Cut into squares.

High Altitude (3500-6500 ft): No change.

Nutritional Info: 1 Serving: Calories 400 (Calories from Fat 180); Total Fat 20g (Saturated Fat 10g, Trans Fat 1.5g); Cholesterol 85mg; Sodium 920mg; Total Carbohydrate 35g (Dietary Fiber 1g, Sugars 13g); Protein 19g. % Daily Value: Vitamin A 10%; Vitamin C 8%; Calcium 25%; Iron 15%. Exchanges: 1-1/2 Starch, 1 Other Carbohydrate, 2 Lean Meat, 2-1/2 Fat. Carbohydrate Choices: 2.

Betty's Kitchen Tip

• Serve with a baked potato, carrot sticks and a crunchy dill pickle.

italian pork chops

Prep Time: 10 Minutes
Start to Finish: 25 Minutes
Servings: 4

EASY QUICK

- 1/2 cup Original Bisquick® mix
- 1/3 cup Italian dressing
- 1/2 cup Progresso® garlic herb bread crumbs
- 4 boneless pork loin chops, 1/2 inch thick (1-1/2 lb)
- 2 tablespoons vegetable oil

1 In separate shallow dishes, place Bisquick mix, dressing and bread crumbs. Coat pork chops with Bisquick mix. Dip coated pork chops into dressing, then coat with bread crumbs.

2 In 12-inch nonstick skillet, heat oil over medium-high heat. Cook pork in oil about 5 minutes or until golden brown; reduce heat to low. Carefully turn pork. Cook 10 to 15 minutes longer or until pork is no longer pink in center. Serve immediately.

High Altitude (3500-6500 ft): No change.

Nutritional Info: 1 Serving: Calories 510 (Calories from Fat 280); Total Fat 31g (Saturated Fat 7g, Trans Fat 0g); Cholesterol 110mg; Sodium 720mg; Total Carbohydrate 20g (Dietary Fiber 0g, Sugars 4g); Protein 40g. % Daily Value: Vitamin A 0%; Vitamin C 0%; Calcium 8%; Iron 15%. Exchanges: 1-1/2 Starch, 5 Lean Meat, 3 Fat. Carbohydrate Choices: 1.

Betty's Kitchen Tip

• Serve cooked spaghetti on the side, and drizzle warm pasta sauce over spaghetti and chops.

creamy chicken and vegetables with noodles

Prep Time: 15 Minutes
Start to Finish: 15 Minutes
Servings: 4

EASY QUICK

- 5 cups uncooked medium egg noodles (10 oz)
- 2 cups Green Giant® Valley Fresh Steamers™ frozen mixed vegetables (from 12-oz bag), thawed, drained
- 6 medium green onions, sliced (6 tablespoons)
- 1 container (8 oz) garden vegetable cream cheese spread

- 1-1/4 cups milk
- 1-1/2 cups chopped deli rotisserie chicken (from 2-lb chicken)
- 1/2 teaspoon garlic salt
- 1/4 teaspoon pepper
- 2 tablespoons French-fried onions (from 2.8-oz can), if desired

1 Cook noodles as directed on package. Meanwhile, spray 12-inch skillet with cooking spray; heat over medium heat. Cook mixed vegetables and green onions in skillet about 4 minutes, stirring frequently, until crisp-tender.

2 Stir in cream cheese and milk until blended. Stir in chicken, garlic salt and pepper; cook until hot.

3 Drain noodles; stir into chicken mixture. Sprinkle with French-fried onions.

High Altitude (3500-6500 ft): No change.

Nutritional Info: 1 Serving: Calories 550; Total Fat 24g (Saturated Fat 13g); Sodium 830mg; Total Carbohydrate 53g (Dietary Fiber 6g); Protein 30g. Exchanges: 2-1/2 Starch, 1/2 Other Carbohydrate, 1 Vegetable, 3 Medium-Fat Meat, 1-1/2 Fat. Carbohydrate Choices: 3-1/2.

Betty's Kitchen Tips

Variation: Choose 2 cups of your family's favorite frozen vegetable to use in place of the mixed vegetables. Corn, peas and green beans would all be good choices.

Time-Saver: Rotisserie chicken from the deli is a convenient way to get dinner on the table in a hurry! Serve the chicken with coleslaw and potato salad—also from the deli—then use the leftovers in this easy one-dish meal.

turkey à la king

Prep Time: 30 Minutes
Start to Finish: 30 Minutes
Servings: 6

2-1/2 cups Original Bisquick® mix
1/3 cup grated Parmesan cheese
1/4 teaspoon dried thyme leaves
2-2/3 cups milk
1 package (20 oz) lean ground turkey
1 small clove garlic, finely chopped

1 cup sliced fresh mushrooms (3 oz)
1/2 cup chopped red bell pepper
1 cup frozen sweet peas
1/2 teaspoon salt
1/4 teaspoon pepper

1 Heat oven to 425°F. Spray cookie sheet with cooking spray. In medium bowl, mix 2-1/4 cups of the Bisquick mix, 2 tablespoons of the Parmesan cheese, the thyme and 2/3 cup of the milk until soft dough forms. Drop dough by 6 large spoonfuls onto cookie sheet.

2 Bake 8 to 10 minutes or until biscuits are golden brown.

3 Meanwhile, in 12-inch nonstick skillet, cook turkey over medium-high heat 5 to 7 minutes, stirring occasionally, until no longer pink. Add garlic, mushrooms and bell pepper. Cook 3 to 4 minutes, stirring occasionally, until vegetables are crisp-tender. Stir in remaining 1/4 cup Bisquick mix until blended. Stir in peas, salt, pepper and remaining 2 cups milk. Cook until mixture bubbles and thickens. Stir in remaining Parmesan cheese.

4 Split biscuits and place bottoms on individual serving plates. Spoon 1/3 cup turkey mixture over each biscuit bottom. Top with biscuit tops and remaining turkey mixture.

High Altitude (3500-6500 ft): No change.

Nutritional Info: 1 Serving: Calories 430 (Calories from Fat 140); Total Fat 15g (Saturated Fat 6g, Trans Fat 2g); Cholesterol 75mg; Sodium 1020mg; Total Carbohydrate 42g (Dietary Fiber 2g, Sugars 9g); Protein 32g. % Daily Value: Vitamin A 20%; Vitamin C 20%; Calcium 25%; Iron 15%. Exchanges: 2 Starch, 1 Other Carbohydrate, 3-1/2 Lean Meat, 1/2 Fat. Carbohydrate Choices: 3.

Betty's Kitchen Tip

• For a richer sauce, use 1 cup half-and-half and 1-2/3 cups milk. Fat free half-and-half will give you the same great richness as regular but with less fat and calories.

chicken-parmesan potatoes

Prep Time: 5 Minutes
Start to Finish: 30 Minutes
Servings: 5

- 1 box (4.7 oz) Betty Crocker® au gratin potatoes
- 3 cups chopped deli rotisserie chicken (from 2-lb chicken)
- 2-1/4 cups hot water
- 2/3 cup milk
- 1 bag (12 oz) Green Giant® Valley Fresh Steamers™ frozen cut green beans
- 1/2 cup grated Parmesan cheese

1 In 10-inch skillet, mix potatoes and sauce mix (from potato box) and remaining ingredients except cheese. Heat to boiling over high heat, stirring occasionally.

2 Reduce heat. Cover; simmer about 25 minutes, stirring occasionally, until potatoes are tender. Stir in cheese. Let stand 5 minutes before serving.

High Altitude (3500-6500 ft): No change.

Nutritional Info: 1 Serving: Calories 320; Total Fat 10g (Saturated Fat 4g); Sodium 1190mg; Total Carbohydrate 27g (Dietary Fiber 2g); Protein 31g. Exchanges: 1-1/2 Starch, 1 Vegetable, 3 Lean Meat. Carbohydrate Choices: 2.

EASY QUICK LOW FAT

Betty's Kitchen Tips

Substitution: Either freshly grated or canned Parmesan cheese will work in this recipe.

Variation: For Ham-Parmesan Potatoes, substitute 3 cups chopped fully cooked ham (about 1 lb) for the chicken.

quick chicken and dumplings

Prep Time: 10 Minutes
Start to Finish: 30 Minutes
Servings: 4

EASY QUICK

1-1/2 cups milk
1 cup frozen green peas and carrots
1 cup cut-up cooked chicken
1 can (10 3/4 oz) condensed creamy chicken mushroom soup

1 cup Original Bisquick® mix
1/3 cup milk
Paprika, if desired

1 Heat 1-1/2 cups milk, the peas and carrots, chicken and soup to boiling in 3-quart saucepan, stirring frequently.

2 Stir Bisquick mix and 1/3 cup milk until soft dough forms. Drop dough by 8 spoonfuls onto chicken mixture (do not drop directly into liquid). Sprinkle with paprika.

3 Cook uncovered over low heat 10 minutes. Cover and cook 10 minutes longer.

High Altitude (3500-6500 ft): No change.

Nutritional Info: 1 Serving: Calories 330 (Calories from Fat 120); Total Fat 13g (Saturated Fat 4.5g, Trans Fat 1.5g); Cholesterol 45mg; Sodium 1000mg; Total Carbohydrate 34g (Dietary Fiber 1g, Sugars 7g); Protein 18g. % Daily Value: Vitamin A 15%; Vitamin C 0%; Calcium 15%; Iron 10%. Exchanges: 2 Starch, 1 Vegetable, 1 Medium-Fat Meat, 1-1/2 Fat. Carbohydrate Choices: 2.

Betty's Kitchen Tip

• More mushrooms would make this dish even more delicious! Add one jar (4.5 oz) Green Giant® sliced mushrooms with the veggies.

take-it-easy noodle dinner

Prep Time: 20 Minutes
Start to Finish: 20 Minutes
Servings: 4

QUICK

- 1 lb ground turkey or lean (at least 80%) ground beef
- 1 medium onion, coarsely chopped (1/2 cup)
- 1 cup water
- 1 can (14.5 oz) stewed tomatoes, undrained
- 1 box (9 oz) Green Giant® frozen baby sweet peas, thawed
- 1 package (3 oz) chicken- or beef-flavor ramen noodle soup mix

1 In 12-inch nonstick skillet, cook turkey and onion over medium heat about 8 minutes, stirring occasionally, until turkey is no longer pink; drain.

2 Stir in water, tomatoes, peas and seasoning packet from soup mix. Break up noodles; stir into turkey mixture. Heat to boiling, stirring occasionally; reduce heat. Cover; simmer about 6 minutes, stirring occasionally, until noodles are tender.

High Altitude (3500-6500 ft): No change.

Nutritional Info: 1 Serving: Calories 310; Total Fat 13g (Saturated Fat 3.5g); Sodium 740mg; Total Carbohydrate 22g (Dietary Fiber 4g); Protein 27g. Exchanges: 1/2 Starch, 1/2 Other Carbohydrate, 2 Vegetable, 3 Lean Meat, 1/2 Fat. Carbohydrate Choices: 1-1/2.

Betty's Kitchen Tips

Substitution: If you're a broccoli fan, feel free to substitute a 9-oz box of frozen broccoli cuts for the peas.

Serve-With: Toss a fruit salad and purchase crunchy breadsticks to round out this simple supper.

beef and salsa skillet

Prep Time: 10 Minutes
Start to Finish: 30 Minutes
Servings: 6

- 1   lb lean (at least 80%) ground beef
- 1   jar (16 oz) Old El Paso® Thick 'n Chunky salsa (2 cups)
- 1   can (15 oz) Progresso® dark red kidney beans, undrained
- 1   can (7 oz) Green Giant® Niblets® whole kernel sweet corn, undrained

- 1   can (8 oz) tomato sauce
- 2   teaspoons chili powder
- 1-1/2   cups Original Bisquick® mix
- 1/2   cup water
- 1/2   cup shredded Colby-Monterey Jack cheese (2 oz), if desired

1. In 12-inch skillet, cook beef over medium-high heat 5 to 7 minutes, stirring occasionally, until thoroughly cooked; drain. Stir in salsa, beans, corn, tomato sauce and 1 teaspoon of the chili powder. Heat to boiling; reduce heat.

2. In medium bowl, stir Bisquick mix, remaining 1 teaspoon chili powder and the water until soft dough forms. Drop dough by 6 spoonfuls onto simmering beef mixture.

3. Cook uncovered 10 minutes. Cover; cook 8 minutes longer. Sprinkle with cheese. Cover; cook about 2 minutes or until cheese is melted.

High Altitude (3500-6500 ft): No change.

Nutritional Info: 1 Serving: Calories 410; Total Fat 13g (Saturated Fat 4.5g); Sodium 1450mg; Total Carbohydrate 49g (Dietary Fiber 7g); Protein 23g. Exchanges: 2-1/2 Starch, 1/2 Other Carbohydrate, 1 Vegetable, 1-1/2 Medium-Fat Meat, 1 Fat. Carbohydrate Choices: 3.

Betty's Kitchen Tips

Substitution: Use ground turkey for the ground beef for an equally delicious one-dish dinner.

Serve-With: Complete this meal with a salad of sliced oranges, sliced avocado and red onion rings drizzled with your favorite vinaigrette dressing.

ginger asian beef

Prep Time: 30 Minutes
Start to Finish: 30 Minutes
Servings: 5

QUICK

- 1 lb lean (at least 80%) ground beef
- 1 box (5.6 oz) Hamburger Helper® beef pasta
- 3-2/3 cups hot water
- 2 tablespoons soy sauce
- 1 tablespoon honey
- 1 teaspoon ground ginger
- 1 bag (16 oz) frozen stir-fry vegetables

1 In 10-inch skillet, cook beef over medium heat 8 to 10 minutes, stirring occasionally, until brown; drain.

2 Stir in sauce mix and uncooked pasta (from Hamburger Helper box), water, soy sauce, honey and ginger. Heat to boiling, stirring occasionally.

3 Stir in frozen vegetables; reduce heat. Cover; simmer 10 minutes, stirring occasionally. Uncover; cook until sauce is desired thickness.

High Altitude (3500-6500 ft): No change.

Nutritional Info: 1 Serving: Calories 310; Total Fat 11g (Saturated Fat 4g); Sodium 1110mg; Total Carbohydrate 31g (Dietary Fiber 3g); Protein 21g. Exchanges: 1-1/2 Starch, 1 Vegetable, 2 Medium-Fat Meat. Carbohydrate Choices: 2.

Betty's Kitchen Tips

Substitution: For a change of pace, use Asian Helper® beef fried rice or Mongolian-style beef for the Hamburger Helper® pasta mix.

Serve-With: Refreshing orange slices and hot or iced tea make excellent accompaniments to this easy meal.

saucy chicken thighs with mushrooms and pea pods

Prep Time: 30 Minutes
Start to Finish: 30 Minutes
Servings: 6

QUICK

1	tablespoon vegetable oil
1-1/4	lb boneless skinless chicken thighs
1	package (8 oz) sliced fresh mushrooms (3 cups)
1	box (6.5 oz) Hamburger Helper® stroganoff

1-3/4	cups milk
1	box (9 oz) Green Giant® frozen sugar snap peas, thawed, drained

1 In 10-inch nonstick skillet, heat oil over medium-high heat. Cook chicken in oil 8 to 10 minutes, turning once, until golden brown. Remove chicken from skillet; set aside. Drain all but 1 tablespoon of the drippings from skillet. Add mushrooms to drippings; cook and stir about 5 minutes or until softened.

2 Stir in sauce mix (from Hamburger Helper box) and milk. Arrange chicken in single layer over mushrooms. Reduce heat. Cover; simmer about 10 minutes, stirring occasionally.

3 Meanwhile, fill 2-quart saucepan 2/3 full of water. Heat to boiling. Stir in uncooked pasta (from Hamburger Helper box). Gently boil uncovered 10 to 12 minutes, stirring occasionally, until tender.

4 Stir sugar snap peas into chicken mixture. Cook uncovered 3 to 4 minutes or until juice of chicken is clear when center of thickest part is cut (165°F) and peas are crisp-tender.

5 Drain pasta; place on large platter with sides. Top with chicken and sauce.

High Altitude (3500-6500 ft): No change.

Nutritional Info: 1 Serving: Calories 320; Total Fat 12g (Saturated Fat 3.5g); Sodium 710mg; Total Carbohydrate 26g (Dietary Fiber 1g); Protein 27g. Exchanges: 1 Starch, 1-1/2 Vegetable, 3 Lean Meat, 1/2 Fat. Carbohydrate Choices: 2.

Betty's Kitchen Tips

Variation: Stroganoff doesn't have to feature beef—versatile and popular boneless chicken thighs are terrific in this dish.

Serve-With: This easy, six-ingredient recipe already contains meat, pasta and veggies, so stop at the store for a can of Pillsbury® crescent dinner rolls and dessert from the bakery, and you have a complete, delicious meal in no time!

FROM THE GRILL

p. 97

96

107

105

chicken and grilled vegetable stacked sandwiches

Prep Time: 25 Minutes
Start to Finish: 25 Minutes
Servings: 4 sandwiches

QUICK

Garlic-Lemon Mayonnaise
- 1/4   cup mayonnaise or salad dressing
- 1   clove garlic, finely chopped
- 1   tablespoon fresh lemon juice

Sandwiches
- 1   small zucchini, cut lengthwise into 4 thin slices
- 2   portabella mushroom caps (about 6 oz)
- 2   tablespoons olive or vegetable oil

- 1/2   teaspoon salt
- 1/8   teaspoon pepper
- 1/2   loaf (1-lb size) French bread, cut in half horizontally, then cut crosswise into 4 sections
- 1/4   lb thinly sliced cooked chicken (from deli)
- 1   plum (Roma) tomato, thinly sliced
- 2   oz smoked mozzarella or provolone cheese, thinly sliced
- 1/4   cup packed fresh basil leaves

1 In small bowl, mix ingredients for Garlic-Lemon Mayonnaise; set aside.

2 Heat gas or charcoal grill. Brush zucchini and mushroom caps with oil; sprinkle both sides with salt and pepper. Place vegetables on grill over medium-high heat. Cover grill; cook 6 minutes, turning once, until just tender. Slice mushroom caps; cool.

3 Spread Garlic-Lemon Mayonnaise on cut sides of bread. On bottom halves of bread, layer zucchini, mushrooms, chicken, tomato, cheese and basil. Cover with top halves of bread.

High Altitude (3500-6500 ft): No change.

Nutritional Info: 1 Sandwich: Calories 430; Total Fat 24g (Saturated Fat 5g); Sodium 1180mg; Total Carbohydrate 38g (Dietary Fiber 2g); Protein 15g. Exchanges: 1-1/2 Starch, 1/2 Other Carbohydrate, 2 Vegetable, 1 Lean Meat, 4 Fat. Carbohydrate Choices: 2-1/2.

Betty's Kitchen Tips

Purchasing: Fresh lemon juice makes all the difference in the Garlic-Lemon Mayonnaise. Choose heavy lemons; they will contain the most juice. Bring lemons to room temperature before juicing. It's easier to get juice from a warm lemon than a cold one.

Variation: Personalize this sandwich by grilling your favorite summertime veggies. Try yellow summer squash, bell peppers, onions or eggplant.

all-american bbq rubbed chicken

Prep Time: 35 Minutes
Start to Finish: 35 Minutes
Servings: 4

- 4 bone-in chicken breasts (about 3 lb)
- 1 tablespoon packed brown sugar
- 1 tablespoon chili powder
- 1 tablespoon paprika
- 2 teaspoons garlic powder
- 1 teaspoon ground cumin
- 1 teaspoon salt
- 1/2 teaspoon pepper
- 1 tablespoon olive oil or vegetable oil

1 Heat gas or charcoal grill. Using hands, gently loosen skin on chicken, forming pocket between meat and skin. In small bowl, mix remaining ingredients. Spread half of rub under skin on chicken. Spread remaining rub on top, bottom and sides of chicken.

2 Carefully brush oil on grill rack. Place chicken, skin sides up, on grill over medium heat. Cover grill; cook 25 minutes, turning once, until juice of chicken is clear when thickest part is cut to bone (165°F).

High Altitude (3500-6500 ft): No change.

Nutritional Info: 1 Serving: Calories 470; Total Fat 21g (Saturated Fat 5g); Sodium 740mg; Total Carbohydrate 6g (Dietary Fiber 1g); Protein 64g. Exchanges: 1/2 Other Carbohydrate, 9 Very Lean Meat, 3 Fat. Carbohydrate Choices: 1/2.

Betty's Kitchen Tips

Time-Saver: Make a second batch of the rub, without the oil, to keep on hand for quick seasoning. (Add oil just before rubbing on chicken.) This rub also makes a great summertime hostess gift—place spice mixture (without oil) in a small jar tied with a ribbon and attach the recipe card.

Success Hint: If the chicken starts to get too dark, turn grill temperature down or move pieces away from coals to cook more slowly.

balsamic chicken breast salad

Prep Time: 25 Minutes
Start to Finish: 1 Hour
Servings: 4

2/3 cup olive oil
1/3 cup balsamic vinegar
2 cloves garlic, finely chopped
1 tablespoon Dijon mustard
1-1/2 teaspoons sugar
1/2 teaspoon salt
1/4 teaspoon pepper

4 boneless skinless chicken breasts (about 1-1/4 lb)
2 cups grape tomatoes (12 oz), cut into halves
4 oz mozzarella cheese, cut into bite-size strips (1 cup)
1 shallot, finely chopped (3 tablespoons)
8 cups salad greens

1 In medium bowl, beat oil, vinegar, garlic, mustard, sugar, salt and pepper with whisk until well blended. Reserve 1/2 cup of dressing for salad; set aside.

2 Place chicken in resealable food-storage plastic bag; pour remaining dressing over chicken. Seal bag; turn to coat chicken with marinade. Refrigerate 30 minutes.

3 Heat gas or charcoal grill. In medium bowl, toss tomatoes, cheese, shallot and 2 tablespoons of the reserved dressing; set aside.

4 Remove chicken from marinade; discard marinade. Carefully brush oil on grill rack. Place chicken on grill over medium heat. Cover grill; cook 12 to 15 minutes, turning once, until juice of chicken is clear when center of thickest part is cut (165°F). Let stand 5 minutes; cut into 1/2-inch strips.

5 Divide salad greens among 4 plates. Top with tomato mixture and chicken; drizzle with remaining dressing.

High Altitude (3500-6500 ft): No change.

Nutritional Info: 1 Serving: Calories 490; Total Fat 29g (Saturated Fat 7g); Sodium 660mg; Total Carbohydrate 15g (Dietary Fiber 3g); Protein 42g. Exchanges: 1/2 Other Carbohydrate, 2 Vegetable, 5-1/2 Very Lean Meat, 5 Fat. Carbohydrate Choices: 1.

Betty's Kitchen Tips

Serve-With: For a heartier meal, serve chicken and tomato salad over cooked pasta instead of salad greens.

Variation: Substitute balls or cubes of fresh mozzarella to add a special touch to this main-dish salad.

blue cheese and bacon chicken burgers

Prep Time: 30 Minutes
Start to Finish: 30 Minutes
Servings: 4 sandwiches

QUICK

5	slices bacon, cut into 1/2-inch pieces
1	slice white sandwich bread
2	tablespoons milk
1	lb ground chicken
1/3	cup crumbled blue cheese
4	hamburger buns, split
4	leaves lettuce
1	medium tomato, sliced

1 In 10-inch skillet, cook bacon until crisp; drain on paper towels. Crumble bacon; set aside.

2 Heat gas or charcoal grill. In medium bowl, mash bread and milk with fork until well mixed. Stir in chicken, cheese and bacon. Shape into 4 patties, 1/2 inch thick.

3 Carefully brush oil on grill rack. Place patties on grill over medium heat. Cover grill; cook 9 to 12 minutes, turning once, until meat thermometer inserted in center of patties reads 165°F.

4 Place burgers on bottom halves of buns. Top with lettuce and tomato. Cover with top halves of buns.

High Altitude (3500-6500 ft): No change.

Nutritional Info: 1 Sandwich: Calories 350; Total Fat 16g (Saturated Fat 6g); Sodium 690mg; Total Carbohydrate 27g (Dietary Fiber 1g); Protein 25g. Exchanges: 1 Starch, 1/2 Other Carbohydrate, 1/2 Vegetable, 3 Lean Meat, 1 Fat. Carbohydrate Choices: 2.

Betty's Kitchen Tips

Time-Saver: Make these mouthwatering burgers even quicker by using 1/4 cup Betty Crocker® Bac~Os® bacon bits or chips instead of cooking the bacon.

Substitution: Other soft, crumbled cheeses will work well in this recipe. Try feta or goat cheese.

apricot-sesame glazed chicken

Prep Time: 1 Hour
Start to Finish: 1 Hour
Servings: 4

3 tablespoons Dijon mustard
3 tablespoons soy sauce
1 cut-up whole chicken (3 to 3-1/2 lb)

3/4 cup apricot preserves
1 tablespoon sesame seed

1 In small bowl, mix mustard and soy sauce. Brush 3 tablespoons of mixture over chicken. Stir 6 tablespoons of the apricot preserves and the sesame seed into remaining mustard mixture; set aside.

2 Heat gas or charcoal grill for indirect cooking. For two-burner gas grill, heat one burner to medium; place chicken on unheated side. For one-burner gas grill, place chicken on grill over low heat. For charcoal grill, move medium coals to edge of firebox; place chicken on grill rack over drip pan.

3 Cover grill; cook 15 minutes. Turn chicken. Cover grill; cook 20 to 30 minutes longer, turning occasionally, until juice of chicken is clear when thickest piece is cut to bone (165°F).

4 Brush chicken with reserved apricot mixture. Cook, turning and brushing frequently, 3 to 5 minutes, just until browned. Remove chicken from grill; spoon remaining 6 tablespoons apricot preserves over chicken.

High Altitude (3500-6500 ft): No change.

Nutritional Info: 1 Serving: Calories 710; Total Fat 32g (Saturated Fat 9g); Sodium 1150mg; Total Carbohydrate 44g (Dietary Fiber 1g); Protein 62g. Exchanges: 1 Starch, 2 Other Carbohydrate, 8 Lean Meat, 1-1/2 Fat. Carbohydrate Choices: 3.

Betty's Kitchen Tips

Variation: This glaze also works great on boneless skinless chicken breasts. Brush chicken as directed in Step 1. Grill over direct medium heat about 15 minutes or until juice of chicken is clear when center of thickest part is cut (165°F). Proceed as directed in Step 4.

Substitution: For Orange-Sesame Glazed Chicken, substitute orange marmalade for the apricot preserves.

grilled chicken breasts with cucumber-peach salsa

Prep Time: 30 Minutes
Start to Finish: 30 Minutes
Servings: 4

QUICK LOW FAT

- 1/2 cup chopped cucumber
- 1/3 cup peach preserves
- 1 tablespoon chopped fresh or 1 teaspoon dried mint leaves
- 1/4 teaspoon salt
- 2 tablespoons chopped red onion
- 1 peach or nectarine, peeled, chopped (3/4 cup)
- 4 boneless skinless chicken breasts (about 1-1/4 lb)

1 Heat gas or charcoal grill. In small bowl, mix cucumber, 2 tablespoons of the preserves, the mint, salt, onion and peach; set aside.

2 Carefully brush oil on grill rack. Place chicken on grill over medium heat. Cover grill; cook 10 to 15 minutes, turning and brushing 2 or 3 times with remaining preserves, until juice of chicken is clear when center of thickest part is cut (165°F). Discard any remaining preserves. Serve chicken with salsa.

High Altitude (3500-6500 ft): No change.

Nutritional Info: 1 Serving: Calories 270; Total Fat 5g (Saturated Fat 1.5g); Sodium 240mg; Total Carbohydrate 23g (Dietary Fiber 1g); Protein 32g. Exchanges: 1/2 Starch, 1 Other Carbohydrate, 4 Very Lean Meat, 1/2 Fat. Carbohydrate Choices: 1-1/2.

Betty's Kitchen Tips

Do-Ahead: The salsa can be made up to 24 hours in advance and refrigerated. Making it ahead allows the flavors to blend.

Success Hint: If you're using a charcoal grill, plan on about 40 minutes to prep the grill and heat charcoal to the correct temperature. Gas and electric grills take about 10 minutes.

grilled chili chicken with southwest relish

Prep Time: 1 Hour 10 Minutes
Start to Finish: 2 Hours 10 Minutes
Servings: 6

Relish

1	can (15 oz) Progresso® black beans, drained, rinsed
1	can (11 oz) Green Giant® Niblets® whole kernel sweet corn, drained
2/3	cup chopped red onion
1/4	cup chopped fresh cilantro
3	tablespoons lime juice
1	tablespoon olive or vegetable oil
1	medium avocado, pitted, peeled and chopped
1	clove garlic, finely chopped

Chicken

1	teaspoon chili powder
1/2	teaspoon paprika
1	cut-up whole chicken (3 to 3-1/2 lb)

1 In medium glass or plastic bowl, mix all relish ingredients. Cover; refrigerate at least 1 hour to blend flavors.

2 Heat gas or charcoal grill. Mix chili powder and paprika; sprinkle over chicken. Carefully brush oil on grill rack. Place chicken, skin sides up, on grill over medium heat. Cover grill; cook 15 minutes.

3 Turn chicken. Cover grill; cook 20 to 40 minutes longer, turning occasionally, until juice of chicken is clear when thickest piece is cut to bone (165°F). Serve chicken with relish.

High Altitude (3500-6500 ft): No change.

Nutritional Info: 1 Serving: Calories 420; Total Fat 20g (Saturated Fat 4.5g); Sodium 220mg; Total Carbohydrate 26g (Dietary Fiber 8g); Protein 33g. Exchanges: 1 Starch, 1-1/2 Vegetable, 4 Lean Meat, 1-1/2 Fat. Carbohydrate Choices: 2.

Betty's Kitchen Tips

Do-Ahead: Prepare the relish ahead of time, so when you get home from work, all you need to do is pop the chicken on the grill.

Variation: Add even more color by using Green Giant® Mexicorn® whole kernel corn with red and green peppers.

chicken pizza mexicana

Prep Time: 20 Minutes
Start to Finish: 20 Minutes
Servings: 4

QUICK

2	cups shredded taco-seasoned cheese blend (8 oz)
1	package (14 oz) prebaked original Italian pizza crust (12 inch)
1-1/2	cups chopped cooked chicken
2	plum (Roma) tomatoes, thinly sliced
1	small jalapeño chile, seeded, finely chopped

1 Heat gas or charcoal grill. Sprinkle cheese evenly over pizza crust. Top with remaining ingredients.

2 Place pizza on grill over medium heat. Cover grill; cook 8 to 10 minutes or until crust is crisp and cheese is melted. (If crust browns too quickly, place a piece of foil between crust and grill.)

High Altitude (3500-6500 ft): No change.

Nutritional Info: 1 Serving: Calories 610; Total Fat 23g (Saturated Fat 13g); Sodium 890mg; Total Carbohydrate 62g (Dietary Fiber 3g); Protein 37g. Exchanges: 4 Starch, 3-1/2 Lean Meat, 2 Fat. Carbohydrate Choices: 4.

Betty's Kitchen Tips

Variation: For mini pizzas, use two 6-inch prebaked crusts and simply divide ingredients equally between the two crusts. Grilling time should be about the same.

Success Hint: Keep a spray bottle filled with water near the grill. Use it to douse any flare-ups that might occur.

chicken kabobs

Prep Time: 30 Minutes
Start to Finish: 1 Hour 30 Minutes
Servings: 8 appetizers or 4 main-dish servings

Bee Yinn Low
Rasa Malaysia
www.rasamalaysia.com

8	(6-inch) bamboo skewers
1/4	cup finely chopped onion
2	cloves garlic, finely chopped (1 teaspoon)
1	tablespoon chopped fresh parsley
1/2	teaspoon paprika
1/2	teaspoon crushed red pepper flakes
1/2	teaspoon ground cumin

1/4	teaspoon salt
1/4	cup olive oil
2	tablespoons lemon juice
1	package (1 lb) boneless skinless chicken breasts, cut into 32 (1-inch) pieces
1	red or yellow bell pepper, cut into 24 (1-inch) pieces

1 Soak the skewers in water for 30 minutes. In shallow glass or plastic dish or resealable food-storage plastic bag, mix onion, garlic, parsley, paprika, pepper flakes, cumin, salt, 2 tablespoons of the olive oil and lemon juice. Add chicken; turning to coat with marinade. Cover dish or seal bag; refrigerate, turning chicken occasionally, at least 1 hour to marinate.

2 Heat gas or charcoal grill. Thread chicken and bell pepper pieces on skewers.

3 Place kabobs on grill over medium heat. Cook 9 to 11 minutes, turning occasionally; brushing with remaining 2 tablespoons oil, until chicken is no longer pink in center.

High Altitude (3500-6500 ft): No change.

Nutritional Info: 1 Appetizer Serving: Calories 140; Total Fat 9g (Saturated Fat 1.5g); Sodium 105mg; Total Carbohydrate 2g (Dietary Fiber 0g); Protein 13g. Exchanges: 2 Lean Meat, 1/2 Fat. Carbohydrate Choices: 0.

grilled chicken pasta salad with caramelized onion, broccoli and mango

Prep Time: 1 Hour
Start to Finish: 1 Hour 30 Minutes
Servings: 8 (1-1/3 cups each)

Jenny Flake
Picky Palate
www.pickypalate.com

QUICK

1   package (8 oz) uncooked campanelle or rotini pasta
3   boneless skinless chicken breasts (1 lb)
1   tablespoon olive oil
1   medium onion, finely chopped (3/4 cup)
3   cups fresh broccoli florets

2   ripe mangoes, seed removed, peeled and cut up
1   red bell pepper, chopped
1   medium zucchini, quartered lengthwise, then cut crosswise into slices (1 cup)
1   bottle (8 oz) Italian dressing
1/2 teaspoon salt

1   Heat gas or charcoal grill. Cook pasta as directed on package; drain. Rinse with cold water to cool; drain well.

2   Meanwhile, place chicken on grill over medium heat. Cover grill; cook 15 to 20 minutes, turning once or twice until juice of chicken is clear when center of thickest part is cut (170°F). Cool slightly. Cut into 3/4-inch cubes.

3   In 8-inch nonstick skillet, heat oil over medium-high heat. Stir in onion; cook uncovered 5 minutes, stirring occasionally.

4   Reduce heat to medium-low. Cook 10 to 15 minutes longer, stirring every 5 minutes, until onion is deep golden brown (onion will shrink during cooking). Cool slightly.

5   In large bowl, combine pasta, chicken, caramelized onion and remaining ingredients; toss gently to coat. Cover; refrigerate 30 minutes to blend flavors.

High Altitude (3500-6500 ft): No change.

Nutritional Info: 1 Serving: Calories 360; Total Fat 13g (Saturated Fat 1.5g); Sodium 810mg; Total Carbohydrate 42g (Dietary Fiber 4g); Protein 19g. Exchanges: 2 Starch, 2 Vegetable, 2 Lean Meat, 1 Fat. Carbohydrate Choices: 3.

Betty's Kitchen Tip

• One pound of boneless skinless chicken breasts will give you two cups of cooked chicken.

peppercorn t-bones

Prep Time: 25 Minutes
Start to Finish: 25 Minutes
Servings: 6

6	beef T-bone steaks, 1 inch thick (about 1-1/2 lb)
3	cloves garlic, cut in half
1-1/2	tablespoons black peppercorns, crushed
1/3	cup butter or margarine, softened
1-1/2	tablespoons Dijon mustard
3/4	teaspoon Worcestershire sauce
1/4	teaspoon lime juice

Salt and pepper, if desired

1 Heat gas or charcoal grill. Trim fat on beef steaks to 1/4-inch thickness. Rub garlic on beef. Press crushed peppercorns into beef. In small bowl, mix remaining ingredients except salt and pepper; set aside.

2 Place beef on grill 4 to 5 inches from medium heat. Cover grill; cook 10 to 14 minutes or until desired doneness is reached, turning once. Sprinkle with salt and pepper. Serve with butter mixture.

High Altitude (3500-6500 ft): No change.

Nutritional Info: 1 Serving: Calories 290; Total Fat 19g (Saturated Fat 10g); Sodium 210mg; Total Carbohydrate 2g (Dietary Fiber 0g); Protein 28g. Exchanges: 4 Medium-Fat Meat. Carbohydrate Choices: 0.

Betty's Kitchen Tip

• To crush peppercorns, place them in a resealable food-storage plastic bag and use a rolling pin to crush them into smaller pieces.

chicken with peppers and artichokes

Prep Time: 30 Minutes
Start to Finish: 1 Hour
Servings: 4

LOW FAT

1   jar (6 oz) Progresso® marinated artichoke hearts, drained, marinade reserved
1/3 cup dry white wine or chicken broth
4   boneless skinless chicken breasts (about 1-1/4 lb)

2   medium red bell peppers, cut lengthwise into quarters
4   medium green onions, sliced (1/4 cup)
1/4 teaspoon pepper

1 Refrigerate artichokes. In shallow glass or plastic dish, mix reserved marinade and wine. Add chicken and bell peppers, turning to coat with marinade. Cover; refrigerate for at least 30 minutes but no longer than 24 hours, turning occasionally.

2 Heat gas or charcoal grill. Remove chicken and bell peppers from marinade; reserve marinade. Place chicken on grill over medium heat. Cover grill; cook 5 minutes. Turn chicken; add bell peppers to grill. Cover grill; cook 10 to 15 minutes or until

peppers are tender and juice of chicken is clear when center of thickest part is cut (165°F).

3 Strain marinade. In 1-quart saucepan, mix marinade, artichokes, onions and pepper. Heat to boiling; boil and stir 1 minute. Serve with chicken and bell peppers.

High Altitude (3500-6500 ft): No change.

Nutritional Info: 1 Serving: Calories 200; Total Fat 5g (Saturated Fat 1.5g); Sodium 210mg; Total Carbohydrate 9g (Dietary Fiber 5g); Protein 27g. Exchanges: 1-1/2 Vegetable, 3-1/2 Very Lean Meat, 1/2 Fat. Carbohydrate Choices: 1/2.

Betty's Kitchen Tips

Success Hint: We recommend a nonmetal dish for marinating. Most marinades contain acidic ingredients, such as vinegar or lemon juice, which react with metal, causing off flavors in the food and possibly damaging the container.

Purchasing: When bell peppers are at their peak, choose from a variety of vibrant colors—red, orange, yellow and green.

SELECT SANDWICHES

p.112

116

119

118

indian curry burgers with chutney mayo

Prep Time: 35 Minutes
Start to Finish: 35 Minutes
Servings: 4 sandwiches

Chutney Mayo

1/4	cup mayonnaise or salad dressing
3	tablespoons mango chutney, finely chopped
1	teaspoon lemon juice

Burgers

1	tablespoon vegetable oil
1	medium onion, chopped (1/2 cup)
1	jalapeño chile, seeded, finely chopped
2	tablespoons curry powder
1	teaspoon ground cumin

1	teaspoon ground ginger
1	teaspoon salt
1/4	teaspoon pepper
1	lb lean (at least 80%) ground beef
4	kaiser rolls, split
4	leaves lettuce
1	medium mango, seed removed, peeled and sliced

1 In small bowl, mix chutney mayo ingredients. Cover; refrigerate until serving time.

2 In 8-inch skillet, heat oil over medium heat. Cook onion and chile in oil 3 to 5 minutes, stirring occasionally, until tender. Add curry powder, cumin, ginger, salt and pepper; cook and stir 2 minutes longer.

3 Heat gas or charcoal grill. In large bowl, mix beef and onion mixture. Shape mixture into 4 patties, 1/4 inch thick. Place patties on grill over medium heat.

Cover grill; cook 5 to 8 minutes, turning once, until meat thermometer inserted in center of patties reads 160°F. During last 2 minutes of cooking, place rolls, cut sides down, on grill until toasted.

4 Spread chutney mayo on cut sides of rolls. Place burgers on bottom halves; top with lettuce and mango. Cover with top halves of rolls.

High Altitude (3500-6500 ft): No change.

Nutritional Info: 1 Sandwich: Calories 470; Total Fat 22g (Saturated Fat 6g); Sodium 1080mg; Total Carbohydrate 40g (Dietary Fiber 4g); Protein 26g. Exchanges: 2 Starch, 1 Vegetable, 2-1/2 Medium-Fat Meat, 1-1/2 Fat. Carbohydrate Choices: 2-1/2.

Betty's Kitchen Tips

Time-Saver: In a hurry? Instead of fresh mangoes, use peeled sliced mangoes from a jar.

Variation: To broil patties instead of grilling, set oven control to broil. Place patties on broiler pan. Broil 4 to 6 inches from heat 5 to 8 minutes, turning once.

grilled bacon-cheeseburgers

Prep Time: 35 Minutes
Start to Finish: 35 Minutes
Servings: 12 sandwiches

- 3 lb lean (at least 80%) ground beef
- 1 medium onion, finely chopped (1/2 cup)
- 3/4 teaspoon pepper
- 12 hamburger buns, split
- 1 cup blue cheese dressing
- 12 slices bacon, crisply cooked, broken in half

1 Heat gas or charcoal grill. In large bowl, mix beef, onion and pepper. Shape into 12 patties, 3/4 inch thick.

2 Place patties on grill over medium heat. Cover grill; cook 13 to 15 minutes, turning once, until meat thermometer inserted in center of patties reads 160°F. During last 2 minutes of cooking, place buns, cut sides down, on grill until toasted.

3 Place burgers on bottom halves of buns. Top each burger with 4 teaspoons dressing and 2 pieces of bacon. Cover with top halves of buns.

High Altitude (3500-6500 ft): No change.

Nutritional Info: 1 Sandwich: Calories 460; Total Fat 28g (Saturated Fat 8g); Sodium 610mg; Total Carbohydrate 24g (Dietary Fiber 1g); Protein 27g. Exchanges: 1-1/2 Starch, 3-1/2 Medium-Fat Meat, 2 Fat. Carbohydrate Choices: 1-1/2.

Betty's Kitchen Tips

Time-Saver: Use your microwave to cook the bacon. Place bacon slices on microwave plate or rack lined with paper towels. Place paper towels between layers; cover with paper towels. For 1 to 8 slices, microwave on high for about 30 seconds per slice or until crisp.

Purchasing: When making your shopping list, put ground beef with the other perishables you'll buy. You'll want to use it within 2 days after purchase.

classic chicken panini

Prep Time: 20 Minutes
Start to Finish: 20 Minutes
Servings: 4 sandwiches

4	boneless skinless chicken breasts (1 lb)
1/2	teaspoon salt-free seasoning blend
1/4	cup fat-free mayonnaise or salad dressing
2	teaspoons white or flavored vinegar
1/2	teaspoon garlic powder
4	whole wheat English muffins, split

4	slices (3/4 oz each) fat-free mozzarella process cheese product
4	thin slices red onion
1	plum (Roma) tomato, cut into 8 slices

1 Heat closed medium-size contact grill for 5 minutes. Position drip tray to catch drippings. Sprinkle chicken with seasoning blend. When grill is heated, place chicken on grill. Close grill; cook 4 to 5 minutes or until juice of chicken is clear when center of thickest part is cut (165°F).

2 Meanwhile, in small bowl, mix the mayonnaise, vinegar and garlic powder. Spread on English muffin halves. Place chicken on bottoms of English muffins. Top with cheese, onion and tomato. Cover with tops of muffins.

3 Place sandwiches on grill. Close grill, pressing to flatten sandwiches; cook 2 to 3 minutes or until toasted.

High Altitude (3500-6500 ft): No change.

Nutritional Info: 1 Sandwich: Calories 350; Total Fat 8g (Saturated Fat 2g); Sodium 650mg; Total Carbohydrate 36g (Dietary Fiber 5g); Protein 34g. Exchanges: 2-1/2 Starch, 3-1/2 Very Lean Meat, 1 Fat. Carbohydrate Choices: 2-1/2.

Betty's Kitchen Tips

Substitution: Regular tomatoes can be substituted for the plum tomatoes but may add more moisture to the sandwiches during grilling.

Variation: Try this sandwich with other types of cheese, such as reduced-fat Swiss, provolone or Cheddar.

grilled backyard beer burgers

Prep Time: 25 Minutes
Start to Finish: 25 Minutes
Servings: 6 sandwiches

QUICK

1-1/2	lb lean (at least 80%) ground beef
1	small onion, finely chopped (1/4 cup)
1/4	cup regular or nonalcoholic beer
1	tablespoon Worcestershire sauce
1	teaspoon salt
1/4	teaspoon pepper
2	cloves garlic, finely chopped
6	rye or whole wheat hamburger buns, split

Ketchup, if desired

Pickle planks, if desired

1 Heat gas or charcoal grill. In medium bowl, mix all ingredients except buns, ketchup and pickles. Shape mixture into 6 patties, 3/4 inch thick.

2 Place patties on grill over medium heat. Cover grill; cook 13 to 15 minutes, turning once, until meat thermometer inserted in center of patties reads 160°F. During last 2 minutes of cooking, place buns, cut sides down, on grill until toasted.

3 Serve burgers on buns with ketchup and pickles.

High Altitude (3500-6500 ft): No change.

Nutritional Info: 1 Sandwich: Calories 310; Total Fat 14g (Saturated Fat 5g); Sodium 680mg; Total Carbohydrate 20g (Dietary Fiber 3g); Protein 25g. Exchanges: 1-1/2 Starch, 2-1/2 Medium-Fat Meat. Carbohydrate Choices: 1.

Betty's Kitchen Tips

Variation: For Burgundy Burgers, substitute 1/4 cup Burgundy wine for the beer.

Success Hint: Avoid pressing down on a hamburger patty while it's cooking—you'll squeeze out much of the flavorful juices.

greek pita burgers with spinach, feta and tzatziki sauce

Prep Time: 30 Minutes
Start to Finish: 30 Minutes
Servings: 8 sandwiches

QUICK LOW FAT

Sauce

1/2	medium cucumber, peeled, seeded and shredded
1	container (8 oz) plain yogurt
4	medium green onions, chopped (1/4 cup)
1	clove garlic, finely chopped
1	tablespoon olive oil
1	teaspoon lemon juice
1/4	teaspoon salt

Burgers

1	lb lean (at least 80%) ground beef

1/2	cup Green Giant® frozen (thawed) chopped spinach, squeezed to drain
1/3	cup crumbled feta cheese
1/4	cup finely chopped red onion
2	cloves garlic, finely chopped
1/2	teaspoon salt
1/4	teaspoon pepper
8	whole wheat hamburger buns, split
2	medium tomatoes, sliced
4	leaves romaine lettuce, torn in half

1 Place shredded cucumber in clean dish towel; squeeze to remove any excess liquid. In small bowl, mix cucumber and remaining sauce ingredients. Cover; refrigerate until serving time.

2 Heat gas or charcoal grill. In large bowl, mix all burger ingredients except buns, tomatoes and lettuce. Shape into 8 patties, 1/4 inch thick. Place patties on grill over medium heat. Cover grill; cook 5 to 8 minutes, turning once, until meat thermometer inserted in center of patties reads 160°F.

3 Spoon 2 tablespoons sauce on bottom half of each bun. Top with burger, tomato and lettuce. Cover with top halves of buns.

High Altitude (3500-6500 ft): No change.

Nutritional Info: 1 Sandwich: Calories 240; Total Fat 9g (Saturated Fat 3g); Sodium 540mg; Total Carbohydrate 27g (Dietary Fiber 2g); Protein 12g. Exchanges: 1-1/2 Starch, 1 Vegetable, 1 Medium-Fat Meat, 1/2 Fat. Carbohydrate Choices: 2.

Betty's Kitchen Tips

Do-Ahead: The tzatziki sauce can be made ahead and kept, covered in the refrigerator, for up to one day.

Purchasing: Try using Greek yogurt, which is thicker and creamier than plain yogurt.

blue cheese burgers

Prep Time: 30 Minutes
Start to Finish: 30 Minutes
Servings: 6 sandwiches

QUICK LOW FAT

1/4	cup old-fashioned or quick-cooking oats
2	tablespoons water
1-1/2	lb extra-lean (at least 90%) ground beef
1/2	cup crumbled reduced-fat blue cheese (4 oz)
1/4	cup finely chopped fresh chives
1/2	teaspoon Worcestershire sauce
1/8	teaspoon red pepper sauce
1/2	teaspoon coarse ground black pepper
1/2	teaspoon ground mustard
1/4	teaspoon salt
6	leaves leaf lettuce
6	slices tomato
6	whole wheat burger buns, split

1 Heat gas or charcoal grill. In large bowl, mix oats and water. Stir in beef, blue cheese, chives, Worcestershire sauce, pepper sauce, pepper, mustard and salt until well mixed. Shape mixture into 6 patties, about 3/4 inch thick.

2 Place patties on grill over medium heat. Cover grill; cook 11 to 13 minutes, turning once, until thermometer inserted in center of patties reads 160°F.

3 Layer lettuce, tomato and burgers on bottom halves of buns; cover with top half of buns.

Contact Grill Directions: Heat closed contact grill 5 minutes. Place patties on bottom grill surface. Close grill; cook 6 to 7 minutes or until meat thermometer inserted in center of patties reads 160°F.

High Altitude (3500-6500 ft): No change.

Nutritional Info: 1 Sandwich: Calories 300; Total Fat 10g (Saturated Fat 4.5g); Sodium 490mg; Total Carbohydrate 22g (Dietary Fiber 4g); Protein 30g. Exchanges: 1-1/2 Starch, 3-1/2 Lean Meat. Carbohydrate Choices: 1-1/2.

Betty's Kitchen Tip

• You could use ground turkey breast instead of the ground beef. Be sure to cook until thermometer inserted in center of turkey patties reads 165°F.

beef and chorizo burgers with roasted chile mayonnaise

Prep Time: 40 Minutes
Start to Finish: 40 Minutes
Servings: 4 sandwiches

Roasted Chile Mayonnaise

1/4	cup mayonnaise or salad dressing
1	clove garlic, finely chopped
2	teaspoons lime juice
1	tablespoon chopped fresh cilantro
1	small poblano chile

Burgers

1	lb lean (at least 80%) ground beef
1/2	lb bulk chorizo sausage or Italian pork sausage, crumbled
3/4	teaspoon salt
1/4	teaspoon pepper
4	slices (1 oz each) Monterey Jack cheese
4	hamburger buns, split
1	medium tomato, coarsely chopped

1 Heat gas or charcoal grill. In small bowl, mix mayonnaise, garlic, lime juice and cilantro. Cover; refrigerate.

2 Remove stem, seeds and membranes from chile; cut chile lengthwise into quarters. Place skin side down on grill. Cover grill; cook over medium heat about 10 minutes or until skin is blackened and blistered.

3 Immediately place chile in bowl. Cover tightly with plastic wrap; cool 5 minutes. Peel off blackened skin; rinse with water. Set aside.

4 In large bowl, mix beef, chorizo, salt and pepper. Shape mixture into 4 patties, 1/2 inch thick.

5 Place patties on grill over medium heat. Cover grill; cook 11 to 13 minutes, turning once, until meat thermometer inserted in center of patties reads 160°F. During last 2 minutes of cooking, top each patty with cheese and place buns, cut sides down, on grill. Cook until cheese is melted and buns are toasted. Remove burgers and buns from grill; cover to keep warm.

6 Finely chop roasted chile; stir into mayonnaise mixture. Spread 1 tablespoon mixture on cut sides of buns. Place burgers on bottom halves of buns; top with tomato. Cover with top halves of buns.

High Altitude (3500-6500 ft): No change.

Nutritional Info: 1 Sandwich: Calories 560; Total Fat 35g (Saturated Fat 14g); Sodium 1580mg; Total Carbohydrate 27g (Dietary Fiber 1g); Protein 36g. Exchanges: 1-1/2 Starch, 1/2 Vegetable, 4 High-Fat Meat, 1/2 Fat. Carbohydrate Choices: 2.

chicken burritos

Prep Time: 20 Minutes
Start to Finish: 40 Minutes
Servings: 10 burritos

1	tablespoon vegetable oil
1	lb boneless skinless chicken breasts, cut into 1-inch pieces
1-1/2	cups water
2	teaspoons lime juice
1	cup Old El Paso® Thick 'n Chunky salsa
1	box (6.4 oz) Chicken Helper® chicken fried rice
1	can (15 oz) Progresso® black beans, drained, rinsed
1	can (11 oz) Green Giant® Mexicorn® whole kernel corn with red and green peppers, drained
10	Old El Paso® flour tortillas for burritos (8 inch; from two 11-oz packages)

Sour cream, shredded lettuce and chopped tomatoes, if desired

1 In 10-inch skillet, heat oil over medium heat. Cook chicken in oil 8 to 10 minutes, stirring occasionally, until no longer pink in center.

2 Stir in water, lime juice, salsa and sauce mix (from Chicken Helper box) until blended. Stir in beans, corn and uncooked rice (from Chicken Helper box). Heat to boiling; reduce heat. Cover; simmer 20 to 25 minutes or until rice is tender.

3 Heat tortillas as directed on package. Spoon slightly less than 1 cup chicken mixture down center of each warmed tortilla. Fold bottom 1/3 of tortilla over filling; fold sides in toward center, leaving top open. Top with sour cream, lettuce and tomatoes.

High Altitude (3500-6500 ft): No change.

Nutritional Info: 1 Burrito: Calories 350; Total Fat 7g (Saturated Fat 1.5g); Sodium 930mg; Total Carbohydrate 52g (Dietary Fiber 6g); Protein 19g. Exchanges: 3-1/2 Starch, 1/2 Vegetable, 1 Lean Meat, 1/2 Fat. Carbohydrate Choices: 3-1/2.

Betty's Kitchen Tips

Leftovers: Use leftover tortillas to make quick quesadillas another day. Sprinkle shredded cheese and chopped tomato, green onion and chiles (or your favorite fillings) on half of each tortilla. Fold tortilla over filling. Bake on ungreased cookie sheet at 350°F for about 5 minutes until cheese is melted. Cut into wedges.

Time-Saver: Make this recipe faster by substituting cooked chicken and eliminating the first step. In Step 2, stir in 3-1/2 cups cubed cooked chicken after rice is tender.

mozzarella-stuffed mushroom pizza burgers

Prep Time: 40 Minutes
Start to Finish: 40 Minutes
Servings: 4 sandwiches

1-1/2 lb lean (at least 80%) ground beef	1 package (8 oz) sliced fresh mushrooms (about 3 cups)
1 teaspoon Italian seasoning	1 clove garlic, finely chopped
1 teaspoon salt	4 hamburger buns, split
1/2 teaspoon pepper	1/2 cup pizza sauce, warmed
1 cup shredded mozzarella cheese (4 oz)	
1 tablespoon olive oil or vegetable oil	

1 In large bowl, mix beef, Italian seasoning, salt and pepper. Shape mixture into 8 patties, 4-1/2 inches in diameter and 1/4 inch thick. Press 1/4 cup of the cheese into a ball with hands; press flat into 3-1/2-inch-diameter patty. Repeat with remaining cheese. Place cheese patties on top of 4 beef patties; top with remaining beef patties. Pinch edges together to seal.

2 In 10-inch skillet, heat oil over medium-high heat. Add mushrooms; cook 4 minutes, stirring occasionally, until lightly browned. Add garlic; cook 1 minute longer. Remove from heat.

3 Heat gas or charcoal grill. Place patties on grill over medium heat. Cover grill; cook 11 to 13 minutes, turning once, until meat thermometer inserted in center of patties reads 160°F. During last 2 minutes of cooking, place buns, cut sides down, on grill until toasted.

4 Place burgers on bottom halves of buns. Top with pizza sauce and mushroom mixture. Cover with top halves of buns.

High Altitude (3500-6500 ft): No change.

Nutritional Info: 1 Sandwich: Calories 560; Total Fat 30g (Saturated Fat 12g); Sodium 1080mg; Total Carbohydrate 27g (Dietary Fiber 2g); Protein 43g. Exchanges: 1-1/2 Starch, 1 Vegetable, 5 Medium-Fat Meat, 1 Fat. Carbohydrate Choices: 2.

Betty's Kitchen Tips

Variation: Try 1/2 cup shredded Cheddar and 1/2 cup mozzarella; or use 1 cup pizza cheese blend.

Success Hint: The melted cheese inside the burgers can be hot, so it's good to give your guests a warning before they take a big bite.

chicken souvlaki sandwiches

Prep Time: 15 Minutes
Start to Finish: 15 Minutes
Servings: 6 sandwiches

EASY QUICK

- 3 cups chopped cooked chicken
- 1 cup chopped peeled cucumber
- 1/2 cup crumbled feta cheese (2 oz)
- 1/3 cup finely chopped red onion
- 1/3 cup sour cream
- 2 tablespoons chopped fresh dill weed
- 2 tablespoons mayonnaise or salad dressing
- 1 tablespoon red wine vinegar
- 1/4 teaspoon salt
- 1/8 teaspoon pepper
- 6 pita fold breads (5 inch), warmed

1 In medium bowl, place all ingredients except pita breads; toss until evenly coated.

2 Divide mixture evenly down center of each pita bread; fold in half.

High Altitude (3500-6500 ft): No change.

Nutritional Info: 1 Sandwich: Calories 340; Total Fat 14g (Saturated Fat 5g); Sodium 690mg; Total Carbohydrate 27g (Dietary Fiber 1g); Protein 26g. Exchanges: 1-1/2 Starch, 1/2 Vegetable, 3 Lean Meat, 1 Fat. Carbohydrate Choices: 2.

Betty's Kitchen Tips

Substitution: You can use 1 to 2 teaspoons dried dill weed for the fresh dill in this recipe.

Do-Ahead: If you've chopped some extra cucumber or red onion, save it to quickly spruce up a salad for the next day.

monterey skillet hamburgers

Prep Time: 10 Minutes
Start to Finish: 25 Minutes
Servings: 4 sandwiches

EASY QUICK

1   lb lean (at least 80%) ground beef
1   can (4.5 oz) Old El Paso® chopped green chiles, drained
2   tablespoons chopped fresh cilantro
1   teaspoon chili powder

1/2   teaspoon salt
1/8   teaspoon ground red pepper (cayenne)
1   medium red onion, thinly sliced
1   medium avocado, pitted, peeled and sliced
4   slices (1 oz each) Monterey Jack cheese

1 In medium bowl, mix beef, chiles, cilantro, chili powder, salt and red pepper. Shape mixture into 4 patties, 1/2 inch thick.

2 Spray 10-inch nonstick skillet with cooking spray; heat over medium-high heat. Cook onion in skillet 1 to 2 minutes, stirring occasionally, just until tender. Remove from skillet.

3 In same skillet, cook patties over medium heat 10 to 12 minutes, turning once, until meat thermometer inserted in center of patties reads 160°F. Top patties with onion, avocado and cheese. Cover; heat until cheese is melted. Serve burgers on buns if desired.

High Altitude (3500-6500 ft): No change.

Nutritional Info: 1 Sandwich: Calories 380; Total Fat 27g (Saturated Fat 11g); Sodium 640mg; Total Carbohydrate 8g (Dietary Fiber 3g); Protein 27g. Exchanges: 1/2 Fruit, 1/2 Vegetable, 3-1/2 Medium-Fat Meat, 2 Fat. Carbohydrate Choices: 1/2.

Betty's Kitchen Tips

How-To: To peel and slice an avocado quickly, cut ripe avocado lengthwise in half around the pit. Hit the pit with the blade of a sharp knife so it sticks; twist the knife to easily remove the pit. Remove the peel with your fingers, then slice the avocado.

Success Hint: Keep cilantro fresh by placing the bunch of stems in a tall glass with an inch of water. Cover with a plastic bag; refrigerate up to 1 week. Replace water as needed.

ranch chicken fillet sandwiches

Prep Time: 35 Minutes
Start to Finish: 1 Hour 35 Minutes
Servings: 4 sandwiches

1/2	cup ranch dressing
1	tablespoon chopped fresh chives
4	boneless skinless chicken breasts (about 1-1/4 lb)
4	slices Canadian bacon
4	whole-grain sandwich buns, split
2	tablespoons mayonnaise or salad dressing
2	tablespoons chopped fresh parsley
1	medium cucumber, thinly sliced
1	large tomato, sliced

1 In shallow glass or plastic dish, mix 1/4 cup of the dressing and the chives. Add chicken; turn to coat. Cover; refrigerate 1 to 2 hours, turning chicken occasionally.

2 Heat gas or charcoal grill. Place chicken on grill over medium heat. Cover grill; cook 15 to 20 minutes, turning once or twice, until juice of chicken is clear when center of thickest part is cut (165°F). During last 2 minutes of cooking, place bacon on grill until heated and, if desired, place buns, cut sides down, on grill until toasted.

3 In small bowl, mix remaining 1/4 cup dressing, the mayonnaise and parsley; spread on cut sides of buns. On bottom halves of buns, layer bacon, chicken, cucumber and tomato. Cover with top halves of buns.

High Altitude (3500-6500 ft): No change.

Nutritional Info: 1 Sandwich: Calories 480; Total Fat 25g (Saturated Fat 5g); Sodium 880mg; Total Carbohydrate 22g (Dietary Fiber 4g); Protein 43g. Exchanges: 1 Starch, 1 Vegetable, 5-1/2 Lean Meat, 1-1/2 Fat. Carbohydrate Choices: 1-1/2.

Betty's Kitchen Tips

Success Hint: Remove the seeds from the cucumber, if desired, before slicing, or look for English cucumbers, which are virtually seedless.

Time-Saver: Use a kitchen scissors to quickly chop chives and parsley.

garlic and mustard burgers

Prep Time: 30 Minutes
Start to Finish: 30 Minutes
Servings: 4 sandwiches

QUICK

- 1 lb lean (at least 80%) ground beef
- 3 tablespoons country-style Dijon mustard
- 5 cloves garlic, finely chopped
- 4 slices (1 oz each) Monterey Jack cheese
- 4 kaiser rolls, split
- 1 jar (7 oz) roasted red bell peppers, drained

Lettuce leaves

1 Heat gas or charcoal grill. In medium bowl, mix beef, mustard and garlic. Shape mixture into 4 patties, 3/4 inch thick.

2 Place patties on grill over medium heat. Cover grill; cook 13 to 15 minutes, turning once, until meat thermometer inserted in center of patties reads 160°F. During last 2 minutes of cooking, top each patty with cheese and place rolls, cut sides down, on grill. Cook until cheese is melted and rolls are toasted.

3 Serve burgers on rolls with roasted peppers and lettuce.

High Altitude (3500-6500 ft): No change.

Nutritional Info: 1 Sandwich: Calories 460; Total Fat 25g (Saturated Fat 11g); Sodium 830mg; Total Carbohydrate 27g (Dietary Fiber 2g); Protein 32g. Exchanges: 1-1/2 Starch, 1/2 Vegetable, 3-1/2 Medium-Fat Meat, 1-1/2 Fat. Carbohydrate Choices: 2.

Betty's Kitchen Tips

Substitution: Fresh tomato slices can be substituted for the roasted red bell peppers.

Special Touch: Sprinkle fresh herbs or garlic cloves over heated coals for an added flavor boost.

SALADS & BREADS

p. 135

142

139

140

southwest pasta salad

Prep Time: 30 Minutes
Start to Finish: 30 Minutes
Servings: 12 (1 cup each)

QUICK

Bonnie St. Dennis
Spencerport, NY
Suddenly Salad Contest Winner

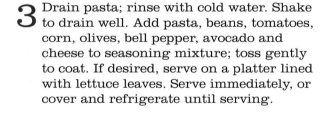

2 boxes Betty Crocker® Suddenly Salad® classic pasta salad mix
1/2 cup cold water
1/3 cup olive oil
2 tablespoons cider vinegar
1 tablespoon chopped fresh cilantro
1 to 2 tablespoons red pepper sauce, if desired
1/2 teaspoon ground cumin
1 can (15 oz) Progresso® black or pinto beans, rinsed and drained
1 can (14.5 oz) diced tomatoes with jalapeños, drained

1 can (11 oz) Green Giant® Mexicorn® whole kernel corn with red and green peppers, drained
1/2 cup sliced ripe olives
1/2 cup chopped red, yellow or green bell pepper
1 medium avocado, peeled, cut into 1/2-inch cubes
8 oz pepper Jack cheese, cut into 1/2-inch cubes (2 cups)
Romaine lettuce leaves, if desired

1 Empty pasta mixes into 4-quart saucepan 2/3 full of boiling water. Gently boil uncovered 12 minutes, stirring occasionally.

2 Meanwhile, in large bowl, stir together seasoning mixes, cold water, olive oil, vinegar, cilantro, pepper sauce and cumin.

3 Drain pasta; rinse with cold water. Shake to drain well. Add pasta, beans, tomatoes, corn, olives, bell pepper, avocado and cheese to seasoning mixture; toss gently to coat. If desired, serve on a platter lined with lettuce leaves. Serve immediately, or cover and refrigerate until serving.

High Altitude (3500-6500 ft): No change.

Nutritional Info: 1 Serving: Calories 340; Total Fat 14g (Saturated Fat 4g); Sodium 960mg; Total Carbohydrate 43g (Dietary Fiber 5g); Protein 11g. Exchanges: 2-1/2 Starch, 1/2 Other Carbohydrate, 1/2 High-Fat Meat, 1-1/2 Fat. Carbohydrate Choices: 3.

Betty's Kitchen Tips

Do Ahead: Make this salad up to 24 hours before serving. Give it a stir before serving.

Variation: If you love cilantro, add extra or sprinkle some extra over the salad before serving.

Special Touch: Wrap the salad up in lettuce leaves for a fresh new dinner idea.

banana bread

Prep Time: 15 Minutes
Start to Finish: 3 Hours 25 Minutes
Servings: 2 Loaves (24 slices each)

- 1-1/4 cups sugar
- 1/2 cup butter or margarine, softened
- 2 eggs
- 1-1/2 cups mashed very ripe bananas (3 medium)
- 1/2 cup buttermilk
- 1 teaspoon vanilla
- 2-1/2 cups Gold Medal® all-purpose flour
- 1 teaspoon baking soda
- 1 teaspoon salt
- 1 cup chopped nuts, if desired

1 Move oven rack to low position so that tops of pans will be in center of oven. Heat oven to 350°F. Grease the bottoms only of 2 (8x4-inch) loaf pans or 1 (9x5-inch) loaf pan with shortening or cooking spray.

2 In large bowl, mix sugar and butter with spoon. Stir in eggs until well blended. Stir in bananas, buttermilk and vanilla; beat until smooth. Stir in flour, baking soda and salt just until moistened. Stir in nuts. Divide batter evenly between pans.

3 Bake 8-inch loaves about 1 hour, 9-inch loaf about 1 hour 15 minutes, or until toothpick inserted in center comes out clean. Cool in pans on cooling rack for 10 minutes.

4 Loosen sides of loaves from pans; remove from pans and place top side up on cooling rack. Cool completely, about 2 hours, before slicing. Wrap tightly and store at room temperature up to 4 days, or refrigerate up to 10 days.

High Altitude (3500-6500 ft): No change.

Nutritional Info: 1 Slice: Calories 70; Total Fat 2g (Saturated Fat 1.5g); Sodium 95mg; Total Carbohydrate 12g (Dietary Fiber 0g); Protein 1g. Exchanges: 1/2 Starch, 1/2 Other Carbohydrate, 1/2 Fat. Carbohydrate Choices: 1.

EASY LOW FAT

Betty's Kitchen Tips

Variation: Like chocolate? Stir 1/2 cup chocolate chips into the batter before you pour it into the pan.

Success Hint: For a quick and refreshingly different breakfast, top slices of banana bread with your favorite fruit-flavored yogurt, sliced fresh bananas and some chopped nuts.

ground beef fajita taco salad

Prep Time: 30 Minutes
Start to Finish: 30 Minutes
Servings: 6

QUICK

Creamy Guacamole Dressing

1	medium ripe avocado, pitted, peeled and cut into chunks
1/4	cup sour cream
3	tablespoons milk
2	tablespoons lime juice
2	tablespoons chopped fresh cilantro
2	tablespoons olive or vegetable oil
1/2	teaspoon salt
1/2	teaspoon ground cumin
1/8	teaspoon ground red pepper (cayenne)

Salad

2	teaspoons vegetable oil
2	medium bell peppers, cut into bite-size strips
1	medium onion, cut into thin wedges
1	lb lean (at least 80%) ground beef
1	package (1 oz) Old El Paso® taco seasoning mix
2/3	cup water
6	cups torn romaine lettuce
1	medium tomato, chopped (3/4 cup)
1	cup shredded Cheddar cheese (4 oz)
2	cups crushed tortilla chips (about 4 oz)

1 In blender, place all dressing ingredients. Cover; blend on medium speed 30 seconds or until smooth. Pour into small bowl. Cover; refrigerate until serving time.

2 In 12-inch nonstick skillet, heat oil over medium heat. Cook bell peppers and onion in oil 6 minutes, stirring occasionally, until tender. Remove vegetables from skillet; set aside.

3 In same skillet, cook beef over medium-high heat 5 to 7 minutes, stirring occasionally, until thoroughly cooked; drain. Add taco seasoning mix and water; heat as directed on package.

4 Place 1 cup lettuce on each of 6 plates. Top with beef mixture, vegetables, tomato, cheese and chips. Serve with dressing.

High Altitude (3500-6500 ft): No change.

Nutritional Info: 1 Serving: Calories 470; Total Fat 31g (Saturated Fat 10g); Sodium 890mg; Total Carbohydrate 25g (Dietary Fiber 5g); Protein 21g. Exchanges: 1-1/2 Starch, 1/2 Vegetable, 3 High-Fat Meat, 1 Fat. Carbohydrate Choices: 1-1/2.

Betty's Kitchen Tips

How-To: If the dressing is too thick, thin it with a little additional milk.

Purchasing: A ripe avocado will be relatively firm, but will give to gentle pressure when squeezed.

turkey chutney pasta salad

Prep Time: 25 Minutes
Start to Finish: 25 Minutes
Servings: 4 (1-1/4 cups each)

QUICK

S. Averett
Westminster, MD
Suddenly Salad Contest Winner

1	box Betty Crocker® Suddenly Salad® Caesar pasta salad mix
1/4	cup mayonnaise
1/4	cup sour cream
2	tablespoons mango chutney
2	teaspoons curry powder
2	cups cubed cooked turkey breast
1/4	cup chopped cashews
2	tablespoons golden raisins
1	green onion, finely chopped
1/4	cup chopped fresh cilantro

1 Empty pasta mix into 3-quart saucepan 2/3 full of boiling water. Gently boil uncovered 12 minutes, stirring occasionally.

2 Meanwhile, in large bowl, stir together seasoning and crouton blend, mayonnaise, sour cream, chutney and curry powder. Stir in turkey, cashews and raisins.

3 Drain pasta; rinse with cold water. Shake to drain well. Stir pasta into salad mixture. Spoon onto serving platter. Top with green onion and cilantro. Serve immediately, or cover and refrigerate 1 hour to chill.

High Altitude (3500-6500 ft): No change.

Nutritional Info: 1 Serving: Calories 480; Total Fat 19g (Saturated Fat 4g); Sodium 780mg; Total Carbohydrate 48g (Dietary Fiber 2g); Protein 28g. Exchanges: 2-1/2 Starch, 1/2 Other Carbohydrate, 3 Lean Meat, 2 Fat. Carbohydrate Choices: 3.

Betty's Kitchen Tips

Purchasing: Find chutney in the condiment section of the grocery store by the pickles and olives. It gives the salad its sweet tangy flavor, you won't want to skip it.

Variation: This salad is also a great way to use up leftover cooked chicken.

zucchini bread

Prep Time: 15 Minutes
Start to Finish: 3 Hours 25 Minutes
Servings: 2 Loaves (24 slices each)

EASY

3	cups shredded zucchini (2 to 3 medium)
1-2/3	cups sugar
2/3	cup vegetable oil
2	teaspoons vanilla
4	eggs
3	cups Gold Medal® all-purpose or whole wheat flour

2	teaspoons baking soda
1	teaspoon salt
1	teaspoon ground cinnamon
1/2	teaspoon ground cloves
1/2	teaspoon baking powder
1/2	cup coarsely chopped nuts
1/2	cup raisins, if desired

1 Move oven rack to low position so that tops of pans will be in center of oven. Heat oven to 350°F. Grease bottoms only of 2 (8x4-inch) loaf pans or 1 (9x5-inch) loaf pan with shortening or cooking spray.

2 In large bowl, stir zucchini, sugar, oil, vanilla and eggs until well mixed. Stir in remaining ingredients except nuts and raisins. Stir in nuts and raisins. Divide batter evenly between 8-inch pans or pour into 9-inch pan.

3 Bake 8-inch loaves 50 to 60 minutes, 9-inch loaf 1 hour 10 minutes to 1 hour 20 minutes, or until toothpick inserted in

center comes out clean. Cool in pans on cooling rack 10 minutes.

4 Loosen sides of loaves from pans; remove from pans and place top side up on cooling rack. Cool completely, about 2 hours, before slicing. Wrap tightly and store at room temperature up to 4 days, or refrigerate up to 10 days.

Pumpkin Bread: Substitute 1 can (15 oz) pumpkin (not pumpkin pie mix) for the zucchini.

Cranberry Bread: Omit zucchini, cinnamon, cloves and raisins. Stir in 1/2 cup milk and 2 teaspoons grated orange peel with the oil. Stir 3 cups fresh or frozen (thawed and drained) cranberries into batter. Bake 60 to 70 minutes.

High Altitude (3500-6500 ft): No change.

Nutritional Info: 1 Slice: Calories 100; Total Fat 4.5g (Saturated Fat 1g); Sodium 120mg; Total Carbohydrate 14g (Dietary Fiber 0g); Protein 1g. Exchanges: 1/2 Starch, 1/2 Other Carbohydrate, 1 Fat. Carbohydrate Choices: 1.

Betty's Kitchen Tip

• To make muffins, grease bottoms only of 24 regular-size muffin cups. Fill cups about 3/4 full. Bake 20 to 25 minutes or until tops spring back when touched lightly.

blt pasta salad

Prep Time: 25 Minutes
Start to Finish: 25 Minutes
Servings: 16 (1/2 cup each)

1   package (7 oz) uncooked rotini pasta
8   slices bacon, cut into 1/2 inch pieces
1   cup mayonnaise or salad dressing
1   tablespoon lemon juice
2   teaspoons sugar
1   large tomato, seeded, chopped (1 cup)
4   medium green onions, sliced (1/4 cup)
4   cups thinly shredded iceberg lettuce

1 Cook pasta as directed on package. Drain; rinse with cold water to cool. Drain well.

2 Meanwhile, in 10-inch skillet, cook bacon over medium heat 8 to 10 minutes, stirring occasionally, until crisp. Drain on paper towels; set aside.

3 In large bowl, stir together mayonnaise, lemon juice and sugar with whisk until mixture is smooth. Stir the pasta into the mayonnaise mixture.

4 Gently stir in bacon, tomato and green onions. Stir in lettuce just before serving.

High Altitude (3500-6500 ft): No change.

Nutritional Info: 1 Serving: Calories 180; Total Fat 13g (Saturated Fat 2.5g); Sodium 220mg; Total Carbohydrate 13g (Dietary Fiber 1g); Protein 4g. Exchanges: 1/2 Starch, 1/2 Vegetable, 1/2 High-Fat Meat, 1-1/2 Fat. Carbohydrate Choices: 1.

QUICK

Robert Cowling
Blog Chef
www.blogchef.net

Betty's Kitchen Tips

Variation: Instead of simply tossing all of the ingredients together, layer the onions, pasta, bacon and tomatoes on the lettuce and drizzle with the dressing.

Health Twist: Upgrade the fiber and nutrients in this hearty salad by using whole wheat penne.

gazpacho-style chicken salad

Prep Time: 25 Minutes
Start to Finish: 25 Minutes
Servings: 2

QUICK LOW FAT

4	cups packed torn green and/or red leaf lettuce
1	package (6 oz) refrigerated grilled chicken breast strips
1	medium tomato, chopped (3/4 cup)
1	cup chopped peeled cucumber
3/4	cup chopped yellow bell pepper
1/3	cup thinly sliced red onion

Dressing

1/2	cup spicy Bloody Mary mix
3	tablespoons red wine vinegar
2	tablespoons olive oil
1/2	teaspoon salt
1/4	teaspoon pepper
1/4	teaspoon red pepper sauce
1	clove garlic, finely chopped

1 Place lettuce on serving platter. Arrange chicken in a pile in center of lettuce. Place tomato, cucumber, bell pepper and onion on top of lettuce, around the chicken.

2 In tightly covered container, shake all dressing ingredients. Spoon 1/4 cup dressing over salad; gently toss to coat. Serve immediately. Reserve remaining dressing for another use.

High Altitude (3500-6500 ft): No change.

Nutritional Info: 1 Serving: Calories 240; Total Fat 8g (Saturated Fat 1.5g); Sodium 720mg; Total Carbohydrate 13g (Dietary Fiber 3g); Protein 29g. Exchanges: 3 Vegetable, 3 Lean Meat. Carbohydrate Choices: 1.

Betty's Kitchen Tips

Did You Know? This recipe is a twist on two summertime favorites. It has the fresh garden flavors found in gazpacho served in a Cobb-style salad! You can easily serve 4 people by doubling the salad ingredients and using all of the dressing.

Variation: Change up the flavor of the dressing by experimenting with different types of vinegar. Try white wine vinegar or cider vinegar.

italian new potato salad

Prep Time: 30 Minutes
Start to Finish: 1 Hour 30 Minutes
Servings: 8

- 3/4 lb fresh green beans
- 1-1/2 lb small red potatoes (10 to 12), quartered
- 1/4 cup water
- 1/2 cup reduced-fat Italian dressing or balsamic vinaigrette dressing
- 1/4 cup chopped red onion
- 1 can (2-1/4 oz) sliced ripe olives, drained

1 Cut beans in half if desired. In 2-quart microwavable casserole, place beans, potatoes and water. Cover and microwave on High 10 to 12 minutes, rotating dish 1/2 turn every 4 minutes, until potatoes are tender; drain.

2 In large glass or plastic bowl, toss beans, potatoes and dressing. Add onion and olives; toss. Cover and refrigerate 1 to 2 hours or until chilled.

High Altitude (3500-6500 ft): After microwaving vegetables, let covered casserole stand 5 minutes before draining.

Nutritional Info: 1 Serving: Calories 120; Total Fat 3.5g (Saturated Fat 0.5g); Sodium 270mg; Total Carbohydrate 19g (Dietary Fiber 3g); Protein 2g. Exchanges: 1/2 Starch, 1/2 Other Carbohydrate, 1 Vegetable, 1/2 Fat. Carbohydrate Choices: 1.

Betty's Kitchen Tips

Success Hint: Avoid overcooking the small red potatoes as they will fall apart. You should be able to just pierce the potatoes with a fork when they are done.

Substitution: One small bell pepper, coarsely chopped (1/2 cup), can be substituted for the sliced ripe olives.

texas coleslaw

Prep Time: 15 Minutes
Start to Finish: 1 Hour 15 Minutes
Servings: 16

EASY LOW FAT

- 1   bag (16 oz) coleslaw mix (shredded cabbage and carrots)
- 1/2   cup chopped fresh cilantro
- 2   cans (11 oz each) Green Giant® Mexicorn® whole kernel corn with red and green peppers, drained

- 3   tablespoons vegetable oil
- 3   tablespoons lime or lemon juice
- 1/2   teaspoon salt
- 3/4   teaspoon ground cumin

1 In very large (4-quart) bowl, toss coleslaw mix, cilantro and corn.

2 In container with tight-fitting lid, shake oil, lime juice, salt and cumin until well mixed. Pour over coleslaw mixture; toss.

3 Cover; refrigerate 1 to 2 hours to blend flavors before serving.

High Altitude (3500-6500 ft): No change.

Nutritional Info: 1 Serving: Calories 70; Total Fat 3g (Saturated Fat 0g); Sodium 190mg; Total Carbohydrate 10g (Dietary Fiber 1g); Protein 1g. Exchanges: 1-1/2 Vegetable, 1/2 Fat. Carbohydrate Choices: 1/2.

Betty's Kitchen Tips

Variation: If your family likes things hot and spicy, add 1 jalapeño chile, seeded and finely chopped, to the coleslaw mixture.

Substitution: Two cups Green Giant® Niblets® frozen corn, cooked as directed on the bag and rinsed with cold water, can be used instead of the canned corn.

asian chopped salad with lime dressing

Prep Time: 25 Minutes
Start to Finish: 25 Minutes
Servings: 4

QUICK

- -

Lime Dressing

1/3	cup frozen (thawed) limeade concentrate
1/4	cup vegetable oil
1	tablespoon rice vinegar or white vinegar
1	teaspoon grated gingerroot
1/4	teaspoon salt

Salad

2	cups chopped escarole
1	cup chopped cooked chicken
1	large papaya, peeled, seeded and chopped (2 cups)
1	small jicama, peeled, chopped (1 cup)
1	large yellow or red bell pepper, chopped (1 cup)
1/2	cup dry-roasted peanuts
1/4	cup chopped fresh cilantro

- -

1 In tightly covered container, shake all dressing ingredients.

2 In large bowl, mix all salad ingredients except peanuts and cilantro. Pour dressing over salad; toss to coat. Top with peanuts and cilantro.

High Altitude (3500-6500 ft): No change.

Nutritional Info: 1 Serving: Calories 400; Total Fat 24g (Saturated Fat 4g); Sodium 330mg; Total Carbohydrate 28g (Dietary Fiber 4g); Protein 15g. Exchanges: 1/2 Fruit, 1 Other Carbohydrate, 1-1/2 Vegetable, 1-1/2 Lean Meat, 4 Fat. Carbohydrate Choices: 2.

Betty's Kitchen Tips

Substitution: When papayas aren't available, you can use peaches or nectarines.

Variation: It's easy to make this a seafood salad. Just use 1 cup cooked small shrimp or crabmeat instead of the chicken.

spring raspberry salad

Prep Time: 20 Minutes
Start to Finish: 20 Minutes
Servings: 8 (1 cup each)

Cheri Liefeld
Adventures In The Kitchen
www.adventuresinthekitchen.com

QUICK

1/4	cup chopped walnuts
2	tablespoons sugar
1	bag (5 oz) torn mixed salad greens
2	containers (6 oz each) fresh raspberries (2 cups)
1/2	small red onion, thinly sliced (1/2 cup)
1/2	cup chopped dates
1/3	cup balsamic vinaigrette dressing
2	oz goat cheese, crumbled

1 In 8-inch nonstick skillet cook walnuts and sugar over low heat about 10 minutes, stirring constantly, until sugar is melted and walnuts are coated; cool and break apart.

2 In large bowl, combine salad greens, raspberries, onion and dates. Just before serving, pour dressing over salad; toss gently to coat salad. Top with cheese and walnuts.

High Altitude (3500-6500 ft): No change.

Nutritional Info: 1 Serving: Calories 160; Total Fat 8g (Saturated Fat 2g); Sodium 150mg; Total Carbohydrate 19g (Dietary Fiber 4g); Protein 3g. Exchanges: 1 Fruit, 1 Vegetable, 1/2 High-Fat Meat, 1/2 Fat. Carbohydrate Choices: 1.

Betty's Kitchen Tip

• For a heartier version, add 1/4 cup diced smoked ham or cut-up chicken to the pizza toppings.

caribbean jerk chicken and pasta salad

Prep Time: 25 Minutes
Start to Finish: 1 Hour 25 Minutes
Servings: 6 (1 cup each)

Melanie Gadzia Smith
Topeka, KS
Suddenly Salad Contest Winner

1 box Betty Crocker® Suddenly Salad® chipotle ranch pasta salad mix	1/2 teaspoon crushed red pepper flakes
1/3 cup mayonnaise	2 packages (6 oz each) refrigerated grilled chicken strips, chopped
1 tablespoon packed brown sugar	1-1/2 cups chopped fresh pineapple
1 tablespoon fresh lime juice	3 medium green onions, sliced
1 teaspoon grated gingerroot	2 teaspoons chopped fresh cilantro

1 Empty pasta mix into 3-quart saucepan 2/3 full of boiling water. Gently boil uncovered 15 minutes, stirring occasionally.

2 Meanwhile, in large bowl, stir together seasoning mix, mayonnaise, brown sugar, lime juice, gingerroot and red pepper flakes. Stir in chicken, pineapple, green onions and cilantro.

3 Drain pasta; rinse with cold water. Shake to drain well. Stir pasta into salad mixture. Cover and refrigerate 1 hour to chill. Stir before serving.

High Altitude (3500-6500 ft): No change.

Nutritional Info: 1 Serving: Calories 300; Total Fat 13g (Saturated Fat 2g); Sodium 670mg; Total Carbohydrate 30g (Dietary Fiber 1g); Protein 18g. Exchanges: 1-1/2 Starch, 1/2 Other Carbohydrate, 2 Lean Meat, 1 Fat. Carbohydrate Choices: 2.

Betty's Kitchen Tips

Do-Ahead: Need dinner now? We love the salad after it's chilled a bit but you also can serve it immediately after making it.

Leftovers: Do you have some grilled or rotisserie chicken in your refrigerator from last night? Use it in this tasty salad.

fattoush pasta salad

Prep Time: 30 Minutes
Start to Finish: 30 Minutes
Servings: 10 (1 cup each)

Leah Lyon
Ada, OK
Suddenly Salad Contest Winner

QUICK

1	box Betty Crocker® Suddenly Salad® classic pasta salad mix
1/3	cup olive oil
1/4	cup fresh lemon juice
2	teaspoons all purpose Greek seasoning
1-1/2	cups coarsely chopped cucumber
1	cup coarsely chopped romaine lettuce
1	cup crumbled feta cheese (4 oz)
1	cup grape tomatoes, halved
1/2	cup thinly sliced zucchini, slices cut into quarters
1/3	cup thinly sliced radishes
1/3	cup chopped red onion
1/3	cup chopped fresh flat leaf parsley
1	tablespoon finely chopped fresh mint leaves
2	cups garlic flavored croutons

1 Empty pasta mix into 3-quart saucepan 2/3 full of boiling water. Gently boil uncovered 12 minutes, stirring occasionally.

2 Drain pasta; rinse with cold water. Shake to drain well.

3 In large bowl, stir together seasoning mix, oil, lemon juice and Greek seasoning. Add pasta and all remaining ingredients; toss gently. Cover and refrigerate 1 hour to chill.

High Altitude (3500-6500 ft): No change.

Nutritional Info: 1 Serving: Calories 230; Total Fat 12g (Saturated Fat 3g); Sodium 790mg; Total Carbohydrate 25g (Dietary Fiber 1g); Protein 5g. Exchanges: 1-1/2 Starch, 2-1/2 Fat. Carbohydrate Choices: 1-1/2.

Betty's Kitchen Tips

Did You Know? "Fattoush" is an Eastern Mediterranean salad made from vegetables like cucumber, radishes and tomatoes plus toasted or fried pieces of pita bread. The vegetables are cut into relatively large pieces compared with Tabbouleh, where the ingredients are finely chopped.

Purchasing: All purpose Greek seasoning is a ground specialty seasoning blend that is found where the herbs and spices are located in the grocery store.

confetti chicken 'n couscous salad

Prep Time: 25 Minutes
Start to Finish: 25 Minutes
Servings: 6 (1-1/2 cups each)

QUICK

1 box (10 oz) couscous
2 cups chopped cooked chicken
2 medium carrots, finely chopped (1-1/2 cups)
1 medium red bell pepper, finely chopped (1 cup)
1/2 cup chopped fresh chives

Dressing
1/3 cup fresh lemon juice
2/3 cup grated Parmesan cheese
1/2 cup olive or vegetable oil
1-1/2 teaspoons salt

1 Prepare couscous according to package directions.

2 In large serving bowl, mix chicken, carrot, bell pepper and chives. Add cooked couscous; fluff with fork until well mixed. Cool slightly.

3 In tightly covered container, shake all dressing ingredients. Pour over salad; toss gently to coat. Serve immediately.

High Altitude (3500-6500 ft): No change.

Nutritional Info: 1 Serving: Calories 490; Total Fat 25g (Saturated Fat 5g); Sodium 820mg; Total Carbohydrate 41g (Dietary Fiber 3g); Protein 24g. Exchanges: 2-1/2 Starch, 1 Vegetable, 2 Lean Meat, 3-1/2 Fat. Carbohydrate Choices: 3.

Betty's Kitchen Tips

Do Ahead: If you're going to make this recipe ahead of time and store it in the refrigerator, you may need to add a little bit more olive oil and/or lemon juice when ready to serve. When made ahead, the couscous will absorb these ingredients over time.

Variation: Chopped chives add a fresh touch to this salad. For a little more "zing," substitute chopped green onions.

black bean and corn salad

Prep Time: 15 Minutes
Start to Finish: 1 Hour 15 Minutes
Servings: 10 (1/2 cup each)

EASY   LOW FAT

Shreya Sasaki
RecipeMatcher
www.recipematcher.com

1/2	cup balsamic vinaigrette dressing
1/4	teaspoon black pepper
1	tablespoon chopped fresh cilantro
1/8	teaspoon ground red pepper (cayenne)
1/4	teaspoon ground cumin
2	cans (15 oz each) black beans, drained, rinsed
1	can (11 oz) Green Giant® Niblets® whole kernel sweet corn
1	small onion, chopped (1/2 cup)
8	medium green onions, chopped (1/2 cup)
1	small red bell pepper, chopped (1/2 cup)

1 In small bowl, stir together dressing, pepper, cilantro, red pepper and cumin. Set aside.

2 In large bowl, mix remaining ingredients. Toss with dressing to coat. Cover; refrigerate for at least 1 hour or overnight to blend flavors. Just before serving, stir mixture to coat beans and corn with the dressing.

High Altitude (3500-6500 ft): No change.

Nutritional Info: 1 Serving: Calories 130; Total Fat 0.5g (Saturated Fat 0g); Sodium 70mg; Total Carbohydrate 24g (Dietary Fiber 7g); Protein 6g. Exchanges: 1-1/2 Starch. Carbohydrate Choices: 1-1/2.

Betty's Kitchen Tips

Success Hint: This delightfully fresh salad can be served as a side dish or as an appetizer with tortilla chips.

Variation: You can determine the spice level of this salad by increasing or decreasing the amount of cayenne pepper.

pumpkin chocolate chip bread

Prep Time: 25 Minutes
Start to Finish: 4 Hours 10 Minutes
Servings: 1 loaf (16 slices)

Bread
- 1/2   cup butter, softened
- 1   cup granulated sugar
- 2   eggs
- 1   cup canned pumpkin (not pumpkin pie mix)
- 2   cups Gold Medal® all-purpose flour
- 1   teaspoon baking soda
- 1   teaspoon ground cinnamon

- 1   teaspoon pumpkin pie spice
- 1/2   cup miniature semisweet chocolate chips
- 1/4   cup chopped walnuts

Glaze
- 1/2   cup powdered sugar
- 2   to 3 teaspoons milk or whipping (heavy) cream

1 Heat oven to 350°F. Grease bottom only of 9x5-inch loaf pan with shortening or cooking spray.

2 In large bowl, mix butter, granulated sugar, eggs and pumpkin with wire whisk. Stir in flour, baking soda, cinnamon and pumpkin pie spice. Stir in chocolate chips and walnuts. Spread in pan.

3 Bake 55 to 65 minutes or until toothpick inserted in center comes out clean. Cool 10 minutes; remove from pan to cooling rack. Cool completely, about 2 hours.

4 In small bowl, stir powdered sugar and milk until smooth and thin enough to drizzle. Drizzle over loaf. Let glaze set up before slicing, about 30 minutes.

High Altitude (3500-6500 ft): No change.

Nutritional Info: 1 Slice: Calories 230; Total Fat 9g (Saturated Fat 5g); Sodium 130mg; Total Carbohydrate 33g (Dietary Fiber 1g); Protein 3g. Exchanges: 1/2 Starch, 1-1/2 Other Carbohydrate, 2 Fat. Carbohydrate Choices: 2.

Betty's Kitchen Tips

Variation: For a different flavor, try sweetened dried cranberries instead of chocolate chips.

Special Touch: Instead of the glaze, sprinkle some brown sugar and additional chopped walnuts on top of the bread before baking.

supreme chicken salad

Prep Time: 20 Minutes
Start to Finish: 20 Minutes
Servings: 4

Leah Lyon
Ada, OK
Suddenly Salad Contest Winner

8	cups packed torn romaine lettuce
2	cups chopped cooked chicken
2	large mangoes, seed removed, peeled and cut up (2 cups)
1	cup fresh raspberries (6 oz)
1/2	cup crumbled goat cheese (2 oz)
1/4	cup roasted salted sunflower nuts
1/2	cup raspberry vinaigrette dressing

1 Place 2 cups lettuce on each of 4 serving plates. Evenly arrange chicken, mangoes, raspberries, cheese and sunflower nuts on lettuce.

2 Drizzle the salad with dressing and then serve immediately.

High Altitude (3500-6500 ft): No change.

Nutritional Info: 1 Serving: Calories 430; Total Fat 24g (Saturated Fat 6g); Sodium 930mg; Total Carbohydrate 27g (Dietary Fiber 6g); Protein 26g. Exchanges: 1 Fruit, 2 Vegetable, 3 Lean Meat, 3 Fat. Carbohydrate Choices: 2.

Betty's Kitchen Tips

Time-Saver: A mango slicer/pitter makes chopping up this delicious tropical fruit super easy and quick.

Do-Ahead: This salad is great for picnics! Simply toss together all of the ingredients except the dressing, and take the dressing along to drizzle just before eating.

mini banana breads

Prep Time: 15 Minutes
Start to Finish: 2 Hours 55 Minutes
Servings: 10 loaves (8 slices each)

EASY LOW FAT

1-1/4 cups sugar	1 teaspoon vanilla
1/2 cup butter or margarine, softened	2-1/2 cups Gold Medal® all-purpose flour
2 eggs	1 teaspoon baking soda
1-1/2 cups mashed ripe bananas (3 to 4 medium)	1 teaspoon salt
1/2 cup buttermilk	1 cup chopped nuts, if desired

1 Heat oven to 350°F. Grease bottoms only of 10 (4-1/2 x 2-1/2 x 1-1/2 -inch) mini loaf pans with shortening or cooking spray.

2 In large bowl, mix sugar and butter with spoon. Stir in eggs until well blended. Add bananas, buttermilk and vanilla; mix until smooth. Stir in flour, baking soda and salt just until moistened. Stir in nuts. Divide batter among pans (about 1/2 cup each).

3 Bake 30 to 35 minutes or until toothpick inserted in centers comes out clean. Cool 5 minutes. Loosen sides of loaves from pans; remove from pans to cooling racks. Cool completely, about 2 hours. Wrap tightly and store at room temperature up to 4 days, or refrigerate up to 10 days.

High Altitude (3500-6500 ft): No change.

Nutritional Info: 1 Slice: Calories 45; Total Fat 1.5g (Saturated Fat 1g); Sodium 60mg; Total Carbohydrate 7g (Dietary Fiber 0g); Protein 0g. Exchanges: 1/2 Other Carbohydrate, 1/2 Fat. Carbohydrate Choices: 1/2.

Betty's Kitchen Tips

Special Touch: Package loaves with a colorful dish towel or pot holder for a bake sale or hostess gift.

Success Hint: Cool quick breads completely before slicing. Cutting while warm causes crumbling. For easiest cutting, store bread, tightly covered, for 24 hours.

summer salad with asiago, pears and cashews

Prep Time: 15 Minutes
Start to Finish: 15 Minutes
Servings: 5 (1 cup each)

EASY QUICK

Heidi Harris
www.savory.tv

Dressing

1/4	cup olive oil
1	tablespoon balsamic vinegar
2	teaspoons honey
1/2	teaspoon Dijon mustard
1/8	teaspoon salt
1/8	teaspoon pepper

Salad

1	bag (5 oz) mixed spring greens
1/2	cup shaved Asiago cheese
1	medium ripe pear, thinly sliced
1/2	cup cashew halves and pieces

1 In small jar with tight-fitting lid, shake dressing ingredients.

2 In medium bowl, toss greens with dressing; arrange on serving platter. Top with remaining salad ingredients. Serve immediately.

High Altitude (3500-6500 ft): No change.

Nutritional Info: 1 Serving: Calories 270; Total Fat 21g (Saturated Fat 5g); Sodium 210mg; Total Carbohydrate 14g (Dietary Fiber 2g); Protein 5g. Exchanges: 1/2 Other Carbohydrate, 1 Vegetable, 1/2 High-Fat Meat, 3-1/2 Fat. Carbohydrate Choices: 1.

Betty's Kitchen Tips

Did You Know? Asiago is a very hard Italian cheese that can easily be shredded or grated. It has a pungent, sharp flavor.

Success Hint: If the pears you purchase are very firm, place them in a brown bag on your counter for a day or two to ripen them.

pumpkin-cranberry pecan bread with tipsy whipped cream

Prep Time: 15 Minutes
Start to Finish: 3 Hours 10 Minutes
Servings: 1 loaf (12 slices)

Charlene Chambers
Ormond Beach, FL

EASY Celebrate the Season-Fall Baking Contest

Bread

1/2	cup unsalted butter, melted
1/2	cup granulated sugar
1/4	cup packed light brown sugar
2	eggs
1-1/4	cups canned pumpkin (not pumpkin pie mix)
3/4	cup milk
2-1/2	cups Gold Medal® all-purpose flour
1	teaspoon baking powder
3/4	teaspoon baking soda
3/4	teaspoon salt
1/2	teaspoon ground cinnamon
1/2	teaspoon ground allspice
1/2	teaspoon ground nutmeg
1/2	teaspoon ground ginger
1	cup chopped pecans, toasted
1/2	cup sweetened dried cranberries

Topping (optional)

1	cup whipping (heavy) cream
1	tablespoon Grand Marnier or orange juice
1	tablespoon powdered sugar

1 Heat oven to 325°F. Spray 9x5-inch loaf pan with baking spray with flour.

2 In large bowl, beat butter, granulated sugar and brown sugar with electric mixer on low speed until smooth. Mix in eggs, pumpkin and milk. Stir in flour, baking powder, baking soda, salt and spices until blended. Stir in pecans and cranberries. Spoon batter into pan.

3 Bake 1 hour 5 minutes to 1 hour 15 minutes or until toothpick inserted in center comes out clean (crack on top surface should look dry). Cool 10 minutes; remove from pan to cooling rack. Cool completely, about 1 hour 30 minutes.

4 In chilled large deep bowl, beat topping ingredients with electric mixer on low speed until mixture begins to thicken. Gradually increase speed to high and beat until stiff peaks form. Slice bread; serve with a dollop of topping.

High Altitude (3500-6500 ft): No change.

Nutritional Info: 1 Slice: Calories 330; Total Fat 16g (Saturated Fat 6g); Sodium 380mg; Total Carbohydrate 41g (Dietary Fiber 3g); Protein 5g. Exchanges: 1 Starch, 1-1/2 Other Carbohydrate, 1/2 High-Fat Meat, 2-1/2 Fat. Carbohydrate Choices: 3.

spinach and caesar pasta salad

Prep Time: 25 Minutes
Start to Finish: 25 Minutes
Servings: 8 (2 cups each)

Thelma Babin
Houma, LA
Suddenly Salad Contest Winner

1   box Betty Crocker® Suddenly Salad®
     Caesar pasta salad mix
1   package (12 oz) turkey bacon, cooked and
     cut into small pieces
1   container (10 oz) washed fresh baby
     spinach leaves
1   package (8 oz) sliced fresh mushrooms
5   hard-cooked eggs, sliced
1/4   cup sugar
1/3   cup ketchup
1/4   cup cider vinegar
1/4   cup vegetable oil
1   tablespoon water

1   Empty pasta mix into 3-quart saucepan
     about 2/3 full of boiling water. Gently
     boil uncovered 12 minutes, stirring
     occasionally.

2   Drain pasta; rinse with cold water. Shake
     to drain well.

3   In large bowl, gently toss together pasta,
     bacon, spinach, mushrooms and eggs. In
     small bowl, stir together seasoning and
     crouton blend, sugar, ketchup, vinegar, oil
     and water. Just before serving, gently toss
     salad ingredients with seasoning mixture.
     Serve immediately.

High Altitude (3500-6500 ft): No change.

Nutritional Info: 1 Serving: Calories 340; Total Fat 18g
(Saturated Fat 4g); Sodium 1040mg; Total Carbohydrate 31g
(Dietary Fiber 1g); Protein 16g. Exchanges: 1-1/2 Starch, 1/2
Other Carbohydrate, 1-1/2 Medium-Fat Meat, 2 Fat. Carbohydrate
Choices: 2.

Betty's Kitchen Tips

Time-Saver: Slash prep time in this recipe by
using precooked bacon. If you do that, note
you will be using regular bacon, as opposed
to turkey bacon, which means the nutritional
information will change.

Variation: Toss in crumbled blue cheese for a
special and unique taste.

spirited eggnog bread with rum glaze

Prep Time: 15 Minutes
Start to Finish: 2 Hours 30 Minutes
Servings: 1 loaf (24 slices)

EASY LOW FAT

2-1/4	cups Gold Medal® all-purpose flour
3/4	cup granulated sugar
1	cup eggnog or half-and-half
3	tablespoons vegetable oil
2	tablespoons rum or 4-1/2 teaspoons water plus 1 teaspoon rum extract
3-1/2	teaspoons baking powder
1/2	teaspoon salt

1/4	teaspoon ground nutmeg
1	egg
1/2	cup chopped pistachio nuts or slivered almonds, if desired

Rum Glaze

1/2	cup powdered sugar
2	teaspoons eggnog or half-and-half
1	teaspoon rum or 1/2 teaspoon rum extract

1 Heat oven to 350°F. Grease bottom only of 8x4- or 9x5-inch loaf pan.

2 In large bowl, mix all ingredients except nuts and Rum Glaze; beat 30 seconds with spoon. Stir in nuts. Pour into pan.

3 Bake 55 to 65 minutes or until toothpick inserted in center comes out clean. Cool 10 minutes. Loosen sides of loaf from pan; remove from pan to cooling rack. Cool completely.

4 In small bowl, mix glaze ingredients until thin enough to drizzle. Drizzle over loaf. Sprinkle with additional ground nutmeg and chopped pistachio nuts, if desired.

High Altitude (3500-6500 ft): No change.

Nutritional Info: 1 Slice: Calories 110; Total Fat 3g (Saturated Fat 1g); Sodium 130mg; Total Carbohydrate 19g (Dietary Fiber 0g); Protein 2g. Exchanges: 1-1/2 Other Carbohydrate, 1/2 Fat. Carbohydrate Choices: 1.

Betty's Kitchen Tip

• Wrap the unglazed bread in plastic wrap and place in a holiday basket. Place the glaze in a decorative container and put extra pistachios for the garnish in a separate holiday container or decorative see-through bag. Include a premium container of ground nutmeg or, for the avid cook, buy whole nutmeg and enclose a small nutmeg grater.

seaside blt pasta salad

Prep Time: 20 Minutes
Start to Finish: 1 Hour 20 Minutes
Servings: 6 (1-1/3 cups each)

Mary Shivers
Ada, OK
Suddenly Salad Contest Winner

1	box Betty Crocker® Suddenly Salad® ranch & bacon pasta salad mix
3/4	cup mayonnaise
2	tablespoons milk
2	tablespoons lemon juice
3	cans (6 oz each) lump crab meat, rinsed and drained
1/4	cup thinly sliced green onions
4	slices bacon, crisply cooked and crumbled (1/4 cup)
2	cups thinly sliced iceberg lettuce
2	medium tomatoes, chopped and drained (1-1/2 cups)

1 Empty pasta mix into 3-quart saucepan about 2/3 full of boiling water. Gently boil uncovered 12 minutes, stirring occasionally.

2 Meanwhile, in large bowl, stir together seasoning mix, mayonnaise, milk and lemon juice. Stir in crab meat, green onions and bacon.

3 Drain pasta; rinse with cold water. Shake to drain well. Stir pasta into salad mixture. Cover and refrigerate 1 hour to chill. Just before serving, gently toss with lettuce and tomatoes to coat.

High Altitude (3500-6500 ft): No change.

Nutritional Info: 1 Serving: Calories 490; Total Fat 26g (Saturated Fat 4g); Sodium 850mg; Total Carbohydrate 38g (Dietary Fiber 2g); Protein 25g. Exchanges: 2 Starch, 1/2 Other Carbohydrate, 3 Lean Meat, 3 Fat. Carbohydrate Choices: 2-1/2.

Betty's Kitchen Tips

Prize-Winner: Prize-Winning Recipe 2009! Love seafood? Take a few minutes and toss a tasty twist on BLT salad.

Health Twist: Slim down this salad by using fat-free mayo and turkey bacon.

Success Hint: Drain the tomatoes to keep the salad from getting watery. To drain tomatoes, place in a strainer after chopping and let stand for 10 minutes.

chicken alfredo salad

Prep Time: 30 Minutes
Start to Finish: 1 Hour
Servings: 4

1 box (6.8 oz) Chicken Helper® fettuccine Alfredo	1 cup Green Giant® Select® frozen broccoli florets (from 22-oz bag)
1/2 cup water	2 cups chopped cooked chicken
1/2 cup sour cream	1 small zucchini, chopped (1 cup)
1/2 cup milk	1 small red bell pepper, chopped (1/2 cup)
4-1/2 teaspoons red wine vinegar	

1 In 4-cup microwavable measuring cup, mix sauce mix (from Chicken Helper box) and water. Microwave uncovered on High about 2 minutes or until sauce is thickened. Stir in sour cream, milk and vinegar with wire whisk until smooth; cover and refrigerate.

2 Fill 2-quart saucepan 2/3 full of water. Heat to boiling. Stir in uncooked fettuccine (from Chicken Helper box). Gently boil uncovered about 15 minutes, stirring occasionally, until tender. During last 5 to 8 minutes of cooking, add broccoli; cook until crisp-tender. Drain well.

3 In large bowl, mix fettuccine, broccoli, chicken, zucchini and bell pepper. Spoon sauce over mixture; toss to coat. Cover; refrigerate salad about 30 minutes before serving.

High Altitude (3500-6500 ft): No change.

Nutritional Info: 1 Serving: Calories 380; Total Fat 13g (Saturated Fat 5g); Sodium 960mg; Total Carbohydrate 40g (Dietary Fiber 3g); Protein 27g. Exchanges: 2-1/2 Starch, 1 Vegetable, 2-1/2 Lean Meat, 1/2 Fat. Carbohydrate Choices: 2-1/2.

Betty's Kitchen Tips

Leftovers: This salad is a great way to use leftover cooked chicken. You can also use rotisserie chicken, or look for refrigerated cooked chicken at your grocery store.

Variation: Try other combinations of veggies in this salad, such as peas, yellow summer squash, green pepper or tomato.

sesame singapore shrimp salad

Prep Time: 25 Minutes
Start to Finish: 25 Minutes
Servings: 4 (1-1/2 cups each)

Roxanne Chan
Albany, CA
Suddenly Salad Contest Winner

QUICK

1	box Betty Crocker® Suddenly Salad® classic pasta salad mix
2/3	cup Asian toasted sesame salad dressing
1/2	teaspoon crushed red pepper flakes
2	cups angel hair or regular coleslaw mix
1-1/2	cups coarsely chopped cooked and peeled shrimp
1/4	cup chopped dry roasted peanuts
1/4	cup finely chopped basil leaves
1	mango, peeled and cut into 1/2-inch cubes (1 cup)
1	green onion, chopped

Black sesame seeds

1. Empty pasta mix into 3-quart saucepan about 2/3 full of boiling water. Gently boil uncovered 12 minutes, stirring occasionally.

2. Meanwhile, in large bowl, stir together seasoning mix, salad dressing and pepper flakes. Add coleslaw, shrimp, peanuts, basil leaves, mango and green onion; toss gently to coat.

3. Drain pasta; rinse with cold water. Shake to drain well. Stir pasta into salad mixture. Sprinkle with sesame seeds. Serve immediately, or cover and refrigerate until serving.

High Altitude (3500-6500 ft): No change.

Nutritional Info: 1 Serving: Calories 550; Total Fat 20g (Saturated Fat 3g); Sodium 1580mg; Total Carbohydrate 64g (Dietary Fiber 3g); Protein 28g. Exchanges: 2 Starch, 1/2 Fruit, 1-1/2 Other Carbohydrate, 1/2 Vegetable, 3 Lean Meat, 2 Fat. Carbohydrate Choices: 4.

Betty's Kitchen Tips

Time-Saver: Buy peeled and precut mango in the produce section of your supermarket. You may need to chop it more finely.

Purchasing: Look for black sesame seeds in the Asian section of your supermarket.

Do-Ahead: Make this salad up to 24 hours before serving, but wait until just before serving to top with sesame seeds.

antipasto curly pasta salad

Prep Time: 30 Minutes
Start to Finish: 30 Minutes
Servings: 6 (1 cup each)

Frances Blackwelder
Grand Junction, CO
Suddenly Salad Contest Winner

QUICK

- 1 box Betty Crocker® Suddenly Salad® classic pasta salad mix
- 3 tablespoons cold water
- 2 tablespoons vegetable oil
- 1 teaspoon Dijon mustard
- 1 cup cubed salami
- 4 oz Provolone cheese, cut into 1/2-inch cubes (1 cup)

- 1/2 cup finely chopped red onion
- 1 jar (7.5 oz) marinated artichoke hearts, drained and chopped
- 1 can (6 oz) pitted small ripe olives, drained
- 1 jar (4 oz) sliced pimientos, drained and chopped
- 1/2 cup shredded or grated Parmesan cheese

1 Empty pasta mix into 3-quart saucepan about 2/3 full of boiling water. Gently boil uncovered 12 minutes, stirring occasionally.

2 Meanwhile, in large bowl, stir together seasoning mix, water, oil and mustard. Add salami, cheese, onion, artichoke hearts, olives and pimentos; toss gently to combine.

3 Drain pasta; rinse with cold water. Shake to drain well. Add pasta to salad mixture; toss gently. Sprinkle with Parmesan cheese. Serve immediately, or cover and refrigerate until serving.

High Altitude (3500-6500 ft): No change.

Nutritional Info: 1 Serving: Calories 490; Total Fat 24g (Saturated Fat 9g); Sodium 2000mg; Total Carbohydrate 48g (Dietary Fiber 5g); Protein 21g. Exchanges: 2 Starch, 1 Other Carbohydrate, 2 High-Fat Meat, 1-1/2 Fat. Carbohydrate Choices: 3.

Betty's Kitchen Tips

Special Touch: For a heartier salad, stir in a can of kidney beans that you've rinsed and drained.

Do-Ahead: Make this salad a day ahead, but wait until just before serving to top with the cheese.

Variation: Use a 3-oz package of sliced pepperoni instead of the salami.

fennel & three bean salad

Prep Time: 20 Minutes
Start to Finish: 1 Hour 20 Minutes
Servings: 12 (1/2 cup each)

Rachel Rappaport
Coconut & Lime
www.coconutlime.blogspot.com

Salad

1/3	lb green beans
1	can (15 oz) Progresso® cannellini (white kidney) beans, rinsed, drained
1	can (15 oz) Progresso® dark red kidney beans, rinsed, drained
1/2	medium sweet onion, very thinly sliced (1/2 cup)
1	medium bulb fennel, very thinly sliced (1 cup)

Dressing

1/4	cup olive oil
2	tablespoons red wine vinegar
2	tablespoons Dijon mustard
1	tablespoon finely chopped fresh basil
1	clove garlic, finely chopped
1/4	teaspoon pepper
1/8	teaspoon salt

1 Remove ends of green beans. Place steamer basket in 1/2 inch of water in 2-quart saucepan or skillet (water should not touch bottom of basket). Place green beans in steamer basket. Cover tightly and heat to boiling; reduce heat. Steam 10 to 12 minutes or until crisp-tender.

2 In large bowl, stir together green beans and remaining salad ingredients; set aside.

3 In small jar with tight-fitting lid, shake all dressing ingredients. Pour dressing over salad ingredients; toss gently. Refrigerate 1 hour to blend flavors. Serve at room temperature and refrigerate any leftovers.

High Altitude (3500-6500 ft): No change.

Nutritional Info: 1 Serving: Calories 120; Total Fat 5g (Saturated Fat 0.5g); Sodium 90mg; Total Carbohydrate 14g (Dietary Fiber 4g); Protein 5g. Exchanges: 1 Starch, 1 Fat. Carbohydrate Choices: 1.

Betty's Kitchen Tip

• Fennel bulbs are sometimes labeled as anise in the grocery store. Look for a long bulb of celery-like stems with bright green, feathery leaves that smell a bit like licorice.

grilled honey mustard chicken salad

Prep Time: 25 Minutes
Start to Finish: 25 Minutes
Servings: 6 (1-1/3 cups each)

QUICK

Mackenzie Severson
Germantown, MD
Suddenly Salad Contest Winner

- 1   box Betty Crocker® Suddenly Salad® classic pasta salad mix
- 1/2   cup mayonnaise
- 1   tablespoon honey mustard
- 2   cups cubed grilled chicken
- 2   cups washed fresh baby spinach leaves

- 1   cup cherry tomatoes, halved
- 1   stalk celery, chopped (1/3 cup)
- 1   cup shredded Cheddar cheese (4 oz)
- 3   hard-cooked eggs, coarsely chopped
- 3   slices bacon, crisply cooked and crumbled

1 Empty pasta mix into 3-quart saucepan 2/3 full of boiling water. Gently boil uncovered 12 minutes, stirring occasionally.

2 Drain pasta; rinse with cold water. Shake to drain.

3 In large bowl, stir together seasoning mix, mayonnaise and honey mustard. Add pasta, chicken, spinach, tomatoes, celery, cheese and eggs; toss gently to coat. Top with crumbled bacon. Serve immediately, or cover and refrigerate 1 hour to chill.

High Altitude (3500-6500 ft): No change.

Nutritional Info: 1 Serving: Calories 500; Total Fat 30g (Saturated Fat 9g); Sodium 1210mg; Total Carbohydrate 30g (Dietary Fiber 1g); Protein 27g. Exchanges: 1-1/2 Starch, 1/2 Other Carbohydrate, 3-1/2 Medium-Fat Meat, 2 Fat. Carbohydrate Choices: 2.

Betty's Kitchen Tips

Time-Saver: Use rotisserie chicken for the grilled chicken and precooked bacon rather than cooking your own.

Variation: Use your favorite chopped lettuce in place of the spinach leaves.

Health Twist: Try fat-free mayo, low-fat cheese and turkey bacon.

italian pasta salad

Prep Time: 30 Minutes
Start to Finish: 1 Hour 30 Minutes
Servings: 24 (1/2 cup each)

LOW FAT

Rachel Rappaport
Coconut & Lime
www.coconutlime.blogspot.com

Dressing

1/4	cup marinade from the artichoke hearts (see salad ingredients below)
1/4	cup olive oil
2	tablespoons red wine vinegar
2	tablespoons finely chopped basil
1	tablespoon finely chopped Italian parsley
2	teaspoons Dijon mustard
1/4	teaspoon salt
1/2	teaspoon pepper

Salad

1	package (12 oz) rainbow rotini pasta
1	jar (12 oz) marinated artichoke hearts, drained, marinade reserved
8	oz mozzarella cheese, cut into 1/2-inch cubes
1	English (seedless) cucumber, chopped (about 2 cups)
1	pint (2 cups) cherry tomatoes, cut in half
1	cup finely chopped red onion
1	cup sliced radishes
1	stalk celery, chopped (1/3 cup)
1/3	cup sliced green olives
4	medium green onions, sliced (1/4 cup)

1 In small jar with tight-fitting lid, shake dressing ingredients.

2 Cook pasta as directed on package; drain. Rinse with cold water to cool; drain well.

3 In large bowl, stir together remaining salad ingredients with pasta. Pour dressing over top; toss gently to coat. Refrigerate at least 1 hour before serving.

High Altitude (3500-6500 ft): No change.

Nutritional Info: 1 Serving: Calories 130; Total Fat 5g (Saturated Fat 1.5g); Sodium 210mg; Total Carbohydrate 16g (Dietary Fiber 2g); Protein 5g. Exchanges: 1/2 Starch, 2 Vegetable, 1 Fat. Carbohydrate Choices: 1.

Betty's Kitchen Tip

• English cucumbers, also called hothouse cucumbers, have very small seeds and thin skins that don't require peeling, so they work well for this salad.

double-orange scones with orange butter

Prep Time: 15 Minutes
Start to Finish: 35 Minutes
Servings: 8 scones

EASY

Scones
2	cups Gold Medal® all-purpose flour
4	tablespoons sugar
2-1/2	teaspoons baking powder
2	teaspoons grated orange peel
1/3	cup cold butter or margarine

1/2	cup mandarin orange segments (from 11 oz-can), chopped, drained
1/4	cup milk
1	egg, slightly beaten

Orange Butter
1/2	cup butter or margarine, softened
2	tablespoons orange marmalade

1 Heat oven to 400°F. Lightly spray cookie sheet with cooking spray.

2 In large bowl, mix flour, 3 tablespoons of the sugar, the baking powder and orange peel. Cut in 1/3 cup butter, using pastry blender (or pulling 2 table knives through ingredients in opposite directions), until mixture looks like coarse crumbs. Add orange segments, milk and egg; stir with fork just until mixture leaves side of bowl and soft dough forms.

3 Place dough on floured surface. Knead lightly 10 times. On cookie sheet, roll or pat dough into 7-inch round. Sprinkle with remaining 1 tablespoon sugar. Cut into 8 wedges; separate slightly. Bake 15 to 20 minutes or until golden brown.

4 Meanwhile, in small bowl, beat 1/2 cup butter until light and fluffy; stir in marmalade. Serve with warm scones.

High Altitude (3500-6500 ft): No change.

Nutritional Info: 1 Scone: Calories 350; Total Fat 20g (Saturated Fat 12g); Sodium 300mg; Total Carbohydrate 37g (Dietary Fiber 1g); Protein 4g. Exchanges: 1-1/2 Starch, 1 Other Carbohydrate, 4 Fat. Carbohydrate Choices: 2-1/2.

Betty's Kitchen Tips

How-To: When grating orange peel, be sure to grate only the orange part of the skin. The white part, or pith, is very bitter.

Did You Know? Like biscuits, scones are small quick breads leavened with baking powder or baking soda. Both biscuits and scones can be sweet or savory.

FAVORITE CAKES

p. 166

170

164

169

honey-rhubarb cake

Prep Time: 20 Minutes
Start to Finish: 2 Hours 15 Minutes
Servings: 15

Cake

1/4	cup butter or margarine
4	cups chopped fresh or frozen rhubarb, thawed if frozen
1/2	cup honey
1/2	cup granulated sugar
1	box Betty Crocker® SuperMoist® yellow cake mix
1-1/4	cups water
1/3	cup vegetable oil
3	eggs

Sweetened Whipped Cream

1	cup whipping (heavy) cream
3	tablespoons powdered sugar
1/2	teaspoon vanilla

1 Heat oven to 350°F for shiny metal or glass pan (or 325°F for dark or nonstick pan). In 13x9-inch pan, melt butter in oven. Remove pan from oven; turn pan so butter evenly coats bottom of pan. Spread rhubarb evenly in pan. Drizzle with honey and granulated sugar.

2 In large bowl, beat cake mix, water, oil and eggs with electric mixer on low speed 30 seconds. Beat on medium speed 2 minutes, scraping bowl occasionally. Pour over rhubarb mixture.

3 Bake 46 to 52 minutes or until toothpick inserted in center comes out clean. Cool cake at least 30 minutes to serve warm, or cool completely, about 1 hour.

4 In chilled medium bowl, beat whipping cream, powdered sugar and vanilla on high speed until soft peaks form. Serve warm cake with a dollop of whipped cream, or frost completely cooled cake with whipped cream. Store loosely covered in refrigerator.

High Altitude (3500-6500 ft): No change.

Nutritional Info: 1 Serving: Calories 360; Total Fat 18g (Saturated Fat 8g); Sodium 270mg; Total Carbohydrate 47g (Dietary Fiber 0g); Protein 3g. Exchanges: 1 Starch, 2 Other Carbohydrate, 3-1/2 Fat. Carbohydrate Choices: 3.

Betty's Kitchen Tip

• To make this recipe easier, top the cake with purchased whipped topping instead of making the Sweetened Whipped Cream.

cherry limeade poke cake

Prep Time: 25 Minutes
Start to Finish: 2 Hours 15 Minutes
Servings: 12

Cake

1	box Betty Crocker® SuperMoist® white cake mix
1-1/4	cups lemon-lime soda
1/3	cup vegetable oil
3	egg whites
4	teaspoons grated lime peel
1	box (4-serving size each) cherry-flavored gelatin
1	cup boiling water

Frosting

1	container (12 oz) Betty Crocker® Whipped fluffy white frosting

Maraschino cherries, if desired

Lime peel twists, if desired

1 Heat oven to 350°F for shiny metal or glass pan (or 325°F for dark or nonstick pan). Spray bottom only of 13x9-inch pan with baking spray with flour.

2 In large bowl, beat cake mix, soda, oil, egg whites and 3 teaspoons of the lime peel with electric mixer on low speed for 30 seconds. Beat on medium speed 2 minutes, scraping bowl occasionally. Pour into prepared pan.

3 Bake 28 to 32 minutes or until toothpick inserted in center comes out clean. Cool 20 minutes.

4 Meanwhile, stir gelatin into boiling water, stirring for 2 minutes to completely dissolve gelatin. Poke cake every inch with tines of meat fork or table knife. Pour cherry mixture slowly over cake, allowing mixture to fill holes in cake. Cool completely, about 1 hour longer.

5 In small bowl, mix frosting and remaining 1 teaspoon grated lime peel. Spread evenly over cake. Top each serving with cherry and lime twists.

High Altitude (3500-6500 ft): No change.

Nutritional Info: 1 Serving: Calories 410; Total Fat 13g (Saturated Fat 3.5g); Sodium 410mg; Total Carbohydrate 68g (Dietary Fiber 0g); Protein 4g. Exchanges: 1-1/2 Starch, 3 Other Carbohydrate, 2-1/2 Fat. Carbohydrate Choices: 4-1/2.

"healthified" strawberry shortcake squares

Prep Time: 30 Minutes
Start to Finish: 1 Hour 30 Minutes
Servings: 15

Cake

- 3 cups Bisquick Heart Smart® mix
- 1 cup sugar
- 2 tablespoons canola oil or 1/4 cup unsweetened applesauce
- 1 cup fat-free (skim) milk
- 2 teaspoons vanilla
- 1 whole egg
- 1 egg white

Topping

- 6 cups sliced fresh strawberries
- 2 tablespoons sugar
- 2 tablespoons water
- 1 teaspoon lemon juice
- 1 container (8 oz) frozen reduced-fat or fat-free whipped topping, thawed

1 Heat oven to 350°F. Spray bottom and sides of 13x9-inch pan with cooking spray. In large bowl, beat cake ingredients with electric mixer on low speed 30 seconds, scraping bowl occasionally. Pour into pan.

2 Bake 30 to 35 minutes or until toothpick inserted in center comes out clean. Cool completely, about 1 hour.

3 In medium bowl, mix the strawberries, 2 tablespoons sugar, the water and lemon juice. Cover; refrigerate for 30 minutes to 1 hour.

4 To serve, cut cake into squares; place on individual dessert plates. Top each serving with strawberries and whipped topping.

High Altitude (3500-6500 ft): No change.

Nutritional Info: 1 Serving: Calories 230; Total Fat 6g (Saturated Fat 2g); Sodium 230mg; Total Carbohydrate 41g (Dietary Fiber 1g); Protein 4g. Exchanges: 1 Starch, 1/2 Fruit, 1 Other Carbohydrate, 1 Fat. Carbohydrate Choices: 3.

Betty's Kitchen Tips

What is "Healthified"? We've replaced ingredients with great-tasting alternatives to create better-for-you recipes that are just as tasty as the original.

Purchasing: Choose the brightest, firmest, freshest strawberries that you can find. Strawberries are available all year long but are in season from April to June.

apple cake

Prep Time: 15 Minutes
Start to Finish: 50 Minutes
Servings: 9

EASY

2	cups Original Bisquick® mix
2	tablespoons sugar
1/2	cup milk
2	tablespoons butter or margarine, softened
1	egg
1	medium unpeeled red apple, thinly sliced (about 1 cup)
1/4	cup butter or margarine, melted
2	tablespoons sugar
1/2	teaspoon ground cinnamon

1 Heat oven to 400°F. Spray 9-inch square pan with cooking spray. In medium bowl, stir Bisquick mix, 2 tablespoons sugar, the milk, 2 tablespoons butter and egg until well blended. Spread batter evenly in pan.

2 Arrange the apple slices in 3 rows, overlapping slices slightly, on batter. Brush 1/4 cup melted butter over tops of apple slices.

3 In small bowl, mix 2 tablespoons sugar and the cinnamon; sprinkle over apples.

4 Bake 16 to 18 minutes or until edges are golden brown. Cool 15 minutes before serving. Cut with serrated knife into 9 squares.

High Altitude (3500-6500 ft): No change.

Nutritional Info: 1 Serving: Calories 220 (Calories from Fat 110); Total Fat 12g (Saturated Fat 6g, Trans Fat 1.5g); Cholesterol 45mg; Sodium 390mg; Total Carbohydrate 25g (Dietary Fiber 1g, Sugars 8g); Protein 3g. % Daily Value: Vitamin A 6%; Vitamin C 0%; Calcium 4%; Iron 4%. Exchanges: 1 Starch, 1/2 Other Carbohydrate, 2-1/2 Fat. Carbohydrate Choices: 1-1/2.

Betty's Kitchen Tip

• Try this interesting apple cake with 1/4 cup dried cranberries or raisins added with the apples.

easy tiramisu

Prep Time: 25 Minutes
Start to Finish: 2 Hours 10 Minutes
Servings: 15

Cake

1	box (1 lb 2.25 oz) Betty Crocker® SuperMoist® white cake mix
1	cup water
1/3	cup vegetable oil
1/4	cup brandy
3	egg whites

Espresso Syrup

1/4	cup instant espresso coffee granules
1/2	cup boiling water
2	tablespoons corn syrup

Topping

1	package (8 oz) cream cheese, softened
1/2	cup powdered sugar
2	cups whipping (heavy) cream
1	tablespoon unsweetened baking cocoa, if desired

1 Heat oven to 350°F (325°F for dark or nonstick pan). Grease bottom only of 13x9-inch pan with shortening or cooking spray. In large bowl, beat cake mix, 1 cup water, the oil, brandy and egg whites with electric mixer on low speed 30 seconds. Beat on medium speed 2 minutes, scraping bowl occasionally. Pour into pan.

2 Bake as directed on box for 13x9-inch pan. Cool 15 minutes.

3 In small bowl, stir espresso granules and 1/2 cup boiling water until mixed. Stir in corn syrup. Pierce top of cake every 1/2 inch with long-tined fork. Brush top of cake with espresso syrup. Cool completely, about 1 hour.

4 In medium bowl, beat cream cheese and powdered sugar with electric mixer on low speed until mixed. Beat on high speed until smooth. Gradually beat in whipping cream, beating on high speed about 2 minutes until stiff peaks form. Spread cream mixture over top of cake; sprinkle with cocoa. Store in refrigerator.

High Altitude (3500-6500 ft): No change.

Nutritional Info: 1 Serving: Calories 370; Total Fat 23g (Saturated Fat 11g); Sodium 300mg; Total Carbohydrate 35g (Dietary Fiber 0g); Protein 4g. Exchanges: 1 Starch, 1-1/2 Other Carbohydrate, 4-1/2 Fat. Carbohydrate Choices: 2.

coffee cake with caramel frosting

Prep Time: 15 Minutes
Start to Finish: 1 Hour 50 Minutes
Servings: 15

EASY

- 1/4 cup instant coffee granules
- 1/4 cup boiling water
- 1 box Betty Crocker® SuperMoist® white cake mix
- 1 cup water
- 1/3 cup vegetable oil
- 3 eggs
- 1 container (1 lb) Betty Crocker® Rich & Creamy vanilla frosting
- 1/4 cup caramel topping
- 3 bars (1.4 oz each) chocolate-covered English toffee candy, coarsely chopped

1. Heat oven to 350°F (325°F for dark or nonstick pan). Grease bottom only of 13x9-inch pan with shortening or cooking spray. In small cup, dissolve coffee granules in 1/4 cup boiling water.

2. In large bowl, beat cake mix, 1 cup water, the oil, eggs and coffee mixture with electric mixer on low speed 30 seconds. Beat on medium speed 2 minutes, scraping bowl occasionally. Pour batter into pan.

3. Bake 28 to 33 minutes or until toothpick inserted in center comes out clean. Cool completely, about 1 hour.

4. In medium bowl, mix frosting and caramel topping. Frost cake. Sprinkle with toffee candy. Store loosely covered at room temperature.

High Altitude (3500-6500 ft): No change.

Nutritional Info: 1 Serving: Calories 370; Total Fat 14g (Saturated Fat 4.5g); Sodium 360mg; Total Carbohydrate 57g (Dietary Fiber 0g); Protein 3g. Exchanges: 1-1/2 Starch, 2-1/2 Other Carbohydrate, 2-1/2 Fat. Carbohydrate Choices: 4.

Betty's Kitchen Tip

- For an Irish Cream Cake, substitute 1/4 cup Irish cream liqueur for the caramel topping.

fire engine cake

Prep Time: 1 Hour 20 Minutes
Start to Finish: 3 Hours 5 Minutes
Servings: 12

Cake

1 box Betty Crocker® SuperMoist® devil's food or yellow cake mix

Water, vegetable oil and eggs called for on cake mix box

Platter, tray or cardboard (about 14x10 inches), covered with wrapping paper and plastic food wrap or foil

Frosting and Decorations

2 containers (1 lb each) Betty Crocker® Rich & Creamy vanilla frosting

Black food color

Red gel or paste food color

10 red chewy fruit-flavored gumdrops (not sugar coated)

6 yellow chewy fruit-flavored gumdrops (not sugar coated)

4 creme-filled chocolate sandwich cookies

2 pieces black licorice coil

1. Heat oven to 350°F (325°F for dark or nonstick pans). Grease bottoms and sides of 3 (8x4-inch) loaf pans with shortening or cooking spray.

2. Make cake mix as directed on box, using water, oil and eggs. Divide batter evenly among pans. Bake 27 to 32 minutes or until toothpick inserted in center comes out clean. Cool 10 minutes. Remove cakes from pans; place rounded sides up on cooling racks. Cool completely, about 1 hour.

3. Spoon 1/2 cup of the frosting into small bowl; stir in enough black food color to make gray. Place 1/2 cup of the remaining white vanilla frosting in a small resealable food-storage plastic freezer bag; cut small tip off 1 bottom corner of bag. Spoon remaining white vanilla frosting into large bowl; stir in enough red food color until desired red color.

4. Trim rounded tops from each cake to make flat surface. Cut cakes and arrange pieces on platter as shown in diagram on BettyCrocker.com attaching pieces with thin layer of red frosting, to form fire engine. To "crumb-coat" cake, spread thin layer of red frosting over entire cake to seal in crumbs. Refrigerate or freeze cake 30 to 60 minutes.

5. Frost area between cab and back of engine with gray frosting. Place remaining gray frosting in small resealable food-storage plastic freezer bag; cut small tip off 1 bottom corner of bag. Frost remaining fire engine with red frosting. Pipe on windshield, windows and ladder with white frosting. Trim and discard thin slice (about 1/8 inch) off bottoms of 4 red and 4 yellow gumdrops; attach trimmed gumdrops for headlights and tail lights with white frosting. Attach remaining gumdrops on top of engine for lights. For wheels, pipe 1/2-inch circle of gray frosting on center of each cookie for hubcap; attach wheels to cake. Attach licorice coils on sides of cake for hoses.

6. Pipe gray frosting around wheels and bottom edge of engine. For bumpers, pipe 1 or 2 lines of gray frosting on front and back of engine.

High Altitude (3500-6500 ft): No change.

Nutritional Info: 1 Serving (Cake and Frosting): Calories 580; Total Fat 24g (Saturated Fat 5g); Sodium 550mg; Total Carbohydrate 88g (Dietary Fiber 1g); Protein 3g. Exchanges: 1 Starch, 5 Other Carbohydrate, 4-1/2 Fat. Carbohydrate Choices: 6.

strawberry cream angel cake

Prep Time: 40 Minutes
Start to Finish: 3 Hours 30 Minutes
Servings: 12

1	box Betty Crocker® white angel food cake mix
1-1/4	cups cold water

Strawberry Cream

1-1/2	cups whipping (heavy) cream
3/4	cup strawberry glaze (from a 13.5-oz container)

Garnish

1	quart strawberries, finely chopped
2	tablespoons granulated sugar

1 Move oven rack to lowest position (remove other racks). Heat oven to 350°F. In extra-large glass or metal bowl, beat cake mix and cold water with electric mixer on low speed 30 seconds. Beat on medium speed 1 minute. Pour into ungreased 10-inch angel food (tube) cake pan. (Do not use fluted tube cake pan or 9-inch angel food pan or batter will overflow.)

2 Bake 37 to 47 minutes or until top is dark golden brown and cracks feel very dry and are not sticky. Do not underbake. Immediately turn pan upside down onto glass bottle until cake is completely cool, about 2 hours.

3 In medium bowl, beat whipping cream on high speed until stiff peaks form. Fold strawberry glaze into whipped cream.

4 On serving plate, place cake with browned side down. Frost top and sides of cake with strawberry cream mixture. Refrigerate for at least 30 minutes before serving.

5 In small bowl, mix strawberries and sugar; refrigerate until serving. Spoon about 1/4 cup chopped strawberry mixture over each serving. Store covered in refrigerator.

High Altitude (3500-6500 ft): No change.

Nutritional Info: 1 Serving: Calories 270; Total Fat 9g (Saturated Fat 6g); Sodium 330mg; Total Carbohydrate 41g (Dietary Fiber 1g); Protein 4g. Exchanges: 1-1/2 Starch, 1-1/2 Other Carbohydrate, 1-1/2 Fat. Carbohydrate Choices: 3.

Betty's Kitchen Tip

• Strawberry glaze can be found in the produce section of most supermarkets.

butter rum-glazed applesauce cake

Prep Time: 20 Minutes
Start to Finish: 1 Hour 25 Minutes
Servings: 9

. . . .

Cake

1/3	cup butter (do not use margarine)
3/4	cup granulated sugar
1	cup applesauce
1	teaspoon vanilla
1-1/2	cups Gold Medal® all-purpose flour
1	teaspoon baking soda
1	teaspoon ground cinnamon
1/2	teaspoon salt

Butter Rum Glaze

2	tablespoons butter (do not use margarine)
1	cup powdered sugar
1/2	teaspoon rum flavor
3 to 4	teaspoons half-and-half or milk

. . . .

1 Heat oven to 350°F. Grease bottom and sides of 8-inch square pan with shortening or cooking spray.

2 In 1-1/2-quart saucepan, melt 1/3 cup butter over medium heat. Cook 2 to 2-1/2 minutes, stirring occasionally, until butter just begins to brown. Immediately remove from heat. Stir in granulated sugar, applesauce and vanilla.

3 In large bowl, mix flour, baking soda, cinnamon and salt. Stir in applesauce mixture. Pour batter into pan.

4 Bake 30 to 35 minutes or until toothpick inserted in center comes out clean.

5 In 1-1/2-quart saucepan, melt 2 tablespoons butter over medium heat; cook about 3 minutes or until butter just begins to brown. Immediately remove from heat. Stir in remaining glaze ingredients until smooth and spreadable. Pour over warm cake. Cool 30 minutes. Serve warm.

High Altitude (3500-6500 ft): No change.

Nutritional Info: 1 Serving: Calories 300; Total Fat 10g (Saturated Fat 6g); Sodium 340mg; Total Carbohydrate 51g (Dietary Fiber 1g); Protein 2g. Exchanges: 1-1/2 Starch, 2 Other Carbohydrate, 2 Fat. Carbohydrate Choices: 3-1/2.

Betty's Kitchen Tip

• After adding glaze, sprinkle the top of the warm cake with a bit of cinnamon.

apple-crisp orange pound cake

Prep Time: 20 Minutes
Start to Finish: 2 Hours
Servings: 8

Priscilla Yee
Concord, CA
Celebrate the Season-Fall Baking Contest

Filling

2	cups chopped peeled baking apples (about 2 medium)
1/4	cup apple jelly
1	tablespoon Gold Medal® all-purpose flour
1/2	teaspoon apple pie spice

Cake and Topping

1-1/3	cups Gold Medal® all-purpose flour
1-1/4	cups sugar
1	teaspoon grated orange peel
1/4	teaspoon baking powder
1/4	teaspoon salt
3/4	cup cold butter or margarine
1/3	cup sour cream
2	eggs
1	teaspoon vanilla
1/2	cup chopped pecans

1 Heat oven to 350°F. Grease 9-inch round or 8-inch square pan with shortening or cooking spray.

2 In small bowl, mix all filling ingredients; set aside. In medium bowl, mix 1-1/3 cups flour, the sugar, orange peel, baking powder and salt. Cut in butter, using pastry blender (or pulling 2 table knives through ingredients in opposite directions), until small crumbs form. Reserve 1 cup of the crumb mixture for topping. To remaining crumb mixture in bowl, add sour cream, eggs and vanilla; beat with electric mixer on medium speed about 1 minute or until blended.

3 Spread batter in pan. Spoon filling over batter and spread evenly. Sprinkle with reserved crumb mixture and the pecans; pat gently.

4 Bake 65 to 70 minutes or until light golden brown and toothpick inserted in center comes out with a few moist crumbs clinging. Cool 30 minutes. Serve warm if desired.

High Altitude (3500-6500 ft): No change.

Nutritional Info: 1 Serving: Calories 490; Total Fat 26g (Saturated Fat 13g); Sodium 240mg; Total Carbohydrate 60g (Dietary Fiber 2g); Protein 5g. Exchanges: 1-1/2 Starch, 2-1/2 Other Carbohydrate, 5 Fat. Carbohydrate Choices: 4.

Betty's Kitchen Tips

Serve-With: Try a piece of cake warm, topped with a scoop of vanilla ice cream and drizzled with caramel topping!

Success Hint: Braeburn apples work well in this cake; or try another crisp, sweet-tart apple such as Cortland or Gala.

walnut-apricot pound cake

Prep Time: 25 Minutes
Start to Finish: 4 Hours 15 Minutes
Servings: 24

Cake

3	cups Gold Medal® all-purpose flour
1	teaspoon baking powder
1/4	teaspoon salt
2	cups granulated sugar
1-1/4	cups butter, softened
1	teaspoon vanilla
5	eggs
1/2	cup milk
1/2	cup apricot nectar
1-1/2	cups chopped dried apricots (about 9 oz)
1	cup chopped walnuts

Glaze

1	cup powdered sugar
2	tablespoons butter, softened
1/2	teaspoon vanilla
4	to 6 teaspoons apricot nectar

1 Heat oven to 325°F. Spray 10-inch angel food (tube) cake pan with baking spray with flour. Wrap foil around bottom of pan to prevent leaking.

2 In medium bowl, mix flour, baking powder and salt; set aside. In large bowl, beat granulated sugar, 1-1/4 cups butter, 1 teaspoon vanilla and the eggs with electric mixer on low speed 30 seconds. Beat on high speed 5 minutes, scraping bowl occasionally. On low speed, beat in flour mixture alternately with milk and 1/2 cup apricot nectar.

3 Set aside 2 tablespoons of the apricots for topping along with 1/4 cup of the walnuts. Stir remaining apricots and walnuts into batter. Spread in pan.

4 Bake 1 hour 30 minutes or until toothpick inserted in center comes out clean. Cool 20 minutes. Remove cake from pan to cooling rack. Cool completely, about 2 hours.

5 In small bowl, mix powdered sugar, 2 tablespoons butter and 1/2 teaspoon vanilla. Using whisk, mix in 4 to 6 teaspoons apricot nectar, 1 teaspoon at a time, until smooth and consistency of thick syrup. Drizzle glaze over top of cake; spread with spatula or back of spoon, letting some glaze drizzle down side. Sprinkle reserved apricots and walnuts on top of cake.

High Altitude (3500-6500 ft): No change.

Nutritional Info: 1 Serving: Calories 320; Total Fat 15g (Saturated Fat 7g); Sodium 135mg; Total Carbohydrate 41g (Dietary Fiber 1g); Protein 4g. Exchanges: 1 Starch, 1-1/2 Other Carbohydrate, 3 Fat. Carbohydrate Choices: 3.

Betty's Kitchen Tip

• Have pecans on hand instead of walnuts? They would be delicious in this cake as well.

brown sugar-spice cake with caramelized apples

Prep Time: 40 Minutes
Start to Finish: 1 Hour 40 Minutes
Servings: 12

Cake

- 1/2 cup butter or margarine, softened
- 1/2 cup packed brown sugar
- 2 eggs
- 1-1/4 cups Gold Medal® all-purpose flour
- 1 teaspoon baking powder
- 1/2 teaspoon baking soda
- 1/2 teaspoon ground ginger
- 1/2 teaspoon ground nutmeg
- 1/4 teaspoon ground cloves
- 1/4 teaspoon salt
- 1/2 cup sour cream
- 1 cup finely chopped peeled apple (1 medium)

Caramelized Apples

- 6 medium apples, peeled, sliced (about 8 cups)
- 1 cup packed brown sugar

Whipped Cream

- 1 cup whipping (heavy) cream

1 Heat oven to 350°F. Spray bottom only of 9-inch square pan with baking spray with flour.

2 In large bowl, beat butter, 1/2 cup brown sugar and the eggs with electric mixer on low speed until blended; beat on medium speed until well combined. On low speed, beat in flour, baking powder, baking soda, ginger, nutmeg, cloves, salt and sour cream until mixed; beat on medium speed 1 minute. Stir in chopped apple. Spoon batter evenly into pan.

3 Bake 35 to 40 minutes or until toothpick inserted in center comes out clean and top is golden brown. Cool 10 minutes. Run knife around pan to loosen cake. Remove cake to heatproof serving plate. Cool cake about 30 minutes.

4 Meanwhile, in 12-inch skillet, cook sliced apples and 1 cup brown sugar over medium-high heat 20 to 25 minutes, stirring occasionally, or until apples are tender and caramelized.

5 In chilled large deep bowl, beat whipping cream with electric mixer on low speed until cream begins to thicken. Gradually increase speed to high and beat just until soft peaks form. Spoon Caramelized Apples over cake. Top with dollops of whipped cream.

High Altitude (3500-6500 ft): No change.

Nutritional Info: 1 Serving: Calories 370; Total Fat 18g (Saturated Fat 11g); Sodium 230mg; Total Carbohydrate 49g (Dietary Fiber 1g); Protein 3g. Exchanges: 1/2 Starch, 1/2 Fruit, 2-1/2 Other Carbohydrate, 3-1/2 Fat. Carbohydrate Choices: 3.

chocolate malt cake

Prep Time: 20 Minutes
Start to Finish: 1 Hour 50 Minutes
Servings: 24

- 1 box Betty Crocker® SuperMoist® milk chocolate cake mix
- 1/3 cup chocolate malted milk powder

Water, vegetable oil and eggs as called for on cake mix box

Malted Milk Frosting

- 1 cup whipping (heavy) cream
- 1/4 cup chocolate malted milk powder
- 1/2 teaspoon vanilla

Garnish

- 1 cup chocolate-covered malted milk balls, if desired

1 Heat oven to 350°F (325°F for dark or nonstick pan.) Spray bottom only of 15x10x1-inch pan with cooking spray.

2 In large bowl, stir together cake mix and 1/3 cup malted milk powder. Beat in water, oil and eggs with electric mixer on low speed 30 seconds. Beat on medium speed 2 minutes, scraping bowl occasionally. Pour into pan.

3 Bake 29 to 34 minutes or until toothpick inserted in center comes out clean. Cool completely, about 1 hour.

4 In medium bowl, beat cream, 1/4 cup malted milk powder and vanilla on medium speed until stiff peaks form. Spread over cake. Place malted milk balls in small resealable freezer plastic bag; seal bag and crush with rolling pin or meat mallet. Just before serving, top with chopped malted milk balls.

High Altitude (3500-6500 ft): No change.

Nutritional Info: 1 Serving: Calories 160; Total Fat 8g (Saturated Fat 3g); Sodium 160mg; Total Carbohydrate 20g (Dietary Fiber 0g); Protein 2g. Exchanges: 1/2 Starch, 1 Other Carbohydrate, 1-1/2 Fat. Carbohydrate Choices: 1.

Betty's Kitchen Tip

- This cake features the flavors of a chocolate malt, that timeless soda-fountain favorite. Look for the chocolate malted milk powder with the instant drink powder in most grocery stores.

chocolate mocha mousse torte

Prep Time: 30 Minutes
Start to Finish: 2 Hours 45 Minutes
Servings: 12

Chocolate Nut Cake

1	box Betty Crocker® SuperMoist® dark chocolate cake mix
3/4	cup water
1	cup sour cream
1/2	cup vegetable oil
3	eggs
3/4	cup slivered almonds, toasted if desired, finely ground

Chocolate Mocha Mousse

4	oz semisweet baking chocolate, chopped
2	cups whipping (heavy) cream
2	tablespoons instant espresso powder
2/3	cup sugar

Garnish

1/2	cup sliced almonds, toasted if desired

1. Heat oven to 350°F (325°F for dark or nonstick pan.) Spray two 9-inch cake pans with baking spray with flour.

2. In large bowl, beat cake mix, water, sour cream, oil and eggs with electric mixer on low speed until moistened. Beat on medium speed 2 minutes, scraping bowl occasionally. Stir in 3/4 cup almonds. Pour into pans.

3. Bake as directed on box for 9-inch rounds. Cool in pan 10 minutes. Remove from pan to cooling rack. Cool completely, about 1 hour.

4. Meanwhile, place chocolate in medium bowl. In 2-quart saucepan, heat whipping cream just to boiling. Pour hot cream over chocolate; let stand until mixture is melted and smooth when stirred. Whisk in espresso powder and sugar. Refrigerate chocolate mixture 1 hour, stirring occasionally, until cold. Beat cold chocolate mixture with electric mixer on high speed until soft peaks form, about 2 to 3 minutes.

5. Cut each cake layer horizontally to make 2 layers. (To cut, mark side of cake with toothpicks and cut with long, thin knife.) On serving plate, place 1 cake layer, rounded side down, frost top with about 1/4 of the mousse. Top with second layer, rounded side up; frost top with about 1/4 of the mousse. Repeat with remaining two layers of cake and mousse. Sprinkle sliced almonds around top edge of cake. Refrigerate for at least 30 minutes before serving. Store in refrigerator.

High Altitude (3500-6500 ft): No change.

Nutritional Info: 1 Serving: Calories 610; Total Fat 38g (Saturated Fat 15g); Sodium 450mg; Total Carbohydrate 59g (Dietary Fiber 3g); Protein 8g. Exchanges: 1-1/2 Starch, 2-1/2 Other Carbohydrate, 1/2 High-Fat Meat, 6-1/2 Fat. Carbohydrate Choices: 4.

white texas sheet cake

Prep Time: 30 Minutes
Start to Finish: 2 Hours
Servings: 24

- 3 oz white chocolate baking bars or squares, chopped
- 2 tablespoons whipping (heavy) cream
- 1 box Betty Crocker® SuperMoist® white cake mix
- 1 cup sour cream
- 1/2 cup vegetable oil
- 3 eggs

White Chocolate Frosting
- 3 oz white chocolate baking bars or squares, chopped
- 3 tablespoons whipping (heavy) cream
- 1/2 cup butter or margarine, softened
- 3 cups powdered sugar

Garnish
- 1/2 cup chopped pecans, toasted if desired

1 Heat oven to 350°F (325°F for dark or nonstick pan.) Spray bottom and sides of 15x10x1-inch pan with baking spray with flour.

2 In small microwaveable bowl mix 3 oz white chocolate and 2 tablespoons cream; microwave uncovered on High 1 minute, stirring every 30 seconds, until smooth. Cool 10 to 15 minutes.

3 In large bowl, beat cake mix, sour cream, oil, eggs and chocolate mixture with electric mixer on low speed 30 seconds. Beat on medium speed 2 minutes, scraping bowl occasionally. Pour into pan.

4 Bake 20 to 23 minutes or until toothpick inserted in center comes out clean. Cool completely, about 1 hour.

5 In small microwaveable bowl, mix 3 oz white chocolate and 3 tablespoons cream; microwave uncovered on High for 1 minute, stirring every 30 seconds, until smooth. Cool 10 to 15 minutes.

6 In medium bowl, beat butter and 2 cups of the powdered sugar with electric mixer on medium until blended. Add white chocolate mixture; blend well. Add remaining sugar; beat until smooth. Spread frosting over cake, sprinkle with nuts.

High Altitude (3500-6500 ft): No change.

Nutritional Info: 1 Serving: Calories 310; Total Fat 17g (Saturated Fat 7g); Sodium 200mg; Total Carbohydrate 37g (Dietary Fiber 0g); Protein 2g. Exchanges: 1/2 Starch, 2 Other Carbohydrate, 3-1/2 Fat. Carbohydrate Choices: 2-1/2.

Betty's Kitchen Tips

Success Hint: Toasting pecans or other nuts intensifies their flavor. To toast pecans, heat oven to 350°F. Spread pecans in ungreased shallow pan. Bake uncovered 6 to 10 minutes, stirring occasionally until light brown.

Did You Know? White chocolate is made from cocoa butter and adds a wonderful rich flavor to this cake. Find white chocolate in the baking section of most grocery stores.

mermaid cake

Prep Time: 1 Hour 10 Minutes
Start to Finish: 2 Hours 20 Minutes
Servings: 12

- 1 box Betty Crocker® SuperMoist® yellow cake mix
- Water, vegetable oil and eggs called for on cake mix box
- 1-1/2 containers (1 lb each) Betty Crocker® Rich & Creamy vanilla frosting
- Blue liquid food color
- 1 tablespoon purple colored sugar
- 1 tablespoon blue colored sugar

- 1 fashion doll in swimsuit or sleeveless top (11-1/2 inches tall)
- 3 rolls Betty Crocker® Fruit Roll-Ups® Blazin' Blue Green chewy fruit snack (from 5-oz box Blastin' Berry Hot Colors)
- Granulated sugar
- 6 large orange, yellow and/or white gumdrops
- 8 assorted sea creature candies

1 Heat oven to 350°F (325°F for dark or nonstick pans). Grease bottoms and sides of 1 (10-oz) custard cup and 2 (8-inch) round cake pans with shortening or cooking spray.

2 Make cake mix as directed on box, using water, oil and eggs. Pour 2/3 cup batter into custard cup; divide remaining cake batter evenly between cake pans. Bake 23 to 28 minutes (26 to 33 minutes for dark or nonstick pans) or until toothpick inserted in centers comes out clean. Cool 10 minutes. Remove cakes from custard cup and pans; place rounded sides up on cooling racks. Cool completely, about 1 hour.

3 Trim off rounded tops from 8-inch cakes. On serving plate, place 1 round cake layer, cut side down. Spread with 1/3 cup frosting. Top with second round cake layer, cut side down. Trim off rounded top of custard-cup cake to make flat surface. With small amount of frosting, attach custard-cup cake, flat side down, to top of layer cake, lining up rounded edge with layer cake edge. Using doll as a guide, cut and remove rounded piece from custard-cup cake to make seat for doll. (Discard cut-out piece.)

4 Spoon 3/4 cup frosting into small bowl. Tint with blue food color to make light blue; set aside. Frost sides and top of

cake with remaining white frosting. To add waves, frost lower side of cake with blue frosting. Dip a fork in a few drops additional blue food color; swirl in blue frosting on cake to add wave effect. Sprinkle top of cake with colored sugars.

5 Tie hair of fashion doll in ponytail. (Keep swimsuit or clothes on doll.) Wrap body of doll with plastic wrap, covering bustline and leaving arms free and shoulders uncovered. With 2 fruit snack rolls, wrap plastic-wrapped portion of doll, overlapping rolls and pressing to stick together. Wrap third snack roll around legs and extend 2 inches beyond feet; press together to form a fin shape, trimming if necessary. Place doll in seat on cake.

6 To make starfish, on surface sprinkled with granulated sugar, flatten each gumdrop to make 1-1/2-inch round. Using scissors, cut 5 wedges from each gumdrop round to form a star. Pull gently to extend points of stars. Decorate cake and serving plate with starfish and sea creature candies.

High Altitude (3500-6500 ft): No change.

Nutritional Info: 1 Serving (Cake and Frosting): Calories 470; Total Fat 17g (Saturated Fat 4g); Sodium 420mg; Total Carbohydrate 75g (Dietary Fiber 0g); Protein 2g. Exchanges: 1/2 Starch, 4-1/2 Other Carbohydrate, 3-1/2 Fat. Carbohydrate Choices: 5.

malt shoppe memories ice cream cookie cake

Prep Time: 35 Minutes
Start to Finish: 6 Hours 10 Minutes
Servings: 16

Dawn Moore
Warren, PA
Cookie Mix Contest 2010

- 1 pouch (1 lb 1.5 oz) Betty Crocker® double chocolate chunk cookie mix
- 2/3 cup chocolate-flavor malted milk powder
- 1/3 cup vegetable oil
- 2 tablespoons water
- 1 egg

- 1/2 cup hot fudge topping
- 1 cup crushed chocolate-covered malted milk balls
- 2 cups vanilla ice cream, softened
- 2 cups chocolate ice cream, softened
- 1 cup frozen (thawed) whipped topping

1 Heat oven to 350°F. Lightly spray 10-inch springform pan with cooking spray. Or line 9-inch square pan with foil, leaving about 2 inches of foil overhanging at 2 opposite sides of pan; lightly spray foil with cooking spray.

2 In large bowl, stir cookie mix, 1/3 cup of the malted milk powder, the oil, water and egg until soft dough forms. Press 1/2 of dough in bottom of pan. Bake 12 to 13 minutes or until set. Cool completely, about 30 minutes.

3 Meanwhile, on large ungreased cookie sheet, press remaining dough into 10-inch circle. After removing cookie crust from oven, bake dough on cookie sheet 12 to 13 minutes or until set. Cool 5 minutes; remove from cookie sheet to cooling rack. Cool 15 minutes.

4 Spread fudge topping over crust in springform or 9-inch pan. In medium bowl, break apart large cookie until crumbly. Stir in crushed malted milk balls. Sprinkle 1/2 of the crumbled cookie mixture over fudge layer; press lightly.

5 In large bowl, combine both softened ice creams and remaining 1/3 cup malted milk powder until well blended. Spread ice cream mixture over crumbs in pan. Gently spread whipped topping over ice cream. Sprinkle with remaining crumb mixture. Cover with foil. Freeze at least 5 hours or until firm.

6 To serve, remove sides of springform pan or use foil to lift dessert out of 9-inch pan. Let stand 5 minutes. Use hot wet knife to cut into wedges or squares. Store covered in freezer.

High Altitude (3500-6500 ft): No change.

Nutritional Info: 1 Serving: Calories 350; Total Fat 15g (Saturated Fat 7g); Sodium 240mg; Total Carbohydrate 50g (Dietary Fiber 1g); Protein 3g. Exchanges: 1 Starch, 2-1/2 Other Carbohydrate, 3 Fat. Carbohydrate Choices: 3.

easy pineapple upside-down cake

Prep Time: 15 Minutes
Start to Finish: 1 Hour 50 Minutes
Servings: 12

EASY

1/4   cup butter or margarine
1   cup packed brown sugar
1   can (20 oz) sliced pineapple in juice, drained, juice reserved
1   jar (6 oz) maraschino cherries, drained
1   box Betty Crocker® SuperMoist® yellow cake mix
Vegetable oil and eggs called for on cake mix box

1 Heat oven to 350°F (325°F for dark or nonstick pan). In 13x9-inch pan, melt butter in oven. Sprinkle brown sugar evenly over butter. Arrange pineapple slices on brown sugar. Place cherry in center of each pineapple slice, and arrange remaining cherries around slices; press gently into brown sugar.

2 Add enough water to reserved pineapple juice to measure 1-1/4 cups. Make cake batter as directed on box, substituting pineapple juice mixture for the water. Pour batter over pineapple and cherries.

3 Bake 40 to 45 minutes (42 to 48 minutes for dark or nonstick pan) or until toothpick inserted in center comes out clean. Immediately run knife around sides of pan to loosen cake. Place heatproof serving plate upside down onto pan; turn plate and pan over. Leave pan over cake 5 minutes so brown sugar topping can drizzle over cake; remove pan. Cool 30 minutes. Serve warm or cool. Store covered in refrigerator.

High Altitude (3500-6500 ft): No change.

Nutritional Info: 1 Serving: Calories 410; Total Fat 15g (Saturated Fat 5g); Sodium 330mg; Total Carbohydrate 65g (Dietary Fiber 0g); Protein 3g. Exchanges: 1 Starch, 3 Other Carbohydrate, 3 Fat. Carbohydrate Choices: 4.

Betty's Kitchen Tips

Substitution: SuperMoist® butter recipe yellow or white cake mix can also be used to make this popular cake. Make cake batter as directed on box, using reserved pineapple juice as part of the total 1 cup water measurement.

Special Touch: Serve with sweetened whipped cream or an 8-oz container of frozen (thawed) whipped topping if desired. To make same amount of sweetened whipped cream, in chilled medium bowl, beat 1-1/2 cups whipping cream and 2 tablespoons sugar with electric mixer on high speed until soft peaks form.

electric guitar cake

Prep Time: 1 Hour 30 Minutes
Start to Finish: 4 Hours 30 Minutes
Servings: 12

Cake

- 1 box Betty Crocker® SuperMoist® yellow or devil's food cake mix

Water, vegetable oil and eggs called for on cake mix box
Tray or foil-covered cardboard (19x11 inches)

Frosting and Decorations

- 1-1/4 cups Betty Crocker® Rich & Creamy chocolate frosting (from 1-lb container)

Black food color

- 2 3/4 cups Betty Crocker® Rich & Creamy vanilla frosting (from two 1-lb containers)

Desired food color for guitar

- 4 pieces black licorice coil, uncoiled, or string licorice
- 4 small chewy fruit candies in desired color
- 6 chewy fruit-flavored gumdrops (not sugar coated) in desired color
- 2 candy-coated tropical fruit candies in desired color

1. Heat oven to 350°F (325°F for dark or nonstick pan). Make and bake cake mix as directed on box for 13x9-inch pan, using water, oil and eggs. Cool 10 minutes; remove cake from pan to cooling rack. Cool completely, about 1 hour. Refrigerate or freeze cake 1 hour or until firm.

2. Meanwhile, in medium bowl, mix chocolate frosting and black food color to make black frosting. In small bowl, mix 1/3 cup vanilla frosting and black food color to make gray frosting. Place gray frosting and 2/3 cup white vanilla frosting in separate resealable plastic freezer bags; seal bags. Cut small bottom corner off each bag. In another medium bowl, mix remaining vanilla frosting and desired food color to make guitar color.

3. Using serrated knife, cut rounded top off cake to level surface; place cake cut side down. Cut cake as shown in template. Place cake pieces on tray as directed in template, attaching to tray with small amount of frosting.

4. To "crumb-coat" cake, spread thin layer of guitar frosting over top and sides of guitar body to seal in crumbs. With black frosting, crumb-coat top and sides of guitar neck and headstock. Refrigerate or freeze cake 30 to 60 minutes to set frosting.

5. Frost entire cake with same colors. If desired, place remaining black frosting in resealable plastic freezer bag and cut small bottom corner off bag to pipe frosting. To extend guitar neck 1 to 2 inches onto body of guitar, pipe and fill in neck with black frosting. With white vanilla frosting, pipe and fill in contrasting design on body of guitar. On white design, pipe black rectangle about 1 inch from end of neck to create pickup. With gray frosting, pipe on frets, bridge and any additional accents as desired. For strings, add black licorice. Add small fruit candies at ends of strings. For tuning pegs, add gumdrops. For buttons on body, add tropical fruit candies.

High Altitude (3500-6500 ft): No change.

Nutritional Info: 1 Serving (Cake and Frosting): Calories 340; Total Fat 13g (Saturated Fat 3.5g); Sodium 380mg; Total Carbohydrate 53g (Dietary Fiber 0g); Protein 2g. Exchanges: 1/2 Starch, 3 Other Carbohydrate, 2-1/2 Fat. Carbohydrate Choices: 3-1/2.

Betty's Kitchen Tip

- Need help? Download the template by going to BettyCrocker.com, searching for this recipe and clicking on the template download.

monster cake

Prep Time: 45 Minutes
Start to Finish: 2 Hours
Servings: 12

1 box Betty Crocker® SuperMoist®
chocolate fudge cake mix (or other flavor)
Water, vegetable oil and eggs called for on cake
mix package
1 container (1 lb) Betty Crocker® Rich &
Creamy creamy white frosting

Black food color
Neon green food color
Betty Crocker® black decorating icing
(from 4.25-oz tube)
2 pieces black string licorice (5 to 6 inch)

1 Heat oven to 350°F. Spray 13x9-inch pan
with cooking spray. Line bottom of pan
with waxed paper or cooking parchment
paper cut to size.

2 Mix cake batter as directed on box, using
water, oil and eggs. Pour batter into pan.
Bake as directed on box. Cool 10 minutes;
remove from pan to cooling rack. Peel
off waxed or parchment paper. Cool
completely, about 30 minutes.

3 Place cake, bottom side up, on large platter
or foil-covered cookie sheet. Remove
2 tablespoons of white frosting from
container; set aside. Remove 1/3 of the
frosting (about 1/2 cup) to small bowl. Tint
black; set aside. Tint remaining frosting
neon green. Frost sides and top of cake
with neon green frosting.

4 Using picture as a guide, use decorating
icing with a round tip to outline hair. Add
licorice pieces for eyebrows. Use reserved
white frosting to form eyes. Use icing to
outline remaining facial features. Spread
black frosting within the outlines to fill in
the hair.

High Altitude (3500-6500 ft): No change.

Nutritional Info: 1 Serving: Calories 430; Total Fat 18g (Saturated
Fat 4g); Sodium 460mg; Total Carbohydrate 63g (Dietary Fiber
1g); Protein 3g. Exchanges: 1 Starch, 3 Other Carbohydrate, 3-1/2
Fat. Carbohydrate Choices: 4.

Betty's Kitchen Tips

Success Hint: To remove cake from pan, place
cooling rack over pan. Carefully turn over; lift
off pan, leaving cake on cooling rack, and peel
off paper.

Substitution: Use 2 white candy melts or
coating wafers instead of frosting to make the
white part of the eyes.

CUPCAKE BONANZA

p. 187

188

185

201

two-for-one cupcakes

Prep Time: 25 Minutes
Start to Finish: 2 Hours 10 Minutes
Servings: 24 cupcakes

- -

1 box Betty Crocker® SuperMoist®
yellow cake mix (or other flavor)

Water, vegetable oil and eggs as called for on cake
mix package

Black string licorice, cut into 2-inch pieces

2 containers (1 lb each) Betty Crocker® Rich
& Creamy chocolate frosting

Black decorator sugar crystals
Red cinnamon candies
Large black gumdrops
Chocolate wafer cookies
Assorted candies

- -

1 Heat oven to 350°F. Place paper baking cup
in each of 24 regular-size muffin cups.

2 Mix cake batter as directed on box, using
water, oil and eggs. Divide batter evenly
among muffin cups. Bake as directed on
box. Cool 10 minutes; remove from pan to
cooling rack. Cool completely, about
30 minutes.

3 To make spiders, press 4 licorice pieces
into each side of 12 of the cupcakes, letting
about 1-1/2 inches hang over the side of
the cupcake. Spread top of cupcakes with

chocolate frosting; sprinkle with sugar
crystals. Slice black gumdrops in half for
the faces. Press red cinnamon candies in
the center for eyes.

4 To make owls, spread chocolate frosting
on remaining 12 cupcakes. Use candies to
form eyes, beaks and feet on each cupcake.
Cut chocolate wafer cookies into quarters;
place wafer pieces, triangle point up,
behind the eyes for ears. Cut wafer cookies
into thirds for wings; place on cupcakes.

High Altitude (3500-6500 ft): No change.

Nutritional Info: 1 Cupcake: Calories 260; Total Fat 10g
(Saturated Fat 3g); Sodium 250mg; Total Carbohydrate 40g
(Dietary Fiber 0g); Protein 1g. Exchanges: 1/2 Starch, 2 Other
Carbohydrate, 2 Fat. Carbohydrate Choices: 2-1/2.

Betty's Kitchen Tips

Did You Know? Licorice allsorts is a mixture of
several shapes and colors of licorice.

Success Hint: Candy corn pieces can be used
for the owls' beaks, and yellow ring-shaped hard
candies can be used for the owls' eyes.

witchly cupcakes

Prep Time: 40 Minutes
Start to Finish: 2 Hours 10 Minutes
Servings: 24 cupcakes

- 1 box Betty Crocker® SuperMoist® cake mix (any flavor)
- Water, vegetable oil and eggs as called for on cake mix package
- 1 container (1 lb) Betty Crocker® Rich & Creamy vanilla frosting
- 8 drops green food color
- Assorted candies (black licorice twists, candy corn, candy-coated peanut butter pieces)
- 1 tube (0.68 oz) Betty Crocker® black decorating gel

1 Heat oven to 350°F (325°F for dark or nonstick pans). Make cake mix as directed on box for 24 cupcakes, using water, oil and eggs. Cool completely, about 30 minutes.

2 Tint frosting with green food color. Cut licorice twists lengthwise in half; cut each half crosswise into various lengths.

3 Frost cupcakes with frosting. Arrange licorice pieces on each cupcake for hat, candy corn for nose and peanut butter pieces for eyes. Make pupils of eyes with black gel.

High Altitude (3500-6500 ft): No change.

Nutritional Info: 1 Cupcake: Calories 210; Total Fat 9g (Saturated Fat 2g); Sodium 230mg; Total Carbohydrate 31g (Dietary Fiber 0g); Protein 1g. Exchanges: 1/2 Starch, 1-1/2 Other Carbohydrate, 1-1/2 Fat. Carbohydrate Choices: 2.

Betty's Kitchen Tips

Do Ahead: You can make and freeze the unfrosted cupcakes up to 3 months ahead. Frost and decorate the frozen cupcakes, then let thaw at room temperature.

Success Hint: Bake the cupcakes in decorative paper baking cups found at party stores or cake-decorating supply stores.

pull-apart spiderweb cupcakes

Prep Time: 20 Minutes
Start to Finish: 1 Hour 45 Minutes
Servings: 24 cupcakes

1   box Betty Crocker® SuperMoist® white cake mix (or other flavor)
Water, vegetable oil and eggs as called for on cake mix package
Orange gel food coloring

2   containers (12 oz each) Betty Crocker® Whipped fluffy white frosting
1   tube (0.68 oz) Betty Crocker® black decorating gel
Plastic spiders (for decoration)

1 Heat oven to 350°F. Place paper baking cup in each of 24 regular-size muffin cups.

2 Mix cake batter as directed on box, using water, oil and eggs. Divide batter evenly among muffin cups. Bake as directed on box. Cool 10 minutes; remove from pan to cooling rack. Cool completely, about 30 minutes.

3 On large round platter or pizza pan, arrange cupcakes, placing them close together. In medium bowl, mix food coloring and frosting. Spread frosting over cupcakes and spaces in between to create one large circle of frosting. Squeeze one large dot of black gel in center of frosting. With gel, draw concentric circles around the dot, spacing them about 2 inches apart. To create the web design, drag a toothpick from the center dot to the outer edge of the circle (about 12 times). Place plastic spiders on web.

High Altitude (3500-6500 ft):: No change.

Nutritional Info: 1 Serving: Calories 240; Total Fat 10g (Saturated Fat 3g); Sodium 190mg; Total Carbohydrate 36g (Dietary Fiber 0g); Protein 1g. Exchanges: 1 Starch, 1-1/2 Other Carbohydrate, 2 Fat. Carbohydrate Choices: 2-1/2.

Betty's Kitchen Tips

Variation: Use gummy spider candies for more color and to make this dessert completely edible.

Purchasing: Look for black cupcake liners with a spiderweb motif to complete the theme.

Success Hint: To easily transport the spiderweb, build it on a portable deli tray that comes with a cover.

autumn leaf cupcakes

Prep Time: 45 Minutes
Start to Finish: 1 Hour 30 Minutes
Servings: 24 cupcakes

- 1 box Betty Crocker® SuperMoist® devil's food cake mix

Water, vegetable oil and eggs as called for on cake mix package

- 1/2 cup semisweet chocolate chips, melted
- 1/2 cup butterscotch chips, melted
- 1 container (1 lb) Betty Crocker® Rich & Creamy chocolate frosting

1 Heat oven to 350°F (325°F for dark or nonstick pan). Make and bake cake mix as directed on box for 24 cupcakes, using water, oil and eggs. Cool 10 minutes; remove from pan to cooling racks. Cool completely, about 30 minutes.

2 Meanwhile, place 12-inch sheet of waxed paper on cookie sheet; mark an 8-inch square on waxed paper. Alternately place spoonfuls of melted chocolate and butterscotch on waxed paper. With small spatula, swirl together for marbled effect, spreading to an 8-inch square. Refrigerate until firm, about 30 minutes.

3 Remove from refrigerator; let stand about 10 minutes or until slightly softened. Use 1-1/2-inch leaf cookie cutter to make 24 leaf cutouts. Carefully remove cutouts from paper with spatula; place on another waxed paper-lined cookie sheet. Refrigerate until firm, about 5 minutes.

4 Frost cupcakes with chocolate frosting. Garnish with leaf cutouts. Store loosely covered in refrigerator.

High Altitude (3500-6500 ft): No change.

Nutritional Info: 1 Cupcake: Calories 240; Total Fat 11g (Saturated Fat 3.5g); Sodium 250mg; Total Carbohydrate 34g (Dietary Fiber 0g); Protein 2g. Exchanges: 1 Starch, 1-1/2 Other Carbohydrate, 2 Fat. Carbohydrate Choices: 2.

Betty's Kitchen Tip

- To melt chocolate and butterscotch chips, place in separate small microwavable bowls. Microwave uncovered on High 30 to 60 seconds; stir until smooth.

peanut butter cupcakes with chocolate frosting

Prep Time: 40 Minutes
Start to Finish: 1 Hour 35 Minutes
Servings: 24 cupcakes

1	box Betty Crocker® SuperMoist® yellow cake mix
1-1/4	cups water
1/4	cup vegetable oil
3	eggs

3/4	cup creamy peanut butter
1	container Betty Crocker® Rich & Creamy chocolate frosting
1/4	cup creamy peanut butter
1/3	cup chopped peanuts

1 Heat oven to 350°F (325°F for dark or nonstick pans). Place paper baking cup in each of 24 regular-size muffin cups.

2 In large bowl, beat cake mix, water, oil, eggs and 3/4 cup peanut butter with electric mixer on low speed 30 seconds. Beat on medium speed 2 minutes, scraping bowl occasionally. Divide batter evenly among muffin cups (about 2/3 full).

3 Bake 20 to 25 minutes or until toothpick inserted in center comes out clean. Remove from pan to cooling rack. Cool completely, about 30 minutes.

4 In medium bowl, stir together frosting and 1/4 cup peanut butter. Frost cupcakes with frosting. Sprinkle with peanuts; press lightly into frosting.

High Altitude (3500-6500 ft): No change.

Nutritional Info: 1 Cupcake: Calories 260; Total Fat 13g (Saturated Fat 3g); Sodium 250mg; Total Carbohydrate 31g (Dietary Fiber 0g); Protein 4g. Exchanges: 1/2 Starch, 1-1/2 Other Carbohydrate, 1/2 High-Fat Meat, 1-1/2 Fat. Carbohydrate Choices: 2.

Betty's Kitchen Tips

Purchasing: Instead of chopping peanuts, look for chopped nuts mix in the baking section of the supermarket. The package size is usually 1/2 cup and contains a mixture of nuts, including peanuts.

Substitution: Betty Crocker® Rich & Creamy cream cheese frosting can be substituted for the chocolate frosting.

Success Hint: Using an ice cream scoop is an easy way to fill muffin cups. Use one that measures out 1/3 cup batter.

dalmatian cupcakes

Prep Time: 10 Minutes
Start to Finish: 1 Hour 15 Minutes
Servings: 24 cupcakes

EASY

2	packages (3 oz each) cream cheese, softened
1/3	cup sugar
1	egg
1-1/2	cups miniature or regular semisweet chocolate chips
1	box Betty Crocker® SuperMoist® devil's food cake mix
1-1/3	cups water
1/3	cup vegetable oil
3	eggs
1	container Betty Crocker® Rich & Creamy or Whipped vanilla frosting

1. Heat oven to 350°F (325°F for dark or nonstick pans). Place paper baking cup in each of 24 regular-size muffin cups.

2. In medium bowl, beat cream cheese, sugar and 1 egg with electric mixer on medium speed until smooth. Stir in 1 cup of the chocolate chips; set aside.

3. In large bowl, beat cake mix, water, oil and 3 eggs on low speed 30 seconds. Beat on medium speed 2 minutes. Divide batter among muffin cups (1/4 cup in each). Top each with 1 heaping teaspoon cream cheese mixture.

4. Bake 17 to 22 minutes or until tops spring back when touched lightly. Cool 10 minutes in pan. Remove from pan; cool completely, about 30 minutes.

5. Frost with frosting. Sprinkle with remaining 1/2 cup chocolate chips. Store loosely covered in refrigerator.

High Altitude (3500-6500 ft): Makes 30 cupcakes.

Nutritional Info: 1 Cupcake: Calories 250; Total Fat 11g (Saturated Fat 3g); Sodium 180mg; Total Carbohydrate 35g (Dietary Fiber 0g); Protein 1g. Exchanges: 1/2 Starch, 2 Other Carbohydrate, 2 Fat. Carbohydrate Choices: 2.

Betty's Kitchen Tips

Special Touch: How about a Dalmatian-themed party? Serve cupcakes with chocolate chip ice cream, play "pin the spot on the dog," and send kids home with a "doggie bag" filled with dog-themed treats and prizes.

Plan Ahead: Wrap individual cupcakes tightly in plastic wrap, and include in lunch boxes for an extra-special lunchtime treat!

jungle animal cupcakes

Prep Time: 2 Hours 45 Minutes
Start to Finish: 2 Hours 45 Minutes
Servings: 24 cupcakes

Cupcakes and Frosting

- 1 box Betty Crocker® SuperMoist® yellow or devil's food cake mix

Water, vegetable oil and eggs as called for on cake mix box

- 1-1/4 cups Betty Crocker® Rich & Creamy chocolate frosting (from 1-lb container)

Black food color

- 2-1/2 cups Betty Crocker® Rich & Creamy vanilla frosting (from two 1-lb containers)

Yellow food color

Red food color

Lion Decorations

- 1-1/2 cups caramel popcorn
- 12 brown miniature candy-coated chocolate baking bits
- 12 pretzel sticks
- 12 pieces Cheerios® cereal (any flavor)

Tiger Decorations

- 12 brown miniature candy-coated chocolate baking bits
- 12 orange chewy fruit-flavored gumdrops (not sugar coated), cut in half crosswise, top halves discarded

Monkey Decorations

- 12 brown miniature candy-coated chocolate baking bits
- 6 miniature marshmallows, cut in half crosswise, pieces flattened
- 12 small round chocolate-covered creamy mints

Zebra Decorations

- 6 round vanilla wafer cookies
- 24 brown miniature candy-coated chocolate baking bits
- 6 black chewy licorice-flavored gumdrops (not sugar coated), cut in half vertically

1 Heat oven to 350°F (325°F for dark or nonstick pans). Place paper baking cup in each of 24 regular-size muffin cups. Make and bake cake mix as directed on box for cupcakes, using water, oil and eggs. Cool in pans 10 minutes; remove from pans to cooling racks. Cool completely, about 30 minutes. Decorate cupcakes to make 6 lions, 6 tigers, 6 monkeys and 6 zebras.

2 In small bowl, mix 1/2 cup chocolate frosting with black food color to make black frosting. Place in resealable food-storage plastic freezer bag; cut small tip off 1 bottom corner of bag. Will use black frosting to decorate lions, tigers, monkeys and zebras.

3 **Lions and Tigers:** In medium bowl, mix 1 cup vanilla frosting with enough yellow and red food colors to make orange. In small bowl, mix 1 tablespoon orange frosting with 3 tablespoons white vanilla frosting to make lighter orange for muzzles. Frost 12 cupcakes with darker orange frosting. For muzzle, spread or pipe small circle of lighter orange frosting on each cupcake.

4 For lions, place caramel corn around edges of cupcakes for mane. For eyes, add brown baking bits. For whiskers, break about 1/2-inch pieces off each end of pretzel sticks and insert in cupcakes. For ears, add cereal pieces. Using black frosting, pipe on mouth and nose.

5 For tigers, use black frosting to pipe on the stripes, nose and mouth. For eyes, add brown baking bits. For ears, add gumdrop halves.

6 **Monkeys:** Frost 6 cupcakes with chocolate frosting. In small bowl, mix 1 tablespoon chocolate frosting and 2 tablespoons

vanilla frosting to make light brown. For muzzle, spread or pipe circle of light brown on each cupcake that starts in middle and extends to edge; pipe small tuft of hair on opposite edge. For each eye, attach brown baking bit to marshmallow half with frosting; place on cupcakes. With black frosting, pipe on nose and mouth. For ears, add mints.

7 **Zebras:** Cut small horizontal slit in top of 6 cupcakes near edge of paper cup. Insert edge of vanilla wafer cookie into each slit to create elongated face, adding small amount of vanilla frosting to cookie before inserting to help stick. Frost cupcakes with vanilla frosting. For muzzles, frost cookies with black frosting. With black frosting, pipe on stripes and mane. Add brown baking bits for nostrils and eyes. For ears, add black gumdrop halves, cut sides down.

High Altitude (3500-6500 ft): No change.

Nutritional Info: 1 Frosted Cupcake (Undecorated): Calories 270; Total Fat 10g (Saturated Fat 2.5g); Sodium 240mg; Total Carbohydrate 44g (Dietary Fiber 0g); Protein 1g. Exchanges: 1/2 Starch, 2-1/2 Other Carbohydrate, 2 Fat. Carbohydrate Choices: 3.

Betty's Kitchen Tip

• Get a party menu, prep guide, tips, party games, activities and more for a Zoo-rrific Kids Birthday Party!

pecan-bourbon italian cream cups

Prep Time: 40 Minutes
Start to Finish: 1 Hour 40 Minutes
Servings: 20 cupcakes

Susan Scarborough, Fernandina Beach, FL
Celebrate the Season-Fall Baking Contest
Grand Prize Winner

Cake

4	eggs
1/2	cup water
4-1/2	teaspoons bourbon or apple cider
1	teaspoon vanilla
2-1/4	cups cake flour
1-1/2	cups granulated sugar
2	teaspoons baking powder
1	bag (5 oz) glazed pecans, finely chopped
15	tablespoons butter or margarine, softened

1	package (8 oz) cream cheese, softened

Frosting

9	tablespoons butter or margarine, slightly softened
2	tablespoons bourbon or apple cider
1/2	teaspoon finely grated lemon peel
1/8	teaspoon salt
4-1/2	cups powdered sugar
3/4	cup flaked coconut

1 Heat oven to 350°F. Place paper baking cup in each of 20 regular-size muffin cups.

2 In 2-cup glass measure, mix eggs, water, 4-1/2 teaspoons bourbon and the vanilla with wire whisk. In medium bowl, mix flour, granulated sugar and baking powder. Remove 1 tablespoon of the flour mixture to small bowl; add 3/4 cup of the glazed pecans and toss to coat. Set aside. Reserve remaining glazed pecans for frosting.

3 Cut butter into tablespoon-size pieces. Cut 3 tablespoons of the cream cheese into cubes; reserve remaining cheese. Add butter pieces and cream cheese cubes, a few at a time, to flour mixture in medium bowl, beating with electric mixer on low speed. Pour in all but 1/2 cup of the egg mixture. Beat on low 30 seconds, then medium 30 seconds, scraping bowl occasionally. Add remaining egg mixture in a slow stream; beat 30 seconds longer. Stir in reserved pecan mixture.

4 Spoon into muffin cups. Bake 20 to 25 minutes or until tops spring back when lightly touched. Cool 5 minutes; remove from pans to cooling racks. Cool completely, about 30 minutes.

5 Meanwhile, in large bowl, beat 9 tablespoons butter, 2 tablespoons bourbon, the lemon peel, salt and reserved cream cheese with electric mixer on low speed until smooth. Gradually beat in powdered sugar, 1 cup at a time, on low speed until smooth. Stir in 1/2 cup of the reserved glazed pecans and the coconut.

6 Spread frosting on top of each cupcake; sprinkle with remaining glazed pecans.

High Altitude (3500-6500 ft): No change.

Nutritional Info: 1 Cupcake: Calories 480; Total Fat 25g (Saturated Fat 13g); Sodium 250mg; Total Carbohydrate 57g (Dietary Fiber 1g); Protein 4g. Exchanges: 1-1/2 Starch, 2-1/2 Other Carbohydrate, 5 Fat. Carbohydrate Choices: 4.

sour cream chocolate cupcakes

Prep Time: 30 Minutes
Start to Finish: 55 Minutes
Servings: 3 dozen cupcakes

. . . .

Cupcakes

2	cups Gold Medal® all-purpose flour
2	cups granulated sugar
3/4	cup sour cream
1/4	cup shortening
1	cup water
1-1/4	teaspoons baking soda
1	teaspoon salt
1	teaspoon vanilla
1/2	teaspoon baking powder
2	eggs
4	oz unsweetened baking chocolate, melted and cooled

Rich Chocolate Buttercream Frosting

4	cups powdered sugar
1	cup butter or margarine, softened
3	tablespoons milk
1-1/2	teaspoons vanilla
3	oz unsweetened baking chocolate, melted and cooled

. . . .

1 Heat oven to 350°F. Line 36 regular-size muffin cups with paper baking cups. In large bowl, beat all cupcake ingredients with electric mixer on low speed 30 seconds, scraping bowl constantly. Beat on high speed 3 minutes, scraping bowl occasionally. Divide batter evenly among muffin cups, filling each 1/2 full.

2 Bake 20 to 25 minutes or until toothpick inserted in center comes out clean. Remove from pan; place on cooling rack. Cool completely.

3 In medium bowl, beat all frosting ingredients with electric mixer on medium speed until smooth and spreadable. If necessary, stir in additional milk, about 1 teaspoon at a time. Spread frosting over cupcakes.

Nutrition Info: 1 Cupcake: Calories 230; Total Fat 10g (Saturated Fat 5g, Trans Fat nc); Cholesterol 30mg; Sodium 160mg; Total Carbohydrate 33g (Dietary Fiber 0g, Sugars nc); Protein 1g. Exchanges: 1/2 Starch, 1-1/2 Other Carbohydrate, 2 Fat. Carbohydrate Choices: 2.

Betty's Kitchen Tips

Simplify: Use ready-to-spread chocolate frosting instead of the homemade buttercream. You'll still get rave reviews for these sensational sweets!

Time-Saver: Instead of making chocolate cutouts, buy Betty Crocker© chocolate decorator shapes; they are available at many supermarkets or at cake decorating supply stores.

gingerbread cupcakes

Prep Time: 30 Minutes
Start to Finish: 1 Hour 25 Minutes
Servings: 18 cupcakes

Cupcakes

1/2	cup granulated sugar
1/2	cup butter or margarine, softened
1/2	cup molasses
2	eggs
2	cups Gold Medal® all-purpose flour
1	teaspoon baking soda
1/2	teaspoon salt
1-1/2	teaspoons ground ginger
1/2	teaspoon ground cinnamon

1/2	teaspoon ground allspice
3/4	cup water

Frosting

1	package (8 oz) cream cheese, softened
1/4	cup butter or margarine, softened
2	teaspoons grated lemon peel
1	teaspoon ground cinnamon
1	teaspoon vanilla
4	cups (1 lb) powdered sugar
1	to 2 teaspoons milk

1 Heat oven to 375°F. Place paper baking cup in each of 18 regular-size muffin cups.

2 In large bowl, beat granulated sugar, 1/2 cup butter, the molasses and eggs with electric mixer on medium speed, or mix with spoon. Stir in flour, baking soda, salt, ginger, 1/2 teaspoon cinnamon, the allspice and water. Spoon about 1/4 cup batter into each muffin cup.

3 Bake 15 to 18 minutes or until toothpick inserted in center comes out clean. Cool 5 minutes; remove from pans to cooling racks. Cool completely, about 20 minutes.

4 Meanwhile, in medium bowl, beat cream cheese, 1/4 cup butter, the lemon peel, 1 teaspoon cinnamon and the vanilla with electric mixer on low speed until smooth. Gradually beat in powdered sugar, 1 cup at a time, on low speed until smooth. Beat in the milk, 1 teaspoon at a time, until spreadable.

5 Pipe or spread a generous amount of frosting on top of each cupcake. Store covered in refrigerator.

High Altitude (3500-6500 ft): No change.

Nutritional Info: 1 Cupcake: Calories 330; Total Fat 13g (Saturated Fat 8g); Sodium 240mg; Total Carbohydrate 51g (Dietary Fiber 0g); Protein 3g. Exchanges: 1 Starch, 2-1/2 Other Carbohydrate, 2-1/2 Fat. Carbohydrate Choices: 3-1/2.

Betty's Kitchen Tip

• Either light or dark molasses can be used in the cupcake batter.

goin' fishin' cupcakes

Prep Time: 5 Minutes
Start to Finish: 1 Hour 45 Minutes
Servings: 24 cupcakes

EASY

Cupcakes

1 box Betty Crocker® SuperMoist®
devil's food cake mix

Water, vegetable oil and eggs as called for on cake
mix box

1 container Betty Crocker® Rich & Creamy
vanilla or butter cream frosting

Blue food color

Fishing Poles

24 cocktail straws

24 pieces dental floss

24 Betty Crocker® Shark Bites® chewy fruit
snacks (2 to 3 pouches)

1 Heat oven to 350°F (325°F for dark or
nonstick pans). Make and cool cake as
directed on box for 24 cupcakes.

2 Stir together frosting and 2 or 3 drops
food color. Frost cupcakes with blue
frosting; pull up on frosting, using metal
spatula, so frosting looks like waves.

3 To make fishing poles, cut each straw to
make one 3-inch piece. Cut dental floss into
3-1/2-inch lengths. Attach piece of dental
floss to end of each straw, using needle, to
look like fish line. Attach 1 fruit snack to
end of each piece of dental floss. Decorate
each cupcake with a fishing pole. Store
loosely covered.

High Altitude (3500-6500 ft): No change.

Nutritional Info: 1 Cupcake: Calories 220; Total Fat 11g
(Saturated Fat 3g); Sodium 220mg; Total Carbohydrate 30g
(Dietary Fiber 0g); Protein 2g. Exchanges: 1 Starch, 1 Other
Carbohydrate, 2 Fat. Carbohydrate Choices: 2.

Betty's Kitchen Tips

Special Touch: Keep the party theme going by
serving blue raspberry punch with "fishy" ice
cubes. Place 1 Shark Bites® chewy fruit snack
in each section of an ice-cube tray. Fill with
ginger ale or water, and freeze until solid.

Success Hint: Find out what the party boy or
girl's favorite cake flavor is, and use that instead
of the devil's food cake mix.

lemon crème cupcakes

Prep Time: 35 Minutes
Start to Finish: 1 Hour 40 Minutes
Servings: 24 cupcakes

Cupcakes

1   box Betty Crocker® SuperMoist®
    yellow or lemon cake mix

Water, vegetable oil and eggs as called for on cake
mix box

Filling

3/4   cup Betty Crocker® Whipped vanilla
     frosting (from 12-oz container)

1/2   cup marshmallow creme

Frosting

1   container (12 oz) Betty Crocker®
    Whipped butter cream frosting

2   teaspoons grated lemon peel

4   teaspoons fresh lemon juice

1/4   cup Betty Crocker® star decors

1 Heat oven to 350°F (325°F for dark or nonstick pans). Make and bake cake mix as directed on box for 24 cupcakes, using water, oil and eggs. Cool in pans 10 minutes; remove from pans to cooling racks. Cool completely, about 30 minutes.

2 By slowly spinning end of round handle of wooden spoon back and forth, make deep, 3/4-inch-wide indentation in center of top of each cupcake, not quite to bottom (wiggle end of spoon in cupcake to make opening large enough).

3 In small bowl, mix filling ingredients. Spoon into small resealable food-storage plastic bag; seal bag. Cut 3/8-inch tip off one bottom corner of bag. Insert tip of bag into opening in each cupcake; squeeze bag to fill opening.

4 In medium bowl, stir together 1 container butter cream frosting, the lemon peel and lemon juice. Frost the cupcakes. Sprinkle with stars.

High Altitude (3500-6500 ft): No change.

Nutritional Info: 1 Cupcake: Calories 220; Total Fat 9g (Saturated Fat 2.5g); Sodium 170mg; Total Carbohydrate 31g (Dietary Fiber 0g); Protein 1g. Exchanges: 2 Other Carbohydrate, 2 Fat. Carbohydrate Choices: 2.

Betty's Kitchen Tips

Special Touch: Use sugared edible flowers to garnish these cupcakes.

Did You Know? You'll get more lemon juice from a room-temperature lemon than you will get from a cold one.

mini candy bar cupcakes

Prep Time: 20 Minutes
Start to Finish: 1 Hour 10 Minutes
Servings: 72 mini cupcakes

- 5 bars (2.1 oz each) chocolate-covered crispy peanut-buttery candy
- 1 box (1 lb 2.25 oz) Betty Crocker® SuperMoist® white cake mix

Water, vegetable oil and egg whites as called for on cake mix box

- 1 container (12 oz) Betty Crocker® Whipped milk chocolate frosting

1 Heat oven to 350°F (325°F for dark or nonstick pans). Place paper baking cup in each of 72 mini muffin cups. Finely chop enough candy to equal 3/4 cup (about 2 bars).

2 In large bowl, beat cake mix, water, oil and egg whites with electric mixer on low speed 30 seconds. Beat on medium speed 2 minutes, scraping bowl occasionally. Beat in chopped candy on low speed just until blended. Divide batter evenly among muffin cups (2/3 full). Refrigerate any remaining cake batter until ready to use.

3 Bake 12 to 16 minutes or until toothpick inserted in center comes out clean. Cool about 5 minutes; remove from pan to wire rack. Cool completely, about 30 minutes. Frost cupcakes with frosting. Coarsely chop remaining candy. Place candy pieces on frosting, pressing down slightly. Store cupcakes loosely covered at room temperature.

High Altitude (3500-6500 ft): No change.

Nutritional Info: 1 Cupcake: Calories 80; Total Fat 3.5g (Saturated Fat 1.5g); Sodium 65mg; Total Carbohydrate 11g (Dietary Fiber 0g); Protein 0g. Exchanges: 1 Other Carbohydrate, 1/2 Fat. Carbohydrate Choices: 1.

Betty's Kitchen Tips

Success Hint: If frosting is too soft to hold its shape as you pipe it, refrigerate the filled tube for about 5 minutes. A slight chill will thicken the frosting, but do not allow it to refrigerate until it is firm.

Do-Ahead: Bake these cupcakes, but don't frost them. Place in an airtight container and freeze. A few hours before serving, remove them from the freezer, frost and decorate.

chocolate raspberry cupcakes

Prep Time: 50 Minutes
Start to Finish: 1 Hour 50 Minutes
Servings: 26 cupcakes

Cupcakes

24	foil paper baking cups
1	box Betty Crocker® SuperMoist® milk chocolate cake mix

Water, vegetable oil and eggs as called for on cake mix box

2	tablespoons unsweetened baking cocoa
1	teaspoon vanilla

Filling

1	cup seedless raspberry jam

Frosting

5	oz semisweet chocolate
1/3	cup milk
3	tablespoons instant espresso powder
3/4	cup shortening
3/4	cup butter, softened
1-1/2	teaspoons vanilla
1/8	teaspoon coarse kosher salt
5	cups powdered sugar

Garnish

Extra fine edible glitter or decorator sugar crystals, if desired

1 Heat oven to 325°F. Remove and discard paper liners from inside foil baking cups; place foil baking cup in each of 24 regular-size muffin cups. Make cake mix as directed on box using water, oil, eggs and adding cocoa and vanilla. Bake 17 to 20 minutes or until toothpick inserted in center comes out clean. Cool in pans 10 minutes; remove from pans to cooling racks. Cool completely, about 30 minutes.

2 Fit #6 round tip in decorating bag (opening about 1/8 inch in diameter). Spoon jam into decorating bag. Insert tip in center of cupcake, about halfway down. Gently squeeze decorating bag, pulling upwards until cupcake swells slightly and filling comes to the top.

3 In small microwaveable bowl, microwave chocolate on High 1 minute 30 seconds, stirring every 30 seconds, until chocolate can be stirred smooth, set aside.

4 In small microwaveable bowl, microwave milk on High 30 to 45 seconds until very warm. Stir in espresso powder until dissolved. Allow mixture to cool to room temperature, about 10 minutes.

5 In large bowl, mix shortening and butter with electric mixer on medium speed, about 30 seconds or until smooth. Add cooled chocolate, vanilla, salt and milk mixture and continue to beat on medium speed until smooth. On low speed, scraping bowl occasionally, gradually add powdered sugar until frosting is thick and smooth.

6 Fit #1 round tip (opening about 1/2 inch in diameter) into decorating bag. Spoon frosting into decorating bag; use round tip to generously pipe frosting in circular motion, leaving 1/4-inch border around cupcake. Dust with edible glitter.

High Altitude (3500-6500 ft): No change.

Nutritional Info: 1 Cupcake: Calories 370; Total Fat 17g (Saturated Fat 7g); Sodium 190mg; Total Carbohydrate 52g (Dietary Fiber 0g); Protein 2g. Exchanges: 1/2 Starch, 3 Other Carbohydrate, 3-1/2 Fat. Carbohydrate Choices: 3-1/2.

Betty's Kitchen Tip

• To make this recipe for a wedding, double the recipe as many times as needed.

pink champagne cupcakes

Prep Time: 25 Minutes
Start to Finish: 1 Hour 15 Minutes
Servings: 24 cupcakes

Champagne Cupcakes

1	box Betty Crocker® SuperMoist® white cake mix
1-1/4	cups champagne
1/3	cup vegetable oil
3	egg whites
4	or 5 drops red food color

Champagne Frosting

1/2	cup butter or margarine, softened
4	cups powdered sugar
1/4	cup champagne
1	teaspoon vanilla
4	to 5 drops red food coloring

Garnish

Pink decorator sugar crystals

Edible pink pearls

1 Heat oven to 350°F (325°F for dark or nonstick pan). Place paper baking cup in each of 24 regular-size muffin cups.

2 In large bowl, combine dry cake mix and champagne. Add oil, eggs and food color. Beat with electric mixer on medium speed for 2 minutes. Divide batter evenly among muffin cups.

3 Bake 17 to 22 minutes or until toothpick inserted in center comes out clean. Cool 10 minutes; remove from pan to cooling rack. Cool completely, about 30 minutes.

4 In medium bowl, beat frosting ingredients with electric mixer on medium speed until smooth. Frost cupcakes. Sprinkle with pink sugar and pearls.

High Altitude (3500-6500 ft): No change.

Nutritional Info: 1 Cupcake: Calories 230; Total Fat 8g (Saturated Fat 3.5g); Sodium 180mg; Total Carbohydrate 38g (Dietary Fiber 0g); Protein 1g. Exchanges: 1/2 Starch, 2 Other Carbohydrate, 1-1/2 Fat. Carbohydrate Choices: 2-1/2.

Betty's Kitchen Tips

Purchasing: For pink decorator sugar crystals, edible pink pearls and decorative cupcake liners, check out www.fancyflours.com.

Success Hint: Champagne is a sparkling wine, and while many expensive champagnes are available, this is one time you might choose a less expensive bottle. Have the champagne at room temperature when preparing the cake.

strawberry and cream cupcakes

Prep Time: 30 Minutes
Start to Finish: 1 Hour 30 Minutes
Servings: 24 cupcakes

1	box Betty Crocker® SuperMoist® white cake mix
1-1/4	cups strawberry-flavored soda pop

Vegetable oil and egg whites as called for on cake mix box

Red food color

1	container (1 lb) Betty Crocker® Rich & Creamy® cream cheese frosting
1/2	cup Betty Crocker® white candy sprinkles

Fresh strawberries, if desired

1 Heat oven to 350°F (325°F for dark or nonstick pans). Place paper baking cup in each of 24 regular-size muffin cups. Make and bake cake mix as directed on box for 24 cupcakes, substituting soda pop for the water and using oil and egg whites. Cool in pan 10 minutes; remove from pan to cooling rack. Cool completely, about 30 minutes

2 Stir 1 or 2 drops food color into frosting. Frost cupcakes.

3 In small resealable food-storage plastic bag, place sprinkles and 1 drop food color; seal bag. Gently shake and massage sprinkles until mixture is various shades of pink; sprinkle around edges of frosted cupcakes. Garnish with fresh strawberries.

High Altitude (3500-6500 ft): No change.

Nutritional Info: 1 Cupcake: Calories 230; Total Fat 10g (Saturated Fat 3g); Sodium 200mg; Total Carbohydrate 32g (Dietary Fiber 0g); Protein 2g. Exchanges: 1/2 Starch, 1-1/2 Other Carbohydrate, 2 Fat. Carbohydrate Choices: 2.

Betty's Kitchen Tip

• If you have only one 12-cup muffin pan, cover and refrigerate the rest of the batter while baking the first batch. Then bake the rest of the batter in the cooled muffin pan, adding 1 or 2 minutes to the bake time.

baby rattle cupcakes

Prep Time: 45 Minutes
Start to Finish: 1 Hour 45 Minutes
Servings: 24 cupcakes

- 1 box Betty Crocker® SuperMoist® cake mix (any flavor)
- Water, vegetable oil and eggs as called for on cake mix box
- 1 container (1 lb) Betty Crocker® Rich & Creamy vanilla or creamy white frosting
- Betty Crocker® yellow and green decorating icings (from 4.25-oz tubes)

- Betty Crocker® candy sprinkles and decors, if desired
- 8 yards pastel satin or curling ribbon (1/4 inch), if desired
- 24 paper lollipop sticks (4-1/2 inch)
- 24 small gumdrops

1 Heat oven to 350°F for shiny metal pans (or 325°F for dark or nonstick pans). Place paper baking cup in each of 24 regular-size muffin cups. Make and bake cupcakes as directed on box, using water, oil and eggs. Cool 10 minutes; remove from pan. Cool completely, about 30 minutes.

2 Frost cupcakes with vanilla frosting. Pipe designs on cupcakes with yellow and green icings. Decorate as desired with candy sprinkles.

3 With toothpick, poke hole in side of each cupcake. Tie ribbon bow in center of each lollipop stick. Add gumdrop to one end of each stick. Insert other ends of sticks into sides of cupcakes, just below frosting, to form rattles.

High Altitude (3500-6500 ft): No change.

Nutritional Info: 1 Frosted Cupcake (Undecorated): Calories 200; Total Fat 8g (Saturated Fat 1.5g); Sodium 190mg; Total Carbohydrate 30g (Dietary Fiber 0g); Protein 1g. Exchanges: 1/2 Starch, 1-1/2 Other Carbohydrate, 1-1/2 Fat. Carbohydrate Choices: 2.

Betty's Kitchen Tips

How-To: Use a decorating bag and tips to pipe designs on the cupcakes. Or fill a resealable food-storage plastic bag with frosting and snip a small opening in one bottom corner of the bag; squeeze bag to pipe the frosting.

Purchasing: Lollipop sticks can be purchased online at www.wilton.com.

bunny cupcakes

Prep Time: 30 Minutes
Start to Finish: 1 Hour 45 Minutes
Servings: 24 cupcakes

1 box Betty Crocker® SuperMoist®
yellow or white cake mix

Water, vegetable oil and eggs as called for on cake mix box

Betty Crocker® pink cupcake icing

Betty Crocker® white cupcake icing

5 large marshmallows

Pink sugar

Candy decorations and sprinkles, as desired

1 Heat oven to 350°F (325°F for dark or nonstick pans). Place paper baking cup in each of 24 regular-size muffin cups. Make and bake cake mix as directed on box for 24 cupcakes, using water, oil and eggs. Cool in pan 10 minutes; remove from pan to cooling rack. Cool completely, about 30 minutes.

2 Gently frost all 24 cupcakes with the pink icing.

3 Spoon 1 heaping teaspoonful white icing on center of each cupcake. To make ears, cut each large marshmallow crosswise into 5 pieces with kitchen scissors. Using scissors, cut through center of each marshmallow piece to within 1/4 inch of edge. Separate to look like bunny ears; press 1 side of cut edges into pink sugar, flattening slightly. Arrange on each of the white icing mounds. Use candy decorations and sprinkles to make eyes, nose and whiskers. Store loosely covered.

High Altitude (3500-6500 ft): No change.

Nutritional Info: 1 Cupcake (Cake and Frosting only): Calories 250; Total Fat 11g (Saturated Fat 3g); Sodium 180mg; Total Carbohydrate 35g (Dietary Fiber 0g); Protein 1g. Exchanges: 1/2 Starch, 2 Other Carbohydrate, 2 Fat. Carbohydrate Choices: 2.

Betty's Kitchen Tip

• Cupcakes are a nice size for a kids' party. These would be great for an Easter party or a Peter Rabbit-themed birthday party.

sunflower cupcake bouquet

Prep Time: 30 Minutes
Start to Finish: 1 Hour 55 Minutes
Servings: 60 mini cupcakes

1   box Betty Crocker® SuperMoist® white or yellow cake mix

Water, vegetable oil and eggs as called for on cake mix box

2   cans (16 oz each) Betty Crocker® Rich & Creamy creamy white frosting

1   cup powdered sugar

Food coloring

60   black gummy raspberries

Green tissue paper

Green pail or clay pot

Green floral oasis

7   wooden skewers

7   pieces green licorice

7   candy spearmint leaves

1   Heat oven to 350°F. Place miniature paper baking cup in each of 60 mini muffin cups. Make cake mix as directed on box, using water, oil and eggs. Fill muffin cups 3/4 full (about 1 heaping tablespoon each.)

2   Bake 10 to 15 minutes or until toothpick inserted in center comes out clean. Cool in pans 5 minutes. Remove from pans to cooling racks. Cool completely, about 30 minutes.

3   Spoon frosting into a mixing bowl. Stir in powdered sugar and desired food coloring, mixing to blend completely. Fit on open star tip (#18) on a pastry bag and fill with frosting. On each cupcake, pipe 6 lines from the center of the cupcake, out to the edge, making an evenly spaced "spoke-like pattern" on each. With the same tip, start in the center and make a loop by going down one side of each spoke, turning at the edge of the cupcake and following the next spoke back into the center. Repeat ending with 6 loops. Place black gummy raspberry in center of each cupcake.

4   Place 2 sheets of tissue paper inside pail. Cut dry oasis to fit inside pail. Thread wooden skewer through green licorice. Thread spearmint leaf on skewer and then cupcake. Repeat to make 6 additional flowers. Arrange flowers in pail. Place remaining cupcakes on platter.

High Altitude (3500-6500 ft): No change.

Nutritional Info: 1 Mini Cupcake: Calories 270; Total Fat 10g (Saturated Fat 2.5g); Sodium 230mg; Total Carbohydrate 42g (Dietary Fiber 0g); Protein 1g. Exchanges: 3 Other Carbohydrate, 2 Fat. Carbohydrate Choices: 3.

Betty's Kitchen Tip

• We used seven of the cupcakes to make a cute bouquet and arranged the remaining cupcakes on a large platter.

piña colada cupcakes

Prep Time: 15 Minutes
Start to Finish: 1 Hour 45 Minutes
Servings: 24 cupcakes

EASY

- 1 box Betty Crocker® SuperMoist® yellow cake mix
- 1/3 cup vegetable oil
- 1/4 cup water
- 1 teaspoon rum extract
- 1 can (8 oz) crushed pineapple in juice, undrained
- 3 eggs
- 1 teaspoon coconut extract
- 1 teaspoon rum extract
- 1 container (12 oz) Betty Crocker® Whipped vanilla frosting
- 3/4 cup shredded coconut

1. Heat oven to 375°F (350°F for dark or nonstick pan). Place paper baking cup in each of 24 regular-size muffin cups.

2. In large bowl, beat cake mix, oil, water, 1 teaspoon rum extract, the pineapple and eggs with electric mixer on low speed 30 seconds. Beat on medium speed 2 minutes, scraping bowl occasionally. Divide batter evenly among muffin cups.

3. Bake 18 to 24 minutes or until toothpick inserted in center comes out clean. Cool 10 minutes; remove from pan to wire rack. Cool completely, about 30 minutes.

4. Stir coconut extract and 1 teaspoon rum extract into frosting. Spread frosting on cupcakes. Dip tops of frosted cupcakes in coconut. Store cupcakes loosely covered at room temperature.

High Altitude (3500-6500 ft): No change.

Nutritional Info: 1 Cupcake: Calories 210; Total Fat 10g (Saturated Fat 3g); Sodium 170mg; Total Carbohydrate 29g (Dietary Fiber 0g); Protein 2g. Exchanges: 1/2 Starch, 1-1/2 Other Carbohydrate, 2 Fat. Carbohydrate Choices: 2.

Betty's Kitchen Tips

Purchasing: For very white-on-white cupcakes, use Betty Crocker® Whipped whipped cream frosting instead of the vanilla frosting.

Special Touch: Decorate cupcakes with paper umbrellas to evoke feelings of sitting on the beach.

ball game cupcakes

Prep Time: 35 Minutes
Start to Finish: 1 Hour 55 Minutes
Servings: 24 cupcakes

- 1   box Betty Crocker® SuperMoist® yellow cake mix
- 1   cup water
- 1/3 cup vegetable oil
- 3   eggs
- 1   cup miniature semisweet chocolate chips

- 1   container (1 lb) Betty Crocker® Rich & Creamy vanilla frosting

Assorted colors Betty Crocker® decorating icing (in 4.25-oz tubes) or Betty Crocker® Easy Flow decorating icing (in 6.4-oz cans)

Assorted food colors

1 Heat oven to 350°F (325°F for dark or nonstick pans). Place paper baking cup in each of 24 regular-size muffin cups.

2 Make cake batter as directed on box except gently stir chocolate chips into batter. Divide batter evenly among muffin cups (about 2/3 full).

3 Bake 20 to 25 minutes or until toothpick inserted in center comes out clean. Cool 10 minutes; remove from pan to cooling rack. Cool completely, about 30 minutes. Decorate as desired.

4 **Soccer balls:** Frost cupcakes with vanilla frosting. With black icing, pipe a pentagon shape in the center of cupcake, piping a few rows of icing into center of pentagon. Pipe lines from pentagon to edge of cupcake to resemble seams. With toothpick or spatula, spread black icing in center of pentagon to fill in the entire shape.

Basketballs: Color frosting with yellow and red food colors to make orange; frost cupcakes. With black icing, pipe line across center of cupcake. On either side, pipe an arch that curves slightly toward center line.

Tennis balls: Color frosting with yellow and green food colors to make tennis-ball yellow; frost cupcakes. With white icing, pipe curved design to resemble tennis balls.

Baseballs: Frost cupcakes with vanilla frosting. With black, red or blue icing, pipe 2 arches on opposite sides of cupcakes, curving lines slightly toward center. Pipe small lines from each arch to resemble stitches on a baseball.

5 Store cupcakes loosely covered at room temperature.

High Altitude (3500-6500 ft): No change.

Nutritional Info: 1 Cupcake: Calories 260; Total Fat 11g (Saturated Fat 6g); Sodium 150mg; Total Carbohydrate 39g (Dietary Fiber 0g); Protein 2g. Exchanges: 1 Starch, 1-1/2 Other Carbohydrate, 2 Fat. Carbohydrate Choices: 2-1/2.

SPECIAL CHEESECAKES

p.220

212

218

206

almond cheesecake

Prep Time: 40 Minutes
Start to Finish: 7 Hours 45 Minutes
Servings: 16

Crust

1 box Betty Crocker® SuperMoist® yellow cake mix

1/2 cup butter or margarine, softened

Filling

3 packages (8 oz each) cream cheese, softened

3/4 cup sugar

1 cup whipping (heavy) cream

1 teaspoon almond extract

3 eggs

Garnish

1/4 cup sliced almonds

4 teaspoons sugar

Fresh raspberries, if desired

1 Heat oven to 350°F for shiny metal pan (or 325°F for dark or nonstick pan). Spray bottom and side of 10-inch springform pan with baking spray with flour. Wrap outside of side and bottom of pan with foil.

2 Reserve 1/2 cup of the cake mix; set aside. In large bowl, beat remaining cake mix and butter with electric mixer on low speed until crumbly. Press in bottom and 1-1/2 inches up side of pan. Bake 15 minutes or until edges are golden brown. Reduce oven temperature to 325°F for shiny metal pan (or 300°F for dark or nonstick pan).

3 In same large bowl, beat reserved 1/2 cup cake mix and cream cheese on medium speed until well blended. Beat in 3/4 cup sugar, the whipping cream and almond extract on medium speed until smooth and creamy. On low speed, beat in eggs, one at a time, until well blended. Pour batter over crust. Place springform pan in large roasting pan; place on oven rack. Pour enough boiling water into roasting pan to cover half of side of springform pan.

4 Bake 55 to 60 minutes or until edge is set but center jiggles slightly when moved. Cool in pan (in water bath) on cooling rack 20 minutes. Remove pan from water bath. Carefully run knife around side of pan to loosen, but do not remove side of pan. Cool 1 hour 30 minutes at room temperature.

5 Cover loosely; refrigerate at least 4 hours or overnight.

6 Meanwhile, in 1-quart saucepan, cook almonds and 4 teaspoons sugar over low heat about 10 minutes, stirring constantly, until sugar is melted and almonds are coated. Cool on waxed paper; break apart.

7 Carefully remove side of pan before serving. Garnish cheesecake with sugared almonds. Store covered in refrigerator.

High Altitude (3500-6500 feet): No changes.

Nutritional Info: 1 Serving: Calories 440; Total Fat 30g (Saturated Fat 17g); Sodium 390mg; Total Carbohydrate 39g (Dietary Fiber 0g); Protein 6g. Exchanges: 1 Starch, 1-1/2 Other Carbohydrate, 1/2 High-Fat Meat, 5 Fat. Carbohydrate Choices: 2-1/2.

crème brûlée cheesecake bars

Prep Time: 15 Minutes
Start to Finish: 4 Hours 20 Minutes
Servings: 36 bars

Jeanne Holt
St. Paul, MN
Cookie Mix Contest 2010

EASY

1	pouch (1 lb 1.5 oz) Betty Crocker® sugar cookie mix
1	box (4-serving size) French vanilla instant pudding and pie filling mix
2	tablespoons packed brown sugar
1/2	cup butter or margarine, melted
2-1/2	teaspoons vanilla
2	whole eggs
2	packages (8 oz each) cream cheese, softened
1/2	cup sour cream
1/2	cup granulated sugar
3	egg yolks
2/3	cup toffee bits, finely crushed

1 Heat oven to 350°F. Lightly spray bottom and sides of 13x9-inch pan with cooking spray.

2 In large bowl, stir cookie mix, pudding mix, brown sugar, butter, 1 teaspoon of the vanilla and 1 whole egg until soft dough forms. Press dough in bottom and 1/2 inch up sides of pan.

3 In small bowl, beat cream cheese, sour cream and granulated sugar with electric mixer on medium speed until smooth. Add remaining whole egg, 3 egg yolks and remaining 1-1/2 teaspoons vanilla; beat until smooth. Spread over crust in pan.

4 Bake 30 to 35 minutes or until set in center. Immediately sprinkle top with crushed toffee bits. Cool 30 minutes. Refrigerate about 3 hours or until chilled. Cut into 9 rows by 4 rows. Store covered in refrigerator.

High Altitude (3500-6500 feet): No change.

Nutritional Info: 1 Bar: Calories 190; Total Fat 11g (Saturated Fat 6g); Sodium 160mg; Total Carbohydrate 20g (Dietary Fiber 0g); Protein 2g. Exchanges: 1/2 Starch, 1 Other Carbohydrate, 2 Fat. Carbohydrate Choices: 1.

Betty's Kitchen Tip

• To crush the toffee bits, place in a small resealable food-storage plastic bag; pound with a rolling pin or flat side of a meat mallet.

peanut butter brownie cheesecake

Prep Time: 20 Minutes
Start to Finish: 11 Hours 35 Minutes
Servings: 16

- 1 pouch (1 lb 1.5 oz) Betty Crocker® peanut butter cookie mix
- Water, oil and egg as called for on cookie mix pouch
- 1 box Betty Crocker® Ultimate fudge brownie mix (with chocolate syrup pouch)
- Water, oil and eggs as called for on brownie mix box
- 3 packages (8 oz each) cream cheese, softened

- 1 can (14 oz) sweetened condensed milk (not evaporated)
- 4 eggs
- 1 teaspoon vanilla
- 1 cup caramel ice cream topping

1 Heat oven to 325°F. Make dough as directed on cookie pouch. Cover and refrigerate about 1 hour or until firm.

2 Meanwhile, make brownie mix as directed on box for 13x9-inch pan. Cool completely, about 1 hour.

3 Wrap outside bottom and side of 9-inch springform pan with foil to prevent leaking. Spray inside bottom and side of pan with cooking spray. Press cookie dough on bottom and 1/2 inch up sides of pan. Bake crust 13 to 15 minutes or until set.

4 Meanwhile, in large bowl, beat cream cheese with electric mixer on medium speed until fluffy. Gradually beat in

condensed milk until smooth. Beat in eggs one at a time, just until blended. Stir in vanilla.

5 Crumble 2 cups of cooled brownies into coarse crumbs. Fold into cream cheese mixture. Pour over cookie dough crust.

6 Bake 1 hour to 1 hour 10 minutes or until edge of cheesecake is set at least 2 inches from edge of pan but center of cheesecake still jiggles slightly when moved. Run small metal spatula around edge of pan to loosen cheesecake. Turn oven off; open oven door at least 4 inches. Let cheesecake remain in oven 30 minutes. Cool in pan on cooling rack 30 minutes. Refrigerate at least 8 hours or overnight before serving. Cool completely in pan on cooling rack for 1 hour.

7 To serve, carefully run small metal spatula along side of cheesecake to loosen. Remove foil and side of pan. In small microwaveable bowl, microwave caramel topping uncovered on High 10 to 15 seconds until thoroughly heated. Top individual servings with caramel topping. Store cheesecake covered in refrigerator.

High Altitude (3500-6500 feet): No changes.

Nutritional Info: 1 Serving: Calories 580; Total Fat 30g (Saturated Fat 14g); Sodium 470mg; Total Carbohydrate 65g (Dietary Fiber 0g); Protein 10g. Exchanges: 1-1/2 Starch, 3 Other Carbohydrate, 1 High-Fat Meat, 4 Fat. Carbohydrate Choices: 4.

apple-topped cheesecake
with caramel topping

Prep Time: 30 Minutes
Start to Finish: 7 Hours 15 Minutes
Servings: 10

Judy Taylor
Gahanna, OH
Celebrate the Season-Fall Baking Contest

Crust

1	cup Gold Medal® all-purpose flour
1/2	cup finely chopped pecans
1/3	cup sugar
1/2	teaspoon vanilla
1/2	cup cold butter or margarine

Filling

2	packages (8 oz each) cream cheese, softened
1/2	cup sugar
1	teaspoon vanilla
2	eggs

Topping

2	large tart apples, peeled, cut into 1/4-inch slices
1/4	cup sugar
1	teaspoon ground cinnamon
1/2	teaspoon vanilla
3/4	cup caramel topping

1 Heat oven to 350°F. Grease bottom and side of 9-inch springform pan with shortening or cooking spray.

2 In medium bowl, mix flour, pecans, 1/3 cup sugar and 1/2 teaspoon vanilla. Cut in butter, using pastry blender (or pulling 2 table knives through ingredients in opposite directions), until blended. Press dough on bottom and 1/2 inch up side of pan. Bake 12 minutes or until set. Cool 15 minutes.

3 In medium bowl, beat all filling ingredients with electric mixer on medium speed until smooth; spread filling over cooled crust. In another bowl, toss apples with 1/4 cup sugar, the cinnamon and 1/2 teaspoon vanilla. Arrange apples in circular design over filling. Carefully brush apples with 2 tablespoons of the caramel topping.

4 Bake 15 minutes. Reduce oven temperature to 325°F. Bake 1 hour longer. Cool completely in pan on cooling rack, about 1 hour. Refrigerate at least 4 hours.

5 Just before serving, run small metal spatula around edge of pan; carefully remove side of pan. Drizzle each piece of cheesecake with 1 tablespoon remaining caramel topping. Cover and refrigerate any remaining cheesecake.

High Altitude (3500-6500 feet): No changes.

Nutritional Info: 1 Serving: Calories 520; Total Fat 30g (Saturated Fat 15g); Sodium 310mg; Total Carbohydrate 56g (Dietary Fiber 2g); Protein 6g. Exchanges: 1/2 Fruit, 2-1/2 Other Carbohydrate, 1 Milk, 4-1/2 Fat. Carbohydrate Choices: 4.

lemon cheesecake with fresh berry topping

Prep Time: 30 Minutes
Start to Finish: 11 Hours
Servings: 16

Crust

- 1-3/4 cups crushed gingersnap cookies (about 35 cookies)
- 6 tablespoons butter or margarine, melted
- 1 tablespoon brown sugar

Filling

- 3 packages (8 oz each) cream cheese, softened
- 3/4 cup sugar
- 3 eggs
- 1/2 cup whipping (heavy) cream
- 3 tablespoons lemon juice
- 2 tablespoons grated lemon peel

Whipped Cream Topping and Garnish

- 1/2 cup whipping (heavy) cream
- 1 tablespoon powdered sugar
- 1 pint blueberries
- 2 cups raspberries

Lemon twists

1 Heat oven to 350°F. Wrap outside of 9-inch springform pan with foil to prevent leaking. Spray inside bottom and side of pan with cooking spray. In small bowl, mix crust ingredients. Press crust mixture on bottom of pan. Bake crust 5 to 7 minutes or until set. Cool 5 minutes at room temperature. Reduce oven temperature to 325°F.

2 Meanwhile, in large bowl beat cream cheese and sugar with electric mixer on medium speed for 2 minutes. Add eggs, one at a time, beating well after each. On low speed, beat in cream, lemon juice and lemon peel. Pour over crust.

3 Bake 1 hour to 1 hour 10 minutes or until edge of cheesecake is set at least 2 inches from edge of pan but center of cheesecake still jiggles slightly when moved. Run small metal spatula around edge of pan to loosen cheesecake. Turn oven off; open oven door at least 4 inches. Let cheesecake remain in oven 30 minutes. Cool in pan on cooling rack 30 minutes. Loosely cover and refrigerate 8 hours or overnight before serving.

4 Just before serving, run small metal spatula around edge of pan; carefully remove side of pan. In chilled small bowl, beat whipping cream and powdered sugar on high speed until soft peaks form. Spoon onto cheesecake. Top with berries and lemon twists.

High Altitude (3500-6500 feet): No change.

Nutritional Info: 1 Serving: Calories 370; Total Fat 26g (Saturated Fat 16g); Sodium 260mg; Total Carbohydrate 28g (Dietary Fiber 2g); Protein 6g. Exchanges: 1/2 Fruit, 1-1/2 Other Carbohydrate, 1 High-Fat Meat, 3-1/2 Fat. Carbohydrate Choices: 2.

Betty's Kitchen Tip

- Heavy duty foil, available in wider widths, is especially good for wrapping around the outside of the springform pan. The larger width makes it convenient and creates a moisture-proof barrier.

key lime cheesecake

Prep Time: 30 Minutes
Start to Finish: 14 Hours 30 Minutes
Servings: 16

Lime Crust

1/2	cup granulated sugar
1/2	cup butter or margarine, softened
1	cup Gold Medal® all-purpose flour
1	tablespoon grated lime peel
1	teaspoon vanilla

Filling

4	packages (8 oz each) cream cheese, softened
3/4	cup powdered sugar
1/2	cup granulated sugar

2	eggs
2	tablespoons grated lime peel
2	tablespoons Key lime juice
2	tablespoons cornstarch
1	cup sour cream

Key Lime Curd

3/4	cup granulated sugar
1	tablespoon grated lime peel
1/2	cup Key lime juice
2	tablespoons firm butter or margarine, cut up
2	eggs, slightly beaten

1 Heat oven to 400°F. Wrap outside of 10-inch springform pan with foil to prevent leaking. Grease bottom and side of pan. In medium bowl, beat 1/2 cup granulated sugar and 1/2 cup butter with electric mixer on medium speed until smooth. Beat in remaining crust ingredients on low speed just until crumbly. Press evenly in bottom of pan.

2 Bake 8 to 10 minutes or until light golden brown. Cool 10 minutes. Reduce oven temperature to 325°F.

3 In large bowl, beat cream cheese, powdered sugar and 1/2 cup granulated sugar with electric mixer on medium speed until smooth. Beat in 2 eggs, one at a time, on low speed just until well blended. Beat in 2 tablespoons lime peel, 2 tablespoons

lime juice and the cornstarch. Fold in sour cream until blended. Pour over crust.

4 Bake 1 hour 10 minutes to 1 hour 20 minutes or until side of cheesecake is set and slightly puffed but center still moves slightly when pan is tapped. Cool in pan on cooling rack 15 minutes.

5 Run knife along side of pan to loosen cheesecake. Refrigerate uncovered about 3 hours or until chilled. Cover and refrigerate at least 9 hours but no longer than 48 hours.

6 In heavy 1-1/2-quart saucepan, mix 3/4 cup sugar, 1 tablespoon lime peel and 1/2 cup lime juice with wire whisk. Stir in 2 tablespoons butter and 2 eggs. Cook over medium heat about 8 to 10 minutes, stirring constantly, until mixture thickens and coats back of spoon (do not boil). Run knife along side of pan to loosen cheesecake; remove side of pan. Spoon curd on top of cheesecake, spreading evenly over the top. Store in refrigerator.

High Altitude (3500-6500 feet): No changes.

Nutritional Info: 1 Serving: Calories 470; Total Fat 31g (Saturated Fat 19g); Sodium 240mg; Total Carbohydrate 41g (Dietary Fiber 0g); Protein 7g. Exchanges: 1/2 Starch, 2 Other Carbohydrate, 1 High-Fat Meat, 4-1/2 Fat. Carbohydrate Choices: 3.

chocolate-chip toffee cheesecake

Prep Time: 30 Minutes
Start to Finish: 5 Hours 45 Minutes
Servings: 12

Crust

1-1/4	cups finely crushed chocolate graham crackers (18 squares)
2	tablespoons sugar
1/4	cup butter or margarine, melted

Filling

2	packages (8 oz each) cream cheese, softened
1/2	cup sugar
1	teaspoon vanilla
2	eggs
2	cups chocolate-coated toffee bits (from two 8-oz bags)

Topping

1/2	cup semisweet chocolate chips
2	tablespoons whipping (heavy) cream

1 Heat oven to 300°F. In medium bowl, mix crumbs, 2 tablespoons sugar and the butter. In ungreased 9-inch springform pan, press crumb mixture in bottom and 1 to 1-1/2 inches up side.

2 In large bowl, beat cream cheese, 1/2 cup sugar and the vanilla with electric mixer on medium speed until smooth. Add eggs, one at a time, beating until smooth after each addition. Reserve 2 tablespoons of the toffee bits for garnish; gently stir remaining toffee bits into cream cheese mixture. Pour mixture into crust.

3 Bake 50 to 60 minutes or until set. Turn off oven; leave door open 4 inches. Cool cheesecake in oven 30 minutes.

4 Remove cheesecake from oven; place on cooling rack. Without releasing or removing side of pan, run metal spatula carefully along side of cheesecake to loosen. Cool 30 minutes. Run metal spatula along side of cheesecake to loosen again.

Refrigerate uncovered until thoroughly chilled, at least 3 hours.

5 In small microwavable bowl, microwave chocolate chips and whipping cream uncovered on High 20 to 30 seconds or until chips are melted and can be stirred smooth. Cool 5 minutes. Spread topping evenly over top of cheesecake. Sprinkle reserved 2 tablespoons toffee bits around outer edge. Refrigerate until topping is set, about 15 minutes. Remove side of pan before serving.

High Altitude (3500-6500 feet): No changes.

Nutritional Info: 1 Serving: Calories 480; Total Fat 33g (Saturated Fat 20g); Cholesterol 100mg; Sodium 290mg; Total Carbohydrate 41g (Dietary Fiber 1g, Sugars 36g), Protein 6g. Exchanges: 1/2 Starch; 2 Other Carbohydrate. Carbohydrate Choices: 3.

Betty's Kitchen Tips

Variation: You can use mini chocolate chips instead of chocolate-coated toffee bits.

Success Hint: Cool the cheesecake in the oven for 30 minutes to help prevent cracking.

piña colada cheesecake

Prep Time: 30 Minutes
Start to Finish: 9 Hours
Servings: 16

Crust
1-3/4 cups graham cracker crumbs
   6 tablespoons butter or margarine, melted

Filling
   3 packages (8 oz each) cream cheese, softened
 1/4 cup sugar
   3 eggs
 3/4 cup cream of coconut
 1/4 cup light rum
   2 teaspoons grated orange peel

   1 can (8 oz) crushed pineapple in juice, drained, juice reserved

Glaze
Reserved 1/2 cup pineapple juice
   2 teaspoons cornstarch
 1/4 cup sugar

Garnish
   1 can (8 oz) crushed pineapple in juice, drained
   1 jar (24 oz) refrigerated sliced mango, drained, chopped
Fresh mint leaves, if desired

1 Heat oven to 325°F. Wrap outside bottom and side of 10-inch springform pan with foil to prevent leaking. Spray inside bottom and side of pan with cooking spray. In small bowl, mix crust ingredients. Press crust mixture in bottom of pan. Bake 8 to 10 minutes or until set.

2 In large bowl, beat cream cheese and 1/4 cup sugar with electric mixer on medium speed until light and fluffy. Beat in eggs; one at a time; just until blended. On low speed, beat in remaining filling ingredients except pineapple. Gently fold in pineapple. Pour over crust.

3 Bake 1 hour 10 minutes to 1 hour 15 minutes or until edge of cheesecake is set at least 2 inches from edge of pan but center of cheesecake still jiggles slightly when moved. Run small metal spatula around edge of pan to loosen cheesecake. Turn oven off; open oven door at least 4 inches. Let cheesecake remain in oven 30 minutes. Cool in pan on cooling rack 30 minutes. Refrigerate at least 6 hours or overnight before serving.

4 In 1-quart saucepan, mix reserved pineapple juice plus enough water to equal 2/3 cup, cornstarch and sugar. Heat to boiling over medium heat, stirring constantly. Boil 1 minute, stirring constantly, until slightly thickened. Cool 20 minutes at room temperature.

5 In large bowl, toss glaze with pineapple and mango. Spoon onto top of cheesecake. Garnish with mint leaves.

High Altitude (3500-6500 feet): No change.

Nutritional Info: 1 Serving: Calories 360; Total Fat 25g (Saturated Fat 16g); Sodium 230mg; Total Carbohydrate 27g (Dietary Fiber 1g); Protein 6g. Exchanges: 1/2 Fruit, 1-1/2 Other Carbohydrate, 1 High-Fat Meat, 3-1/2 Fat. Carbohydrate Choices: 2.

lemon cheesecake

Prep Time: 15 Minutes
Start to Finish: 6 Hours 50 Minutes
Servings: 16

Crust

1	box Betty Crocker® SuperMoist® yellow cake mix
1/2	cup butter or margarine, softened
1	teaspoon grated lemon peel

Filling

2	packages (8 oz each) cream cheese, softened
3/4	cup sugar
3	containers (3.5 oz each) lemon pudding (from 4-pack container)
1/2	cup sour cream
3	eggs
2	cups frozen (thawed) whipped topping

EASY

1. Heat oven to 300°F. Spray bottom and side of 10-inch springform pan with baking spray with flour. Wrap foil around outside of pan to prevent leaking. Reserve 1/4 cup of the cake mix; set aside. In large bowl, beat remaining cake mix, butter and lemon peel with electric mixer on low speed until crumbly. Press in bottom and 1-1/2 inches up side of pan.

2. In same large bowl, beat reserved cake mix, the cream cheese, sugar, pudding and sour cream on medium speed until smooth and creamy. Beat in eggs, one at a time, until mixed. Pour over crust.

3. Bake 1 hour 20 minutes to 1 hour 35 minutes or until edges are set but center of cheesecake jiggles slightly when moved. Turn oven off; open oven door at least 4 inches. Leave cheesecake in oven 30 minutes longer.

4. Remove cheesecake from oven; place on cooling rack. Without releasing side of pan, run knife around edge of pan to loosen cheesecake. Cool in pan on cooling rack 30 minutes. Cover loosely; refrigerate 4 hours or overnight. Remove side of pan before serving. Pipe or spoon whipped topping around outside edge of cheesecake. Store in refrigerator.

High Altitude (3500-6500 feet): No change.

Nutritional Info: 1 Serving: Calories 380; Total Fat 21g (Saturated Fat 13g); Sodium 400mg; Total Carbohydrate 43g (Dietary Fiber 0g); Protein 5g. Exchanges: 1 Starch, 2 Other Carbohydrate, 4 Fat. Carbohydrate Choices: 3.

Betty's Kitchen Tips

Success Hint: For clean cuts when serving the cheesecake, dip a sharp knife in hot water and dry on a paper towel before each cut.

Special Touch: This is not your ordinary cheesecake! Make sure you allow enough time to savor every last bit of this lemon sensation.

fresh strawberry topped cheesecake

Prep Time: 30 Minutes
Start to Finish: 11 Hours
Servings: 16

Crust

2 cups finely crushed vanilla wafer cookies (about 55 cookies)
1/4 cup butter or margarine, melted

Filling

3 packages (8 oz each) cream cheese, softened
3/4 cup sugar
3 eggs

1 cup whipping (heavy) cream
2 tablespoons Gold Medal® all-purpose flour
1 teaspoon vanilla

Strawberry Topping

1 quart fresh strawberries, sliced in half lengthwise (3 cups)
1/2 cup glaze for strawberries (from 13.5 oz container)

1 Heat oven to 325°F. Wrap outside of 9-inch springform pan with foil to prevent leaking. Spray inside bottom and side of pan with cooking spray. In small bowl, mix crust ingredients. Press crust mixture on bottom and 1 inch up sides of pan. Bake crust 6 to 8 minutes or until set.

2 In large bowl, beat cream cheese with electric mixer on medium speed until fluffy. Gradually beat in sugar until smooth. Beat in eggs, one at a time, just until blended. On low, beat in whipping cream, flour and vanilla until smooth. Pour over crust.

3 Bake 1 hour to 1 hour 10 minutes or until edge of cheesecake is set at least 2 inches from edge of pan but center of cheesecake still jiggles slightly when moved. Run small metal spatula around edge of pan to loosen cheesecake. Turn oven off; open oven door at least 4 inches. Let cheesecake remain in oven 30 minutes. Cool in pan on cooling rack 30 minutes. Refrigerate at least 8 hours or overnight before serving.

4 Just before serving, run metal spatula around edge of pan; carefully remove foil and side of pan. In medium bowl, mix together strawberries and glaze. Arrange strawberries on top of cheesecake.

High Altitude (3500-6500 feet): No change.

Nutritional Info: 1 Serving: Calories 340; Total Fat 25g (Saturated Fat 15g); Sodium 210mg; Total Carbohydrate 22g (Dietary Fiber 1g); Protein 5g. Exchanges: 1/2 Starch, 1 Other Carbohydrate, 1/2 High-Fat Meat, 4 Fat. Carbohydrate Choices: 1-1/2.

Betty's Kitchen Tip

• When making any cheesecake, be sure to have the cream cheese, eggs and other ingredients at room temperature.

praline crumb caramel cheesecake bars

Prep Time: 25 Minutes
Start to Finish: 3 Hours 35 Minutes
Servings: 36 bars

Brenda Watts
Gaffney, SC
Cookie Mix Contest 2010

Cookie Base and Topping

- 1 pouch (1 lb 1.5 oz) Betty Crocker® sugar cookie mix
- 1/2 cup cold butter or margarine
- 1/2 cup chopped pecans
- 1/2 cup toffee bits

Filling

- 2 packages (8 oz each) cream cheese, softened
- 1/2 cup sugar
- 2 tablespoons Gold Medal® all-purpose flour
- 1/2 cup caramel topping
- 1 teaspoon vanilla
- 1 egg

1 Heat oven to 350°F. Spray bottom and sides of 13x9-inch pan with cooking spray.

2 Place cookie mix in bowl; cut in butter, using pastry blender (or pulling 2 table knives through ingredients in opposite directions), until mixture is crumbly. Reserve 1-1/2 cups mixture for topping. Press remaining mixture in bottom of pan. Bake 10 minutes.

3 Meanwhile, in large bowl, beat cream cheese, sugar, flour, 1/4 cup of the caramel topping, vanilla and egg with electric mixer on medium speed until smooth.

4 Spread cream cheese mixture evenly over partially baked cookie base. Sprinkle with reserved crumb topping, the pecans and toffee bits.

5 Bake 35 to 40 minutes or until light golden brown. Cool 30 minutes. Refrigerate about 2 hours or until chilled. Drizzle with remaining 1/4 cup caramel topping. Cut into 9 rows by 4 rows. Store covered in the refrigerator.

High Altitude (3500-6500 feet): No change.

Nutritional Info: 1 Bar: Calories 180; Total Fat 10g (Saturated Fat 5g); Sodium 125mg; Total Carbohydrate 19g (Dietary Fiber 0g); Protein 1g. Exchanges: 1/2 Starch, 1 Other Carbohydrate, 2 Fat. Carbohydrate Choices: 1.

new york cheesecake (lighter recipe)

Prep Time: 30 Minutes
Start to Finish: 14 Hours 5 Minutes
Servings: 16

3/4	cup graham cracker crumbs
2	tablespoons margarine, melted
2	tablespoons sugar
5	packages (8 oz each) reduced-fat cream cheese (Neufchâtel), softened
1-3/4	cups sugar
1/4	cup Gold Medal® all-purpose flour

1	tablespoon grated orange peel
1	tablespoon grated lemon peel
1/4	teaspoon salt
1-1/4	cups fat-free cholesterol-free egg product
2	egg yolks

Berries or cut-up fresh fruit, if desired

1 Move oven rack to lowest position. Heat oven to 425°F. Lightly grease side only of 9-inch springform pan with shortening.

2 In small bowl, mix graham cracker crumbs, margarine and 2 tablespoons sugar; press evenly in bottom of pan.

3 In large bowl, beat cream cheese, 1-3/4 cups sugar, the flour, orange peel, lemon peel and salt with electric mixer on medium speed about 1 minute or until smooth. Beat in egg product and egg yolks, beating on low speed until well blended. Pour over graham cracker mixture.

4 Bake 15 minutes. Reduce oven temperature to 200°F. Bake 1 hour longer. Cheesecake may not appear to be done, but if a small area in the center seems soft, it will become firm as cheesecake cools. (Do not insert a knife to test for doneness because the hole could cause cheesecake to crack.) Turn off oven; leave cheesecake in oven 30 minutes longer. Remove from oven and cool in pan on wire rack away from drafts 30 minutes.

5 Without releasing or removing side of pan, run metal spatula along side of cheesecake to loosen. Refrigerate uncovered about 3 hours or until chilled; cover and continue refrigerating at least 9 hours but no longer than 48 hours.

6 Run metal spatula along side of cheesecake to loosen again. Remove side of pan; leave cheesecake on pan bottom to serve. Serve with berries, if desired. Store covered in refrigerator.

High Altitude (3500-6500 feet): No change.

Nutritional Info: 1 Serving: Calories 330; Total Fat 19g (Saturated Fat 11g); Sodium 400mg; Total Carbohydrate 31g (Dietary Fiber 0g); Protein 10g. Exchanges: 1/2 Starch, 1-1/2 Other Carbohydrate, 1 High-Fat Meat, 2 Fat. Carbohydrate Choices: 2.

mocha-fudge cheesecake

Prep Time: 15 Minutes
Start to Finish: 3 Hours 55 Minutes
Servings: 8

Cheesecake

1	tablespoon instant coffee granules or crystals
3	tablespoons coffee-flavored liqueur
2	packages (8 oz each) cream cheese, softened
3/4	cup granulated sugar
3/4	cup Original Bisquick® mix
1	teaspoon vanilla
3	eggs
3	oz semisweet baking chocolate, melted, cooled

Chocolate Topping

1	oz semisweet baking chocolate, melted, cooled
2	tablespoons powdered sugar
1	tablespoon coffee-flavored liqueur, if desired
1	container (8 oz) sour cream
1	teaspoon vanilla

1 Heat oven to 350°F. Grease 9-inch glass pie plate. In small bowl, mix coffee and liqueur until coffee is dissolved.

2 In large bowl, beat coffee mixture and remaining cheesecake ingredients with electric mixer on high speed 2 minutes, scraping bowl frequently. Pour into pie plate.

3 Bake about 35 minutes or until center is firm and puffed. Cool 5 minutes (cheesecake top will be cracked).

4 In small bowl, mix 1 ounce chocolate, the powdered sugar and 1 tablespoon liqueur until well blended. Stir in sour cream and 1 teaspoon vanilla. Carefully spread topping over cheesecake. Refrigerate at least 3 hours before serving. Store in refrigerator.

EASY

High Altitude (3500-6500 ft): Bake about 40 minutes.

Nutritional Info: 1 Serving: Calories 520; Total Fat 33g (Saturated Fat 19g); Sodium 340mg; Total Carbohydrate 44g (Dietary Fiber 1g); Protein 9g. Exchanges: 1 Starch, 2 Other Carbohydrate, 1 High-Fat Meat, 5 Fat. Carbohydrate Choices: 3.

Betty's Kitchen Tips

Substitution: Cold strong coffee can be used instead of the coffee liqueur.

Success Hint: Softening the cream cheese helps it blend into the other ingredients, ensuring that the final cheesecake is lump-free!

bittersweet chocolate cheesecake

Prep Time: 30 Minutes
Start to Finish: 4 Hours 45 Minutes
Servings: 12

Cheesecake

- 2 packages (8 oz each) cream cheese, softened
- 1 teaspoon vanilla
- 2/3 cup sugar
- 1 tablespoon Gold Medal® all-purpose flour
- 3 eggs
- 8 oz bittersweet baking chocolate, melted, cooled

Fresh raspberries or strawberries, if desired

White Truffle Sauce

- 1 package (6 oz) white chocolate baking bars, chopped
- 2 tablespoons butter or margarine
- 1/2 cup whipping (heavy) cream

1 Heat oven to 275°F. Lightly grease bottom and side of 9-inch springform pan. In medium bowl, beat cream cheese and vanilla with electric mixer on medium speed until smooth. Gradually add sugar, beating until fluffy. Beat in flour. Beat in eggs, one at a time. Beat in chocolate. Pour into pan.

2 Bake about 1 hour 15 minutes or until center is set. (Do not insert a knife because the hole could cause cheesecake to crack.) Cool at room temperature 15 minutes.

3 Run knife around side of pan to loosen cheesecake. Cover and refrigerate about 3 hours or until chilled.

4 In 2-quart saucepan, melt white chocolate and butter over low heat, stirring constantly (mixture will be thick and grainy); remove from heat. Stir in whipping cream until smooth. Cover and refrigerate about 2 hours or until chilled.

5 Run knife around side of pan to loosen cheesecake; remove side of pan. Let cheesecake stand at room temperature 15 minutes before cutting. Serve with sauce and berries. Store in the refrigerator.

High Altitude (3500-6500 feet): No changes.

Nutritional Info: 1 Serving: Calories 430; Total Fat 30g (Saturated Fat 18g); Sodium 160mg; Total Carbohydrate 33g (Dietary Fiber 1g); Protein 6g. Exchanges: 2 Other Carbohydrate, 1 High-Fat Meat, 4-1/2 Fat. Carbohydrate Choices: 2.

Betty's Kitchen Tip

- Bittersweet chocolate differs from semisweet in that it contains more chocolate liquor (the paste that comes from ground cocoa beans) and less sugar.

creamy vanilla-caramel cheesecake

Prep Time: 20 Minutes
Start to Finish: 5 Hours 5 Minutes
Servings: 16

- 15 chocolate or vanilla wafer cookies, crushed (1/2 cup)
- 2 packages (8 oz each) 1/3-less-fat cream cheese (Neufchâtel), softened
- 2/3 cup sugar
- 3 egg whites or 1/2 cup fat-free egg product
- 2 teaspoons vanilla
- 2 cups Yoplait® Original lowfat vanilla yogurt
- 2 tablespoons Gold Medal® all-purpose flour
- 1/3 cup fat-free caramel topping

Pecan halves, if desired

1 Heat oven to 300°F. Spray 9-inch springform pan with cooking spray. Sprinkle cookie crumbs over bottom of pan.

2 Beat cream cheese in medium bowl with electric mixer on medium speed until smooth. Add sugar, egg whites and vanilla. Beat on medium speed about 2 minutes or until smooth. Add yogurt and flour. Beat on low speed until smooth.

3 Carefully spread batter over cookie crumbs in pan. Bake 1 hour. Turn off oven; cool in oven 30 minutes with door closed. Remove from oven; cool 15 minutes. Cover and refrigerate at least 3 hours.

4 Drizzle caramel topping over cheesecake. Garnish with pecan halves. Store covered in the refrigerator.

High Altitude (3500-6500 feet): No changes.

Nutritional Info: 1 Serving: Calories 180; Total Fat 7g (Saturated Fat 4.5g); Sodium 190mg; Total Carbohydrate 21g (Dietary Fiber 0g); Protein 5g. Exchanges: 1-1/2 Starch, 1-1/2 Fat. Carbohydrate Choices: 1-1/2.

Betty's Kitchen Tips

Did You Know? Egg whites provide the protein from eggs but don't contain the cholesterol found in egg yolks. That's very good news for your heart.

Success Hint: Place the springform pan on a cookie sheet before putting it in the oven to keep pesky drips in check.

Variation: If you're an almond or walnut lover, use them in place of the pecans.

trick-or-treat cheesecake

Prep Time: 20 Minutes
Start to Finish: 8 Hours 10 Minutes
Servings: 12

Diane Neibling
Overland Park, KS
Celebrate the Season-Fall Baking Contest

1-1/2 cups crushed chocolate wafer cookies (about 25 cookies)

1/3 cup sugar

1/3 cup butter or margarine, melted

2 packages (8 oz each) cream cheese, softened

1 can (14 oz) sweetened condensed milk (not evaporated)

3 eggs

2 teaspoons vanilla

20 bars (fun-size) candy, unwrapped, cut into quarters (about 2 cups)

1 Heat oven to 300°F. Spray 9-inch springform pan with cooking spray. To minimize cracking, place shallow pan half full of hot water on lower oven rack.

2 In medium bowl, mix cookie crumbs, sugar and butter. Press in bottom of pan. In large bowl, beat cream cheese and sweetened condensed milk with electric mixer until smooth. Beat in eggs, one at a time, just until blended. Stir in vanilla and candy. Pour over crust.

3 Bake 40 to 50 minutes or until edge of cheesecake is set at least 2 inches from edge of pan but center of cheesecake still jiggles slightly when moved. Run small metal spatula around edge of pan to loosen cheesecake. Turn oven off; open door at least 4 inches. Let cheesecake remain in oven 30 minutes. Cool in pan on cooling rack 30 minutes. Refrigerate at least 6 hours or overnight.

4 Just before serving, run small metal spatula around edge of pan; carefully remove side of pan. Cover and refrigerate any remaining cheesecake.

High Altitude (3500-6500 feet): No change.

Nutritional Info: 1 Serving: Calories 550; Total Fat 32g (Saturated Fat 17g); Sodium 380mg; Total Carbohydrate 57g (Dietary Fiber 1g); Protein 9g. Exchanges: 3 Other Carbohydrate, 1 Milk, 5 Fat. Carbohydrate Choices: 4.

Betty's Kitchen Tip

• Use your choice of candy bars, mixing and matching flavors if you like. Buy on sale after Halloween or use your kids' leftovers.

COOKIES GALORE

p.265

236

248

247

inside-out peanut butter cookies

Prep Time: 45 Minutes
Start to Finish: 2 Hours
Servings: 1-1/2 dozen sandwich cookies

Karen Warner
Louisville, OH
Cookie Contest 2009

1	pouch (1 lb 1.5 oz) Betty Crocker® double chocolate chunk cookie mix
1/4	cup vegetable oil
2	tablespoons water
1	egg

1/2	cup marshmallow creme (from 7-oz jar)
1	bag (10 oz) peanut butter chips (1-2/3 cups)
2	tablespoons shortening

1 Heat oven to 350°F. Make cookie dough, using oil, water and egg, and bake as directed on package. Cool completely.

2 Spoon about 1 teaspoon of marshmallow creme on the bottom of half of the cookies. Top each with a second cookie, bottom side down; gently press together.

3 In small saucepan, heat peanut butter chips and shortening over low heat, stirring frequently, until melted and smooth. Spoon about 2 teaspoons peanut butter mixture over each cookie, spreading with back of spoon over top and side. Place on waxed paper. Let stand 30 minutes or until set.

High Altitude (3500-6500 ft): No change.

Nutritional Info: 1 Sandwich Cookie: Calories 250; Total Fat 12g (Saturated Fat 3.5g); Sodium 170mg; Total Carbohydrate 32g (Dietary Fiber 0g); Protein 3g. Exchanges: 1 Starch, 1 Other Carbohydrate, 2-1/2 Fat. Carbohydrate Choices: 2.

Betty's Kitchen Tips

Leftovers: Use the remaining marshmallow creme to make easy s'mores—just spread on a graham cracker, top with a piece of chocolate candy bar (softened slightly in the microwave) and a second graham cracker.

Special Touch: If you love peanut butter cups, you'll love these cookies. My children received a candy for Valentine's Day that gave me the idea to make these chocolate sandwich cookies with peanut butter on the outside.

funny face cookies

Prep Time: 1 Hour
Start to Finish: 1 Hour 15 Minutes
Servings: 2 dozen cookies

- 1 pouch (1 lb 1.5 oz) Betty Crocker® sugar cookie mix
- 1/3 cup butter or margarine, softened
- 1 tablespoon Gold Medal® all-purpose flour
- 1 egg

Green, red and yellow food color

- 2 pouches (7 oz each) Betty Crocker® cookie icing in desired colors

Betty Crocker® decors, if desired

Assorted candies and coconut, if desired

1. Heat oven to 375°F. In medium bowl, stir cookie mix, butter, flour and egg until soft dough forms. Divide dough into thirds; stir food color into each third of dough.

2. On floured surface, roll dough to about 1/4-inch thickness. Carefully cut with 2- to 2-1/2-inch round cookie cutter. On ungreased cookie sheets, place cutouts about 1 inch apart.

3. Bake 7 to 9 minutes or until edges are light golden brown. Cool 1 minute; remove from cookie sheets. Cool completely, about 15 minutes.

4. Spread or pipe cookie icing on cooled cookies. Decorate as desired with decors, candies and coconut.

High Altitude (3500-6500 ft): No change.

Nutritional Info: 1 Frosted Cookie (Undecorated): Calories 180; Total Fat 7g (Saturated Fat 4g); Sodium 80mg; Total Carbohydrate 28g (Dietary Fiber 0g); Protein 1g. Exchanges: 1/2 Starch, 1-1/2 Other Carbohydrate, 1-1/2 Fat. Carbohydrate Choices: 2.

Betty's Kitchen Tip

- When decorating, set the cookies in a shallow baking pan first. The edges of the pan help keep the candies and coconut contained so cleanup is easy.

chocolate and orange pecan shortbread

Prep Time: 1 Hour 30 Minutes
Start to Finish: 2 Hours 15 Minutes
Servings: About 2 dozen cookies

Amy Tong
Carson, CA
Celebrate the Season-Holiday Cookie Contest

1-1/2 cups unsalted butter, softened	3-1/2 cups Gold Medal® all-purpose flour
1 cup sugar	1/4 teaspoon salt
2 tablespoons grated orange peel	1-1/2 cups finely chopped pecans
1 teaspoon vanilla	1 cup miniature semisweet chocolate chips
1 teaspoon orange extract	

1 Heat oven to 350°F. In large bowl, beat butter and sugar with electric mixer on medium speed until combined. Beat in orange peel, vanilla and orange extract. On low speed, beat in flour and salt. Stir in pecans and chocolate chips.

2 Divide dough in half; shape into 2 flat disks. Wrap 1 disk in plastic wrap.

3 On floured surface, roll unwrapped dough about 1/2 inch thick. Cut into 2-1/2-inch circles with plain or fluted cookie cutter (or cut into desired shapes). On ungreased cookie sheet, place cookies about 1 inch apart. Repeat with second disk.

4 Bake 15 to 19 minutes or until edges begin to brown. Remove from cookie sheet to cooling rack.

High Altitude (3500-6500 ft): No change.

Nutritional Info: 1 Cookie: Calories 290; Total Fat 19g (Saturated Fat 9g); Sodium 25mg; Total Carbohydrate 28g (Dietary Fiber 1g); Protein 3g. Exchanges: 1 Starch, 1 Other Carbohydrate, 3-1/2 Fat. Carbohydrate Choices: 2.

Betty's Kitchen Tip

• Don't use too much flour on your work surface when rolling the dough, as it could affect the texture of the baked cookies.

mint chocolate chip cookies

Prep Time: 25 Minutes
Start to Finish: 40 Minutes
Servings: 3 dozen cookies

Patti Bullock
Corpus Christi, TX
Cookie Mix Contest 2010

1	pouch (1 lb 1.5 oz) Betty Crocker® sugar cookie mix
1/2	cup butter or margarine, softened
1/4	to 1/2 teaspoon mint extract
6	to 8 drops green food color
1	egg
1	cup crème de menthe baking chips
1	cup semisweet chocolate chunks

1 Heat oven to 350°F. In large bowl, stir cookie mix, butter, mint extract, food color and egg until soft dough forms. Stir in baking chips and chocolate chunks.

2 Using a small cookie scoop or a teaspoon, drop dough 2 inches apart on an ungreased cookie sheet.

3 Bake 8 to 10 minutes or until set. Cool 3 minutes; remove from cookie sheet to cooling rack. Store cooled cookies tightly covered at room temperature.

High Altitude (3500-6500 ft): No change.

Nutritional Info: 1 Cookie: Calories 130; Total Fat 7g (Saturated Fat 3.5g); Sodium 60mg; Total Carbohydrate 16g (Dietary Fiber 0g); Protein 1g. Exchanges: 1 Other Carbohydrate, 1-1/2 Fat. Carbohydrate Choices: 1.

Betty's Kitchen Tip

• What's more delicious than warm cookies right out of the oven, with a cold glass of milk or hot cup of coffee? Make sure to cool the leftover cookies before storing.

oatmeal shortbread santas

Prep Time: 55 Minutes
Start to Finish: 1 Hour 40 Minutes
Servings: 1 dozen cookies

2/3	cup butter or margarine, softened		6	miniature marshmallows, cut in half
1/2	cup packed brown sugar		1	tablespoon red decorating sugar
1	teaspoon vanilla		24	blue miniature candy-coated chocolate candies
1	cup Gold Medal® all-purpose flour		12	red miniature candy-coated chocolate candies
3/4	cup quick-cooking oats			
1/4	teaspoon baking powder			
2	cans (6.4 oz each) Betty Crocker® Easy Flow white decorating icing			

1 In large bowl, beat butter, brown sugar and vanilla with electric mixer on medium speed until creamy. Stir in flour, oats and baking powder. Gather dough into ball. Wrap in plastic wrap; refrigerate 30 minutes.

2 Heat oven to 350°F. On well-floured surface, roll dough 1/4 inch thick. Cut with 3- to 3-1/2-inch heart-shaped cookie cutter. On ungreased cookie sheet, place cutouts 2 inches apart.

3 Bake 8 to 10 minutes or until edges are light golden brown. Cool 1 minute; remove from cookie sheet to cooling rack. Cool completely.

4 Turn cookies so pointed ends are up. Using desired tip, pipe frosting on upper 1/3 of cookie. Place 1 marshmallow half at tip of each cookie for hat; sprinkle with red sugar. Using small dots of frosting, attach 2 blue candies on each cookie for eyes. Pipe small frosting mustache below eyes; place red candy in center for mouth. Pipe frosting on lower 1/3 of each cookie for beard. Store cookies in single layer, loosely covered.

High Altitude (3500-6500 ft): No change.

Nutritional Info: 1 Cookie: Calories 190; Total Fat 11g (Saturated Fat 7g); Sodium 85mg; Total Carbohydrate 20g (Dietary Fiber 0g); Protein 2g. Exchanges: 1 Starch, 1/2 Other Carbohydrate, 2 Fat. Carbohydrate Choices: 1.

Betty's Kitchen Tips

Success Hint: These cookies are fragile when they are hot, but they are very sturdy once they have cooled.

Variation: Use any small round blue and red candies for the eyes and noses.

cranberry pistachio cookies

Prep Time: 1 Hour
Start to Finish: 1 Hour
Servings: 4 dozen cookies

Virginia Kocen
Norco, CA
Cookie Mix Contest 2010

- 1 pouch (1 lb 1.5 oz) Betty Crocker® sugar cookie mix
- 1 box (4-serving size) pistachio instant pudding and pie filling mix
- 1/4 cup Gold Medal® all-purpose flour
- 1/2 cup butter or margarine, melted
- 2 eggs
- 1 cup dry-roasted salted pistachio nuts, chopped
- 1/2 cup dried cranberries, chopped

1 Heat oven to 350°F. In large bowl, stir cookie mix, pudding mix and flour. Stir in butter and eggs until soft dough forms. Add nuts and cranberries; mix well.

2 Using small cookie scoop or teaspoon, drop dough 2 inches apart on ungreased cookie sheet. Press with fingers to slightly flatten.

3 Bake 9 to 11 minutes or until edges are light golden brown. Cool 2 minutes; remove from cookie sheet to cooling rack. Store cooled cookies tightly covered at room temperature.

High Altitude (3500-6500 ft): No change.

Nutritional Info: 1 Cookie: Calories 90; Total Fat 4.5g (Saturated Fat 1.5g); Sodium 85mg; Total Carbohydrate 12g (Dietary Fiber 0g); Protein 1g. Exchanges: 1 Other Carbohydrate, 1 Fat. Carbohydrate Choices: 1.

Betty's Kitchen Tip

• Use a food processor to quickly chop the nuts and cranberries.

lime christmas wreaths

Prep Time: 1 Hour 10 Minutes
Start to Finish: 2 Hours 45 Minutes
Servings: 2-1/2 dozen cookies

1/2	cup butter, softened	2-1/2	cups Gold Medal® all-purpose flour
1/4	cup sour cream	1/2	teaspoon baking soda
3/4	cup granulated sugar	1/4	teaspoon salt
1	egg	1	cup powdered sugar
2	tablespoons grated lime peel	2	to 3 tablespoons lime juice
1	tablespoon lime juice	Colored sugars, if desired	
1	teaspoon vanilla	White or colored sprinkles, if desired	

1 In large bowl, beat butter, sour cream and granulated sugar with electric mixer on medium speed until creamy. Add egg, lime peel, lime juice and vanilla; beat until smooth. On low speed, beat in flour, baking soda and salt until dough forms. Gather dough into ball; divide in half. Shape each half into a disk; wrap in plastic wrap. Refrigerate 1 hour.

2 Heat oven to 375°F. Place pastry cloth on work surface; sprinkle with flour. With floured cloth-covered rolling pin, roll 1 disk of dough 1/8 inch thick. Cut with floured 3-inch fluted cutter. With 1-inch scalloped or fluted canapé cutter, cut out center of each circle. On ungreased cookie sheet, place wreath cutouts 1 inch apart. Cut each small cutout in half; brush backs of small cutouts with water and place on wreaths for bows. Repeat with second disk of dough.

3 Bake 6 to 8 minutes or until edges start to brown. Remove from cookie sheet to cooling rack; cool completely.

4 In small bowl, mix powdered sugar and 2 tablespoons of the lime juice with wire whisk. Stir in remaining 1 tablespoon lime juice, 1 teaspoon at a time, until glaze is thin. Working with a few cookies at a time, brush glaze over cookies and immediately decorate with sugars and sprinkles as desired. Let stand until set. Store in layers with waxed paper between.

High Altitude (3500-6500 ft): No change.

Nutritional Info: 1 Cookie: Calories 110; Total Fat 3.5g (Saturated Fat 2g); Sodium 65mg; Total Carbohydrate 17g (Dietary Fiber 0g); Protein 1g. Exchanges: 1/2 Starch, 1/2 Other Carbohydrate, 1/2 Fat. Carbohydrate Choices: 1.

Betty's Kitchen Tip

• Silicone brushes work very well for brushing the glaze onto these cookies. The brushes can be purchased in most kitchen stores.

chocolate-peanut butter cookies

Prep Time: 45 Minutes
Start to Finish: 45 Minutes
Servings: About 3 dozen cookies

- -

1	can (14 oz) sweetened condensed milk
3/4	cup peanut butter
2	cups Original Bisquick® mix
1/4	cup sugar
1	teaspoon vanilla
1/3	cup sugar

About 36 milk chocolate-covered caramel candies

- -

1 Heat oven to 375°F. In large bowl, stir milk and peanut butter until smooth. Stir in Bisquick® mix, 1/4 cup sugar and the vanilla.

2 Shape dough into 1-1/4-inch balls. Roll tops in 1/3 cup sugar. On ungreased cookie sheet, place balls, sugar sides up, about 2 inches apart.

3 Bake 8 to 10 minutes or until bottoms of cookies just begin to brown. Immediately press chocolate candy into top of each cookie. Remove from cookie sheet to cooling rack.

High Altitude (3500-6500 ft): No change.

Nutritional Info: 1 Cookie: Calories 130 (Calories from Fat 50); Total Fat 6g (Saturated Fat 2g, Trans Fat 0g); Cholesterol 0mg; Sodium 140mg; Total Carbohydrate 16g (Dietary Fiber 0g, Sugars 11g); Protein 3g. % Daily Value: Vitamin A 0%; Vitamin C 0%; Calcium 6%; Iron 2%. Exchanges: 1 Starch, 1 Fat. Carbohydrate Choices: 1.

Betty's Kitchen Tip

• Try chocolate kisses, chocolate hearts or chocolate stars instead of the chocolate-caramel candies for something different.

chocolate-filled orange-rosemary butter balls

Prep Time: 1 Hour
Start to Finish: 1 Hour 30 Minutes
Servings: 2-1/2 dozen sandwich cookies

Cookies
1	cup butter, softened
1/2	cup powdered sugar
1	tablespoon grated orange peel
1	tablespoon finely chopped fresh rosemary leaves
1/4	teaspoon salt
1	teaspoon vanilla

2	cups Gold Medal® all-purpose flour
1/2	teaspoon baking powder
1/4	cup coarse white decorator sugar crystals, if desired

Filling
1/2	cup dark chocolate chips
2	tablespoons whipping (heavy) cream

1 Heat oven to 400°F. In large bowl, beat butter, powdered sugar, orange peel, rosemary, salt and vanilla with electric mixer on low speed until mixed; beat on medium speed until creamy. On low speed, beat in flour and baking powder until dough forms.

2 In small bowl, place decorator sugar. Shape dough into 60 (1-inch) balls. Roll in sugar. On ungreased cookie sheets, place balls 2 inches apart. Press lightly with tines of fork to flatten slightly.

3 Bake 6 to 8 minutes or just until edges start to brown. Remove from cookie sheets to cooling racks; cool completely.

4 Meanwhile, in small microwavable bowl, microwave chocolate chips and whipping cream uncovered on High in 15-second intervals until chips can be stirred smooth. Refrigerate until cooled and mixture starts to set, about 10 minutes.

5 For each sandwich cookie, spread about 1/2 teaspoon filling on bottom of 1 cookie. Press bottom of second cookie over filling. Let stand until set.

High Altitude (3500-6500 ft): No change.

Nutritional Info: 1 Sandwich Cookie: Calories 110; Total Fat 7g (Saturated Fat 4.5g); Sodium 75mg; Total Carbohydrate 10g (Dietary Fiber 0g); Protein 1g. Exchanges: 1/2 Other Carbohydrate, 1-1/2 Fat. Carbohydrate Choices: 1/2.

Betty's Kitchen Tips

Special Touch: Place filled cookies sideways in individual petit four paper cups or mini paper baking cups.

Success Hint: If you bake 2 cookie sheets at a time, switch their positions in the oven halfway through baking.

caramel cashew thumbprints

Prep Time: 45 Minutes
Start to Finish: 1 Hour
Servings: 5 dozen cookies

LOW FAT

3/4	cup butter, softened		1/4	teaspoon salt
3/4	cup powdered sugar		1/3	cup finely chopped cashews
1	teaspoon vanilla		15	milk chocolate squares with caramel filling (from 9.5 oz bag), unwrapped, cut into quarters
1	egg			
2	cups Gold Medal® all-purpose flour			
1/4	teaspoon baking powder			

1 Heat oven to 375°F. In large bowl, beat butter and powdered sugar with electric mixer on low speed until mixed; beat on medium speed until creamy. Add vanilla and egg; beat until mixed, scraping bowl if necessary. On low speed, beat in flour, baking powder and salt until dough forms. Stir in cashews.

2 Shape dough into 1-inch balls. On ungreased cookie sheet, place balls 2 inches apart. Press thumb into center of each cookie to make indentation, but do not press all the way to the cookie sheet.

3 Bake 7 to 9 minutes or until edges start to brown. Quickly remake indentation with end of wooden spoon handle if necessary. Remove from cookie sheet to cooling rack.

4 Place 1 chocolate candy quarter in the thumbprint of each warm cookie. Let stand 3 minutes to melt; with tip of small knife, swirl slightly to fill thumbprint. If desired, sprinkle with additional chopped cashews. Cool completely.

High Altitude (3500-6500 ft): No change.

Nutritional Info: 1 Cookie: Calories 50; Total Fat 3g (Saturated Fat 2g); Sodium 30mg; Total Carbohydrate 6g (Dietary Fiber 0g); Protein 0g. Exchanges: 1/2 Other Carbohydrate, 1/2 Fat. Carbohydrate Choices: 1/2.

Betty's Kitchen Tip

• Serve these beautiful cookies in colored mini cupcake liners or on an attractive plate.

nutty fun in the sun cookies

Prep Time: 25 Minutes
Start to Finish: 1 Hour
Servings: 3 dozen cookies

- 1/2 cup butter or margarine, softened
- 2 eggs
- 5 drops yellow food color, if desired
- 1 pouch (1 lb 1.5 oz) Betty Crocker® walnut chocolate chip cookie mix
- 2 tablespoons ground flaxseed or flaxseed meal
- 1/2 cup roasted salted sunflower nuts
- 1/2 cup sliced almonds
- 1/2 cup shredded coconut

1 Heat oven to 375°F. In medium bowl, mix butter, eggs and food color. Stir in cookie mix until soft dough forms. Stir in remaining ingredients.

2 On ungreased cookie sheets, drop dough by teaspoonfuls 2 inches apart. Bake 9 to 11 minutes or until light golden brown. Cool 1 to 2 minutes; remove from cookie sheets to cooling racks.

High Altitude (3500-6500 ft): No change.

Nutritional Info: 1 Cookie: Calories 120; Total Fat 7g (Saturated Fat 3g); Sodium 85mg; Total Carbohydrate 12g (Dietary Fiber 1g); Protein 1g. Exchanges: 1 Other Carbohydrate, 1-1/2 Fat. Carbohydrate Choices: 1.

Betty's Kitchen Tip

• Flaxseed contains several essential nutrients, including calcium, iron, niacin and vitamin E. You can easily store flaxseed in the refrigerator or freezer for up to 6 months.

snowflake mittens

Prep Time: 1 Hour
Start to Finish: 1 Hour 45 Minutes
Servings: 21 cookies

- 1 pouch (1 lb 1.5 oz) Betty Crocker® sugar cookie mix
- 1 tablespoon Gold Medal® all-purpose flour
- 1/3 cup butter, softened
- 1 egg
- 1 tablespoon grated lemon peel

- 1 container (1 lb) Betty Crocker® Rich & Creamy creamy white frosting
- 3 drops blue food color
- 1 can (6.4 oz) Betty Crocker® Easy Flow white decorating icing

White snowflake sprinkles or other white sprinkles, if desired

1 Heat oven to 375°F. In large bowl, stir cookie mix, flour, butter, egg and lemon peel until dough forms; gather into ball. Divide dough in half; shape into 2 disks. Wrap 1 disk in plastic wrap.

2 On floured surface, roll unwrapped disk 1/4 inch thick. Cut with 3-1/2-inch mitten-shaped cookie cutter. On ungreased large cookie sheet, place cutouts 1 inch apart. Repeat with second disk. Reroll scraps and cut out additional cookies.

3 Bake 8 to 10 minutes or until edges are light golden brown. Cool 1 minute before removing from cookie sheet to cooling rack; cool completely.

4 Using 1/2 cup of the creamy white frosting, frost cuffs of mittens. Stir food color into remaining white frosting. Frost remaining portion of mittens with blue frosting. With decorating icing and small round tip, pipe small snowflake on each mitten. Decorate with snowflake sprinkles. With star tip, decorate cuffs of mittens with decorating icing, if desired. Let dry.

High Altitude (3500-6500 ft): No change.

Nutritional Info: 1 Cookie: Calories 130; Total Fat 5g (Saturated Fat 2.5g); Sodium 90mg; Total Carbohydrate 18g (Dietary Fiber 0g); Protein 1g. Exchanges: 1/2 Starch, 1/2 Other Carbohydrate, 1 Fat. Carbohydrate Choices: 1.

Betty's Kitchen Tips

Special Touch: Spoon some of the blue frosting into a small resealable food-storage plastic bag; cut off a tiny corner of bag and pipe each child's name across the cuff of a mitten.

Do-Ahead: Bake the cookies a day ahead and store them in an airtight container. Get the frosting and decorating items ready, and let the kids help decorate.

oma's german chocolate chip cookies

Prep Time: 1 Hour 15 Minutes
Start to Finish: 1 Hour 15 Minutes
Servings: 24 cookies

Doreen Howarth
San Antonio, TX
Cookie Contest 2009

- 1 pouch (1 lb 1.5 oz) Betty Crocker® oatmeal chocolate chip cookie mix
- 1 egg
- 1 tablespoon unsweetened baking cocoa
- 1 container (1 lb) Betty Crocker® Rich and Creamy coconut pecan frosting
- 1 oz sweet baking chocolate, grated

1 Heat oven to 375°F. In large bowl, stir cookie mix, egg, cocoa and 3/4 cup of the frosting until soft dough forms.

2 Shape dough into 24 (1-1/4-inch) balls. On ungreased cookie sheets, place balls about 2 inches apart. Bake 11 to 13 minutes, or until set. Cool 1 to 2 minutes. Remove from cookie sheet to cooling rack. Cool completely, about 30 minutes.

3 Spread remaining frosting evenly over cookies. Sprinkle with chocolate.

High Altitude (3500-6500 ft): No change.

Nutritional Info: 1 Cookie: Calories 160; Total Fat 5g (Saturated Fat 2g); Sodium 110mg; Total Carbohydrate 26g (Dietary Fiber 0g); Protein 2g. Exchanges: 1/2 Starch, 1 Other Carbohydrate, 1 Fat. Carbohydrate Choices: 2.

Betty's Kitchen Tip

- Don't want to grate chocolate? A sprinkling of baking cocoa in place of the grated chocolate on each cookie is a nice substitute.

lemon-coconut cream drops

Prep Time: 45 Minutes
Start to Finish: 1 Hour 45 Minutes
Servings: 3 dozen cookies

- 1   bag (7 oz) flaked coconut
     (about 2-2/3 cups)
- 1   pouch (1 lb 1.5 oz) Betty Crocker®
     sugar cookie mix
- 1   cup macadamia nuts, finely chopped
- 1   package (8 oz) cream cheese, softened

- 1/2 cup butter or margarine, softened
- 1   egg
- 1   tablespoon grated lemon peel
- 2   drops yellow food color
- 1   cup white vanilla baking chips (6 oz)

1 Heat oven to 350°F. Spray 2 cookie sheets with cooking spray.

2 In food processor, place coconut. Cover; process, using quick on-and-off motion, until finely chopped. In large bowl, mix coconut, cookie mix and 1/2 cup of the macadamia nuts. Set aside.

3 In medium bowl, beat cream cheese and butter with electric mixer on medium speed about 30 seconds or until smooth. Beat in egg, lemon peel and food color until well blended. On low speed, beat in coconut mixture until stiff dough forms.

4 On cookie sheets, drop dough by rounded teaspoonfuls 2 inches apart. Bake 8 to 10 minutes or until edges begin to brown. Cool 1 to 2 minutes; remove from cookie sheets to cooling rack. Cool completely, about 30 minutes.

5 Place baking chips in small resealable freezer plastic bag. Microwave on High 45 to 50 seconds until softened. Gently squeeze bag until chips are smooth; cut tiny tip off one corner of bag. Squeeze bag to drizzle over cookies. Sprinkle with remaining 1/2 cup macadamia nuts. Let stand until drizzle hardens, about 10 minutes.

High Altitude (3500-6500 ft): No change.

Nutritional Info: 1 Cookie: Calories 200; Total Fat 14g (Saturated Fat 8g); Sodium 95mg; Total Carbohydrate 17g (Dietary Fiber 1g); Protein 2g. Exchanges: 1 Other Carbohydrate, 3 Fat. Carbohydrate Choices: 1.

Betty's Kitchen Tip

- These pretty cookies with a light lemony flavor are nice for Easter, weddings and other spring or summer occasions.

butter pecan thumbprints

Prep Time: 1 Hour 10 Minutes
Start to Finish: 1 Hour 40 Minutes
Servings: 3 dozen cookies

Mary Shivers
Ada, OK
Celebrate the Season-Fall Baking Contest

1	cup packed light brown sugar
1/2	cup unsalted butter, softened
1	egg, beaten
2	teaspoons vanilla
1-1/2	cups Gold Medal® all-purpose flour
1/4	teaspoon baking soda
1/8	teaspoon kosher (coarse) salt
1-1/2	cups finely chopped pecans

Filling

1/3	cup packed light brown sugar
2	tablespoons Gold Medal® all-purpose flour
1	cup finely chopped pecans
2	tablespoons unsalted butter, softened

1 Heat oven to 325°F. Grease cookie sheet with shortening or cooking spray or line with cooking parchment paper or silicone baking mat.

2 In large bowl, beat 1 cup brown sugar, 1/2 cup butter, the egg and vanilla with electric mixer on low speed. Stir in 1-1/2 cups flour, the baking soda and salt. Stir in 1-1/2 cups pecans.

3 In small bowl, mix 1/3 cup brown sugar, 2 tablespoons flour and 1 cup pecans. Stir in 2 tablespoons butter with fork until mixture is crumbly.

4 Shape dough into 1-1/2-inch balls. Place 2 inches apart on cookie sheet. Press thumb into center of each cookie to make indentation, but do not press all the way to the cookie sheet. Fill each indentation with about 1 teaspoon of filling.

5 Bake 10 to 15 minutes or until edges are golden brown. Cool 5 minutes; remove from cookie sheet to cooling rack.

High Altitude (3500-6500 ft): No change.

Nutritional Info: 1 Cookie: Calories 150; Total Fat 9g (Saturated Fat 2.5g); Sodium 20mg; Total Carbohydrate 16g (Dietary Fiber 1g); Protein 1g. Exchanges: 1 Other Carbohydrate, 2 Fat. Carbohydrate Choices: 1.

Betty's Kitchen Tip

• Use a thimble or the end of a wooden spoon to make uniform indentations in cookie dough.

best-ever chewy gingerbread cookies

Prep Time: 1 Hour 30 Minutes
Start to Finish: 3 Hours 30 Minutes
Servings: 7-1/2 dozen cookies

LOW FAT

Shannon Bills, Indio, CA
Celebrate the Season-
Holiday Cookie Contest

1	cup plus 2 tablespoons unsalted butter, softened
1	cup packed brown sugar
1	egg
1/4	cup plus 2 tablespoons molasses
2-1/2	cups Gold Medal® all-purpose flour
2-1/4	teaspoons baking soda

1/2	teaspoon kosher (coarse) salt
1	tablespoon ground ginger
1	tablespoon ground cinnamon
2	teaspoons ground cloves
1-1/2	teaspoons ground nutmeg
1/2	teaspoon ground allspice
2/3	cup granulated or coarse sugar

1 In large bowl, beat butter and brown sugar with electric mixer on medium speed until light and fluffy, about 5 minutes. Beat in egg and molasses. Stir in remaining ingredients except granulated sugar. Cover; refrigerate at least 2 hours.

2 Heat oven to 350°F. Line cookie sheets with cooking parchment paper or silicone baking mat. In small bowl, place granulated sugar. Shape dough into 1-inch balls; roll in sugar. On cookie sheets, place balls 2 inches apart.

3 Bake 8 to 10 minutes or just until set and soft in center. Cool 2 minutes; remove from cookie sheets to cooling racks. Store tightly covered up to 1 week.

High Altitude (3500-6500 ft): No change.

Nutritional Info: 1 Cookie: Calories 50; Total Fat 2.5g (Saturated Fat 1.5g); Sodium 45mg; Total Carbohydrate 8g (Dietary Fiber 0g); Protein 0g. Exchanges: 1/2 Other Carbohydrate, 1/2 Fat. Carbohydrate Choices: 1/2.

Betty's Kitchen Tips

Purchasing: Look for cooking parchment paper with the waxed paper, foil and plastic wrap at the grocery store. Silicone baking mats are also becoming widely available and are now sold in a variety of stores.

Success Hint: You can use light or dark molasses in this recipe.

cinnamon-raisin oatmeal cookies

Prep Time: 1 Hour
Start to Finish: 1 Hour
Servings: 2-1/2 dozen cookies

1	cup packed brown sugar
1	cup butter or margarine, softened
2	teaspoons vanilla
2	eggs
1- 3/4	cups Gold Medal® all-purpose flour
1	teaspoon baking soda
1	teaspoon ground cinnamon
1/4	teaspoon salt
1	cup old-fashioned oats
1	cup Fiber One® original bran cereal
1/2	cup raisins

1 Heat oven to 350°F. In large bowl, beat brown sugar and butter with electric mixer on medium speed until creamy. On low speed, beat in vanilla and eggs until well blended. Beat in flour, baking soda, cinnamon and salt until well blended. With spoon, stir in oats, cereal and raisins.

2 Onto ungreased cookie sheet, drop dough by heaping tablespoonfuls about 2 inches apart.

3 Bake 12 to 15 minutes or until set and golden brown. Immediately remove from cookie sheet to cooling rack.

High Altitude (3500-6500 ft): No change.

Nutritional Info: 1 Cookie: Calories 140; Total Fat 7g (Saturated Fat 4g); Sodium 130mg; Total Carbohydrate 18g (Dietary Fiber 1g); Protein 1g. Exchanges: 1/2 Starch, 1/2 Other Carbohydrate, 1-1/2 Fat. Carbohydrate Choices: 1.

Betty's Kitchen Tip

• This oatmeal cookie boasts the addition of high-fiber bran cereal.

cran-orange 'n date-nut cookies

Prep Time: 55 Minutes
Start to Finish: 1 Hour
Servings: 3-1/2 dozen cookies

Barbara Estabrook
Rhinelander, WI
Cookie Mix Contest 2006

1/3   cup dried cranberries
1/4   cup chopped orange slice candies
1/4   cup coarsely chopped dates
  2   tablespoons fresh orange juice
  1   pouch (1 lb 1.5 oz) Betty Crocker®
      sugar cookie mix
  2   tablespoons Gold Medal® all-purpose flour
1/2   teaspoon ground cinnamon

1/4   teaspoon ground ginger
1/3   cup butter or margarine, melted
  1   teaspoon grated orange peel
  1   egg
  1   cup chopped pistachio nuts
1/2   cup flaked coconut

1 Heat oven to 375°F. In small bowl, mix cranberries, candies, dates and orange juice; set aside. In large bowl, stir cookie mix, flour, cinnamon and ginger until blended. Stir in butter, orange peel and egg until soft dough forms. Stir in cranberry mixture, nuts and coconut.

2 Onto ungreased cookie sheets, drop dough by teaspoonfuls 2 inches apart.

3 Bake 10 to 12 minutes or until edges are light golden brown. Cool 5 minutes; remove from cookie sheets to cooling racks. Store cooled cookies tightly covered.

High Altitude (3500-6500 ft): No change.

Nutritional Info: 1 Cookie: Calories 100; Total Fat 4.5g (Saturated Fat 1.5g); Sodium 50mg; Total Carbohydrate 13g (Dietary Fiber 0g); Protein 1g. Exchanges: 1/2 Starch, 1/2 Other Carbohydrate, 1 Fat. Carbohydrate Choices: 1.

Betty's Kitchen Tip

• Use a spring-loaded scoop to make quick work out of dropping cookie dough. The cookies will be the same size, so they'll bake evenly and for the same time. Look for the scoops at kitchen specialty stores.

ginger-brown sugar cookies

Prep Time: 45 Minutes
Start to Finish: 45 Minutes
Servings: 3 dozen cookies

- 1 cup packed brown sugar
- 3/4 cup butter or margarine, softened
- 1 teaspoon vanilla
- 1 egg
- 2 cups Gold Medal® all-purpose flour
- 1/2 teaspoon baking soda
- 1/2 teaspoon ground ginger
- 1/2 cup finely chopped crystallized ginger
- 2 tablespoons granulated sugar

1 Heat oven to 375°F. In large bowl, beat brown sugar, butter, vanilla and egg with electric mixer on medium speed, or mix with spoon. Stir in remaining ingredients except granulated sugar.

2 Shape dough by rounded teaspoonfuls into 1-inch balls. Place about 2 inches apart on ungreased cookie sheet. Flatten to 1/2-inch thickness with greased bottom of glass dipped in granulated sugar.

3 Bake 8 to 10 minutes or until edges are set. Remove from the cookie sheet to a cooling rack.

High Altitude (3500-6500 ft): No change.

Nutritional Info: 1 Cookie: Calories 90; Total Fat 4g (Saturated Fat 2.5g); Sodium 50mg; Total Carbohydrate 12g (Dietary Fiber 0g); Protein 1g. Exchanges: 1/2 Starch, 1/2 Other Carbohydrate, 1/2 Fat. Carbohydrate Choices: 1.

Betty's Kitchen Tip

• For a frosty white finish, dip half of each cookie in a thin vanilla glaze or melted white chocolate. Let stand on waxed paper until coating sets.

glazed bohemian anise cookies

Prep Time: 1 Hour 5 Minutes
Start to Finish: 1 Hour 50 Minutes
Servings: 2-1/2 dozen cookies

David Dahlman
Chatsworth, CA
Celebrate the Season-Holiday Cookie Contest

Cookies

3/4	cup butter, softened
1/2	cup sugar
1	egg
1	teaspoon grated lemon peel
1-3/4	cups Gold Medal® all-purpose flour
1	teaspoon ground cinnamon
1/4	teaspoon ground cloves
1/4	teaspoon ground nutmeg

1/4	teaspoon pepper
1	teaspoon anise seed
2	tablespoons Gold Medal® all-purpose flour

Glaze and Topping

3/4	cup white vanilla baking chips
1	teaspoon oil
1/4	teaspoon anise extract
1/4	cup chopped almonds, toasted

1 Heat oven to 350°F. In large bowl, beat butter and sugar with electric mixer on medium speed until smooth. Beat in egg and lemon peel. Stir in 1-3/4 cups flour, the cinnamon, cloves, nutmeg, pepper and anise seed.

2 Shape dough into 1-1/4-inch balls. On ungreased cookie sheet, place balls about 1 inch apart. Dip bottom of drinking glass in 2 tablespoons flour; press each ball until about 1/4 inch thick.

3 Bake 11 to 14 minutes or until edges are light golden brown. Remove from cookie sheet to cooling rack. Cool 15 minutes.

4 In a small microwavable bowl, microwave baking chips and oil on High 10 seconds; stir. Microwave in 10-second intervals until mixture can be stirred smooth. Stir in anise extract. Spoon into small resealable food-storage plastic bag; cut off tiny corner of bag. Squeeze bag to drizzle glaze over cookies. Immediately sprinkle with almonds. Let stand until set, about 30 minutes.

High Altitude (3500-6500 ft): No change.

Nutritional Info: 1 Cookie: Calories 130; Total Fat 8g (Saturated Fat 4.5g); Sodium 40mg; Total Carbohydrate 14g (Dietary Fiber 0g); Protein 1g. Exchanges: 1 Other Carbohydrate, 1-1/2 Fat. Carbohydrate Choices: 1.

Betty's Kitchen Tip

• To toast almonds, heat oven to 350°F. Spread almonds in ungreased shallow pan. Bake uncovered 6 to 10 minutes, stirring occasionally, until light brown.

raspberry pistachio thumbprints

Prep Time: 1 Hour 20 Minutes
Start to Finish: 1 Hour 50 Minutes
Servings: 3-1/2 dozen cookies

Laura Murphy, Columbus, MS
Celebrate the Season-Holiday Cookie Contest
Grand Prize Winner

1	cup butter or margarine, softened
1/2	cup powdered sugar
2	cups Gold Medal® all-purpose flour
1/4	teaspoon salt
1	teaspoon vanilla
1	cup finely chopped roasted pistachio nuts
1	jar (12 oz) red raspberry jam
2	tablespoons powdered sugar

1 Heat oven to 325°F. In large bowl, beat butter and 1/2 cup powdered sugar with electric mixer on medium speed until creamy. Stir in flour, salt, vanilla and nuts.

2 Shape dough into 1-1/4-inch balls. On ungreased cookie sheet, place balls about 1 inch apart. Press thumb into center of each cookie to make indentation, but do not press all the way to the cookie sheet.

3 Bake 15 to 17 minutes or until set but not browned. Quickly remake indentation with end of wooden spoon handle if necessary. Remove from cookie sheet to cooling rack; cool completely, about 30 minutes.

4 Fill each thumbprint with about 1 rounded teaspoonful of jam. Sprinkle 2 tablespoons powdered sugar over jam-filled centers.

High Altitude (3500-6500 ft): No change.

Nutritional Info: 1 Cookie: Calories 110; Total Fat 6g (Saturated Fat 3g); Sodium 60mg; Total Carbohydrate 13g (Dietary Fiber 0g); Protein 1g. Exchanges: 1/2 Starch, 1/2 Other Carbohydrate, 1 Fat. Carbohydrate Choices: 1.

Betty's Kitchen Tips

Success Hint: A food processor works great for finely chopping the pistachio nuts.

Substitution: You can use strawberry jam or your favorite flavor for the raspberry.

pecan candied jewels

Prep Time: 1 Hour 10 Minutes
Start to Finish: 1 Hour 20 Minutes
Servings: 3-1/2 dozen cookies

Susan Rodgers
Round Rock, TX
Celebrate the Season-Holiday Cookie Contest

Cookies

1/4	cup unsalted butter, softened
1/2	cup packed brown sugar
2	tablespoons granulated sugar
2	eggs
1/4	cup apple juice
1-1/2	cups Gold Medal® all-purpose flour
1-1/4	teaspoons baking soda
1/2	teaspoon ground cloves
1/8	teaspoon ground nutmeg
1/8	teaspoon ground cinnamon

2	cups chopped pecans (8 oz)
1-1/2	cups chopped pitted dates (8 oz)
1/2	cup finely chopped candied cherries (4 oz)
1/2	cup finely chopped candied pineapple (4 oz)
2/3	cup finely chopped dried apricots (4 oz)

Glaze

2	tablespoons water
2	tablespoons packed brown sugar
2	tablespoons orange juice
1	tablespoon corn syrup

1 Heat oven to 350°F. Line cookie sheet with cooking parchment paper or silicone baking mat.

2 In large bowl, beat butter, 1/2 cup brown sugar and the granulated sugar with electric mixer on medium-high speed. Add eggs, one at a time, beating after each. On medium-low speed, beat in apple juice, flour, baking soda, cloves, nutmeg and cinnamon. Stir in nuts and fruit until incorporated (mixture will be stiff and sticky).

3 On cookie sheet, drop dough by heaping teaspoonfuls about 2 inches apart.

4 Bake 10 to 12 minutes or until edges are golden brown. Remove from cookie sheet to cooling rack; cool 10 minutes.

5 In 1-quart saucepan, heat all glaze ingredients to boiling; cook and stir until sugar is dissolved. Brush over tops of cookies.

High Altitude (3500-6500 ft): No change.

Nutritional Info: 1 Cookie: Calories 130; Total Fat 5g (Saturated Fat 1g); Sodium 50mg; Total Carbohydrate 19g (Dietary Fiber 1g); Protein 1g. Exchanges: 1/2 Starch, 1 Other Carbohydrate, 1 Fat. Carbohydrate Choices: 1.

Betty's Kitchen Tip

• Use red or green candied cherries or use a combination of both.

chocolate chip-oatmeal shortbread cookies

Prep Time: 1 Hour 5 Minutes
Start to Finish: 1 Hour 20 Minutes
Servings: 4-1/2 dozen cookies

Laurie DeHamer
Granville, IA
Celebrate the Season-Holiday Cookie Contest

1	cup butter, softened
1	cup powdered sugar
1-1/2	cups Gold Medal® all-purpose flour
1/2	teaspoon baking soda
2	teaspoons vanilla
1	cup quick-cooking oats
1	bag (12 oz) miniature semisweet chocolate chips

1 Heat oven to 325°F. In large bowl, beat butter and powdered sugar with electric mixer on medium speed until light and fluffy. Stir in flour, baking soda, vanilla and oats. Stir in chocolate chips.

2 On ungreased cookie sheets, drop dough by teaspoonfuls 2 inches apart.

3 Bake 11 to 13 minutes or until lightly browned. Cool 1 minute; remove from cookie sheets to cooling racks.

High Altitude (3500-6500 ft): No change.

Nutritional Info: 1 Cookie: Calories 90; Total Fat 5g (Saturated Fat 3.5g); Sodium 35mg; Total Carbohydrate 10g (Dietary Fiber 0g); Protein 1g. Exchanges: 1/2 Other Carbohydrate, 1 Fat. Carbohydrate Choices: 1/2.

Betty's Kitchen Tip

• Both old-fashioned and quick-cooking oats are whole oats that have been steamed and rolled. Because the quick-cooking variety is cut into small pieces before steaming, it gives baked goods a softer texture.

candy corn roll-up cookies

Prep Time: 1 Hour 10 Minutes
Start to Finish: 3 Hours 5 Minutes
Servings: About 3-1/2 dozen cookies

1 cup butter or margarine, softened	1 teaspoon baking soda
1-1/2 cups powdered sugar	1 teaspoon cream of tartar
1 egg	1/8 teaspoon orange gel food color
Grated peel of 1 medium orange	1/8 teaspoon yellow gel food color
(1 to 2 tablespoons)	Coarse sugar, if desired
2-1/2 cups Gold Medal® all-purpose flour	

1 In large bowl, beat butter, powdered sugar, egg and orange peel with electric mixer on medium speed, or mix with spoon. Stir in flour, baking soda and cream of tartar.

2 Divide dough into thirds. Tint one portion orange and one portion yellow; leave remaining portion plain. Flatten each portion into a disk. Wrap in plastic wrap; refrigerate 20 minutes.

3 On separate sheets of lightly floured waxed paper, roll each portion of dough into 12x9-inch rectangle. Place orange rectangle on top of yellow rectangle, using waxed paper ends to help flip dough over. Top with plain dough rectangle. Starting on a long side, and using waxed paper as an aid, roll dough into a cylinder. Wrap in plastic; refrigerate 1 hour.

4 Heat oven to 375°F. Cut dough into 1/4-inch slices. On ungreased cookie sheet, place slices about 1 inch apart. Sprinkle with coarse sugar.

5 Bake 7 to 8 minutes or until edges are set. Cool 1 minute; remove from cookie sheet to cooling rack.

High Altitude (3500-6500 ft): No change.

Nutritional Info: 1 Cookie: Calories 90; Total Fat 4.5g (Saturated Fat 3g); Sodium 65mg; Total Carbohydrate 10g (Dietary Fiber 0g); Protein 1g. Exchanges: 1/2 Starch, 1 Fat. Carbohydrate Choices: 1/2.

Betty's Kitchen Tip

• For a fun look, turn these into lollipop cookies. Before baking, place paper lollipop sticks on cookie sheet and lay bottom of dough slices on top of sticks. Bake as directed in the recipe.

cherry-topped chocolate tassies

Prep Time: 25 Minutes
Start to Finish: 1 Hour 10 Minutes
Servings: 2 dozen cookies

1/2	cup butter, softened
1	package (3 oz) cream cheese, softened
1	cup Gold Medal® all-purpose flour
1/8	teaspoon salt
1	cup miniature semisweet chocolate chips
24	large maraschino cherries, drained

1 Heat oven to 350°F. Spray 24 mini muffin cups with cooking spray.

2 In medium bowl, beat butter and cream cheese with electric mixer on medium speed until well mixed. On low speed, beat in flour and salt until dough forms.

3 Shape dough into 24 (1-1/4-inch) balls. Press in bottoms and up sides of muffin cups. Fill each cup with about 2 teaspoons chocolate chips. Top each with a cherry.

4 Bake 13 to 16 minutes or until edges of cups are golden brown. Cool 10 minutes. Remove from muffin cups to cooling rack; cool completely.

High Altitude (3500-6500 ft): No change.

Nutritional Info: 1 Cookie: Calories 110; Total Fat 7g (Saturated Fat 4.5g); Sodium 50mg; Total Carbohydrate 10g (Dietary Fiber 0g); Protein 1g. Exchanges: 1/2 Other Carbohydrate, 1-1/2 Fat. Carbohydrate Choices: 1/2.

Betty's Kitchen Tip

• These tassies are fragile when they're hot, so it's important to let them cool 10 minutes before removing from the muffin cups. They set up once they are cooled.

pumpkin whoopie pies

Prep Time: 1 Hour
Start to Finish: 1 Hour 15 Minutes
Servings: 1-1/2 dozen sandwich cookies

Cookies

- 1 pouch (1 lb 1.5 oz) Betty Crocker® sugar cookie mix
- 1 tablespoon Gold Medal® all-purpose flour
- 1/2 cup canned pumpkin (not pumpkin pie mix)
- 1/3 cup butter or margarine, softened
- 2 teaspoons ground cinnamon
- 1 egg

Filling

- 2/3 cup marshmallow creme (from 7-oz jar)
- 1/3 cup butter or margarine, softened
- 2/3 cup powdered sugar

1 Heat oven to 375°F. In large bowl, stir together cookie mix and flour. Add remaining cookie ingredients; stir until stiff dough forms.

2 Onto ungreased cookie sheets, drop dough by 36 rounded teaspoonfuls 2 inches apart. Lightly press tops with floured fingertips to flatten slightly.

3 Bake 8 to 10 minutes or until set. Cool 2 minutes; remove from cookie sheets to cooling racks. Cool completely, about 15 minutes.

4 In medium bowl, beat filling ingredients with electric mixer until light and fluffy. For each whoopie pie, spread about 2 teaspoons of the filling on bottom of 1 cooled cookie. Top with second cookie, bottom side down; gently press together. Store tightly covered in refrigerator. Sprinkle with additional powdered sugar just before serving.

High Altitude (3500-6500 ft): No change.

Nutritional Info: 1 Cookie: Calories 210; Total Fat 10g (Saturated Fat 5g); Sodium 135mg; Total Carbohydrate 29g (Dietary Fiber 0g); Protein 1g. Exchanges: 1/2 Starch, 1-1/2 Other Carbohydrate, 2 Fat. Carbohydrate Choices: 2.

Betty's Kitchen Tip

- Use the leftover canned pumpkin to make Pumpkin Swirl Brownies (page 288).

oh so good chocolate cherry cookies

Prep Time: 1 Hour 10 Minutes
Start to Finish: 1 Hour 30 Minutes
Servings: 36 cookies

Ann Rozzi
Rochester, NY
Cookie Contest 2009

1	pouch (1 lb 1.5 oz) Betty Crocker® double chocolate chunk cookie mix
1/4	cup vegetable oil
2	tablespoons water
1	egg
1/4	cup almonds, finely chopped
36	maraschino cherries, from 2 jars, drained, pat dry
1	cup semi sweet chocolate chips (from 12-oz. bag)
1/4	cup whipping (heavy) cream

1 Heat oven to 350°F. In a large bowl, stir cookie mix, oil, water and egg until soft dough forms. Stir in almonds. Drop dough by rounded teaspoonfuls 2 inches apart onto ungreased cookie sheet. Place 1 cherry on each cookie. Bake 8 to 10 minutes. Cool 1 minute before removing from cookie sheet.

2 Meanwhile, in small microwavable bowl, microwave chocolate chips and cream uncovered on High 30 to 45 seconds; stir until smooth. Spoon generous teaspoon on each cookie and spread over cookie. Allow chocolate to set until firm, about 30 minutes.

High Altitude (3500-6500 ft): No change.

Nutritional Info: 1 Cookie: Calories 110; Total Fat 5g (Saturated Fat 2g); Sodium 65mg; Total Carbohydrate 16g (Dietary Fiber 0g); Protein 1g. Exchanges: 1 Other Carbohydrate, 1 Fat. Carbohydrate Choices: 1.

Betty's Kitchen Tip

• To dress up these cookies, lightly drizzle the melted chocolate back and forth over the top.

pumpkin-pecan spice cookies

Prep Time: 1 Hour 5 Minutes
Start to Finish: 1 Hour 35 Minutes
Servings: 3-1/2 dozen cookies

Debra Keil
Owasso, OK
Celebrate the Season-Fall Baking Contest

1-1/2	cups packed light brown sugar
1/2	cup butter or margarine, softened
2	eggs
1/2	cup canned pumpkin (not pumpkin pie mix)
3	teaspoons vanilla
2-3/4	cups Gold Medal® all-purpose flour
2	teaspoons baking powder
1	teaspoon ground cinnamon
1/2	teaspoon salt

1/2	teaspoon ground ginger
1/4	teaspoon ground nutmeg
1/8	teaspoon ground allspice
1/8	teaspoon ground cloves
Pinch ground cardamom	
1-1/3	cups finely chopped pecans
1/2	cup white vanilla baking chips
4	oz vanilla-flavored candy coating (almond bark), chopped

1 Heat oven to 350°F. Grease cookie sheet with shortening or cooking spray, or line with cooking parchment paper or silicone baking mat.

2 In large bowl, beat brown sugar, butter, eggs, pumpkin and vanilla with electric mixer on medium speed. Stir in flour, baking powder and spices. Stir in pecans and baking chips. Drop dough by tablespoonfuls onto cookie sheet.

3 Bake 10 to 14 minutes or until edges are lightly browned. Remove to cooling rack. Cool completely, about 30 minutes.

4 Place candy coating in small resealable freezer plastic bag; seal bag. Microwave on High about 1 minute or until softened. Gently squeeze bag until coating is smooth; cut off tiny corner of bag. Squeeze bag to drizzle coating over cookies. Let stand until set.

High Altitude (3500-6500 ft): No change.

Nutritional Info: 1 Cookie: Calories 140; Total Fat 7g (Saturated Fat 3g); Sodium 80mg; Total Carbohydrate 18g (Dietary Fiber 0g); Protein 2g. Exchanges: 1 Other Carbohydrate, 1-1/2 Fat. Carbohydrate Choices: 1.

Betty's Kitchen Tips

Purchasing: When buying canned pumpkin, check the label to be sure it's not pumpkin pie mix, which contains sugar and spices.

Substitution: Try cooked winter squash in place of the pumpkin.

dark chocolate apricot cookies

Prep Time: 1 Hour
Start to Finish: 3 Hours
Servings: 3 dozen cookies

Pat Muzzy
Roseville, MN
Cookie Mix Contest 2010

1	pouch (1 lb 1.5 oz) Betty Crocker® sugar cookie mix
1/2	cup butter or margarine, softened
1/4	teaspoon orange extract
1	egg
1	cup chopped dried apricots
1	package (12 oz) dark chocolate chips

1 Heat oven to 375°F. In large bowl, stir cookie mix, butter, orange extract and egg until soft dough forms. Stir in apricots until blended.

2 On ungreased cookie sheet, drop dough by rounded teaspoonfuls 2 inches apart.

3 Bake 8 to 10 minutes or until edges are light golden brown. Cool 3 minutes; remove from cookie sheet to cooling rack. Cool completely, about 15 minutes.

4 In small microwavable bowl, microwave chocolate chips uncovered on High for 1 to 2 minutes, stirring every 30 seconds, until chips are melted. Dip each cookie halfway into melted chocolate, letting excess drip off. Place on waxed paper; let stand until chocolate is set, at least 2 hours. To quickly set chocolate, refrigerate cookies 15 minutes. Store between sheets of waxed paper in tightly covered container at room temperature.

High Altitude (3500-6500 ft): No change.

Nutritional Info: 1 Cookie: Calories 140; Total Fat 7g (Saturated Fat 3.5g); Sodium 60mg; Total Carbohydrate 19g (Dietary Fiber 1g); Protein 1g. Exchanges: 1/2 Starch, 1 Other Carbohydrate, 1 Fat. Carbohydrate Choices: 1.

Betty's Kitchen Tip

• Dried fruit can be sticky to chop. Try dipping a kitchen scissor in water to cut the dried apricots into small pieces.

cherry-almond refrigerator cookies

Prep Time: 1 Hour 15 Minutes
Start to Finish: 3 Hours 30 Minutes
Servings: 5 to 6 dozen cookies

1/2	cup slivered almonds	1	teaspoon almond extract
1	cup butter or margarine, softened	2-1/2	cups Gold Medal® all-purpose flour
1	cup granulated sugar	1-1/2	teaspoons baking powder
1/2	cup packed brown sugar	1/2	teaspoon salt
1	egg	1	cup chopped red candied cherries

1 Sprinkle almonds in ungreased heavy skillet. Cook over medium heat 5 to 7 minutes, stirring frequently until nuts begin to brown, then stirring constantly until nuts are light brown. Cool 10 minutes. In food processor, process almonds until finely chopped; set aside.

2 In large bowl, beat butter, granulated sugar and brown sugar with electric mixer on medium speed until smooth and creamy. Add egg and almond extract; beat on medium speed until smooth. On low speed, beat in flour, baking powder and salt until dough forms. Stir in cherries and chopped almonds.

3 Form dough into 2 (8-inch) logs. Wrap in plastic wrap or waxed paper. Refrigerate at least 2 hours.

4 Heat oven to 375°F. Cut dough into 1/8- to 1/4-inch slices. On ungreased cookie sheets, place slices 2 inches apart.

5 Bake 7 to 9 minutes or until edges start to turn golden brown. Cool 1 minute; remove from cookie sheets to cooling racks.

High Altitude (3500-6500 ft): No change.

Nutritional Info: 1 Cookie: Calories 80; Total Fat 3.5g (Saturated Fat 2g); Sodium 60mg; Total Carbohydrate 12g (Dietary Fiber 0g); Protein 1g. Exchanges: 1/2 Starch, 1/2 Other Carbohydrate, 1/2 Fat. Carbohydrate Choices: 1.

Betty's Kitchen Tips

Do-Ahead: These are ideal holiday cookies. You can keep the logs of dough in the refrigerator up to 2 weeks and bake them as you need fresh cookies. You can also double-wrap them and freeze up to 1 month.

Variation: Add an elegant look to these cookies by piping with powdered sugar drizzle. It is quick and easy if you line up rows of cookies so you can just pipe along a long row. Just be sure to separate the cookies slightly as they set so they don't stick together.

citrus-kissed fig thumbprints

Prep Time: 55 Minutes
Start to Finish: 55 Minutes
Servings: 4 dozen cookies

Edwina Gadsby
Great Falls, MT
Cookie Mix Contest 2010

LOW FAT

1	pouch (1 lb 1.5 oz) Betty Crocker® sugar cookie mix
3	tablespoons Gold Medal® all-purpose flour
1/2	cup butter or margarine, melted
1	teaspoon grated lemon peel
1	teaspoon grated orange peel
1/2	teaspoon vanilla
1	egg
1/3	cup fig preserves
1	teaspoon coarse sugar, if desired

1 Heat oven to 375°F. In large bowl, stir cookie mix, flour, butter, lemon peel, orange peel, vanilla and egg until soft dough forms.

2 Roll dough into 1-inch balls. On ungreased cookie sheets, place balls 2 inches apart. Press thumb into center of each cookie to make indentation, but do not press all the way to the cookie sheet. Spoon about 1/4 teaspoon preserves into each indentation.

3 Bake 7 to 9 minutes or until edges are light golden brown. Cool 2 minutes; remove from cookie sheets to cooling racks. Sprinkle with coarse sugar. Store cooled cookies tightly covered at room temperature.

High Altitude (3500-6500 ft): No change.

Nutritional Info: 1 Cookie: Calories 70; Total Fat 3g (Saturated Fat 1.5g); Sodium 45mg; Total Carbohydrate 10g (Dietary Fiber 0g); Protein 0g. Exchanges: 1/2 Other Carbohydrate, 1/2 Fat. Carbohydrate Choices: 1/2.

Betty's Kitchen Tip

• Grating lemon and orange peel is a breeze when you use a handheld Microplane® grater. Look for them where kitchen supplies are sold.

memory lane oatmeal peanut butter crème sandwiches

Prep Time: 1 Hour
Start to Finish: 1 Hour 15 Minutes
Servings: 20 sandwich cookies

Nancy Elliott
Houston, TX
Cookie Mix Contest 2010

Cookies

- 1 pouch (1 lb 1.5 oz) Betty Crocker® oatmeal cookie mix
- 1/4 cup packed brown sugar
- 1/2 cup butter or margarine, softened
- 1/2 cup creamy peanut butter
- 1 tablespoon water
- 1 egg

Filling

- 1 cup creamy peanut butter
- 1/2 cup Betty Crocker® Rich & Creamy vanilla frosting (from 1-lb container)
- 4 teaspoons milk

1 Heat oven to 375°F. In large bowl, stir cookie mix, brown sugar, butter, 1/2 cup peanut butter, the water and egg until soft dough forms.

2 Roll dough into 40 (1-1/4-inch) balls. On ungreased cookie sheet, place balls 2 inches apart. Press with fingers to slightly flatten.

3 Bake 9 to 10 minutes or until light golden brown. Cool 3 minutes; remove from cookie sheet to cooling rack. Cool completely, about 15 minutes.

4 In small bowl, stir filling ingredients until well blended. For each sandwich cookie, spread about 1 tablespoon filling on bottom of 1 cookie; top with another cookie, bottom side down. Press together lightly, twisting slightly. Store tightly covered at room temperature.

High Altitude (3500-6500 ft): No change.

Nutritional Info: 1 Sandwich Cookie: Calories 300; Total Fat 17g (Saturated Fat 5g); Sodium 230mg; Total Carbohydrate 31g (Dietary Fiber 1g); Protein 7g. Exchanges: 1 Starch, 1 Other Carbohydrate, 1/2 Medium-Fat Meat, 3 Fat. Carbohydrate Choices: 2.

Betty's Kitchen Tip

• Spray your measuring cup with cooking spray before measuring the peanut butter, and the peanut butter will slide right out!

peppermint candy canes

Prep Time: 1 Hour 10 Minutes
Start to Finish: 1 Hour 40 Minutes
Servings: 5-1/2 dozen cookies

1/3	cup butter, softened
1/4	cup shortening
1/2	cup sugar
1	egg
1-1/4	cups Gold Medal® all-purpose flour
1/4	teaspoon baking powder
1/4	teaspoon salt
1	teaspoon peppermint extract
5	drops red food color
3-1/2	oz vanilla-flavored candy coating (almond bark)

1 Heat oven to 375°F. In large bowl, beat butter, shortening and sugar with electric mixer on medium speed until light and fluffy. Beat in egg. Stir in flour, baking powder, salt, peppermint extract and food color until mixed.

2 Place dough in cookie press. Fit 1/2-inch star template in press. On ungreased large cookie sheets, press 15-inch lines of dough 3 inches apart. Score at 3-inch intervals. Pull top of dough into a curve, forming candy cane.

3 Bake 5 to 7 minutes or until edges just start to brown. Immediately and carefully remove from cookie sheets to cooling racks; cool completely.

4 Place waxed paper under cooling racks. In small resealable freezer plastic bag, place candy coating; seal bag. Microwave on High 1 minute or until softened. Gently squeeze bag until coating is smooth; cut off tiny corner of bag. Squeeze bag to pipe coating diagonally over each candy cane for striped effect. Move position of cookie before coating sets completely so coating doesn't adhere to cooling rack.

LOW FAT

High Altitude (3500-6500 ft): No change.

Nutritional Info: 1 Cookie: Calories 40; Total Fat 2.5g (Saturated Fat 1g); Sodium 20mg; Total Carbohydrate 4g (Dietary Fiber 0g); Protein 0g. Exchanges: 1/2 Fat. Carbohydrate Choices: 0.

Betty's Kitchen Tips

Success Hint: These cookies are very fragile when they are warm, but are quite sturdy once cooled. To remove them from the cookie sheet, slide the spatula under the curved end first.

Packaging: Once the cookies are cooled, they can be stacked in containers; they won't stick together or break easily.

gluten free peanut butter cookie cups

Prep Time: 55 Minutes
Start to Finish: 1 Hour 30 Minutes
Servings: 5 dozen cookies

Michelle Bowman
Sammamish, WA
Celebrate the Season-Holiday Cookie Contest

1   box (19 oz) Betty Crocker® Gluten-Free chocolate chip cookie mix
1   egg
1/2   cup butter, softened

1   teaspoon vanilla
1/2   cup creamy peanut butter
60   miniature chocolate-covered peanut butter cup candies, unwrapped

1 Heat oven to 375°F. Place mini paper baking cup in each of 24 mini muffin cups.

2 In large bowl, mix cookie mix, egg, butter and vanilla with spoon. Stir in peanut butter. Roll dough into 1-inch balls. Place in muffin cups.

3 Bake 9 to 11 minutes or until just lightly browned. Immediately press peanut butter cup candy into center of each cookie. Cool 5 minutes before removing from pans to cooling rack; cool completely. Repeat with remaining dough.

High Altitude (3500-6500 ft): No change.

Nutritional Info: 1 Cookie: Calories 100; Total Fat 5g (Saturated Fat 2g); Sodium 80mg; Total Carbohydrate 11g (Dietary Fiber 0g); Protein 1g. Exchanges: 1/2 Starch, 1/2 Other Carbohydrate, 1 Fat. Carbohydrate Choices: 1.

Betty's Kitchen Tip

• Cooking gluten free? Always read labels to make sure each recipe ingredient is gluten free. Products and ingredient sources can change.

here's my heart gingerbread pals

Prep Time: 1 Hour 25 Minutes
Start to Finish: 2 Hours 25 Minutes
Servings: 2-1/2 dozen cookies

1/4 cup light molasses	1 teaspoon ground cinnamon
2 tablespoons water	1/2 teaspoon baking soda
2/3 cup butter or margarine	1/2 teaspoon salt
1/2 cup packed brown sugar	1/4 teaspoon ground cloves
1 egg	4 oz vanilla-flavored candy coating (almond bark)
2-1/4 cups Gold Medal® all-purpose flour	4 teaspoons red decorating sugar
1 teaspoon ground ginger	

1 In 3-quart saucepan, cook and stir molasses and water over medium heat until hot; remove from heat. Stir in butter and brown sugar until smooth. Stir in remaining ingredients except candy coating and decorating sugar. Divide dough in half; shape into 2 disks. Wrap each in plastic wrap; refrigerate 1 hour.

2 Heat oven to 350°F. On floured surface, roll 1 disk of dough 1/8 inch thick. Cut with floured 3- to 3-1/2-inch gingerbread boy and girl cookie cutters. With 1-inch heart-shaped cutter, cut out small heart in center of each cookie. On 1 ungreased cookie sheet, place gingerbread cutouts. On second ungreased cookie sheet, place hearts. Repeat with second disk.

3 Bake hearts 5 to 7 minutes, gingerbread cookies 7 to 9 minutes, or until set. Remove from the cookie sheets to the cooling racks.

4 In small microwavable bowl, microwave candy coating on High 1 minute; stir until smooth. Frost each heart with coating; immediately sprinkle with red sugar. Place dot of melted coating on back of heart; place on hand of each gingerbread cookie or near cutout heart on body of cookie. Decorate as desired.

High Altitude (3500-6500 ft): No change.

Nutritional Info: 1 Cookie: Calories 110; Total Fat 5g (Saturated Fat 3g); Sodium 95mg; Total Carbohydrate 15g (Dietary Fiber 0g); Protein 1g. Exchanges: 1/2 Starch, 1/2 Other Carbohydrate, 1 Fat. Carbohydrate Choices: 1.

Betty's Kitchen Tips

Time-Saver: These saucepan cookies are easy to stir up—you don't need a mixer.

Success Hint: You could use Betty Crocker® frosting to decorate the hearts and cookies if you prefer. But the frosting doesn't set up, so store the cookies in a single layer if you do.

pb&j sandwich cookies

Prep Time: 45 Minutes
Start to Finish: 1 Hour 15 Minutes
Servings: 1-1/2 dozen sandwich cookies

- 1 pouch (1 lb 1.5 oz) Betty Crocker® peanut butter cookie mix

Vegetable oil and egg called for on cookie mix package

- 1/3 cup Betty Crocker® Rich & Creamy vanilla frosting (from 1-lb container)
- 2 tablespoons creamy peanut butter
- 1/3 cup favorite jelly, jam or preserves

1 Heat oven to 375°F. Make cookies as directed on pouch, using oil and egg. Cool completely, about 30 minutes.

2 In small bowl, stir frosting and peanut butter until smooth.

3 For each sandwich cookie, spread generous teaspoon of peanut butter mixture on bottom of 1 cookie; spread scant teaspoon jelly over peanut butter mixture. Top with another cookie.

Triple PB&J Sandwich Cookies: Make cookies as directed. In microwavable bowl, microwave 1 bag (10 oz) peanut butter chips and 2 teaspoons shortening uncovered on High about 1 minute or until almost melted; stir until smooth. If necessary, microwave at additional 5-second intervals. Dip half of each sandwich cookie into mixture. Immediately roll outside of frosted edge in chopped peanuts. Lay flat to dry.

High Altitude (3500-6500 ft): No change.

Nutritional Info: 1 Sandwich Cookie: Calories 130; Total Fat 6g (Saturated Fat 1.5g); Sodium 100mg; Total Carbohydrate 17g (Dietary Fiber 0g); Protein 1g. Exchanges: 1 Other Carbohydrate, 1 Fat. Carbohydrate Choices: 1.

Betty's Kitchen Tip

• You can make sandwich cookies with Betty Crocker® oatmeal, chocolate chip and sugar cookie mixes, too.

chewy cranberry-oatmeal cookies with orange icing

Prep Time: 45 Minutes
Start to Finish: 1 Hour
Servings: 2 dozen cookies

Ungala Gillespie
St. Petersburg, FL
Celebrate the Season-Holiday Cookie Contest

Cookies

3/4	cup butter or margarine, softened
1	cup packed light brown sugar
2	eggs
2	teaspoons vanilla
2	teaspoons grated orange peel
2	cups quick-cooking oats
1	cup Gold Medal® all-purpose flour

2/3	teaspoon baking soda
1	teaspoon ground cinnamon
1	cup sweetened dried cranberries

Icing

1	cup powdered sugar
1/4	teaspoon vanilla
3	to 4 teaspoons orange juice

1 Heat oven to 350°F. In large bowl, beat butter, brown sugar, eggs, vanilla and orange peel with electric mixer on medium speed, or mix with spoon. Stir in remaining cookie ingredients.

2 On ungreased cookie sheet, drop dough by tablespoonfuls 2 inches apart.

3 Bake 11 to 14 minutes or until golden brown. Remove from cookie sheet to cooling rack; cool completely, about 15 minutes.

4 In small bowl, stir powdered sugar, vanilla and enough orange juice until thin enough to drizzle. Spoon into small resealable food-storage plastic bag; cut off tiny corner of bag. Squeeze bag to drizzle icing over cookies.

High Altitude (3500-6500 ft): No change.

Nutritional Info: 1 Cookie: Calories 180; Total Fat 7g (Saturated Fat 4g); Sodium 85mg; Total Carbohydrate 27g (Dietary Fiber 1g); Protein 2g. Exchanges: 1/2 Starch, 1-1/2 Other Carbohydrate, 1-1/2 Fat. Carbohydrate Choices: 2.

Betty's Kitchen Tip

• You'll need 1 medium orange for the grated peel in the cookie dough and the juice in the icing.

monster-style cookies

Prep Time: 45 Minutes
Start to Finish: 45 Minutes
Servings: 1-1/2 dozen cookies

3/4	cup creamy peanut butter
1/2	cup butter or margarine, softened
3/4	cup packed brown sugar
1/2	cup granulated sugar
1	teaspoon vanilla
2	eggs
1-1/4	cups Gold Medal® all-purpose flour
1	teaspoon baking soda
2-1/2	cups quick-cooking or old-fashioned oats
1/2	cup white vanilla baking chips
1/2	cup sweetened dried cranberries

1 Heat oven to 375°F. In large bowl, beat peanut butter and butter with electric mixer on medium speed until creamy. Add brown sugar and granulated sugar; beat until fluffy. Beat in vanilla and eggs until well mixed. On low speed, beat in flour and baking soda. Stir in oats, baking chips and cranberries.

2 Onto ungreased cookie sheets, drop dough by 1/4 cupfuls about 3 inches apart.

3 Bake 11 to 15 minutes or until edges are golden brown. Cool 1 minute; remove from cookie sheets to cooling racks.

High Altitude (3500-6500 ft): No change.

Nutritional Info: 1 Cookie: Calories 310; Total Fat 14g (Saturated Fat 6g); Sodium 220mg; Total Carbohydrate 38g (Dietary Fiber 2g); Protein 6g. Exchanges: 1 Starch, 1-1/2 Other Carbohydrate, 1/2 High-Fat Meat, 2 Fat. Carbohydrate Choices: 2-1/2.

Betty's Kitchen Tips

Variation: To make 3-1/2 dozen smaller cookies, simply drop the dough by tablespoonfuls onto the cookie sheets (about 2 inches apart) instead of 1/4 cupfuls. Bake 8 to 10 minutes.

Substitution: Have semisweet chocolate chips on hand? Go ahead and use them instead of the vanilla chips.

caramel s'more cups

Prep Time: 30 Minutes
Start to Finish: 1 Hour 30 Minutes
Servings: 2 dozen cookies

Lindsay Weiss
Overland Park, KS
Cookie Contest 2009

1   pouch (1 lb 1.5 oz) Betty Crocker® chocolate chip cookie mix
1/2   cup butter or margarine, softened
1   egg

24   round chewy caramels in milk chocolate, from 3 (1.91-oz) rolls, unwrapped
72   mini marshmallows (about 3/4 cup)
1/3   cup semisweet chocolate chips

1   Heat oven to 350°F. Spray 24 mini muffin cups with cooking spray.

2   Make cookie dough as directed on package, using butter and egg. Shape dough into 24 (1-1/2-inch) balls. Place 1 ball in each muffin cup.

3   Bake 13 to 15 minutes or until edges begin to brown. Remove from oven; firmly press 1 candy into center of each cookie until flush with cookie top. Top each with 3 marshmallows. Bake 2 to 4 minutes longer or until marshmallows are puffed.

Cool 10 to 15 minutes. Loosen edges of cookies with small metal spatula and remove to cooling racks. Cool completely.

4   Place chocolate chips in small resealable freezer plastic bag. Microwave on High about 1 minute or until softened. Gently squeeze bag until chocolate is smooth; cut off tiny corner of bag. Squeeze bag to drizzle chocolate over marshmallows. Let stand until hardened, about 10 minutes.

High Altitude (3500-6500 ft): No change.

Nutritional Info: 1 Cookie: Calories 170; Total Fat 8g (Saturated Fat 4g); Sodium 125mg; Total Carbohydrate 25g (Dietary Fiber 0g); Protein 1g. Exchanges: 1/2 Starch, 1 Other Carbohydrate, 1-1/2 Fat. Carbohydrate Choices: 1-1/2.

Betty's Kitchen Tips

Success Hint: Need to make a sweet treat for a bake sale? These would be a hit! Place a dozen of the cups on a pretty plate and cover with cellophane wrap. Tie with a brightly-colored bow and attach a fancy price tag.

Variation: These cookies taste heavenly when they are warm but are also a delicious treat after they have cooled.

simple turtle cookie cups

Prep Time: 45 Minutes
Start to Finish: 1 Hour 15 Minutes
Servings: 36 cookies

Marilyn Blankschien
Clintonville, WI
Cookie Contest 2009

1	pouch (1 lb 1.5 oz) Betty Crocker® double chocolate chunk cookie mix
3	tablespoons vegetable oil
1	tablespoon water
1	egg
36	round milk chocolate-covered chewy caramels, unwrapped
36	pecan halves

1 Heat oven to 375°F. Place miniature paper baking cups in each of 36 mini muffin cups.

2 In large bowl stir cookie mix, oil, water, and egg until soft dough forms. Shape dough into 36 (1-1/4 inch) balls; place in muffin cups.

3 Bake 8 to 9 minutes or until edges are set. Immediately press one milk chocolate-covered caramel into center of each cookie cup. Cool two minutes. Top with pecan halves. Cool completely, about 30 minutes. Remove from pans with narrow spatula.

High Altitude (3500-6500 ft): No change.

Nutritional Info: 1 Cookie: Calories 110; Total Fat 5g (Saturated Fat 2g); Sodium 75mg; Total Carbohydrate 15g (Dietary Fiber 0g); Protein 1g. Exchanges: 1 Other Carbohydrate, 1 Fat. Carbohydrate Choices: 1.

Betty's Kitchen Tip

• Egg substitutes can replace eggs at a savings of 5 grams of fat each. Use 1/4 cup egg substitute for each egg called for in a recipe.

chocolate hazelnut cookies

Prep Time: 1 Hour 10 Minutes
Start to Finish: 1 Hour 55 Minutes
Servings: 36 cookies

Christine Riccitelli
Incline Village, NY
Cookie Contest 2009

1 pouch (1 lb 1.5 oz) Betty Crocker® chocolate chip cookie mix	1/2 cup hazelnuts (filberts), toasted, skins removed, chopped
1/3 cup butter or margarine, softened	3/4 cup white vanilla baking chips
1 cup hazelnut spread with cocoa	2 teaspoons oil
1 egg	

1 Heat oven to 375°F. In large bowl stir cookie mix, butter, chocolate spread and egg until soft dough forms, stir in hazelnuts. Drop by rounded teaspoonfuls 2 inches apart onto ungreased cookie sheet.

2 Bake 8 to 11 minutes or until edges are set. Cool 1 to 2 minutes. Remove from cookie sheets to cooling rack. Cool completely, about 30 minutes.

3 Place baking chips and oil in small resealable freezer plastic bag. Microwave on High for 45 to 60 seconds, turning bag over after 25 seconds. Squeeze bag until chips are melted and smooth. Cut small tip off one corner of bag, and drizzle over cookies. Let stand until set, about 10 minutes.

High Altitude (3500-6500 ft): No change.

Nutritional Info: 1 Cookie: Calories 160; Total Fat 8g (Saturated Fat 3.5g); Sodium 80mg; Total Carbohydrate 19g (Dietary Fiber 0g); Protein 1g. Exchanges: 1/2 Starch, 1 Other Carbohydrate, 1-1/2 Fat. Carbohydrate Choices: 1.

Betty's Kitchen Tip

• To toast hazelnuts, spread on a baking sheet. Bake at 350°F 12 minutes or until light golden brown. Cool slightly, place the nuts in a clean kitchen towel and rub them vigorously to remove the skins.

dark chocolate-glazed orange macaroons

Prep Time: 1 Hour
Start to Finish: 2 Hours 15 Minutes
Servings: 2-1/2 dozen cookies

Holly Bauer
West Bend, WI
Celebrate the Season-Holiday Cookie Contest

2-2/3 cups firmly packed flaked coconut
2/3 cup sugar
1/4 cup Gold Medal® all-purpose flour
4 egg whites
1/2 cup finely chopped pecans
1 tablespoon grated orange peel
2 teaspoons vanilla
1/2 teaspoon almond extract
3 oz dark baking chocolate, chopped

1 Heat oven to 325°F. Line cookie sheet with cooking parchment paper or silicone baking mat.

2 In large bowl, mix coconut, sugar and flour. Stir in egg whites, pecans, orange peel, vanilla and almond extract. On cookie sheet, drop dough by tablespoonfuls 2 inches apart.

3 Bake 18 to 22 minutes or until golden. Remove from cookie sheet to cooling rack; cool completely.

4 In small resealable freezer plastic bag, place chocolate; seal bag. Microwave on High about 1 minute or until softened. Gently squeeze bag until chocolate is smooth; cut off tiny corner of bag. Squeeze bag to drizzle chocolate over cookies. Let stand until set.

High Altitude (3500-6500 ft): No change.

Nutritional Info: 1 Cookie: Calories 100; Total Fat 5g (Saturated Fat 3.5g); Sodium 30mg; Total Carbohydrate 10g (Dietary Fiber 1g); Protein 1g. Exchanges: 1/2 Starch, 1 Fat. Carbohydrate Choices: 1/2.

Betty's Kitchen Tip

• When you need to separate eggs, be sure to take them out of the refrigerator just before using, because chilled eggs separate easier than room-temperature eggs.

choco-cherry double delights

Prep Time: 45 Minutes
Start to Finish: 1 Hour
Servings: 2-1/2 dozen cookies

Diana Neves
Lafayette, CA
Cookie Mix Contest 2010

1-1/3   cups whole maraschino cherries, well drained
1   pouch (1 lb 1.5 oz) Betty Crocker® double chocolate chunk cookie mix
2   tablespoons vegetable oil

1   tablespoon water
1   egg, beaten
1/2   cup chopped macadamia nuts
1   teaspoon powdered sugar

1 Heat oven to 375°F. Carefully cut 15 of the maraschino cherries in half; set aside for topping cookies. Chop remaining cherries.

2 In large bowl, stir cookie mix, oil, water and egg until soft dough forms. Stir in chopped cherries and nuts.

3 On ungreased cookie sheet, drop dough by rounded teaspoonfuls 2 inches apart. Press 1 cherry half lightly into center of each cookie.

4 Bake 7 to 9 minutes or until set. Cool 2 minutes; remove from cookie sheet to cooling rack. Cool completely, about 15 minutes. Before serving, sprinkle with powdered sugar. Store loosely covered at room temperature.

High Altitude (3500-6500 ft): No change.

Nutritional Info: 1 Cookie: Calories 110; Total Fat 4g (Saturated Fat 1.5g); Sodium 75mg; Total Carbohydrate 17g (Dietary Fiber 0g); Protein 1g. Exchanges: 1/2 Starch, 1/2 Other Carbohydrate, 1 Fat. Carbohydrate Choices: 1.

Betty's Kitchen Tips

Storage: Because of their high fat content, macadamia nuts should be kept in the refrigerator or freezer. All types of nuts keep well in the freezer, so you can always be prepared when the cookie-baking bug strikes!

Substitution: Have almonds, walnuts or pecans on hand, but no macadamia nuts? Go ahead and use them in this recipe!

red velvet rich and creamy cookies

Prep Time: 1 Hour
Start to Finish: 1 Hour 15 Minutes
Servings: 3 dozen cookies

Joanne Opdahl
Venice, CA
Cookie Mix Contest 2010

1	pouch (1 lb 1.5 oz) Betty Crocker® sugar cookie mix
1/3	cup unsweetened baking cocoa
1/4	cup butter or margarine, softened
1/4	cup sour cream
1	tablespoon red food color
1	egg
3/4	to 1 cup Betty Crocker® Rich & Creamy cream cheese frosting (from 1-lb container)
1/4	cup chopped nuts

1 Heat oven to 375°F. In large bowl, stir cookie mix, cocoa, butter, sour cream, food color and egg until soft dough forms.

2 Roll dough into 1-inch balls. On ungreased cookie sheet, place balls 2 inches apart.

3 Bake 8 to 9 minutes or until set. Cool 2 minutes; remove from cookie sheet to cooling rack. Cool completely, about 15 minutes.

4 Frost cooled cookies with frosting. Sprinkle with nuts. Store tightly covered at room temperature.

High Altitude (3500-6500 ft): No change.

Nutritional Info: 1 Cookie: Calories 110; Total Fat 4.5g (Saturated Fat 1.5g); Sodium 70mg; Total Carbohydrate 16g (Dietary Fiber 0g); Protein 1g. Exchanges: 1/2 Starch, 1/2 Other Carbohydrate, 1 Fat. Carbohydrate Choices: 1.

Betty's Kitchen Tips

Success Hint: Chopped walnuts are delicious sprinkled on these frosted cookies, or try chopped pecans. Lightly toast them first, if you like, to bring out the flavor.

Storage: Put the leftover cream cheese frosting in its container in the refrigerator and use it to frost some cupcakes. It would be great on carrot cake cupcakes!

white chocolate cranberry cookies

Prep Time: 55 Minutes
Start to Finish: 1 Hour 25 Minutes
Servings: 3 dozen cookies

Laura Abeloe
Grand Junction, CO
Celebrate the Season-Holiday Cookie Contest

3/4	cup butter or margarine, softened		1-3/4	cups Gold Medal® all-purpose flour
3/4	cup packed light brown sugar		1/2	teaspoon baking soda
1/2	cup granulated sugar		1/4	teaspoon salt
2	teaspoons vanilla		1	cup white vanilla baking chips (6 oz)
1	teaspoon almond extract, if desired		1	cup sweetened dried cranberries
1	egg			

1 Heat oven to 350°F. In large bowl, beat butter, brown sugar, granulated sugar, vanilla, almond extract and egg with electric mixer on medium speed until well mixed. Stir in flour, baking soda and salt. Stir in baking chips and cranberries.

2 On ungreased cookie sheet, drop dough by rounded tablespoonfuls about 2 inches apart.

3 Bake 12 to 15 minutes or until light brown. Cool 2 to 3 minutes; remove from cookie sheet to cooling rack.

High Altitude (3500-6500 ft): No change.

Nutritional Info: 1 Cookie: Calories 130; Total Fat 6g (Saturated Fat 3.5g); Sodium 70mg; Total Carbohydrate 18g (Dietary Fiber 0g); Protein 1g. Exchanges: 1/2 Starch, 1/2 Other Carbohydrate, 1 Fat. Carbohydrate Choices: 1.

Betty's Kitchen Tip

• When using brown sugar in baking, it's important to firmly pack the brown sugar into the measuring cup for best results.

double trouble

Prep Time: 25 Minutes
Start to Finish: 55 Minutes
Servings: 24 cookies

Whitney Miller
Poplarville, MS
Cookie Contest 2009

1   pouch (1 lb 1.5 oz) Betty Crocker® double chocolate chunk cookie mix

1/2   cup butter or margarine, softened

1   egg

1   cup cocoa-flavored rice cereal

1 Heat oven to 375°F. In large bowl, stir cookie mix, softened butter and egg until soft dough forms. Gently stir in cereal.

2 Onto ungreased cookie sheet, carefully drop dough by rounded tablespoonfuls about 2 inches apart.

3 Bake 8 to 10 minutes or until edges are set. Cool 1 to 2 minutes; remove from cookie sheets to cooling rack.

High Altitude (3500-6500 ft): No change.

Nutritional Info: 1 Cookie: Calories 130; Total Fat 6g (Saturated Fat 3.5g); Sodium 130mg; Total Carbohydrate 18g (Dietary Fiber 0g); Frotein 1g. Exchanges: 1/2 Starch, 1/2 Other Carbohydrate, 1 Fat. Carbohydrate Choices: 1.

Betty's Kitchen Tip

• There's nothing better to sweeten your day than a piece of chocolate—and it's not just because of the delicious taste. Studies show that eating it increases the amount of serotonin, an antidepressant, and releases feel-good endomorphins in your brain.

chocolate-mint layered cookie slices

Prep Time: 1 Hour 10 Minutes
Start to Finish: 4 Hours 40 Minutes
Servings: 3-1/2 dozen cookies

3/4	cup butter or margarine, softened		1/4	teaspoon salt
3/4	cup sugar		1-1/2	cups semisweet chocolate chips (9 oz)
1	egg		1	tablespoon Gold Medal® all-purpose flour
1	teaspoon vanilla		9	drops green food color
2-1/4	cups Gold Medal® all-purpose flour		1	teaspoon mint extract
1/4	teaspoon baking powder		1	teaspoon shortening

1 In large bowl, beat butter and sugar with electric mixer on medium speed until creamy. Beat in egg and vanilla. On low speed, beat in 2-1/4 cups flour, the baking powder and salt until dough forms. Divide dough in half (about 1-1/4 cups each); place 1 portion in medium bowl.

2 In small microwavable bowl, microwave 1/2 cup of the chocolate chips on High 30 to 60 seconds or until melted, stirring twice. Stir until smooth; cool. Add melted chocolate to dough in medium bowl; knead until combined. To remaining dough, add 1 tablespoon flour, the food color and mint extract; mix until blended. Wrap each portion of dough in waxed paper; refrigerate 30 minutes.

3 Pat chocolate dough into rectangle shape. Place between sheets of waxed paper. Roll to 10x6-inch rectangle, patting into shape with fingers as needed to retain rectangle shape. Repeat with green dough; remove top sheet of waxed paper. Remove top sheet of waxed paper from chocolate dough. Turn upside down over green dough, pressing firmly; remove waxed paper. With sharp knife or pizza cutter, cut lengthwise into 3 equal strips. Stack strips so you have 1 long rectangle, about 1-1/2 inches high and 2 inches wide, pressing firmly. Wrap in plastic wrap; refrigerate 1 hour.

4 Heat oven to 350°F. Trim edges of dough log, if desired. Cut into 1/4-inch slices. On ungreased cookie sheet, place slices 2 inches apart. Bake 10 to 12 minutes or until edges start to brown. Remove from cookie sheet to cooling rack; cool completely.

5 In small microwavable bowl, microwave remaining 1 cup chocolate chips and the shortening uncovered on High 60 to 90 seconds or until melted, stirring twice. Stir until melted. Dip one edge of each cookie in chocolate. Place on waxed paper; let stand until set, about 1-1/2 to 2 hours.

High Altitude (3500-6500 ft): No change.

Nutritional Info: 1 Cookie: Calories 100; Total Fat 5g (Saturated Fat 3g); Sodium 45mg; Total Carbohydrate 13g (Dietary Fiber 0g); Protein 1g. Exchanges: 1 Other Carbohydrate, 1 Fat. Carbohydrate Choices: 1.

chocolate marble cookies

Prep Time: 1 Hour
Start to Finish: 1 Hour 40 Minutes
Servings: 36 cookies

Marie Patton
Glendale, AZ
Cookie Contest 2009

1	pouch (1 lb 1.5 oz) Betty Crocker® sugar cookie mix
1/2	cup butter or margarine, softened
1	egg
1	tablespoon water
1	teaspoon vanilla
2	oz semisweet baking chocolate, melted

1 Heat oven to 350°F. Lightly spray 2 large cookie sheets with cooking spray.

2 In large bowl stir cookie mix, butter, egg, water and vanilla until soft dough forms. Cover, and refrigerate until firm; about 30 minutes.

3 Divide dough in half. Stir melted chocolate into 1 half of dough. Shape about 1/2 teaspoon each of chocolate and white dough into 1-inch ball of marbled dough. Place about 1 inch apart on prepared cookie sheet. Press bottom of glass into dough to grease, then dip into granulated sugar; press on shaped dough until about 1/4 inch thick.

4 Bake 8 to 11 minutes or until set and edges just begin to brown. Cool 1 minute; remove from cookie sheets to wire rack.

High Altitude (3500-6500 ft): No change.

Nutritional Info: 1 Cookie: Calories 90; Total Fat 4.5g (Saturated Fat 2g); Sodium 60mg; Total Carbohydrate 12g (Dietary Fiber 0g); Protein 0g. Exchanges: 1 Other Carbohydrate, 1 Fat. Carbohydrate Choices: 1.

Betty's Kitchen Tip

• Consider getting the kids to help - after all, making cookies is where many on Betty's staff got their start! Look over your baking equipment and consider buying the kids a mixing spoon or whisk that's just their size.

almond poppy tea cookies

Prep Time: 1 Hour
Start to Finish: 1 Hour
Servings: 3 dozen cookies

Joan Cassette
Colbert, WA
Cookie Mix Contest 2010

1	pouch (1 lb 1.5 oz) Betty Crocker® sugar cookie mix
1/3	cup Gold Medal® all-purpose flour
1	tablespoon poppy seeds
1/2	cup butter or margarine, softened
1	package (3 oz) cream cheese, softened

2	teaspoons almond extract
1	egg
1/4	cup sliced almonds, if desired
1	cup powdered sugar
3	to 4 teaspoons water

1 Heat oven to 350°F. In large bowl, stir cookie mix, flour, poppy seeds, butter, cream cheese, 1 teaspoon of the almond extract and egg until soft dough forms.

2 Roll dough into 1-1/4-inch balls. On ungreased cookie sheet, place balls 2 inches apart. Press with fingers to slightly flatten. Top each with 5 sliced almonds arranged to form a star.

3 Bake 9 to 11 minutes or until edges are light golden brown. Cool 3 minutes; remove from cookie sheet to cooling rack.

4 In small bowl, mix powdered sugar, remaining 1 teaspoon almond extract and enough water to give glaze spreading consistency. Spread glaze over warm cookies. Store cooled cookies tightly covered in single layer at room temperature.

High Altitude (3500-6500 ft): No change.

Nutritional Info: 1 Cookie: Calories 110; Total Fat 5g (Saturated Fat 2.5g); Sodium 70mg; Total Carbohydrate 15g (Dietary Fiber 0g); Protein 1g. Exchanges: 1/2 Starch, 1/2 Other Carbohydrate, 1 Fat. Carbohydrate Choices: 1.

Betty's Kitchen Tip

• Here's a recipe that proves holiday cookies don't have to be difficult or time-consuming to make. The simple addition of sliced almonds arranged in the shape of a star on top of each cookie makes them a standout!

jumbo childhood fantasy cookies

Prep Time: 20 Minutes
Start to Finish: 1 Hour 15 Minutes
Servings: 36 cookies

Edwina Gadsby
Great Falls, MT
Cookie Contest 2009

- 1   pouch (1 lb 1.5 oz) Betty Crocker® oatmeal chocolate chip cookie mix
- 1   pouch (1 lb 1.5 oz) Betty Crocker® peanut butter cookie mix
- 1/2 cup butter or margarine, softened
- 2   eggs
- 1   cup milk chocolate chips
- 1   cup candy-coated peanut butter pieces
- 1/2 cup chopped walnuts, toasted if desired

1 Heat oven to 350°F. In large bowl stir cookie mixes, butter and eggs until soft dough forms. Stir in chocolate chips, peanut butter pieces and walnuts.

2 On large ungreased cookie sheets, drop dough by scant 1/4 cupfuls about 2 inches apart. Bake 13 to 16 minutes or until light golden brown.

3 Cool 1 to 2 minutes; remove from cookie sheets to cooling rack. Cool completely, about 30 minutes.

High Altitude (3500-6500 ft): No change.

Nutritional Info: 1 Cookie: Calories 200; Total Fat 9g (Saturated Fat 3.5g); Sodium 160mg; Total Carbohydrate 26g (Dietary Fiber 0g); Protein 3g. Exchanges: 1 Starch, 1 Other Carbohydrate, 1-1/2 Fat. Carbohydrate Choices: 2.

Betty's Kitchen Tip

- It is important to space drop cookies 2 inches apart on a pan (or as directed in a recipe). This will help to prevent cookies from running together during baking.

lime-ginger cookies

Prep Time: 50 Minutes
Start to Finish: 1 Hour 10 Minutes
Servings: 36 cookies

Brenda Wright
Muncie, IN
Cookie Contest 2009

1	pouch (1 lb 1.5 oz) Betty Crocker® sugar cookie mix
1/2	cup butter or margarine, softened
1	egg
1	tablespoon grated lime peel

3/4 teaspoon ground ginger
1/4 cup sugar
1/2 cup white vanilla baking chips
1/2 teaspoon vegetable oil
Shredded lime peel, if desired

1 Heat oven to 375°F. In medium bowl, stir cookie mix, butter, egg, lime peel and 1/2 teaspoon of the ginger until soft dough forms.

2 In small bowl, mix sugar and remaining 1/4 teaspoon ginger. Shape dough into 36 (1-inch) balls. Roll balls in sugar mixture. On ungreased cookie sheets, place balls 2 inches apart. Bake 7 to 9 minutes, or until edges begin to brown and center is set. Cool 1 to 2 minutes. Carefully remove from cookie sheets to cooling rack. Cool completely, about 30 minutes.

3 Place baking chips and oil in small resealable freezer plastic bag. Microwave on High for 45 to 60 seconds, turning bag over after 25 seconds. Squeeze bag until chips are melted and smooth. Cut small tip off one corner of bag, and drizzle over cookies. Sprinkle with shredded lime peel. Let stand until set, about 10 minutes.

High Altitude (3500-6500 ft): No change.

Nutritional Info: 1 Cookie: Calories 100; Total Fat 5g (Saturated Fat 2.5g); Sodium 65mg; Total Carbohydrate 14g (Dietary Fiber 0g); Protein 1g. Exchanges: 1 Other Carbohydrate, 1 Fat. Carbohydrate Choices: 1.

Betty's Kitchen Tip

• Whole limes can be stored in a plastic bag in the refrigerator for up to 10 days. Once the limes are sliced, they will keep in the refrigerator for up to 5 days.

BROWNIES & BARS

p.287

311

306

307

merry cherry swirl brownies

Prep Time: 25 Minutes
Start to Finish: 2 Hours 20 Minutes
Servings: 48 brownies

Cherry-Cream Cheese Filling

2	packages (8 oz each) cream cheese, softened
1/2	cup sugar
1/2	cup drained chopped red or green maraschino cherries
1	tablespoon red or green maraschino cherry juice
1	egg

Brownies

4	oz unsweetened baking chocolate
1	cup butter or margarine
2	cups sugar
2	teaspoons vanilla
4	eggs
1-1/2	cups Gold Medal® all-purpose flour
1/2	teaspoon salt
1	cup coarsely chopped nuts

1 Heat oven to 350°F. Grease bottom and sides of 13x9-inch pan with shortening or cooking spray.

2 In medium bowl, beat all filling ingredients with spoon until smooth; set aside.

3 In 2-quart saucepan, melt chocolate and butter over low heat, stirring frequently, until smooth; remove from heat. Cool 5 minutes.

4 In large bowl, beat chocolate mixture, 2 cups sugar, the vanilla and 4 eggs with electric mixer on medium speed 1 minute, scraping bowl occasionally. Beat in flour and salt on low speed 30 seconds, scraping bowl occasionally. Beat on medium speed for 1 minute. Stir in nuts.

5 Spread 1/2 of batter (about 2-1/2 cups) in pan. Spread filling over batter. Carefully spread remaining batter over filling. Gently swirl through batters with knife for marbled design.

6 Bake 45 to 50 minutes or until toothpick inserted in center comes out clean. Cool completely, about 1 hour. Cut into 8 rows by 6 rows. Store covered in refrigerator.

High Altitude (3500-6500): No change.

Nutritional Info: 1 Brownie: Calories 170; Total Fat 10g (Saturated Fat 5g); Sodium 90mg; Total Carbohydrate 16g (Dietary Fiber 0g); Protein 2g. Exchanges: 1 Other Carbohydrate, 2 Fat. Carbohydrate Choices: 1.

Betty's Kitchen Tip

• Try chopped walnuts or pecans in these dressed-up brownies.

cookies 'n creme brownies

Prep Time: 25 Minutes
Start to Finish: 2 Hours 25 Minutes
Servings: 20 brownies

- 1 box (1 lb 2.3 oz) Betty Crocker® fudge brownie mix
- 1/4 cup water
- 1/2 cup vegetable oil
- 2 eggs
- 1 cup coarsely chopped creme-filled chocolate sandwich cookies (about 7 cookies)
- 1/2 cup powdered sugar
- 2 to 4 teaspoons milk

1 Heat oven to 350°F. Grease or spray bottom only of 13x9-inch pan. In large bowl, stir brownie mix, water, oil and eggs until well blended. Spread in pan. Sprinkle cookies over batter.

2 Bake 28 to 30 minutes or until toothpick inserted 2 inches from side of pan comes out almost clean. Cool completely, about 1 hour 30 minutes.

3 In small bowl, stir together powdered sugar and milk until smooth and thin enough to drizzle. Drizzle over brownies. For brownies, cut into 5 rows by 4 rows. Store covered at room temperature.

High Altitude (3500-6500): No change.

Nutritional Info: 1 Brownie: Calories 180; Total Fat 7g (Saturated Fat 1.5g); Sodium 115mg; Total Carbohydrate 29g (Dietary Fiber 0g); Protein 1g. Exchanges: 1 Starch, 1 Other Carbohydrate, 1 Fat. Carbohydrate Choices: 2.

Betty's Kitchen Tip

• With the variety of cookies available, you can easily substitute mint-flavored chocolate sandwich cookies, peanut butter chocolate sandwich cookies or double chocolate cookies to suit your taste.

cranberry-almond triangles

Prep Time: 35 Minutes
Start to Finish: 1 Hour 35 Minutes
Servings: 24 bars

3/4   cup Gold Medal® all-purpose flour
3/4   cup quick-cooking oats
1/2   cup powdered sugar
3/4   cup butter, softened
1/3   cup cherry-flavored sweetened dried
      cranberries

1/4   cup packed brown sugar
1/4   cup light corn syrup
2   tablespoons whipping cream
3/4   cup sliced almonds
1/2   cup milk chocolate chips

1 Heat oven to 350°F. Line 8-inch square pan with foil; spray foil with cooking spray.

2 In large bowl, beat flour, oats and powdered sugar with electric mixer on low speed until mixed. Add 1/2 cup of the butter. Mix on low speed until well combined (mixture will be crumbly). Press mixture in pan. Sprinkle with cranberries; lightly push into dough. Bake 15 minutes or until very light golden brown.

3 In 1-quart saucepan, stir brown sugar, corn syrup, remaining 1/4 cup butter and the whipping cream. Cook over medium-high heat until smooth and mixture boils, stirring frequently. Boil 4 minutes, stirring frequently. Stir in almonds.

4 Sprinkle chocolate chips over partially baked crust; let stand 2 minutes. Spread melted chips over cranberries. Immediately spoon hot almond mixture over chocolate; spread carefully.

5 Bake 15 to 20 minutes or until bubbly and almonds start to brown. Cool completely. Use foil to lift bars from pan; remove foil. Cut into 4 rows by 3 rows; cut each square diagonally into 2 triangles.

High Altitude (3500-6500): No change.

Nutritional Info: 1 Bar: Calories 150; Total Fat 9g (Saturated Fat 4.5g); Sodium 45mg; Total Carbohydrate 16g (Dietary Fiber 1g); Protein 1g. Exchanges: 1 Other Carbohydrate, 2 Fat. Carbohydrate Choices: 1.

Betty's Kitchen Tip

• Dried fruits tend to darken as they are exposed to air. For the brightest color, use a fresh package of sweetened dried cranberries.

butter pecan chews

Prep Time: 20 Minutes
Start to Finish: 2 Hours 35 Minutes
Servings: 36 bars

Lisa Chambers, Fort Ashby, WV
Celebrate the Season-Holiday Cookie Contest
3rd Place Winner

1-1/2	cups Gold Medal® all-purpose flour
3	tablespoons granulated sugar
3/4	cup butter or margarine, softened
3	eggs, separated
2-1/2	cups packed light brown sugar
1	teaspoon vanilla
1/2	teaspoon salt
1	cup chopped pecans
3/4	cup flaked coconut
2	tablespoons powdered sugar

1 Heat oven to 375°F. Grease 13x9-inch pan with butter.

2 In medium bowl, mix flour, granulated sugar and butter. Press mixture in bottom of pan. Bake 12 to 14 minutes or until light brown.

3 Meanwhile, in large bowl, beat egg yolks, brown sugar, vanilla and salt with electric mixer. Stir in pecans and coconut. In small bowl, beat egg whites with electric mixer until foamy. Fold into egg yolk mixture.

4 Remove partially baked crust from oven. Spread filling evenly over crust. Reduce oven temperature to 350°F.

5 Bake 25 to 30 minutes or until deep golden brown and center is set. Sprinkle powdered sugar over bars. Cool on cooling rack. Cut into 6 rows by 6 rows.

High Altitude (3500-6500): No change.

Nutritional Info: 1 Bar: Calories 160; Total Fat 7g (Saturated Fat 3.5g); Sodium 75mg; Total Carbohydrate 22g (Dietary Fiber 0g); Protein 1g. Exchanges: 1-1/2 Other Carbohydrate, 1-1/2 Fat. Carbohydrate Choices: 1-1/2.

Betty's Kitchen Tip

• With a flavor like pecan pie, these rich and buttery bars would be perfect for Thanksgiving or Christmas and would also be great to take to a potluck gathering or bake sale.

cranberry-macadamia bars

Prep Time: 15 Minutes
Start to Finish: 1 Hour 15 Minutes
Servings: 36 bars

EASY

- 1 pouch (1 lb 1.5 oz) Betty Crocker® sugar cookie mix
- 1/3 cup butter or margarine, melted
- 1 egg
- 1/3 cup butter or margarine

- 1/4 cup packed brown sugar
- 1 cup sweetened dried cranberries
- 1 cup macadamia nuts, coarsely chopped
- 1/2 cup white vanilla baking chips
- 1 teaspoon vegetable oil

1 Heat oven to 350°F. Grease bottom only of 9-inch square pan with shortening or cooking spray.

2 In medium bowl, stir cookie mix, melted butter and egg until soft dough forms. Press in bottom of pan. Bake 15 minutes.

3 In 1-quart saucepan over medium heat, cook 1/3 cup butter, brown sugar and cranberries, stirring constantly, until

mixture boils. Spoon over partially baked cookie base and spread evenly. Sprinkle with nuts. Bake 10 to 15 minutes longer or until light golden brown. Cool completely.

4 In small resealable food-storage plastic bag, place baking chips and oil; seal bag. Microwave on High 30 to 45 seconds or until softened. Gently squeeze bag until mixture is smooth. Cut off tiny corner of bag; squeeze bag to drizzle over bars. Cut into 6 rows by 6 rows.

High Altitude (3500-6500): No change.

Nutritional Info: 1 Bar: Calories 150; Total Fat 8g (Saturated Fat 3.5g); Sodium 70mg; Total Carbohydrate 17g (Dietary Fiber 0g); Protein 1g. Exchanges: 1/2 Starch, 1/2 Other Carbohydrate, 1-1/2 Fat. Carbohydrate Choices: 1.

Betty's Kitchen Tip
• Cut these special bars into triangles to create a new look for your cookie tray.

chocolate-covered cherry brownies

Prep Time: 20 Minutes
Start to Finish: 2 Hours 30 Minutes
Servings: 48 brownies

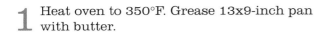

Brownies

3/4	cup butter or margarine
3	oz unsweetened baking chocolate
1-1/2	cups sugar
1	teaspoon vanilla
3	eggs
1	cup Gold Medal® all-purpose flour
1/4	teaspoon salt
1	cup marshmallow creme
1/2	cup chopped maraschino cherries, well drained

Chocolate-Cherry Glaze

1	cup semisweet chocolate chips (6 oz)
6	tablespoons butter or margarine
1	tablespoon light corn syrup
2	tablespoons maraschino cherry juice

1 Heat oven to 350°F. Grease 13x9-inch pan with butter.

2 In 2-quart heavy saucepan, heat 3/4 cup butter and the baking chocolate over low heat, stirring constantly, until melted. Remove from heat. Stir in sugar, vanilla and eggs until blended. Stir in flour and salt until smooth. Spread in pan.

3 In small bowl, mix marshmallow creme and cherries. Spoon by teaspoonfuls onto batter. Swirl lightly with knife.

4 Bake 30 to 40 minutes or until marshmallow mixture is light golden brown. Cool completely, about 1 hour.

5 In 1-quart heavy saucepan, heat chocolate chips, 6 tablespoons butter and the corn syrup over low heat, stirring constantly, until melted. Stir in cherry juice. Spread over bars. Refrigerate 30 minutes or until glaze is set. Cut into 8 rows by 6 rows.

High Altitude (3500-6500): No change.

Nutritional Info: 1 Brownie: Calories 120; Total Fat 7g (Saturated Fat 4g); Sodium 50mg; Total Carbohydrate 14g (Dietary Fiber 0g); Protein 1g. Exchanges: 1 Other Carbohydrate, 1-1/2 Fat. Carbohydrate Choices: 1.

Betty's Kitchen Tip

• Chop maraschino cherries easily by snipping them with kitchen scissors. Drain on paper towels to absorb moisture.

no-bake chocolate-peanut butter candy bars

Prep Time: 15 Minutes
Start to Finish: 45 Minutes
Servings: 32 bars

EASY

24	creme-filled chocolate sandwich cookies
4	cups miniature marshmallows
1/4	cup butter or margarine
1	cup semisweet chocolate chips (6 oz)
1	can (14 oz) sweetened condensed milk (not evaporated)
1	bag (10 oz) peanut butter chips (1-2/3 cups)

1/4	cup creamy peanut butter
1	cup coarsely chopped honey-roasted peanuts
4	Nature Valley® peanut butter crunchy granola bars (2 pouches from 8.9-oz box), crushed
1	teaspoon vegetable oil

1 Line bottom and sides of 13x9-inch (3-quart) glass baking dish with foil, leaving foil hanging over 2 opposite sides of pan. In food processor bowl with metal blade, place cookies. Cover; process until cookies are finely chopped.

2 In 2-quart saucepan, cook marshmallows and butter over low heat, stirring constantly, until melted. Stir in chopped cookies and 3/4 cup of the chocolate chips until well mixed. Press in bottom of baking dish.

3 In medium microwavable bowl, microwave milk and peanut butter chips uncovered on High 30 seconds. Stir; microwave 30 to 60 seconds longer, stirring every 30 seconds, until smooth and creamy. Stir in peanut butter until smooth. Stir in peanuts and crushed granola bars. Spread over chocolate layer. If peanut butter mixture starts to set, microwave uncovered on High 15 to 30 seconds or until warm and spreadable.

4 In small microwavable bowl, microwave remaining 1/4 cup chocolate chips and the oil uncovered on High 30 to 45 seconds or until chips are melted and can be stirred smooth. Drizzle chocolate diagonally over peanut butter layer. Refrigerate 30 minutes or until set. To cut bars, remove from pan, using foil to lift. Cut into 8 rows by 4 rows. Store covered in cool place.

High Altitude (3500-6500 ft): No change.

Nutritional Info: 1 Bar: Calories 240; Total Fat 12g (Saturated Fat 4g); Sodium 130mg; Total Carbohydrate 29g (Dietary Fiber 1g); Protein 5g. Exchanges: 2 Starch, 2 Fat. Carbohydrate Choices: 2.

chocolate covered strawberry tarts

Prep Time: 45 Minutes
Start to Finish: 1 Hour 15 Minutes
Servings: 36 tarts

Megan Link
Lake Quivira, KS
Cookie Contest 2009

- 1 pouch (1 lb 1.5 oz) Betty Crocker® double chocolate chunk cookie mix
- 1/4 cup vegetable oil
- 1 egg
- 2 tablespoons water
- 1/3 cup strawberry jam
- 1/2 cup frozen (thawed) whipped topping
- 1 cup Betty Crocker® Whipped Strawberry Mist frosting (from a 12-oz container)
- 3 tablespoons miniature semisweet chocolate chips

1 Heat oven to 350°F. Place miniature paper baking cup in each of 36 mini muffin cups.

2 In medium bowl, stir cookie mix, oil, egg and water until soft dough forms. Drop dough by teaspoonfuls into baking cups.

3 Bake 8 to 10 minutes or until edges are set. Gently press end of wooden spoon into bottoms and against sides of baking cups to flatten, being careful not to make holes in dough. Cool completely, about 30 minutes.

4 Spoon about 1/2 teaspoon jam into each cookie cup.

5 In medium bowl, fold whipped topping into frosting until well combined. Spoon frosting mixture into decorating bag fitted with medium star tip, and pipe into the center of each tart. Top with chocolate chips. Store loosely covered.

High Altitude (3500-6500): No change.

Nutritional Info: 1 Tart: Calories 110; Total Fat 4.5g (Saturated Fat 1.5g); Sodium 70mg; Total Carbohydrate 17g (Dietary Fiber 0g); Protein 0g. Exchanges: 1 Other Carbohydrate, 1 Fat. Carbohydrate Choices: 1.

Betty's Kitchen Tip
- Use low-fat whipped topping to keep fat and calories in check.

chocolate-cream cheese-peanut butter bars

Prep Time: 50 Minutes
Start to Finish: 2 Hours 15 Minutes
Servings: 36 bars

Cookie Base and Topping

- 1 pouch (1 lb 1.5 oz) Betty Crocker® peanut butter cookie mix
- 3 tablespoons vegetable oil
- 1 tablespoon water
- 1 egg

Filling

- 1-1/4 cups semisweet chocolate chips
- 1/4 cup butter or margarine
- 1 package (8 oz) cream cheese, softened
- 2/3 cup crunchy or creamy peanut butter
- 3/4 cup powdered sugar
- 1/2 cup whipping (heavy) cream

1 Heat oven to 350°F. Spray bottom only of 13x9-inch pan with cooking spray. In large bowl, stir cookie base and topping ingredients until soft dough forms. Shape 6 (1-inch) balls of dough. On ungreased cookie sheet, place balls 2 inches apart; flatten in crisscross pattern with fork.

2 Press remaining dough in pan. Bake cookies and base 10 to 12 minutes or until edges are light golden brown. Cool 10 minutes. Reserve cookies for topping.

3 In small microwavable bowl, microwave chocolate chips and butter uncovered on High 1 minute to 1 minute 30 seconds, stirring every 30 seconds, until melted and stirred smooth. Spread evenly over bars. Refrigerate until firm, about 30 minutes.

4 In medium bowl, beat cream cheese, peanut butter, powdered sugar and whipping cream with electric mixer on low speed until blended. Beat on high speed about 2 minutes or until light and fluffy. Spread over chocolate layer.

5 Crush reserved cookies; sprinkle over cream cheese layer. Press in lightly. Refrigerate until set, about 30 minutes. For bars, cut into 9 rows by 4 rows. Store covered in refrigerator.

High Altitude (3500-6500 ft): No change.

Nutritional Info: 1 Bar: Calories 190; Total Fat 12g (Saturated Fat 5g); Sodium 125mg; Total Carbohydrate 17g (Dietary Fiber 0g); Protein 3g. Exchanges: 1 Other Carbohydrate, 2-1/2 Fat. Carbohydrate Choices: 1.

turtle bars

Prep Time: 10 Minutes
Start to Finish: 1 Hour
Servings: 36 bars

EASY

- 1 cup Original Bisquick® mix
- 1 cup quick-cooking oats
- 3/4 cup packed brown sugar
- 1/4 cup butter or margarine, melted
- 1 jar (12.25 oz) caramel topping
- 1-1/2 cup pecan halves
- 1 cup swirled semisweet and white chocolate chips (6 oz)

1 Heat oven to 350°F. Line 13x9-inch pan with foil; spray with cooking spray.

2 In large bowl, stir Bisquick mix, oats, brown sugar and butter until well blended. Press in bottom of pan. Bake 15 to 18 minutes or until golden brown. Remove pan from oven.

3 Spread caramel topping over crust. Sprinkle with pecan halves and chocolate chips. Bake 20 to 30 minutes longer or until caramel is bubbly. For bars, cut into 6 by 6 rows.

High Altitude (3500-6500): No change.

Nutritional Info: 1 Bar: Calories 130 (Calories from Fat 60); Total Fat 6g (Saturated Fat 2g, Trans Fat 0g); Cholesterol 0mg; Sodium 90mg; Total Carbohydrate 18g (Dietary Fiber 1g, Sugars 12g); Protein 1g. % Daily Value: Vitamin A 0%; Vitamin C 0%; Calcium 2%; Iron 4%. Exchanges: 1 Other Carbohydrate, 1-1/2 Fat. Carbohydrate Choices: 1.

Betty's Kitchen Tip

• Lining the pan with foil and spraying the foil makes removing the bars easier and cleanup a breeze. Try this method with all of your bars!

mochachino dessert bars with white mocha drizzle

Prep Time: 20 Minutes
Start to Finish: 1 Hour 45 Minutes
Servings: 20 bars

Brett Youman
Reading, PA
Cookie Mix Contest 2010

1	pouch (1 lb 1.5 oz) Betty Crocker® double chocolate chunk cookie mix
1/4	cup vegetable oil
3	tablespoons strong brewed coffee (room temperature)
1	egg
1/2	cup coarsely chopped macadamia nuts

1/2 cup flaked coconut, toasted
1/2 cup whipping (heavy) cream
3 oz white chocolate baking squares, coarsely chopped
2 tablespoons coarsely chopped macadamia nuts

1 Heat oven to 350°F. Line 9-inch square pan with foil. Spray foil with cooking spray.

2 In large bowl, stir cookie mix, oil, 2 tablespoons of the coffee, egg, 1/2 cup macadamia nuts and coconut until soft dough forms. Spread in bottom of pan.

3 Bake 20 to 25 minutes or just until set. Cool completely, about 1 hour.

4 In small microwavable bowl, microwave whipping cream, white chocolate and remaining 1 tablespoon coffee uncovered on High about 1 minute 30 seconds, stirring every 30 seconds, until chocolate is melted and mixture is smooth.

5 Use foil to lift bars from pan; remove foil. Cut into 5 rows by 4 rows. Place bars on dessert plates. Spoon warm drizzle over bars; sprinkle with 2 tablespoons macadamia nuts. Serve immediately. Store bars tightly covered at room temperature. Store leftover drizzle covered in refrigerator.

High Altitude (3500-6500): No change.

Nutritional Info: 1 Bar: Calories 210; Total Fat 12g (Saturated Fat 5g); Sodium 125mg; Total Carbohydrate 24g (Dietary Fiber 0g); Protein 2g. Exchanges: 1/2 Starch, 1 Other Carbohydrate, 2-1/2 Fat. Carbohydrate Choices: 1-1/2.

Betty's Kitchen Tips

How-To: To toast coconut, heat oven to 350°F. Spread coconut in ungreased shallow pan. Bake uncovered 5 to 7 minutes, stirring occasionally, until golden brown.

Success Hint: Drizzle the bars just before serving so the drizzle is fresh in case you do not serve all the bars the day they are made.

cranberry crumb bars

Prep Time: 20 Minutes
Start to Finish: 4 Hours
Servings: 24 bars

Katie Goodman, Albuquerque, NM
Celebrate the Season-Holiday Cookie Contest
Good Life Eats, www.goodlifeeats.com

Crust and Topping

2-1/2	cups Gold Medal® all-purpose flour
1	cup sugar
1/2	cup ground slivered almonds
1	teaspoon baking powder
1/4	teaspoon salt
1	cup cold butter
1	egg
1/4	teaspoon ground cinnamon

Filling

4	cups fresh or frozen cranberries
1	cup sugar

Juice of 1/2 orange (4 teaspoons)

1	tablespoon cornstarch
1	teaspoon vanilla

Nutritional Info: 1 Bar: Calories 210; Total Fat 9g (Saturated Fat 5g); Sodium 105mg; Total Carbohydrate 30g (Dietary Fiber 1g); Protein 2g. Exchanges: 1 Starch, 1/2 Fruit, 1/2 Other Carbohydrate, 1-1/2 Fat. Carbohydrate Choices: 2.

1 Heat oven to 375°F. Grease 13x9-inch pan with butter or cooking spray.

2 In large bowl, mix flour, 1 cup sugar, the almonds, baking powder and salt. Cut in butter, using pastry blender (or pulling 2 table knives through ingredients in opposite directions), until mixture looks like coarse crumbs. Stir in egg. Press 2-1/2 cups of crumb mixture in bottom of pan. Stir cinnamon into remaining crumb mixture; set aside.

3 In medium bowl, stir all filling ingredients. Spoon evenly over crust. Spoon reserved crumb mixture evenly over filling.

4 Bake 45 to 55 minutes or until top is light golden brown. Cool completely. Refrigerate until chilled. Cut into 6 rows by 4 rows. Store tightly covered in refrigerator.

High Altitude (3500-6500): No change.

Betty's Kitchen Tip

• A food processor works great for grinding the almonds. You will need about 2/3 cup slivered almonds to measure 1/2 cup ground almonds.

pumpkin swirl brownies

Prep Time: 15 Minutes
Start to Finish: 2 Hours 30 Minutes
Servings: 16 brownies

EASY

Filling

1	package (3 oz) cream cheese, softened
1/2	cup canned pumpkin (not pumpkin pie mix)
1	egg
3	tablespoons sugar
1	teaspoon ground cinnamon
1/4	teaspoon ground nutmeg

Brownies

1	box Betty Crocker® Premium Brownies Ultimate Fudge
1/4	cup vegetable oil
2	tablespoons water
1	egg

1 Heat oven to 350°F (325°F for dark or nonstick pan). Grease bottom only of 9-inch square pan with shortening or cooking spray. In small bowl, beat all filling ingredients with electric mixer on low speed until smooth. Set aside.

2 Make brownie batter as directed on box, using 1/4 cup oil, 2 tablespoons water and the egg. Spread 3/4 of the batter in pan. Spoon filling by tablespoonfuls evenly over batter. Spoon remaining brownie batter over filling. Cut through batter several times with knife for marbled design.

3 Bake 40 to 45 minutes or until toothpick inserted 1 inch from side of pan comes out almost clean. Cool completely. Cut into 4 rows by 4 rows. Store covered in the refrigerator.

High Altitude (3500-6500): No change.

Nutritional Info: 1 Brownie: Calories 210; Total Fat 8g (Saturated Fat 3g); Sodium 140mg; Total Carbohydrate 33g (Dietary Fiber 1g); Protein 2g. Exchanges: 1/2 Starch, 1-1/2 Other Carbohydrate, 1-1/2 Fat. Carbohydrate Choices: 2.

Betty's Kitchen Tip

• You can freeze brownies for up to six months. Wrap them up individually and they'll be ready for packing in lunches.

lime cheesecake dessert squares

Prep Time: 20 Minutes
Start to Finish: 6 Hours
Servings: 24 squares

Heather Hunsaker
Austin, TX
Cookie Contest 2009

Crust

1/2	cup cold butter or margarine
1	pouch (1 lb 1.5 oz) Betty Crocker® oatmeal cookie mix

Filling

3	packages (8 oz each) cream cheese
1	cup sugar
1	teaspoon vanilla
3	eggs

1	can (14 oz) sweetened condensed milk (not evaporated)
3/4	cup key lime juice
2	teaspoons grated lime peel
2	tablespoons flour

Topping

3/4	cup reserved cookie crust crumbs
3/4	cup coconut
3/4	cup macadamia nuts, chopped

1 Heat oven to 350°F. Spray 13x9-inch pan with cooking spray.

2 In medium bowl, cut butter into cookie mixture using pastry blender or fork, until mixture is crumbly. Reserve 3/4 cup mixture for topping. Press remaining mixture in bottom of pan. Bake 10 minutes.

3 Meanwhile, in large bowl, beat cream cheese, sugar, and vanilla with electric mixer on medium speed until smooth. Beat in eggs one at a time, mixing well after each addition. Stir in condensed milk, key lime juice, lime peel and flour. Pour filling mixture over crust.

4 In medium bowl, mix reserved cookie crumbs, coconut and macadamia nuts. Sprinkle evenly over top of filling. Bake 30 to 35 minutes or until light golden brown and mixture is set. Cool 1 hour or until completely cooled. Refrigerate at least 4 hours before serving. For bars, cut into 6 rows by 4 rows. Store covered in the refrigerator.

High Altitude (3500-6500): No change.

Nutritional Info: 1 Square: Calories 360; Total Fat 21g (Saturated Fat 12g); Sodium 220mg; Total Carbohydrate 37g (Dietary Fiber 0g); Protein 6g. Exchanges: 1-1/2 Starch, 1 Other Carbohydrate, 4 Fat. Carbohydrate Choices: 2-1/2.

almond fudge bars

Prep Time: 15 Minutes
Start to Finish: 2 Hours
Servings: 32 bars

EASY

- 1 box (18.3 oz) Betty Crocker® fudge brownie mix

Water, vegetable oil and eggs as called for on brownie mix box

- 1 can (14 oz) sweetened condensed milk (not evaporated)
- 1 egg, slightly beaten
- 6 bars (1.61 oz each) milk chocolate, coconut and almond candy, cut into 1/2-inch pieces
- 1 cup sliced almonds

1. Heat oven to 350°F. Spray bottom and sides of 13x9-inch pan with cooking spray.

2. Make brownie mix as directed on brownie box using water, oil and eggs. Bake 20 minutes.

3. Meanwhile, in medium bowl, mix the sweetened condensed milk and egg with whisk. Pour mixture over partially baked brownie base. Sprinkle candy bar pieces evenly over base; top with sliced almonds. Bake 22 to 27 minutes longer or until center is set.

4. Cool completely, about 1 hour 30 minutes. For bars, cut into 8 rows by 4 rows.

High Altitude (3500-6500): No change.

Nutritional Info: 1 Bar: Calories 190; Total Fat 8g (Saturated Fat 3.5g); Sodium 85mg; Total Carbohydrate 26g (Dietary Fiber 1g); Protein 3g. Exchanges: 1 Starch, 1 Other Carbohydrate, 1-1/2 Fat. Carbohydrate Choices: 2.

Betty's Kitchen Tips

Success Hint: Bars can sometimes be difficult to cut. To make it easier, refrigerate them first.

Variation: For even more coconut flavor, you can stir 1/3 cup sweetened flaked coconut into the sweetened condensed milk mixture. Proceed as the recipe directs.

snickerdoodle bars

Prep Time: 20 Minutes
Start to Finish: 1 Hour 45 Minutes
Servings: 24 bars

2-1/3	cups Gold Medal® all-purpose flour
1-1/4	teaspoons baking powder
1/2	teaspoon salt
3/4	cup butter or margarine, softened
1-1/4	cups granulated sugar
1/2	cup packed brown sugar
3	eggs
1	teaspoon vanilla

Cinnamon Filling

1	tablespoon granulated sugar
1	tablespoon ground cinnamon

Glaze

1	cup powdered sugar
1	to 2 tablespoons milk
1/4	teaspoon vanilla

1 Heat oven to 350°F. Spray or grease bottom only of 13x9-inch pan with cooking spray. In small bowl, combine flour, baking powder and salt; set aside.

2 In large bowl, beat butter with electric mixer on high speed until creamy. Beat in sugars. Gradually beat eggs and vanilla into sugar mixture until combined. On low speed, beat in dry ingredients until combined.

3 Spoon half the batter into pan; spread evenly. Sprinkle cinnamon-sugar mixture evenly over batter.

4 Dollop teaspoon size amounts of the remaining batter evenly over cinnamon-sugar mixture.

5 Bake 20 to 25 minutes or until golden brown and toothpick inserted in center comes out clean. Cool completely, about 1 hour.

6 In small bowl, stir glaze ingredients until smooth and thin enough to drizzle. Drizzle over bars. For bars, cut into 6 rows by 4 rows.

High Altitude (3500-6500): No change.

Nutritional Info: 1 Bar: Calories 190; Total Fat 7g (Saturated Fat 4g); Sodium 125mg; Total Carbohydrate 30g (Dietary Fiber 0g); Protein 2g. Exchanges: 1/2 Starch, 1-1/2 Other Carbohydrate, 1-1/2 Fat. Carbohydrate Choices: 2.

Betty's Kitchen Tips

Packaging: Some bars are especially suitable for picnics and traveling, and this is one of them. Bars with soft frostings should be avoided because the frosting may melt. Cut into bars, and pack between sheets of waxed paper in sealed plastic food containers. For optimum packing, wrap each individual brownie or bar cookie in plastic wrap.

Did You Know? The inspiration for these bars comes from the classic snickerdoodle cookie, a favorite butter cookie coated in cinnamon and sugar.

salted caramel turtle triangles

Prep Time: 20 Minutes
Start to Finish: 1 Hour 30 Minutes
Servings: 48 bars

Patty Lok
Los Angeles, CA
Cookie Contest 2009

. . . .

Cookie Base

1	pouch (1 lb 1.5 oz) Betty Crocker® double chocolate chunk cookie mix
1/4	cup butter or margarine, melted
2	tablespoons water
1	egg
2/3	cup pecans, coarsely chopped

Caramel Topping

4	tablespoons butter
1	bag (14 oz) caramels, approximately 35 caramels
1/4	cup whipping (heavy) cream
1/2	teaspoon vanilla
1/8	teaspoon coarse kosher salt, plus additional 1/2 teaspoon for top of bars

. . . .

1 Heat oven to 350°F. Spray 9 x 13-inch pan with cooking spray.

2 In medium bowl, stir together cookie mix, butter, water and egg until soft dough forms. Press dough evenly into prepared pan, sprinkle with 1/3 cup pecans. Bake 11 to 15 minutes or until set in center and edges just begin to pull from sides of pan. Set aside to cool.

3 Meanwhile, in medium saucepan over medium-low heat, melt butter, caramels and cream, stirring frequently until mixture is smooth. Remove from heat. Stir in vanilla and 1/8 teaspoon salt.

4 Spread caramel evenly over cookie base and sprinkle with remaining pecans. Cool completely. Sprinkle top of caramel with additional salt right before serving. To serve, cut into 4 rows by 6 rows and cut each square diagonally into triangles. Store in refrigerator; bring to room temperature before serving.

High Altitude (3500-6500): No change.

Nutritional Info: 1 Bar: Calories 110; Total Fat 5g (Saturated Fat 2.5g); Sodium 110mg; Total Carbohydrate 15g (Dietary Fiber 0g); Protein 1g. Exchanges: 1 Other Carbohydrate, 1 Fat. Carbohydrate Choices: 1.

Betty's Kitchen Tip

• For a no-fuss brownie-turtle sundae, serve the triangles with a scoop of vanilla ice cream topped with a drizzle of hot fudge.

mocha brownies

Prep Time: 30 Minutes
Start to Finish: 2 Hours 10 Minutes
Servings: 24 brownies

Robert Cowling
Blog Chef
www.blogchef.net

Brownies

1/2	cup shortening
1/2	cup butter
2	cups granulated sugar
1	cup unsweetened baking cocoa
4	teaspoons instant coffee granules
1	tablespoon hot water
2	teaspoons vanilla
4	eggs

1	cup Gold Medal® all-purpose flour
1/2	teaspoon salt

Frosting

2	tablespoons milk
2	teaspoons instant coffee granules
2	cups powdered sugar
1/2	cup butter, softened
1	teaspoon vanilla

1 Heat oven to 350°F. Grease 13x9-inch pan with baking spray with flour.

2 In large microwaveable bowl, microwave shortening and butter uncovered on Medium (50%) for 1-1/2 to 2 minutes, stirring once, until shortening and butter are melted. Stir 2 cups granulated sugar and cocoa into butter mixture, until sugar is dissolved.

3 In small bowl mix 4 teaspoons instant coffee granules and hot water until coffee granules are dissolved; stir into cocoa mixture. Stir in vanilla and eggs one at a time until well blended. Stir in flour and salt, until smooth. Spread batter evenly in pan.

4 Bake 25 to 30 minutes, or until toothpick inserted in center comes out clean. Cool completely, about 1 hour.

5 In small microwaveable bowl, microwave milk on High for 20 to 30 seconds until very warm. Stir in 2 teaspoons coffee granules until dissolved. Allow mixture to cool to room temperature, about 10 minutes.

6 In medium bowl, mix remaining frosting ingredients with electric mixer on low speed until combined; increase speed to medium and blend until light and fluffy. Beat in cooled coffee. Spread frosting over the cooled brownies. For brownies, cut into 6 rows by 4 rows.

High Altitude (3500-6500): No change.

Nutritional Info: 1 Brownie: Calories 260; Total Fat 13g (Saturated Fat 7g); Sodium 115mg; Total Carbohydrate 33g (Dietary Fiber 1g); Protein 2g. Exchanges: 1/2 Starch, 2 Other Carbohydrate, 2-1/2 Fat. Carbohydrate Choices: 2.

blueberry cheesecake bars

Prep Time: 40 Minutes
Start to Finish: 4 Hours 10 Minutes
Servings: 28 bars

1	pouch (1 lb 1.5 oz) Betty Crocker® oatmeal cookie mix
1/2	cup butter or margarine, softened
1	egg
3	packages (8 oz each) cream cheese, softened
3/4	cup sugar
1/2	cup whipping (heavy) cream
3	eggs
1	jar (10 oz) blueberry spreadable fruit
1-1/2	cups fresh or frozen (thawed and drained) whole blueberries

1 Heat oven to 350°F. Spray bottom and sides of 13x9-inch pan with cooking spray. In large bowl, beat cookie mix, butter and egg with electric mixer on low speed until soft dough forms. Press in bottom of pan.

2 Bake 15 minutes. Cool 10 minutes. Meanwhile, in another large bowl, beat cream cheese and sugar with mixer on medium speed until fluffy. Add whipping cream and eggs; beat on low speed until well blended.

3 Spread spreadable fruit over partially cooled crust. Sprinkle with blueberries. Pour cream cheese mixture evenly over blueberries, spreading gently to cover.

4 Bake 40 to 45 minutes or until center is set. Cool 30 minutes. Refrigerate at least 2 hours. For bars, cut into 7 rows by 4 rows. Store covered in refrigerator.

High Altitude (3500-6500 ft): In Step 4, bake 45 to 50 minutes.

Nutritional Info: 1 Bar: Calories 260; Total Fat 14g (Saturated Fat 8g); Sodium 180mg; Total Carbohydrate 28g (Dietary Fiber 1g); Protein 4g. Exchanges: 1/2 Starch, 1-1/2 Other Carbohydrate, 3 Fat. Carbohydrate Choices: 2.

Betty's Kitchen Tip

• Using a wet, clean knife makes cutting these bars much easier.

creamy peanut butter-filled bars

Prep Time: 15 Minutes
Start to Finish: 2 Hours
Servings: 36 bars

EASY

1   pouch (1 lb 1.5 oz) Betty Crocker® chocolate chip cookie mix
Butter and egg called for on cookie mix pouch
2   cups powdered sugar
1/2 cup creamy peanut butter
2   tablespoons milk

1   cup honey-roasted peanuts
1   cup semisweet chocolate chips (6 oz)
1/4 cup butter, cut into pieces
1/4 cup whipping (heavy) cream
1   tablespoon multicolored candy sprinkles

1   Heat oven to 375°F. Make cookie dough as directed on package. Press in bottom of ungreased 13x9-inch pan.

2   Bake 12 to 14 minutes or until light golden brown. Cool completely.

3   In medium bowl, beat powdered sugar, peanut butter and milk with electric mixer on medium speed until smooth. Stir in peanuts. Spread over cooled cookie crust.

4   In 2-quart heavy saucepan, heat chocolate chips and butter over low heat, stirring frequently, until melted and smooth. Remove from heat; stir in whipping cream until blended. Spread evenly over peanut butter layer. Top with sprinkles. Refrigerate 1 hour or until set. Cut into 9 rows by 4 rows.

High Altitude (3500-6500): No change.

Nutritional Info: 1 Bar: Calories 200; Total Fat 12g (Saturated Fat 5g); Sodium 115mg; Total Carbohydrate 22g (Dietary Fiber 1g); Protein 3g. Exchanges: 1/2 Starch, 1 Other Carbohydrate, 2 Fat. Carbohydrate Choices: 1-1/2.

Betty's Kitchen Tip

• Make these bars a seasonal treat. Use red and green candy sprinkles for Christmas, mini red, white and blue sprinkles for the 4th of July and pastel-colored mini egg sprinkles for Easter.

caramel apple-nut bars

Prep Time: 15 Minutes
Start to Finish: 2 Hours 20 Minutes
Servings: 36 bars

EASY

2	cups Gold Medal® all-purpose flour
2	cups quick-cooking oats
1-1/2	cups packed brown sugar
1	teaspoon baking soda
1/2	teaspoon salt
1-1/4	cups butter or margarine, softened
1/2	cup caramel topping
3	tablespoons Gold Medal® all-purpose flour
1	medium apple, peeled, chopped (1 cup)
1/2	cup coarsely chopped pecans

1 Heat oven to 350°F. Grease bottom and sides of 13x9-inch pan with shortening or cooking spray. In large bowl, beat 2 cups flour, the oats, brown sugar, baking soda, salt and butter with electric mixer on low speed, or mix with spoon, until crumbly. Press about 3 cups of the mixture in pan. Bake 10 minutes.

2 Meanwhile, in small bowl, mix caramel topping and 3 tablespoons flour. Sprinkle apple and pecans over partially baked crust. Drizzle with caramel mixture. Sprinkle with remaining crust mixture.

3 Bake 20 to 25 minutes or until golden brown. Cool completely, about 1 hour 30 minutes. Cut into 6 rows by 6 rows.

High Altitude (3500-6500): No change.

Nutritional Info: 1 Bar: Calories 160; Total Fat 8g (Saturated Fat 4g); Sodium 150mg; Total Carbohydrate 22g (Dietary Fiber 1g); Protein 1g. Exchanges: 1/2 Starch, 1 Other Carbohydrate, 1-1/2 Fat. Carbohydrate Choices: 1-1/2.

Betty's Kitchen Tip

• Lining the pan with foil not only makes for easy cleanup, but it also makes it easy to remove the bars from the pan and then cut into straight, even bars.

cheryl's chocolate chip blonde brownies

Prep Time: 15 Minutes
Start to Finish: 3 Hours 45 Minutes
Servings: 24 brownies

EASY

2/3 cup butter or margarine, softened	2 teaspoons baking powder
2 cups packed brown sugar	1 teaspoon salt
2 teaspoons vanilla	1 bag (12 oz) semisweet chocolate chips (2 cups)
2 eggs	
2 cups Gold Medal® all-purpose flour	

1 Heat oven to 350°F. Grease bottom only of 13x9-inch pan with cooking spray or butter.

2 In large bowl, beat butter, brown sugar, vanilla and eggs with electric mixer on medium-high speed until blended. On low speed, beat in flour, baking powder and salt until soft dough forms. Spread in pan. Sprinkle chocolate chips evenly over top.

3 Bake 25 to 30 minutes or until edges are golden brown. Cool completely, about 3 hours. Cut into 6 rows by 4 rows.

High Altitude (3500-6500): No change.

Nutritional Info: 1 Brownie: Calories 240; Total Fat 10g (Saturated Fat 6g); Sodium 190mg; Total Carbohydrate 35g (Dietary Fiber 1g); Protein 2g. Exchanges: 1 Starch, 1-1/2 Other Carbohydrate, 2 Fat. Carbohydrate Choices: 2.

Betty's Kitchen Tip

• The Betty Crocker staff prefers to use shortening when greasing brownie pans because it spreads smoothly and evenly and because it tolerates heat better than butter.

crème brûlée squares

Prep Time: 25 Minutes
Start to Finish: 5 Hours 25 Minutes
Servings: 24 bars

Kathy Nasano
Montvale, NJ
Cookie Contest 2009

1	pouch (1 lb 1.5 oz) Betty Crocker® sugar cookie mix
1/2	cup butter, softened
1	egg
5	egg yolks, slightly beaten
1/4	cup granulated sugar
1-1/4	cup whipping (heavy) cream
1	teaspoon vanilla
3	tablespoons packed brown sugar

1 Heat oven to 350°F. Spray bottom and sides of 13x9-inch pan with cooking spray.

2 In large bowl, stir cookie mix, butter and 1 egg until soft dough forms. Press dough in bottom of pan. Bake 15 minutes.

3 Reduce oven temperature to 300°F. In large bowl, beat egg yolks and sugar with wire whisk until well blended; gradually beat in whipping cream and vanilla. Pour over crust. Bake 45 to 50 minutes longer or until knife inserted in center comes out clean. Cool completely, about 1 hour. Refrigerate at least 3 hours before serving.

4 Set oven control to broil. Sprinkle top of bar with brown sugar. Broil with top about 5 inches from heat 2 to 3 minutes or until top is brown and sugar is melted. For bars, cut into 6 rows by 4 rows. Store covered in refrigerator.

High Altitude (3500-6500): No change.

Nutritional Info: 1 Bar: Calories 180; Total Fat 11g (Saturated Fat 6g); Sodium 95mg; Total Carbohydrate 20g (Dietary Fiber 0g); Protein 2g. Exchanges: 1/2 Starch, 1 Other Carbohydrate, 2 Fat. Carbohydrate Choices: 1.

Betty's Kitchen Tip

• This recipe is a spin-off of the classic crème brûlée dessert. The delicious bars can also be topped with various berries (blueberries, strawberries or raspberries).

candy bar brownies

Prep Time: 30 Minutes
Start to Finish: 2 Hours 25 Minutes
Servings: 48 brownies

Brownies

3/4	cup butter or margarine, softened
2	tablespoons water
2/3	cup sugar
1	cup semisweet chocolate chips
1	teaspoon vanilla
2	eggs
1	cup Gold Medal® all-purpose flour
1/2	teaspoon baking powder

Candy Bar Topping

1	cup sugar
1/4	cup butter or margarine
1/4	cup milk
1	cup marshmallow creme
1/2	cup creamy peanut butter
1/2	teaspoon vanilla
1-1/2	cups dry-roasted peanuts
40	caramels, unwrapped
1/4	cup water
1	cup semisweet chocolate chips
1/4	cup butterscotch-flavored chips

1 Heat oven to 350°F (325°F if using dark or nonstick pan). Line 13x9-inch pan with foil, leaving 1 inch of foil overhanging at 2 opposite sides of pan; spray foil with cooking spray.

2 In large microwavable bowl, microwave 3/4 cup butter, 2 tablespoons water and 2/3 cup sugar uncovered on High about 1 minute or until mixture just starts to boil; stir until blended. Stir in 1 cup chocolate chips until melted. Stir in 1 teaspoon vanilla and the eggs until well mixed. Stir in flour and baking powder. Pour batter into pan.

3 Bake 18 to 23 minutes or until toothpick inserted in center comes out clean (do not overbake). Cool completely in pan on cooling rack, about 30 minutes.

4 In 2-quart saucepan, heat 1 cup sugar, 1/4 cup butter and the milk to boiling over medium heat, stirring constantly. Boil 5 minutes, stirring constantly. Stir in

marshmallow creme, 1/4 cup of the peanut butter and 1/2 teaspoon vanilla. Pour over brownies. Sprinkle peanuts over top.

5 In 1-quart saucepan, heat caramels and 1/4 cup water over medium-low heat, stirring constantly, until caramels are melted; pour over peanuts.

6 In medium microwavable bowl, microwave 1 cup chocolate chips and the butterscotch chips uncovered on High about 1 minute or until softened; stir until smooth. Stir in remaining 1/4 cup peanut butter; spread over caramel layer. Refrigerate at least 1 hour. Use foil to lift bars from pan; remove foil. Cut into 8 rows by 6 rows. Store covered in refrigerator.

High Altitude (3500-6500): No change.

Nutritional Info: 1 Brownie: Calories 200; Total Fat 11g (Saturated Fat 5g); Sodium 110mg; Total Carbohydrate 24g (Dietary Fiber 1g); Protein 3g. Exchanges: 1/2 Starch, 1 Other Carbohydrate, 2 Fat. Carbohydrate Choices: 1-1/2.

heavenly chocolate mousse bars

Prep Time: 25 Minutes
Start to Finish: 2 Hours 40 Minutes
Servings: 36 bars

1   pouch (1 lb 1.5 oz) Betty Crocker® sugar cookie mix
Butter and egg called for on cookie mix pouch
1   bag (12 oz) semisweet chocolate chips (2 cups)

1   package (8 oz) cream cheese, softened
1-1/2   cups whipping (heavy) cream

1 Heat oven to 350°F. Make cookie dough as directed on package. Spread in bottom of ungreased 13x9-inch pan.

2 Bake 12 to 15 minutes or until light golden brown. Cool completely.

3 In small microwavable bowl, microwave 1 cup of the chocolate chips uncovered on High 1 minute or until melted. In medium bowl, beat cream cheese with electric mixer until smooth. Beat in melted chocolate. In another bowl, beat 1 cup of the whipping cream with electric mixer on high speed until stiff peaks form. Fold into chocolate-cream cheese mixture until well blended. Spread over cooled cookie base. Cover; refrigerate 1 hour or until set.

4 In same small bowl, microwave remaining 1 cup chocolate chips uncovered on High 1 minute or until melted. Stir in remaining 1/2 cup whipping cream until blended. Spoon warm chocolate mixture over mousse; spread evenly. Refrigerate 30 minutes or until set. Cut into 9 rows by 4 rows. Store in refrigerator.

High Altitude (3500-6500): No change.

Nutritional Info: 1 Bar: Calories 190; Total Fat 13g (Saturated Fat 7g); Sodium 85mg; Total Carbohydrate 17g (Dietary Fiber 0g); Protein 1g. Exchanges: 1 Other Carbohydrate, 2-1/2 Fat. Carbohydrate Choices: 1.

Betty's Kitchen Tip

• Whipping cream will form stiff peaks faster if you chill the bowl and beaters before using.

orange-oat date bars

Prep Time: 20 Minutes
Start to Finish: 3 Hours
Servings: 20 bars

Deborah Puette
Lilburn, GA
Cookie Mix Contest 2010

1	box (8 oz) chopped dates (1-1/2 cups)
1-3/4	cups orange juice
1/3	cup packed brown sugar
1	cup coarsely chopped pecans
1	pouch (1 lb 1.5 oz) Betty Crocker® oatmeal cookie mix
1/2	cup plus 2 tablespoons butter or margarine, melted
1/2	teaspoon powdered sugar

1. Heat oven to 350°F. Spray bottom and sides of 9-inch square pan with cooking spray.

2. In 2-quart saucepan, cook dates and orange juice over medium-low heat 5 minutes, stirring occasionally. Stir in brown sugar; simmer 5 minutes longer, stirring occasionally. Remove from heat; stir in pecans. Set aside.

3. In large bowl, stir cookie mix and butter with fork until mixture is crumbly. Press 2/3 of mixture in bottom of pan. Pour date mixture over crust. Sprinkle with remaining crumb mixture.

4. Bake 30 to 40 minutes or until golden brown. Cool completely, about 2 hours. Sprinkle with powdered sugar. Cut into 5 rows by 4 rows. Store bars covered at room temperature.

High Altitude (3500-6500): No change.

Nutritional Info: 1 Bar: Calories 250; Total Fat 11g (Saturated Fat 4g); Sodium 135mg; Total Carbohydrate 35g (Dietary Fiber 1g); Protein 2g. Exchanges: 1 Starch, 1-1/2 Other Carbohydrate, 2 Fat. Carbohydrate Choices: 2.

Betty's Kitchen Tip

• Dried dates can be stored in an airtight container in a cool, dry place up to 6 months or in the refrigerator up to 1 year.

mojito bars

Prep Time: 15 Minutes
Start to Finish: 2 Hours 20 Minutes
Servings: 24 bars

EASY

3	tablespoons light rum or 1-1/2 teaspoons rum extract plus 3 tablespoons water	1-1/2	cups granulated sugar
16	fresh mint leaves, chopped	1/4	teaspoon salt
3/4	cup butter or margarine, softened	2	teaspoons grated lime peel
1/2	cup powdered sugar	2/3	cup fresh lime juice (from 6 limes)
2	cups Gold Medal® all-purpose flour	2	to 3 drops green food color, if desired
4	eggs	2	tablespoons milk
		1	tablespoon powdered sugar

1 In small bowl, combine rum and chopped mint. Set aside.

2 Heat oven to 350°F. Lightly spray 13x9-inch pan with cooking spray. In large bowl, mix butter and 1/2 cup powdered sugar together with electric mixer on medium speed. Mix in 1-3/4 cup of the flour on low speed, just until well combined. Press in pan. Bake 22 to 25 minutes or until set and lightly browned.

3 Meanwhile, in large bowl, mix eggs and sugar, with whisk. Add remaining 1/4 cup flour and salt, mix with whisk until blended. Mix in lime peel, lime juice, food color and milk.

4 Place strainer over medium bowl; pour rum mixture into strainer. Press mixture with back of spoon through strainer to drain liquid from leaves; discard leaves. Mix strained liquid into egg mixture, with whisk until well combined. Pour over partially baked crust. Bake 25 to 27 minutes longer or until center is set.

5 Cool completely, about 1 hour. Sprinkle with powdered sugar. For bars, cut into 6 rows by 4 rows. Store bars, tightly covered, in the refrigerator.

High Altitude (3500-6500): No change.

Nutritional Info: 1 Bar: Calories 170; Total Fat 7g (Saturated Fat 4g); Sodium 75mg; Total Carbohydrate 24g (Dietary Fiber 0g); Protein 2g. Exchanges: 1/2 Starch, 1 Other Carbohydrate, 1-1/2 Fat. Carbohydrate Choices: 1-1/2.

Betty's Kitchen Tip

• If desired, omit mint leaves and substitute 1/2 teaspoon mint extract. Add extract with the rum as directed.

brownie and strawberry shortcakes

Prep Time: 20 Minutes
Start to Finish: 1 Hour 45 Minutes
Servings: 12 shortcakes

. . . .

  1 box (1 lb 2.4 oz) Betty Crocker® Original
     Supreme Premium brownie mix

Water, vegetable oil and egg called for on brownie
mix box

1-1/4 cups milk
  1 box (4-serving size) white chocolate
     instant pudding and pie filling mix
  1 pint (2 cups) whipping cream
  2 cups sliced fresh strawberries

. . . .

1 Heat oven to 350°F (325°F for dark or
   nonstick pan). Grease 13x9-inch pan
   with shortening or cooking spray. Make
   brownie batter, using water, oil and egg,
   as directed on box. Spread batter in pan.

2 Bake 28 to 33 minutes or until brownie
   springs back when touched lightly in
   center. Cool at least 30 minutes.

3 Meanwhile, in medium bowl, beat milk
   and pudding mix with wire whisk until
   thickened; set aside. In medium deep bowl,
   beat whipping cream with electric mixer
   on low speed until cream begins to thicken.
   Increase speed to high and beat until stiff
   peaks form. Gently fold whipped cream
   into pudding mixture until well combined.
   Cover; refrigerate until serving time.

4 Cut brownies into 6 rows by 4 rows,
   making 24 squares. Place 1 brownie
   square on each of 12 dessert plates; top
   each square with 3 tablespoons pudding
   mixture, a second brownie square, 2
   more tablespoons of pudding mixture
   and 2 tablespoons strawberries. Serve
   immediately.

High Altitude (3500-6500): No change.

Nutritional Info: 1 Serving: Calories 390; Total Fat 20g (Saturated
Fat 10g); Sodium 290mg; Total Carbohydrate 48g (Dietary Fiber
2g); Protein 4g. Exchanges: 1 Starch, 2 Other Carbohydrate,
4 Fat. Carbohydrate Choices: 3.

Betty's Kitchen Tips

Substitution: To save time, use 3 cups frozen
(thawed) whipped topping for the whipped
cream in the recipe.

Storage: Fresh strawberries are best used within
2 or 3 days of purchase or picking. Do not wash
until ready to use. Refrigerate loosely covered.

banana cream squares

Prep Time: 20 Minutes
Start to Finish: 2 Hours 15 Minutes
Servings: 24 squares

Frances Blackwelder
Grand Junction, CO
Cookie Contest 2009

1/2 cup butter or margarine, cold
1 pouch (1 lb 1.5 oz) Betty Crocker® sugar cookie mix
1 egg, slightly beaten
1 package (8 oz) cream cheese, softened

1 can (14 oz) sweetened condensed milk
1 tub (8 oz) frozen whipped topping, thawed
1 box (3.4 oz) instant banana pudding mix
3 medium ripe bananas, sliced

1 Heat oven to 375°F. Spray 13x9-inch baking dish with cooking spray.

2 In medium bowl, cut butter into cookie mix using pastry blender or fork, until mixture is crumbly. Reserve 3/4 cup mixture for topping. Mix egg in remaining mixture until incorporated. Press crumbs evenly in bottom of dish. Bake 13 to 15 minutes or until light golden brown around the edges. Cool completely.

3 In 15x10x1-inch pan, place the reserved topping crumbs in a thin layer. Bake 8 to 10 minutes, stirring occasionally or until light golden brown. Cool completely. Crumble into small pieces. Set aside.

4 In 3-quart mixing bowl, beat cream cheese with electric mixer on medium speed, for 1 minute or until smooth. Add sweetened condensed milk. Beat until well blended. Beat in the whipped topping until smooth. Add the pudding mix and continue to beat for an additional 2 minutes or until everything is well combined.

5 Spread 1/3 of the pudding mixture onto cooled base. Arrange bananas in a single layer over pudding, Top with remaining pudding mixture and refrigerate for about 10 minutes or until set. Sprinkle the cookie crumbs over the pudding.

6 To serve, cut into 24 squares, 4 rows by 6 rows, and serve individually.

High Altitude (3500-6500): No change.

Nutritional Info: 1 Square: Calories 260; Total Fat 12g (Saturated Fat 7g); Sodium 200mg; Total Carbohydrate 35g (Dietary Fiber 0g); Protein 3g. Exchanges: 1 Starch, 1-1/2 Other Carbohydrate, 2 Fat. Carbohydrate Choices: 2.

Betty's Kitchen Tip

• Cream cheese is a soft, unripened cheese made from cow's milk. It has a rich, slightly tangy flavor and creamy spreadable texture.

best lemon bars

Prep Time: 15 Minutes
Start to Finish: 2 Hours
Servings: 24 bars

EASY

Shreya Sasaki
Recipe Matcher
www.recipematcher.com

1	cup butter or margarine, softened
2-1/4	cups Gold Medal® all-purpose flour
2	cups granulated sugar
4	eggs
2	teaspoons grated lemon peel
1/2	cup fresh lemon juice
2	tablespoons powdered sugar

1 Heat oven to 350°F. In medium bowl, mix butter, 2 cups of the flour and 1/2 cup of the granulated sugar. Press into bottom of ungreased 13x9-inch pan.

2 Bake 15 to 20 minutes or until center is set and edges just begin to brown.

3 In medium bowl, mix remaining 1/4 cup flour and remaining 1-1/2 cups granulated sugar with whisk. Add eggs, lemon peel and lemon juice; stir with whisk until well combined. Pour over partially baked crust.

4 Bake 18 to 22 minutes longer or until center is set and edges are golden brown. The bars will firm up as they cool. Cool 1 hour. Sprinkle with powdered sugar. For bars, cut into 6 rows by 4 rows.

High Altitude (3500-6500): No change.

Nutritional Info: 1 Bar: Calories 200; Total Fat 9g (Saturated Fat 5g); Sodium 65mg; Total Carbohydrate 27g (Dietary Fiber 0g); Protein 2g. Exchanges: 1 Starch, 1 Other Carbohydrate, 1-1/2 Fat. Carbohydrate Choices: 2.

Betty's Kitchen Tip

• Add some pizzazz to the bars with stencils or strips of parchment paper. Place stencil on bars, sift powdered sugar over the stencil and then carefully lift the stencil from the bars.

peanut butter rocky road brownies

Prep Time: 20 Minutes
Start to Finish: 2 Hours 30 Minutes
Servings: 24 brownies

1   box (1 lb 2.3 oz) Betty Crocker® fudge brownie mix
Water, vegetable oil and eggs as called for on brownie mix package
1   jar (7 oz) marshmallow creme
1/2   cup creamy peanut butter

1   tablespoon milk
30   miniature chocolate-covered peanut butter cup candies, unwrapped, chopped
1/2   cup chopped salted peanuts
1/4   cup semisweet chocolate chips
1/4   teaspoon vegetable oil

1 Heat oven to 350°F (325°F for dark or nonstick pan). Grease bottom only of 13x9-inch pan with shortening or cooking spray.

2 Make brownie mix as directed on box, using water, oil and eggs. Bake 24 to 26 minutes or until toothpick inserted about 2 inches from side of pan comes out almost clean. Cool completely.

3 In medium bowl, beat marshmallow creme, peanut butter and milk with electric mixer on medium speed until smooth

and creamy. Spread over cooled brownies. Sprinkle with chopped peanut butter candies and peanuts.

4 In small microwavable bowl, microwave chocolate chips and 1/4 teaspoon oil uncovered on High 30 to 60 seconds, stirring once, until melted. Drizzle over brownies. Let stand 30 minutes or until chocolate is set. Cut into 6 rows by 4 rows.

High Altitude (3500-6500): No change.

Nutritional Info: 1 Brownie: Calories 280; Total Fat 14g (Saturated Fat 3.5g); Sodium 160mg; Total Carbohydrate 34g (Dietary Fiber 2g); Protein 4g. Exchanges: 1 Starch, 1-1/2 Other Carbohydrate, 2-1/2 Fat. Carbohydrate Choices: 2.

Betty's Kitchen Tip

• Cut these rich brownies into bite-size squares and serve in decorative papers.

salted peanut chews

Prep Time: 1 Hour
Start to Finish: 1 Hour
Servings: 36 bars

- 1 pouch (1 lb 1.5 oz) Betty Crocker® peanut butter cookie mix
- 3 tablespoons vegetable oil
- 1 tablespoon water
- 1 egg
- 3 cups miniature marshmallows
- 2/3 cup light corn syrup
- 1/4 cup butter or margarine
- 2 teaspoons vanilla
- 1 bag (10 oz) peanut butter chips
- 2 cups crisp rice cereal
- 2 cups salted peanuts

1 Heat oven to 350°F. Spray bottom of 13x9-inch pan with cooking spray.

2 In large bowl, stir cookie mix, oil, water and egg until soft dough forms. Press dough in pan using floured fingers.

3 Bake 12 to 15 minutes or until set. Immediately sprinkle marshmallows over crust; bake 1 to 2 minutes longer or until marshmallows begin to puff.

4 In 4-quart saucepan, cook corn syrup, butter, vanilla and chips over low heat, stirring constantly, until chips are melted. Remove from heat; stir in cereal and nuts. Immediately spoon cereal mixture evenly over marshmallows. Refrigerate 30 minutes or until firm. For bars, cut into 9 rows by 4 rows.

High Altitude (3500-6500 ft): Increase first bake time to 15 to 18 minutes.

Nutritional Info: 1 Bar: Calories 170; Total Fat 9g (Saturated Fat 2g); Sodium 150mg; Total Carbohydrate 20g (Dietary Fiber 0g); Protein 3g. Exchanges: 1/2 Starch, 1 Other Carbohydrate, 1-1/2 Fat. Carbohydrate Choices: 1.

Betty's Kitchen Tips

Time-Saver: Skip the cooking spray and line pan with foil for quick cleanup and easy bar removal.

Variation: For a different flavor, try 1-2/3 cups milk chocolate or semisweet chocolate chips for the peanut butter chips.

chewy chocolate peanut butter bars

Prep Time: 15 Minutes
Start to Finish: 1 Hour 35 Minutes
Servings: 48 bars

EASY

1	cup Gold Medal® all-purpose flour	1	egg yolk
1/2	teaspoon baking powder	1	teaspoon vanilla
1/2	teaspoon salt	1	bag (12 oz) dark chocolate chips (2 cups)
1/2	cup butter, cut into pieces	1/2	cup salted dry-roasted peanuts, coarsely chopped
1/2	cup crunchy peanut butter		
1	cup packed brown sugar		

1 Heat oven to 350°F. Spray 13x9-inch pan with baking spray with flour. In small bowl, stir flour, baking powder and salt; set aside.

2 In medium microwavable bowl, place butter and peanut butter. Microwave on High 30 to 45 seconds or until butter is melted. Add brown sugar and egg yolk; stir until mixed. Stir in vanilla and flour mixture. Stir in 3/4 cup of the chocolate chips. Spread in pan.

3 Bake 20 to 25 minutes or until just firm to the touch. Remove from oven; immediately sprinkle with remaining 1-1/4 cups chocolate chips. Let stand 2 to 3 minutes or until chips have softened. Spread softened chips evenly over top. Sprinkle with chopped peanuts. Cool on cooling rack. Cut into 8 rows by 6 rows. Store in airtight container.

High Altitude (3500-6500): No change.

Nutritional Info: 1 Bar: Calories 110; Total Fat 6g (Saturated Fat 3g); Sodium 70mg; Total Carbohydrate 12g (Dietary Fiber 1g); Protein 1g. Exchanges: 1 Starch, 1/2 Fat. Carbohydrate Choices: 1.

Betty's Kitchen Tip

• When measuring brown sugar for this recipe or any baking recipe, it's important to firmly pack the sugar into a dry measuring cup for best results.

mom's favorite candy bars

Prep Time: 20 Minutes
Start to Finish: 2 Hours 15 Minutes
Servings: 32 bars

Rita Bowen
Orion, IL
Cookie Contest 2009

- 1/2 cup butter
- 1/4 cup light corn syrup
- 3/4 cup chunky peanut butter
- 1 pouch (1 lb 1.5 oz) Betty Crocker® oatmeal cookie mix
- 1 bag (12 oz) semisweet chocolate chips (2 cups)
- 1 cup butterscotch chips
- 1 cup dry-roasted peanuts

1 Heat oven to 375°F. Spray 13x9-inch pan with cooking spray.

2 In 2-quart saucepan melt butter, corn syrup and 1/4 cup of the peanut butter over medium heat stirring frequently until melted. Stir in cookie mix until soft dough forms. Press dough in bottom of prepared pan.

3 Bake 11 to 13 minutes, or until edges begin to brown. Cool completely, about 45 minutes.

4 In medium microwavable bowl, mix chocolate chips, butterscotch chips and remaining 1/2 cup peanut butter. Microwave uncovered on High for 1 to 2 minutes, stirring once, until melted. Stir in peanuts. Spread evenly over cookie bars. Refrigerate about 1 hour or until chocolate is set. For bars, cut into 8 rows by 4 rows.

High Altitude (3500-6500): No change.

Nutritional Info: 1 Bar: Calories 250; Total Fat 13g (Saturated Fat 6g); Sodium 90mg; Total Carbohydrate 27g (Dietary Fiber 1g); Protein 4g. Exchanges: 1 Starch, 1 Other Carbohydrate, 2-1/2 Fat. Carbohydrate Choices: 2.

Betty's Kitchen Tip

- These delightful bars, filled with chocolate, peanuts and butterscotch chips, taste just like Baby Ruth® candy bars!

new orleans praline brownies

Prep Time: 25 Minutes
Start to Finish: 2 Hours 10 Minutes
Servings: 24 brownies

Brownies

    1   box (1 lb 2.3 oz) Betty Crocker®
        fudge brownie mix
Water, vegetable oil and eggs as called for on brownie
mix box
    1/2 cup chopped pecans

Praline Frosting

    1/2   cup whipping (heavy) cream
    6   tablespoons butter
    1-1/2 cups packed brown sugar
    1/8   teaspoon salt
    1/2   cup chopped pecans, toasted
    1-1/2 cups powdered sugar
    1   teaspoon vanilla

1. Heat oven to 350°F. Spray bottom only of 13x9-inch pan with cooking spray.

2. Make brownie mix as directed on box for fudge brownies, using water, oil and eggs. Stir in chopped pecans. Bake as directed. Cool completely, about 1 hour.

3. In medium saucepan, mix cream, butter, brown sugar and salt. Cook over medium heat, stirring frequently, until mixture comes to a boil. Continue cooking for about 1 minute, stirring constantly. Remove from heat. Stir in pecans, powdered sugar and vanilla. Cool 5 minutes, stirring frequently.

4. Spread frosting over brownies. Allow to stand 30 to 45 minutes, or until frosting is set. For bars, cut into 6 rows by 4 rows.

High Altitude (3500-6500): No change.

Nutritional Info: 1 Brownie: Calories 280; Total Fat 13g (Saturated Fat 4g); Sodium 105mg; Total Carbohydrate 41g (Dietary Fiber 0g); Protein 0g. Exchanges: 2-1/2 Other Carbohydrate, 2-1/2 Fat. Carbohydrate Choices: 3.

Betty's Kitchen Tips

How-To: To toast pecans, preheat oven to 350°F. Spread pecans in a single layer in a baking pan. Bake about 5 to 7 minutes or until golden and toasted.

Success Hint: Cut into bars about 45 minutes after spreading frosting over the brownies. This will allow you to cut the brownies while the frosting is still just slightly warm and will minimize any cracks in the frosting.

peanut-buttery fudge bars

Prep Time: 20 Minutes
Start to Finish: 3 Hours 5 Minutes
Servings: 24 bars

Robin Wilson
Altamonte Springs, FL
Cookie Mix Contest 2010

Cookie Base

- 1 pouch (1 lb 1.5 oz) Betty Crocker® peanut butter cookie mix
- 3 tablespoons vegetable oil
- 1 tablespoon water
- 1 egg

Topping

- 1 cup hot fudge topping
- 1 cup Betty Crocker® Rich & Creamy cream cheese frosting (from 1-lb container)
- 1/4 cup creamy peanut butter
- 1 container (8 oz) frozen whipped topping, thawed
- 2 bars (2.1 oz each) chocolate-covered crispy peanut-buttery candy, unwrapped, finely crushed

1. Heat oven to 350°F. Spray bottom only of 13x9-inch pan with cooking spray.

2. In large bowl, stir cookie mix, oil, water and egg until soft dough forms. Press in bottom of pan.

3. Bake 12 to 15 minutes or until light golden brown. Cool completely, about 30 minutes.

4. Spread fudge topping over cooled cookie base. In large bowl, mix frosting and peanut butter. Gently fold in whipped topping and candy until well blended. Spoon mixture over fudge topping and carefully spread to evenly cover. Refrigerate about 2 hours or until chilled. Cut into 6 rows by 4 rows. Store covered in refrigerator.

High Altitude (3500-6500): No change.

Nutritional Info: 1 Bar: Calories 260; Total Fat 12g (Saturated Fat 4g); Sodium 200mg; Total Carbohydrate 36g (Dietary Fiber 0g); Protein 3g. Exchanges: 1 Starch, 1-1/2 Other Carbohydrate, 2 Fat. Carbohydrate Choices: 2-1/2.

Betty's Kitchen Tip

- To crush candy bars, place in small resealable food-storage plastic bag; crush with rolling pan or flat side of meat mallet.

turtle bars supreme

Prep Time: 20 Minutes
Start to Finish: 3 Hours 45 Minutes
Servings: 36 bars

Bev Jones
Brunswick, MO
Cookie Contest 2009

Cookie Base

- 1 teaspoon instant espresso coffee granules or instant coffee granules
- 2 tablespoons hot water
- 1 pouch (1 lb 1.5 oz) Betty Crocker® double chocolate chunk cookie mix
- 1/4 cup vegetable oil
- 1 egg

Filling

- 1 package (8 oz) cream cheese, softened
- 3 cups powdered sugar
- 1/2 cup unsweetened baking cocoa
- 2 eggs
- 2 rolls (1.7 oz each) milk chocolate covered caramels, cut into fourths
- 1 cup chopped pecans

Topping

- 1/4 cup caramel topping
- 1/4 cup chopped pecans

1 Heat oven to 350°F. Spray bottom and sides of 13x9- inch pan with cooking spray. In small bowl, stir coffee granules and water until dissolved, set aside. In large bowl, stir cookie mix, oil, egg and dissolved coffee until soft dough forms. Press in bottom of pan. Bake 10 minutes; cool 15 minutes.

2 In medium mixing bowl, beat cream cheese, powdered sugar, cocoa powder and eggs until smooth; fold in caramels and pecans. Gently spread over cookie base. Bake 30 to 35 minutes, or until set. Cool 30 minutes.

3 Drizzle caramel topping over bars; sprinkle with pecans. Refrigerate 2 hours or until set. For bars, cut into 9 rows by 4 rows. Store covered in refrigerator.

High Altitude (3500-6500): No change.

Nutritional Info: 1 Bar: Calories 190; Total Fat 9g (Saturated Fat 3g); Sodium 95mg; Total Carbohydrate 26g (Dietary Fiber 0g); Protein 2g. Exchanges: 1 Starch, 1 Other Carbohydrate, 1-1/2 Fat. Carbohydrate Choices: 2.

chewy raspberry almond bars

Prep Time: 20 Minutes
Start to Finish: 2 Hours
Servings: 16 bars

- 1-1/2   cups quick-cooking oats
- 1-1/2   cups Gold Medal® all-purpose flour
- 3/4   cup packed light brown sugar
- 1/2   teaspoon salt
- 3/4   cup cold butter or margarine
- 1   egg, beaten
- 3/4   cup seedless red raspberry jam
- 1   cup fresh raspberries (6 oz)
- 1/2   cup sliced almonds

1. Heat oven to 375°F. Spray 9-inch square pan with baking spray with flour.

2. In large bowl, mix oats, flour, brown sugar and salt. Cut in butter, using pastry blender (or pulling 2 table knives through mixture in opposite directions), until mixture looks like coarse crumbs. Reserve 1 cup mixture for topping. To remaining mixture, stir in egg until just moistened.

3. Press dough firmly and evenly into bottom of pan, using fingers or bottom of measuring cup. Spread with jam. Arrange raspberries over jam. Stir almonds into reserved crumb mixture; sprinkle evenly over raspberries.

4. Bake 30 to 35 minutes or until top is golden. Cool completely on cooling rack. Cut into 4 rows by 4 rows.

High Altitude (3500-6500): No change.

Nutritional Info: 1 Bar: Calories 260; Total Fat 11g (Saturated Fat 6g); Sodium 150mg; Total Carbohydrate 36g (Dietary Fiber 2g); Protein 3g. Exchanges: 2 Starch, 1/2 Other Carbohydrate, 1-1/2 Fat. Carbohydrate Choices: 2-1/2.

Betty's Kitchen Tips

Variation: For Chewy Blueberry Almond Bars, substitute fresh blueberries for the raspberries.

Substitution: If you don't have baking spray with flour, grease the pan with cooking spray and dust lightly with flour.

black and white chocolate macadamia bars

Prep Time: 25 Minutes
Start to Finish: 1 Hour 15 Minutes
Servings: 32 bars

Kurt Wait
Redwood, CA
Cookie Contest 2009

Cookie Base

- 1 pouch (1 lb 1.5 oz) Betty Crocker® sugar cookie mix
- 2 tablespoons Gold Medal® all-purpose flour
- 1/3 cup butter or margarine, softened
- 1 egg

Fudge Filling

- 1 bag (12 oz) semisweet chocolate chips (2 cups)
- 1 can (14 oz) sweetened condensed milk (not evaporated)
- 1 egg
- 2 teaspoons vanilla
- 1 cup chopped macadamia nuts
- 1/4 cup white vanilla baking chips
- 1 teaspoon vegetable oil

1 Heat oven to 350°F. Spray 13x9-inch pan with cooking spray.

2 In large bowl, mix cookie mix, flour, butter and egg until well mixed. Press dough into bottom of prepared pan. Bake 16 to 18 minutes or until light golden brown. Cool about 10 minutes.

3 Meanwhile, in small saucepan melt 1 cup of the chocolate chips and half of the sweetened condensed milk over medium-low heat, stirring frequently; remove from heat. Stir in remaining condensed milk, egg and vanilla. Spread over crust. Sprinkle with remaining 1 cup chocolate chips and nuts.

4 Bake 22 to 25 minutes or until set. Cool completely, about 30 minutes.

5 For white chocolate drizzle, place baking chips and oil in small resealable freezer plastic bag. Microwave on medium (50%) for 1 minute to 1 minute 15 seconds, turning bag over after 25 seconds. Squeeze bag until chips are melted and smooth. Cut small tip off one corner of bag, and drizzle over bars. Let stand until set, about 10 minutes. Cut bars into 8 rows by 4 rows.

High Altitude (3500-6500): No change.

Nutritional Info: 1 Bar: Calories 220; Total Fat 11g (Saturated Fat 5g); Sodium 85mg; Total Carbohydrate 27g (Dietary Fiber 1g); Protein 3g. Exchanges: 1 Starch, 1 Other Carbohydrate, 2 Fat. Carbohydrate Choices: 2.

DESSERTS&CANDIES

p.322

319

331

325

chocolate-covered peanut butter candies

Prep Time: 25 Minutes
Start to Finish: 2 Hours 25 Minutes
Servings: 64 candies

* * *

1/2	cup creamy peanut butter
1/4	cup butter or margarine, softened
1/4	cup chopped peanuts
1/2	teaspoon vanilla
2	cups powdered sugar
1	bag (12 oz) semisweet chocolate chips (2 cups)

4	teaspoons shortening

Peanut Butter Icing

1/2	cup powdered sugar
2	tablespoons creamy peanut butter

About 1 tablespoon milk

* * *

1 Line 8- or 9-inch square pan with foil, leaving 1 inch of foil overhanging at 2 opposite sides of pan; grease foil with butter.

2 In medium bowl, mix 1/2 cup peanut butter, the butter, peanuts and vanilla. Stir in 2 cups powdered sugar, 1/2 cup at a time, until stiff dough forms. If dough is crumbly, work in additional 1 tablespoon peanut butter. Pat mixture in pan. Cover; refrigerate about 1 hour or until firm.

3 Use foil to lift candy from pan; remove foil. Cut into 8 rows by 8 rows. Line cookie sheet with waxed paper.

4 In 1-quart heavy saucepan, melt chocolate chips and shortening over low heat, stirring constantly. Dip 1 peanut butter square at a time into chocolate mixture. Place on cookie sheet. Refrigerate uncovered about 30 minutes or until firm.

5 In small bowl, mix 1/2 cup powdered sugar and 2 tablespoons peanut butter. Beat in milk with wire whisk until smooth. If necessary, stir in additional milk, 1 teaspoon at a time, until thin enough to drizzle.

6 Drizzle icing over tops of squares. Refrigerate uncovered 30 minutes or until firm. Refrigerate candies loosely covered.

High Altitude (3500-6500 ft): No change.

Nutritional Info: 1 Candy: Calories 80 (Calories from Fat 35); Total Fat 4.5g (Saturated Fat 1-1/2g, Trans Fat 0g); Sodium 15mg; Total Carbohydrate 9g (Dietary Fiber 0g, Sugars 8g); Protein 1g. Exchanges: 1/2 Other Carbohydrate, 1 Fat. Carbohydrate Choices: 1/2.

Betty's Kitchen Tip

• For easy dipping, use one fork for dipping candy into melted chocolate and another fork to push the candy onto the cookie sheet.

chocolate-strawberry shortcakes

Prep Time: 15 Minutes
Start to Finish: 1 Hour 45 Minutes
Servings: 6

- 1 quart (4 cups) fresh strawberries, sliced
- 1/2 cup sugar
- 2 cups Original Bisquick® mix
- 1/3 cup unsweetened baking cocoa
- 2 tablespoons sugar
- 2/3 cup milk
- 2 tablespoons butter or margarine, melted
- 1/3 cup miniature semisweet chocolate chips
- 1-1/2 cups frozen (thawed) whipped topping

EASY

1 In medium bowl, toss strawberries and 1/2 cup sugar until coated. Let stand for 1 hour.

2 Heat oven to 375°F. Spray cookie sheet with cooking spray. In medium bowl, stir Bisquick mix, cocoa, 2 tablespoons sugar, the milk and butter until soft dough forms. Stir in chocolate chips. Drop dough by about 1/3 cupfuls onto cookie sheet, forming six shortcakes.

3 Bake 12 to 15 minutes or until tops of shortcakes appear dry and cracked. Cool 15 minutes. Using serrated knife, split warm shortcakes. Fill and top with strawberries and whipped topping.

High Altitude (3500-6500 ft): No change.

Nutritional Info: 1 Serving: Calories 450 (Calories from Fat 150); Total Fat 17g (Saturated Fat 9g, Trans Fat 1.5g); Cholesterol 10mg; Sodium 530mg; Total Carbohydrate 70g (Dietary Fiber 5g, Sugars 36g); Protein 6g. % Daily Value: Vitamin A 4%; Vitamin C 110%; Calcium 10%; Iron 15%. Exchanges: 2 Starch, 1/2 Fruit, 2 Other Carbohydrate, 3 Fat. Carbohydrate Choices: 4-1/2.

Betty's Kitchen Tip

- For a pretty garnish, sprinkle additional miniature chocolate chips over tops of shortcakes and tuck a mint leaf into whipped topping.

apple crisp

Prep Time: 20 Minutes
Start to Finish: 1 Hour
Servings: 6

---

6 medium tart cooking apples (Greening, Rome, Granny Smith), sliced (about 6 cups)
3/4 cup packed brown sugar
1/2 cup Gold Medal® all-purpose flour
1/2 cup quick-cooking or old-fashioned oats

1 teaspoon ground cinnamon
1/2 teaspoon ground nutmeg
1/3 cup cold butter or margarine
Cream or ice cream, if desired

---

1 Heat oven to 375°F. Spread apples in ungreased 8-inch square pan.

2 In medium bowl, mix brown sugar, flour, oats, cinnamon and nutmeg. Cut in butter, using pastry blender (or pulling 2 table knives through ingredients in opposite directions), until mixture is crumbly. Sprinkle evenly over apples.

3 Bake 35 to 40 minutes or until topping is golden brown and apples are tender when pierced with fork. Serve warm with cream or ice cream.

Blueberry Crisp: Substitute 6 cups fresh or frozen (thawed and drained) blueberries for the apples.

Rhubarb Crisp: Substitute 6 cups cut-up fresh or frozen (thawed and drained) rhubarb for the apples. Sprinkle 1/2 cup granulated sugar over rhubarb; stir to combine. Continue as directed in Step 2.

High Altitude (3500-6500 ft): No change.

Nutritional Info: 1 Serving: Calories 330; Total Fat 11g (Saturated Fat 7g); Sodium 110mg; Total Carbohydrate 55g (Dietary Fiber 4g); Protein 2g. Exchanges: 1 Starch, 1/2 Fruit, 2 Other Carbohydrate, 2 Fat. Carbohydrate Choices: 3-1/2.

Betty's Kitchen Tips

Variation: Other apple varieties that work well in this dessert are Cortland, Haralson and Honeycrisp Apples.

Time-Saver: Leftover apple crisp makes a tasty breakfast treat. Serve it with a dollop of plain yogurt for a sweet morning.

triple-berry granola crisp

Prep Time: 10 Minutes
Start to Finish: 1 Hour
Servings: 9

EASY LOW FAT

1 bag (10 oz) Cascadian Farm® frozen organic blueberries

1 bag (10 oz) Cascadian Farm® frozen organic strawberries

1 bag (10 oz) Cascadian Farm® frozen organic raspberries

1/4 cup sugar

2 tablespoons Gold Medal® all-purpose flour

1-1/2 cups Cascadian Farm® organic oats & honey granola

Vanilla reduced-fat ice cream or vanilla yogurt, if desired

1 Heat oven to 375°F. In ungreased 8-inch square (2-quart) glass baking dish, stir together frozen berries, sugar and flour until fruit is coated.

2 Bake 20 minutes. Stir; sprinkle with the granola.

3 Bake 15 to 20 minutes longer or until light golden brown and bubbly. Let stand 5 to 10 minutes before serving. Serve warm with ice cream.

High Altitude (3500-6500 ft): No change.

Nutritional Info: 1 Serving: Calories 140; Total Fat 2g (Saturated Fat 0g); Sodium 30mg; Total Carbohydrate 29g (Dietary Fiber 3g); Protein 2g. Exchanges: 1/2 Starch, 1/2 Fruit, 1 Other Carbohydrate, 1/2 Fat. Carbohydrate Choices: 2.

Betty's Kitchen Tip

• If you like, use 3 bags (10 oz each) Cascadian Farm® frozen organic harvest berries in place of the blueberries, strawberries and raspberries.

espresso truffle cups

Prep Time: 30 Minutes
Start to Finish: 1 Hour
Servings: 16 candies

16	(1-inch) foil candy cups (not mini paper baking cups)	1	teaspoon instant espresso coffee powder or granules
1-1/4	cups white vanilla baking chips	1/3	cup dark chocolate chips
1-1/2	teaspoons vegetable oil	16	chocolate-covered espresso beans
2	tablespoons whipping (heavy) cream		Unsweetened baking cocoa, if desired

1 Place candy cups in mini muffin pans. In medium microwavable bowl, microwave baking chips and oil uncovered on High for 1 minute; stir. Microwave in 30-second intervals, stirring after each, until melted and smooth.

2 Spoon 1 teaspoon melted mixture in each candy cup. (There will be mixture left over; set aside for later use.) With back of small spoon, spread mixture in bottoms and most of the way up sides of cups. (If mixture is too liquid, cool for a few minutes so it will coat the cups.) Let stand until completely set.

3 Meanwhile, in small microwavable bowl, mix cream and espresso powder. Microwave uncovered on High 20 seconds or until cream is very hot; stir to combine.

Stir in chocolate chips until melted. If necessary, microwave 15 seconds longer until mixture can be stirred smooth. Refrigerate 10 minutes to cool slightly.

4 When candy cups are set and espresso mixture is cooled, microwave remaining white mixture 30 seconds or just until melted but not warm. Spoon espresso mixture into small resealable food-storage plastic bag; cut 1/4 inch from one bottom corner of bag. Pipe about 1 teaspoon mixture into each candy cup. Spoon enough melted white mixture over to cover. Top each with chocolate-covered coffee bean. Sprinkle with cocoa. Let stand until set, about 30 minutes.

High Altitude (3500-6500 ft): No change.

Nutritional Info: 1 Candy: Calories 110; Total Fat 7g (Saturated Fat 4g); Sodium 15mg; Total Carbohydrate 11g (Dietary Fiber 0g); Protein 1g. Exchanges: 1/2 Other Carbohydrate, 1-1/2 Fat. Carbohydrate Choices: 1.

Betty's Kitchen Tips

Purchasing: If your grocery store doesn't carry chocolate-covered espresso beans, look for them in a coffee shop.

Success Hint: The white chocolate mixture must be melted, but not too warm. If it is warm, just let it stand at room temperature a few minutes.

cinnamon truffles

Prep Time: 40 Minutes
Start to Finish: 2 Hours 10 Minutes
Servings: About 24 truffles

- 1 bag (12 oz) semisweet chocolate chips (2 cups)
- 1 tablespoon butter or margarine
- 1/4 cup whipping (heavy) cream
- 1 teaspoon vanilla
- 1/2 teaspoon ground cinnamon

Powdered sugar, if desired

Unsweetened baking cocoa, if desired

1 In 2-quart heavy saucepan, melt chocolate chips and butter over low heat, stirring constantly; remove from heat. Stir in whipping cream, vanilla and cinnamon. Refrigerate 30 to 60 minutes, stirring frequently, just until firm enough to roll into balls.

2 Line cookie sheet with foil or cooking parchment paper. Drop chocolate mixture by tablespoonfuls onto cookie sheet. Shape into balls. (If mixture is too sticky, refrigerate until firm enough to shape.) Refrigerate about 1 hour or until firm.

3 Sprinkle half of the truffles with powdered sugar and half with cocoa. Store in airtight container in refrigerator. Remove truffles from refrigerator about 30 minutes before serving; serve at room temperature.

High Altitude (3500-6500 ft): No change.

Nutritional Info: 1 Truffle: Calories 90; Total Fat 6g (Saturated Fat 3.5g); Sodium 5mg; Total Carbohydrate 9g (Dietary Fiber 1g); Protein 0g. Exchanges: 1/2 Other Carbohydrate, 1 Fat. Carbohydrate Choices: 1/2.

Betty's Kitchen Tips

Special Touch: Celebrate during the Christmas season by serving the truffles in paper candy cups placed in an ornament box.

Variation: Make truffle "pops" by punching a small hole in the bottom of several silver paper candy cups. Insert 8- to 12-inch lollipop stick through bottom of each cup and then into a truffle. Wrap thin ribbon around the stick. Place in a simple silver cup or pitcher.

apricot-chai almond bark

Prep Time: 35 Minutes
Start to Finish: 1 Hour 35 Minutes
Servings: 24

Aysha Schurman, Ammon, ID
Celebrate the Season-Holiday Cookie Contest
2nd Place Winner

3/4	cup slivered almonds
24	oz vanilla-flavored candy coating (almond bark), chopped
1/4	cup apricot nectar
3	teaspoons ground cinnamon

1	teaspoon ground allspice
1	teaspoon ground cardamom
1	teaspoon vanilla
1	teaspoon grated lemon peel
1/4	cup finely chopped dried apricots

1. Sprinkle almonds in ungreased heavy skillet. Cook over medium heat 5 to 7 minutes, stirring frequently until nuts begin to brown, then stirring constantly until nuts are light brown. Cool for 10 minutes. In food processor, process almonds until finely chopped; set aside.

2. Line 15x10x1-inch pan with waxed paper. In medium microwavable bowl, microwave 12 oz of the candy coating on High for 1 minute; stir. Microwave in 15-second intervals, stirring after each, until melted. Quickly stir in 1/3 cup of the chopped almonds. Spread mixture evenly in pan. Refrigerate 15 minutes or until set.

3. In small bowl, mix apricot nectar, cinnamon, allspice, cardamom, vanilla and lemon peel; set aside. In medium microwavable bowl, microwave remaining 12 oz candy coating on High 1 minute; stir. Microwave in 15-second intervals, stirring after each, until melted. Quickly stir in the apricot nectar mixture and dried apricots.

4. Pour and spread over chilled bark. Sprinkle with remaining chopped almonds. Refrigerate at least 1 hour. Break into 2-inch pieces.

High Altitude (3500-6500 ft): No change.

Nutritional Info: 1 Serving: Calories 180; Total Fat 11g (Saturated Fat 6g); Sodium 25mg; Total Carbohydrate 19g (Dietary Fiber 0g); Protein 2g. Exchanges: 1-1/2 Other Carbohydrate, 2 Fat. Carbohydrate Choices: 1.

Betty's Kitchen Tip

• This bark would be a welcomed gift from the kitchen! Make a few batches and look for decorative tins or other containers at craft stores for packaging.

southern apple crumble

Prep Time: 20 Minutes
Start to Finish: 1 Hour 20 Minutes
Servings: 9

Laura McAllister
Morganton, NC
Cookie Mix Contest 2008

. . . .

Filling

3	large apples, peeled, coarsely chopped (about 3 cups)
1/2	cup granulated sugar
1/4	cup packed brown sugar
1	to 2 teaspoons ground cinnamon
1/4	cup cold butter or margarine, cut into small pieces

Topping

1	pouch (1 lb 1.5 oz) Betty Crocker® oatmeal cookie mix
1/2	cup butter or margarine, melted
1/2	cup chopped pecans

. . . .

1 Heat oven to 300°F. Spray bottom and sides of 8-inch square (2-quart) glass baking dish with cooking spray.

2 In large bowl, toss filling ingredients. Spread mixture in baking dish. In same bowl, stir cookie mix and melted butter until crumbly. Sprinkle over filling.

3 Bake 40 minutes. Remove from oven; sprinkle with pecans. Bake 15 to 20 minutes longer or until topping is golden brown. Serve warm or at room temperature.

High Altitude (3500-6500 ft): No change.

Nutritional Info: 1 Serving: Calories 500; Total Fat 22g (Saturated Fat 10g); Sodium 320mg; Total Carbohydrate 71g (Dietary Fiber 1g); Protein 5g. Exchanges: 1-1/2 Starch, 1/2 Fruit, 2-1/2 Other Carbohydrate, 4-1/2 Fat. Carbohydrate Choices: 5.

Betty's Kitchen Tips

Variation: Use fresh peaches instead of the apples for a juicy peach crumble.

Success Hint: Serve with a scoop of ice cream or a dollop of whipped cream.

impossibly easy
mixed-berry crumble pie

Prep Time: 10 Minutes
Start to Finish: 1 Hour 10 Minutes
Servings: 8

EASY

1 cup Original Bisquick® mix	1 teaspoon ground cinnamon
1/4 cup packed brown sugar	1/4 teaspoon ground nutmeg
1/4 cup chopped nuts	1/2 cup sugar
2 tablespoons firm butter or margarine	1/2 cup milk
1 bag (12 oz) frozen mixed berries (about 2-1/2 cups)	1 tablespoon butter or margarine, softened
	2 eggs

1 Heat oven to 325°F. Spray 9-inch glass pie plate with cooking spray. Stir together 1/2 cup Bisquick mix, brown sugar and nuts in small bowl. Cut in the 2 tablespoons firm butter, using pastry blender or crisscrossing 2 knives, until crumbly; set aside.

2 Mix frozen berries, cinnamon and nutmeg in medium bowl. Spread in pie plate. Stir remaining 1/2 cup Bisquick mix and the remaining ingredients in medium bowl with wire whisk or fork until blended. Pour into pie plate. Sprinkle with nut mixture.

3 Bake 50 to 60 minutes or until top is evenly deep golden brown.

High Altitude (3500-6500 ft): No change.

Nutritional Info: 1 Serving: Calories 260 (Calories from Fat 100); Total Fat 11g (Saturated Fat 3.5g, Trans Fat 0.5g); Cholesterol 65mg; Sodium 270mg; Total Carbohydrate 36g (Dietary Fiber 2g, Sugars 26g); Protein 4g. % Daily Value: Vitamin A 6%; Vitamin C 10%; Calcium 6%; Iron 6%. Exchanges: 1 Starch, 1 Fruit, 1/2 Other Carbohydrate, 2 Fat. Carbohydrate Choices: 2-1/2.

Betty's Kitchen Tip

• Make Caramel Whipped Cream by whipping 1 cup chilled whipping (heavy) cream with 2 tablespoons caramel ice cream topping until stiff peaks form. Dollop onto pie.

super-easy cherry almond fudge

Prep Time: 10 Minutes
Start to Finish: 30 Minutes
Servings: 36 candies

EASY QUICK

Jeanne Trudell, Del Norte, CO
Celebrate the Season-
Holiday Cookie Contest

- 1 bag (12 oz) white vanilla baking chips
- 1 container (1 lb) Betty Crocker® Rich & Creamy cherry frosting
- 1/2 cup chopped red candied cherries (4 oz)
- 1/2 cup slivered almonds, toasted
- 1 teaspoon vanilla

Dash salt

1 Line 9-inch square pan with foil; spray foil with cooking spray. In large microwavable bowl, microwave baking chips uncovered on High 1 minute to 1 minute 30 seconds, stirring every 15 seconds, until melted.

2 Stir frosting into melted chips. Fold in remaining ingredients. Pour and spread into pan. Refrigerate 20 minutes or until set.

3 Using foil, lift fudge out of pan; remove foil. Cut into 6 rows by 6 rows. Store tightly covered.

High Altitude (3500-6500 ft): No change.

Nutritional Info: 1 Candy: Calories 120; Total Fat 6g (Saturated Fat 2.5g); Sodium 40mg; Total Carbohydrate 17g (Dietary Fiber 0g); Protein 1g. Exchanges: 1 Other Carbohydrate, 1 Fat. Carbohydrate Choices: 1.

Betty's Kitchen Tip

- To toast almonds, sprinkle in ungreased heavy skillet. Cook over medium heat 5 to 7 minutes, stirring frequently until nuts begin to brown, then stirring constantly until nuts are light brown.

ginger-cherry-pear crisp with oatmeal topping

Prep Time: 30 Minutes
Start to Finish: 1 Hour 40 Minutes
Servings: 12

1 pouch (1 lb 1.5 oz) Betty Crocker® oatmeal cookie mix
3/4 cup cold butter or margarine
1 cup chopped walnuts
6 medium pears, peeled, cut into 1-inch pieces (about 7 cups)

1 bag (5.5 oz) dried cherries
1/4 cup packed brown sugar
2 teaspoons ground ginger

1 Heat oven to 350°F. Spray bottom only of 13x9-inch (3-quart) glass baking dish with cooking spray.

2 In large bowl, place cookie mix. Cut in butter, using pastry blender (or pulling 2 table knives through ingredients in opposite directions), until particles are the size of peas.

3 Remove 1 cup crumb mixture to small bowl; stir in walnuts. Set aside for topping. Press remaining crumb mixture into bottom of dish.

4 In another large bowl, toss pears, cherries, brown sugar and ginger; spoon over crust. Sprinkle reserved crumb/nut mixture over the fruit.

5 Bake 40 to 50 minutes or until topping is golden brown and edges are bubbly. Cool about 20 minutes. Serve warm.

High Altitude (3500-6500 ft): No change.

Nutritional Info: 1 Serving: Calories 450; Total Fat 20g (Saturated Fat 8g); Sodium 240mg; Total Carbohydrate 63g (Dietary Fiber 4g); Protein 5g. Exchanges: 1-1/2 Starch, 1 Fruit, 1-1/2 Other Carbohydrate, 4 Fat. Carbohydrate Choices: 4.

Betty's Kitchen Tips

Time-Saver: To quickly remove seeds from pears, cut in half and use a melon baller.

Substitution: Pecans can be used instead of the walnuts.

cashew brittle

Prep Time: 1 Hour
Start to Finish: 2 Hours
Servings: About 72 pieces

- -

1-1/2	teaspoons baking soda
1	teaspoon water
1	teaspoon vanilla
1-1/2	cups sugar
1	cup water
1	cup light corn syrup
3	tablespoons butter (do not use margarine)
12	oz cashew halves or unsalted raw Spanish peanuts (2-1/2 cups)

- -

1 Heat oven to 200°F. Grease two 15x12-inch cookie sheets with butter; keep warm in oven. (Keeping cookie sheets warm allows the candy to be spread 1/4 inch thick without it setting up.) Grease long metal spatula with butter; set aside.

2 In small bowl, mix baking soda, 1 teaspoon water and the vanilla; set aside. In 3-quart heavy saucepan, mix sugar, 1 cup water and the corn syrup. Cook over medium heat 25 to 35 minutes, stirring frequently, to 240°F on candy thermometer or until small amount of mixture dropped into cup of very cold water forms a soft ball that flattens when removed from water.

3 Stir in butter and cashews. Cook 10 to 15 minutes, stirring constantly, to 300°F or until small amount of mixture dropped into cup of very cold water separates into hard, brittle threads. (Watch carefully so mixture does not burn.) Immediately remove from heat. Quickly stir in baking soda mixture until light and foamy.

4 Pour half of the mixture onto each cookie sheet and quickly spread about 1/4 inch thick with buttered spatula. Cool

LOW FAT

completely, at least 1 hour. Break into pieces. Store in airtight container at room temperature.

High Altitude (3500-6500 ft): No change.

Nutritional Info: 1 Piece: Calories 70; Total Fat 3g (Saturated Fat 1g); Sodium 35mg; Total Carbohydrate 9g (Dietary Fiber 0g); Protein 1g. Exchanges: 1/2 Other Carbohydrate, 1/2 Fat. Carbohydrate Choices: 1/2.

Betty's Kitchen Tip

• Fill pretty glass jars with brittle pieces for an easy, yet elegant gift.

asian pear pie

Prep Time: 45 Minutes
Start to Finish: 4 Hours 20 Minutes
Servings: 8

Lisa Keys, Middlebury, CT
Celebrate the Season-Fall Baking Contest
3rd Place Winner

2 1/3	cups Gold Medal® all-purpose flour	6	cups thinly sliced peeled pears (about 6 large)
1	teaspoon salt	2	tablespoons fresh lemon juice
3/4	cup shortening	1	tablespoon butter
5	to 7 tablespoons cold ginger ale	1	egg white, lightly beaten
1/2	cup packed light brown sugar	1	tablespoon granulated sugar
1/2	teaspoon five-spice powder		

1 In medium bowl, mix 2 cups of the flour and the 1 teaspoon salt. Cut in shortening, using pastry blender (or pulling 2 table knives through ingredients in opposite directions), until particles are size of small peas. Sprinkle with ginger ale, 1 tablespoon at a time, tossing with fork until all flour is moistened and pastry almost leaves side of bowl. Gather pastry into a ball. Divide in half. Shape into 2 flattened rounds on lightly floured surface. Wrap in plastic wrap; refrigerate about 45 minutes or until dough is firm and cold, yet pliable.

2 Heat oven to 500°F. In small bowl, mix remaining 1/3 cup flour, the brown sugar and five-spice powder. In large bowl, gently toss pears and lemon juice; sprinkle with brown sugar mixture and toss again.

3 On lightly floured surface, roll one round of pastry into circle 2 inches larger than upside-down 9-inch glass pie plate. Fold pastry into fourths and place in pie plate. Unfold pastry and ease into plate, pressing firmly against bottom and side. Spoon filling into pastry-lined plate; dot with butter.

4 Trim overhanging edge of bottom pastry 1/2 inch from rim of plate. Roll other round of pastry. Fold into fourths and cut slits so steam can escape. Place pastry over filling and unfold; trim, seal and flute edge. Brush top with egg white. Sprinkle with granulated sugar. Place pie plate on a cookie sheet. Place in oven.

5 Reduce oven temperature to 400°F. Bake 45 to 50 minutes or until crust is golden brown and juice begins to bubble through slits in crust. Cool on cooling rack at least 2 hours.

High Altitude (3500-6500 ft): No change.

Nutritional Info: 1 Serving: Calories 450; Total Fat 21g (Saturated Fat 6g); Sodium 320mg; Total Carbohydrate 60g (Dietary Fiber 4g); Protein 4g. Exchanges: 2 Starch, 2 Other Carbohydrate, 4 Fat. Carbohydrate Choices: 4.

Betty's Kitchen Tips

Success Hint: Chilling the pastry allows the shortening to become slightly firm, which helps make the baked pastry more flaky. If refrigerated longer than 45 minutes, let pastry soften slightly at room temperature before rolling.

How-To: To prevent excessive browning, cover crust edge with a 2- to 3-inch strip of foil; remove foil during last 15 minutes of baking.

walnut apple-peach crisp with cinnamon-brown sugar crumble

Prep Time: 15 Minutes
Start to Finish: 1 Hour
Servings: 6

EASY

Angela Spengler
Clovis, NM
Celebrate the Season-Fall Baking Contest

3 cups sliced peeled Golden Delicious apples (about 3 medium)
2 cups sliced peeled fresh peaches (about 3 medium)
1/4 cup granulated sugar
1/2 cup old-fashioned oats

1/2 cup packed brown sugar
1/4 cup Gold Medal® all-purpose flour
1/2 teaspoon ground cinnamon
1/4 cup cold butter or margarine
1/4 cup chopped walnuts

1 Heat oven to 375°F. Grease 11x7-inch (2-quart) glass baking dish with shortening or cooking spray.

2 In large bowl, toss apples, peaches and granulated sugar. Pour into baking dish. In same bowl, mix oats, brown sugar, flour and cinnamon. Cut in butter, using pastry blender (or pulling 2 table knives through ingredients in opposite directions), until mixture is crumbly. Stir in walnuts. Sprinkle over fruit.

3 Bake 30 minutes or until the topping is golden and fruit is tender. Cool 15 minutes. Serve warm.

High Altitude (3500-6500 ft): No change.

Nutritional Info: 1 Serving: Calories 310; Total Fat 12g (Saturated Fat 5g); Sodium 85mg; Total Carbohydrate 48g (Dietary Fiber 3g); Protein 3g. Exchanges: 1/2 Starch, 1/2 Fruit, 2 Other Carbohydrate, 2-1/2 Fat. Carbohydrate Choices: 3.

Betty's Kitchen Tips

Substitution: If fresh peaches aren't available, you can use frozen (thawed) sliced peaches.

Did You Know? Old-fashioned and quick-cooking oats can be used interchangeably in most recipes, but you will notice a difference in texture.

Serve-With: This crisp is even more delicious when served with vanilla ice cream!

my lite 'n easy pumpkin cobbler

Prep Time: 20 Minutes
Start to Finish: 1 Hour 45 Minutes
Servings: 12

Jodie Gharbi
Shreveport, LA
Celebrate the Season-Fall Baking Contest

1	can (15 oz) pumpkin (not pumpkin pie mix)
1	can (12 oz) evaporated low-fat milk
2	whole eggs
2	egg whites
3	teaspoons vanilla
1/2	teaspoon almond extract
1/2	cup sugar
1/2	cup artificial no-calorie sweetener
3	teaspoons pumpkin pie spice
1/4	teaspoon salt
1	box Betty Crocker® SuperMoist® yellow cake mix
1	cup fat-free spread, melted
1	cup chopped pecans

1 Heat oven to 350°F. Spray 13x9-inch pan with cooking spray.

2 In large bowl, mix all ingredients except cake mix, spread and pecans with wire whisk; pour into pan. In medium bowl, mix cake mix and spread with pastry blender or fork until large clumps form; spoon randomly over mixture in pan (some clumps will sink). Sprinkle with pecans.

3 Bake 48 to 52 minutes or until toothpick inserted in center comes out clean. Cool on cooling rack 30 minutes. Serve warm with whipped topping or vanilla ice cream, if desired.

High Altitude (3500-6500 ft): No change.

Nutritional Info: 1 Serving: Calories 350; Total Fat 10g (Saturated Fat 2g); Sodium 520mg; Total Carbohydrate 59g (Dietary Fiber 2g); Protein 5g. Exchanges: 1-1/2 Starch, 2-1/2 Other Carbohydrate, 2 Fat. Carbohydrate Choices: 4.

Betty's Kitchen Tips

Serve-With: Fat-free or reduced-fat whipped topping, or vanilla frozen yogurt or reduced-fat ice cream, are good choices to serve with this lighter cobbler.

Storage: Pecans can be stored in an airtight container in the freezer up to 2 years without losing flavor or nutritive value. They thaw quickly and are ready to eat as a snack or use in recipes.

easy apple-cranberry dessert squares

Prep Time: 20 Minutes
Start to Finish: 1 Hour 45 Minutes
Servings: 32

Crust

2-1/2	cups Original Bisquick® mix
1-1/2	cups quick-cooking oats
1	cup packed brown sugar
1	cup cold butter or margarine
1/2	cup chopped pecans

Filling

8	cups thinly sliced peeled apples (about 5 large)
1	bag (6 oz) sweetened dried cranberries
1/2	cup granulated sugar
1	tablespoon ground cinnamon
1	container (8 oz) sour cream
3	eggs
1/2	gallon vanilla ice cream

1 Heat oven to 375°F. Spray 15x10-inch pan with cooking spray.

2 In large bowl, mix Bisquick mix, oats and brown sugar. Cut in butter, using pastry blender (or pulling 2 table knives through ingredients in opposite directions), until mixture is crumbly. Remove 1-1/2 cups crumb mixture to small bowl; stir in pecans. Set aside for topping. Pat remaining crumb mixture into bottom of pan.

3 In large bowl, toss apples, cranberries, granulated sugar and cinnamon. In small bowl, whisk together sour cream and eggs. Pour over apple mixture; toss to coat. Spoon filling over crust; sprinkle reserved crumb/nut mixture over filling.

4 Bake 45 to 55 minutes or until topping is golden brown and apples are tender. Cool 30 minutes. Cut into 8 rows by 4 rows. Serve warm with ice cream.

High Altitude (3500-6500 ft): No change.

Nutritional Info: 1 Serving: Calories 280; Total Fat 14g (Saturated Fat 7g); Sodium 210mg; Total Carbohydrate 35g (Dietary Fiber 2g); Protein 3g. Exchanges: 1/2 Fruit, 1-1/2 Other Carbohydrate, 1/2 Low-Fat Milk, 2-1/2 Fat. Carbohydrate Choices: 2.

Betty's Kitchen Tip

• When choosing apples for this recipe, try 4 cups of a tart apple type (such as Granny Smith) and 4 cups of a sweeter apple (such as Gala) for a flavor variation.

gingerbread marshmallows

Prep Time: 30 Minutes
Start to Finish: 9 Hours
Servings: 77 marshmallows **LOW FAT**

Butter for greasing

1/3	cup powdered sugar
2-1/2	tablespoons unflavored gelatin
1-1/2	teaspoons ground ginger
1	teaspoon ground cinnamon
1/4	teaspoon ground cloves
1/2	cup cold water
1-1/2	cups granulated sugar
1	cup corn syrup
1/4	teaspoon salt
1/4	cup water
1/4	cup molasses

1 Generously grease bottom and sides of 11x7-inch (2-quart) glass baking dish with butter; sprinkle with 1 tablespoon of the powdered sugar. In bowl of stand mixer, sprinkle gelatin, ginger, cinnamon and cloves over 1/2 cup cold water to soften; set aside.

2 In 2-quart saucepan, heat granulated sugar, corn syrup, salt, 1/4 cup water and the molasses over low heat, stirring constantly, until sugar is dissolved. Heat to boiling; cook without stirring about 30 minutes to 240°F on candy thermometer or until small amount of mixture dropped into cup of very cold water forms a ball that holds its shape but is pliable; remove from heat.

3 Slowly pour syrup into softened gelatin while beating on low speed. Increase speed to high; beat 8 to 10 minutes or until mixture is white and has almost tripled in volume. Pour into baking dish, patting lightly with wet hands. Let stand uncovered at least 8 hours or overnight.

4 Sprinkle cutting board with about 1 tablespoon powdered sugar. Place remaining powdered sugar in small bowl.

5 To remove marshmallow mixture, loosen sides from dish and gently lift in one piece onto cutting board. Using sharp knife greased with butter, cut into 1-inch squares (11 rows by 7 rows). Dip bottom and sides of each marshmallow in bowl of powdered sugar; shake off excess sugar but leave a light coating. Store in airtight container at room temperature up to 3 weeks.

High Altitude (3500-6500 ft): No change.

Nutritional Info: 1 Marshmallow: Calories 35; Total Fat 0g (Saturated Fat 0g); Sodium 10mg; Total Carbohydrate 9g (Dietary Fiber 0g); Protein 0g. Exchanges: 1/2 Other Carbohydrate. Carbohydrate Choices: 1/2.

Betty's Kitchen Tip

• Make these homemade treats extra special by putting the marshmallows in small plastic bags tied with curly ribbon. Place bags in oversized mugs along with packages of gourmet cocoa.

caramel-pecan-apple pie

Prep Time: 35 Minutes
Start to Finish: 3 Hours 20 Minutes
Servings: 8

Crust

1   box Pillsbury® refrigerated pie crusts, softened as directed on box

Filling

6   cups thinly sliced peeled apples (6 medium)

3/4   cup sugar

2   tablespoons Gold Medal® all-purpose flour

3/4   teaspoon ground cinnamon

1/4   teaspoon salt

1/8   teaspoon ground nutmeg

1   tablespoon lemon juice

Topping

1/3   cup caramel topping

2   to 4 tablespoons chopped pecans

1   Heat oven to 425°F. Make pie crusts as directed on box for Two-Crust Pie using 9-inch glass pie plate.

2   In large bowl, gently mix all filling ingredients; spoon into crust-lined pie plate. Top with second crust; seal edges and flute. Cut slits or shapes in several places in top crust. Cover crust edge with strips of foil to prevent excessive browning.

3   Bake 40 to 45 minutes or until apples are tender and crust is golden brown, removing foil during last 15 minutes of baking. Immediately after removing pie from oven, drizzle with caramel topping; sprinkle with pecans. Cool on cooling rack at least 2 hours before serving.

High Altitude (3500-6500 ft): No change.

Nutritional Info: 1 Serving: Calories 390; Total Fat 13g (Saturated Fat 5g); Sodium 380mg; Total Carbohydrate 64g (Dietary Fiber 1g); Protein 2g. Exchanges: 1-1/2 Starch, 1/2 Fruit, 2-1/2 Other Carbohydrate, 2-1/2 Fat. Carbohydrate Choices: 4.

Betty's Kitchen Tips

Success Hint: Tart apples, such as Granny Smith, McIntosh or Pippin, would be good choices for this dessert.

Substitution: Two 21-oz cans of apple pie filling can be used instead of the fresh apple filling.

peach and raspberry cobbler

Prep Time: 20 Minutes
Start to Finish: 50 Minutes
Servings: 8

- 2-1/2 cups sliced fresh peaches
- 2 cups fresh raspberries
- 1/2 cup granulated sugar
- 1 tablespoon cornstarch
- 1/2 teaspoon ground cinnamon or ground nutmeg
- 2 cups Original Bisquick® mix
- 1/2 cup milk
- 3 tablespoons butter or margarine, melted
- 2 tablespoons packed brown sugar

1 Heat oven to 375°F. Lightly butter bottom and side of 9x1-1/2-inch deep-dish pie plate or 2-quart casserole.

2 Mix peaches, raspberries, granulated sugar, cornstarch and cinnamon in large bowl. Let stand 10 minutes. Spoon into pie plate.

3 Stir together remaining ingredients in same bowl until dough forms. Drop dough by spoonfuls onto fruit mixture. Bake 25 to 30 minutes or until fruit is bubbly and topping is deep golden brown and thoroughly baked.

High Altitude (3500-6500 ft): No change.

Nutritional Info: 1 Serving: Calories 280 (Calories from Fat 80); Total Fat 9g (Saturated Fat 4g, Trans Fat 1.5g); Cholesterol 15mg; Sodium 410mg; Total Carbohydrate 45g (Dietary Fiber 3g, Sugars 23g); Protein 3g. % Daily Value: Vitamin A 6%; Vitamin C 10%; Calcium 6%; Iron 6%. Exchanges: 1 Starch, 1 Fruit, 1 Other Carbohydrate, 1-1/2 Fat. Carbohydrate Choices: 3.

Betty's Kitchen Tip

- Frozen sliced peaches and raspberries, thawed, can be used instead of the fresh.

pear and apple crumble

Prep Time: 30 Minutes
Start to Finish: 1 Hour 20 Minutes
Servings: 8

Lily Julow
Gainesville, FL
Celebrate the Season-Fall Baking Contest

Topping

1	cup Gold Medal® all-purpose flour
1	teaspoon baking powder
1	teaspoon apple pie spice
1/2	cup cold unsalted butter
3	tablespoons granulated sugar
3	tablespoons packed light brown sugar

Filling

3	large Gala or Golden Delicious apples
3	large ripe but firm pears
2	tablespoons butter
2	tablespoons granulated sugar
1/4	cup fresh lemon juice
2	tablespoons cornstarch
1/2	teaspoon ground cinnamon

1 Heat oven to 375°F. In medium bowl, mix flour, baking powder and apple pie spice. Cut in 1/2 cup butter, using pastry blender (or pulling 2 table knives through ingredients in opposite directions), until mixture looks like rolled oats. Stir in 3 tablespoons granulated sugar and the brown sugar; set aside.

2 Peel and core apples. Cut into quarters, then cut each quarter crosswise in half. Repeat with pears. In 4-quart Dutch oven, combine 2 tablespoons butter, 2 tablespoons granulated sugar and 2 tablespoons of the lemon juice. Heat over medium heat until butter is melted; stir

in apples. Partly cover; cook 5 minutes, stirring occasionally.

3 Add pears; cook and stir 1 to 2 minutes, depending on ripeness of pears. In small bowl, mix remaining 2 tablespoons lemon juice, the cornstarch and cinnamon; add to fruit mixture. Cook 2 to 3 minutes, stirring constantly, until thickened.

4 Carefully spoon fruit mixture into an ungreased 9-1/2-inch glass deep-dish pie plate. Spoon topping evenly over fruit. Place pie plate on cookie sheet.

5 Bake 35 to 40 minutes or until topping is golden brown and fruit is bubbly. Serve warm or cool.

High Altitude (3500-6500 ft): No change.

Nutritional Info: 1 Serving: Calories 350; Total Fat 15g (Saturated Fat 9g); Sodium 85mg; Total Carbohydrate 51g (Dietary Fiber 4g); Protein 2g. Exchanges: 1/2 Starch, 1 Fruit, 2 Other Carbohydrate, 3 Fat. Carbohydrate Choices: 3-1/2.

Betty's Kitchen Tip

• Select heavy lemons, which contain more juice. One medium lemon contains about 3 tablespoons juice, so you will need 2 lemons for this recipe.

apple-raspberry pie

Prep Time: 25 Minutes
Start to Finish: 2 Hours 20 Minutes
Servings: 6

- 1 box Pillsbury® refrigerated pie crusts, softened as directed on box
- 5 cups sliced peeled cooking or baking apples (3 large)
- 3/4 cup sugar
- 1/4 cup cornstarch
- 1 teaspoon grated orange peel
- 1 container (6 oz) fresh raspberries (about 1 cup)
- 1 tablespoon cold butter or margarine, cut into small pieces
- 1 teaspoon sugar

1 Heat oven to 400°F. Make pie crusts as directed on box for Two-Crust Pie using 9-inch glass pie plate.

2 In large bowl, toss apples, 3/4 cup sugar, the cornstarch and orange peel. Spoon half of apple mixture into crust-lined pie plate. Sprinkle evenly with raspberries. Top with remaining apple mixture. Dot with butter. Top with second crust; seal edges and flute.

3 Lightly brush crust with water; sprinkle with 1 teaspoon sugar. Cut slits in several places in top crust. Cover crust edge with strips of foil to prevent excessive browning.

4 Place pie on middle oven rack; place sheet of foil on rack below pie in case of spillover. Bake 45 to 55 minutes or until deep golden brown, removing foil during last 15 minutes of baking. Cool at least 1 hour before serving.

High Altitude (3500-6500 ft): No change.

Nutritional Info: 1 Serving: Calories 480; Total Fat 18g (Saturated Fat 8g); Sodium 360mg; Total Carbohydrate 77g (Dietary Fiber 2g); Protein 2g. Exchanges: 1-1/2 Starch, 1 Fruit, 2-1/2 Other Carbohydrate, 3-1/2 Fat. Carbohydrate Choices: 5.

Betty's Kitchen Tips

Substitution: Frozen unsweetened raspberries can be substituted for the fresh berries. Do not thaw first. Bake at 375°F for 65 to 75 minutes.

Did You Know? Tart apples, such as Granny Smith or Haralson, make flavorful pies. Braeburn or Gala apples provide good texture and a slightly sweeter flavor.

creamy chocolate marble fudge

Prep Time: 40 Minutes
Start to Finish: 3 Hours 40 Minutes
Servings: 96 candies

1   bag (12 oz) white vanilla baking chips
    (2 cups)
6   cups sugar
1   can (12 oz) evaporated milk
1   cup butter or margarine
1   package (8 oz) cream cheese, softened
2   jars (7 oz each) marshmallow creme or
    1 bag (10.5 oz) miniature marshmallows

1   tablespoon vanilla
1   cup milk chocolate chips (6 oz)
1   cup semisweet chocolate chips (6 oz)
2   tablespoons unsweetened baking cocoa
1/2   cup chopped nuts, if desired

1 Butter bottom and sides of 13x9-inch pan or line with foil, leaving 1 inch of foil overhanging at 2 opposite sides of pan. In large bowl, place white baking chips; set aside.

2 In 6-quart Dutch oven, heat sugar, milk, butter and cream cheese to boiling over medium-high heat; cook 6 to 8 minutes, stirring constantly. Reduce heat to medium. Cook about 10 minutes, stirring occasionally, to 225°F on candy thermometer; remove from heat.

3 Quickly stir in marshmallow creme and vanilla. Pour 4 cups hot marshmallow mixture over baking chips in bowl; stir to mix. Into remaining marshmallow mixture, stir milk chocolate chips, semisweet chocolate chips, cocoa and nuts.

4 Pour 1/3 of the white mixture into pan, spreading evenly. Quickly pour 1/3 of the chocolate mixture over top, spreading evenly. Repeat twice. Swirl knife greased with butter through mixtures for marbled design. Cool until set.

5 Refrigerate uncovered about 3 hours or until set. Cut into 12 rows by 8 rows with knife greased with butter. Store covered in refrigerator.

High Altitude (3500-6500 ft): No change.

Nutritional Info: 1 Candy: Calories 130; Total Fat 5g (Saturated Fat 3g); Sodium 35mg; Total Carbohydrate 21g (Dietary Fiber 0g); Protein 1g. Exchanges: 1-1/2 Other Carbohydrate, 1 Fat. Carbohydrate Choices: 1-1/2.

Betty's Kitchen Tip

• To easily scoop the marshmallow creme out of the jars, lightly spray a rubber spatula with cooking spray. The sticky marshmallow won't stick quite as much!

hazelnut marble bark

Prep Time: 20 Minutes
Start to Finish: 1 Hour 20 Minutes
Servings: About 24 pieces

- -

  1   package (6 oz) white chocolate baking bars, chopped

  6   oz semisweet baking chocolate, chopped

  3   oz hazelnuts (filberts), toasted, finely chopped (1/2 cup)

- -

1 Line cookie sheet with foil or waxed paper. In medium microwavable bowl, microwave white chocolate uncovered on High 1 minute, stirring once, until melted. If necessary, continue to microwave on High in 15-second intervals, stirring until smooth. Repeat with semisweet chocolate.

2 Stir 1/4 cup of the hazelnuts into each bowl of chocolate. On cookie sheet, alternately spoon white mixture and semisweet mixture in rows side by side; spread evenly to about 1/4 inch thick. With knife or small metal spatula, cut through mixtures for marbled design. Refrigerate until firm, about 1 hour. Break into pieces.

High Altitude (3500-6500 ft): No change.

Nutritional Info: 1 Piece: Calories 90; Total Fat 6g (Saturated Fat 2.5g); Sodium 5mg; Total Carbohydrate 9g (Dietary Fiber 0g); Protein 1g. Exchanges: 1/2 Other Carbohydrate, 1 Fat. Carbohydrate Choices: 1/2.

Betty's Kitchen Tips

How-To: To toast hazelnuts, heat oven to 350°F. Spread whole nuts on ungreased shallow pan; bake 8 to 10 minutes, stirring occasionally, until skins begin to crack open and flake. To remove skins, if desired, place warm nuts on cloth towel and fold towel over nuts; rub vigorously.

Success Hint: This is an easy candy to make and give as a hostess gift. Package the pieces in a fancy cellophane wrap and pretty container.

roasted almond-cranberry-pear crisp

Prep Time: 25 Minutes
Start to Finish: 1 Hour 30 Minutes
Servings: 8

5 cups sliced peeled pears (about 5 medium)
2 cups fresh or frozen cranberries
1 cup granulated sugar
3 tablespoons Gold Medal® all-purpose flour
6 Nature Valley® roasted almond crunchy granola bars (3 pouches from 8.9-oz box), finely crushed

1/2 cup Gold Medal® all-purpose flour
1/4 cup packed brown sugar
1/4 cup butter or margarine, melted
Whipped cream, if desired

1 Heat oven to 350°F. Spray 8-inch square (2-quart) glass baking dish with cooking spray.

2 In large bowl, mix pears, cranberries, granulated sugar and 3 tablespoons flour. Spoon evenly into baking dish.

3 In medium bowl, mix crushed granola bars, 1/2 cup flour, the brown sugar and butter until crumbly. Sprinkle over pear mixture.

4 Bake 55 to 65 minutes or until top is golden brown and fruit is tender (mixture will be bubbly). Cool slightly. Serve warm or cool with whipped cream.

High Altitude (3500-6500 ft): No change.

Nutritional Info: 1 Serving: Calories 360; Total Fat 9g (Saturated Fat 4g); Sodium 110mg; Total Carbohydrate 67g (Dietary Fiber 5g); Protein 3g. Exchanges: 1 Starch, 1 Fruit, 2-1/2 Other Carbohydrate, 1-1/2 Fat. Carbohydrate Choices: 4-1/2.

Betty's Kitchen Tip

• If your pears are not quite ripe, let them stand at room temperature for 1 or 2 days.

general index

alphabetical index